Electoral Democracy

Electoral Democracy

Edited by
Michael B. MacKuen
and George Rabinowitz

THE UNIVERSITY OF MICHIGAN PRESS
Ann Arbor

Copyright © by the University of Michigan 2003
All rights reserved
Published in the United States of America by
The University of Michigan Press
Manufactured in the United States of America
⊚ Printed on acid-free paper

2006   2005   2004   2003   4   3   2   1

A CIP catalog record for this book is available from the British Library.

Library of Congress Cataloging-in-Publication Data

Electoral democracy / edited by Michael B. MacKuen and George
   Rabinowitz.
      p.   cm.
   Includes bibliographical references and index.
   ISBN 0-472-09820-9 (hc : acid-free) — ISBN 0-472-06820-2 (pb :
acid-free)
   1. Elections—United States.   2. Voting—United States.
3. United States—Politics and government.   4. Democracy.
I. MacKuen, Michael.   II. Rabinowitz, George.

JK1976 .E386   2003
324.973—dc21   2002153621

Contents

Preface

This book presents a set of essays on electoral democracy. They were originally written for a conference that honored Philip E. Converse. We sought the participation of the intellectual leaders in the field of electoral politics and were gratified to have such prominent scholars join in our effort. The contributors were encouraged to think about elections and democracy rather than about Converse and his contributions—the authors were explicitly asked not to write a set of laudatory essays. We wanted these eminent researchers, with the luxury of more space than a typical journal article would provide, either to write a general overview of contemporary research in their areas or to present an extension and explication of their current work. We were confident that Converse would most enjoy stimulating essays and would not much care whether they were directed toward his work. It is some measure of him as a person that we were quite confident of that assessment. We did suspect, however, that the richness of Converse's contributions would make his work relevant to a good many of these essays. For the fact that this suspicion was realized, Converse must be held responsible. His work simply lies so much at the center of what we know about democratic politics that it is impossible to think seriously about competitive elections and electoral systems without thinking about what he has written. This book is dedicated to him as a scholar, a teacher, and a person.

Introduction

Michael B. MacKuen and George Rabinowitz

The great Greek theorists were not enamored of democracy. They felt the mass was too impulsive and too readily manipulated to manage the responsibilities of governance. When we look through the eyes of Thucydides and Aristotle, we see the Greek experience with democratic rule as a history of property appropriation, warfare, demagoguery, and eventually dictatorship. Democracy was a dangerous way to proceed.

This Greek view remained widely accepted in the eighteenth-century United States when nationwide representative democracy was first put into practice. But this deeply felt caution was tempered by a strong belief that citizens should have some say in how government is run. The U.S. Constitution, as it was originally adopted, reflected this duality of thought. Only members of the House of Representatives were directly elected, and the bicameral demands associated with any legislative action, further enhanced by the presidential veto, ensured that the House could not operate with autonomy.

Over time, the selection of leaders in the United States has become decidedly more democratic. The members of the U.S. Senate are directly elected and, for all intents and purposes, so is the president. The scope of the electorate has changed, too, with the elimination of previous systematic exclusions such as poverty, gender, and race. By any reasonable standard, the contemporary United States meets the fundamental standards of representative democracy: adult citizens are allowed to select their leaders in open competitive elections, and these leaders are in a position to determine the policy under which the society operates.

In retrospect, the American experience with democratic government has been far more successful than the classical view might have expected. While going through occasional bouts of demagoguery, volatility, and perhaps irresponsibility, the U.S. government has both reflected the broad-gauged demands of the public and maintained the sorts of stability conducive to economic and social development—this despite the fact the electorate is comprised of ordinary citizens who are only indifferently attentive to public affairs.

To be sure, keen observers had long been aware of the relatively unsophisticated mind-set of most citizens. Such thoughtful analysts as Lord Bryce (1899) and Walter Lippmann (1965) were profoundly aware of how shallow were democracy's public opinion roots. The fact that democratic government was built on the broad public's uncertain judgment gave great pause. Getting directly to the point, this ongoing concern was epitomized by H. L. Mencken's famous quip, "Democracy is the art of running the circus from the monkey cage."

And yet in mid-twentieth-century America, it was quite a shock to the intellectual community when social scientists started to discover the flimsy structure of public opinion on which democratic politics is based. The most critical evidence was presented by Philip E. Converse (1964). Using survey data, he showed that most voters had only a vague sense of public affairs. Converse's work revealed that the public had little understanding of public policy and found that political views were haphazardly disconnected and judgments about politicians and policies were so unstable that the vast majority of Americans apparently held no serious political attitudes at all. What appeared to be genuine opinions were instead "doorstep" opinions manufactured on the spot to please the interviewer.

These early survey analyses first struck a chord of disharmony—they provided detailed scientific evidence about the profound limits of the general public's political understanding and about the indifference with which the public regarded the national policy debate. This unflattering portrait led to twenty years of scientific controversy about whether citizens had real opinions or not.

Even more important, however, was Converse's (1975) emphasis on the mismatch between the framework organizing the political views of ordinary citizens and the framework of elite political debate. When the mass public thinks about politics in quite different ways than the politicians it elects, it is difficult for politicians to translate mass preferences into public policy. For example, if people judge on the basis of partisanship and the state of the times while politicians think ideologically, then the policy guidance that politicians derive from an election might have little to do with actual public policy preferences. Or more subtly, if people see issues as essentially distinctive matters that incorporate different mixtures of principles and interests, then politicians who think in terms of ideological coalitions will find it difficult to craft stable governing coalitions.

The mid-twentieth-century "behavioral revolution" in political science was a precursor to the rebirth of interest in the importance of "institutions." *Institution* in this context refers to established patterns of mutually reinforcing regularities. Institutions might be formally constituted organizations or formal legal rules (e.g., Congress and the rules under which it operates), but they also might include any established patterns of human behavior that govern what is and what is not possible (e.g., what are viewed as legitimate female roles or how attentive people are to news and public affairs). Many of these early behavioral findings fit naturally into an institutional context.

For democratic government, the key institution, far more important than legal voting requirements, campaign finance laws, the party nomination process, or any other formal arrangement, is the underlying structure of public opinion. That, of course, was a critical subject of these early investigators. The nature of that structure—and how it connects elite politics to the mass public—is the key to understanding the mass base of democratic rule. We need to know the sorts of set patterns that more or less permanently shape the way that the public and politicians interact.

Some findings are now widely accepted.

- Parents transmit political values to their children and that this tends to preserve continuities in the politics of social class, ethnic group, and geographic region. Thus, politicians and parties and political regimes could persist in localities, with their original coalitional base kept intact from one generation to the next, barring any fundamental change in their policy orientations.

- Most citizens think about politics in terms of their group orientations—economic groups, religious groups, or ethnic groups. And of course, the principle of group interests undergirds the organization of Washington's K Street politics in a way that legitimizes contemporary elite politics.

- People develop allegiances to the two main political parties that encompass both performance evaluations and a psychological self-identification with abstract symbols. Savvy politicians, understanding the permanent and the transient in political attitudes, shape their electoral appeals to reinforce their partisan supporters while attempting to woo the uncommitted. Modern campaigns both mobilize the base and curry favor with marginal voters. All this leads to a highly stylized—and complex—set of symbolic rhetoric and policy promises.

The importance of this structure is so well known—so ingrained in conventional wisdom—that we can easily forget that it constitutes a form of political institution. But outlining this understanding only shows how powerful electoral theory might develop: it needs to establish a richer base of scientific regularities, one that further expands our ability to think about what is possible and what is not possible in electoral democracy.

For example, we can outline a number of commonplace propositions about the mass-elite connection that produce strong theory.

- If the public were entirely inattentive toward politicians' policy-making, then we might reasonably expect politicians to be entirely indifferent to their constituents' political views. Policy-making would be determined by the internal politics of Washington, with electoral implications a minor afterthought.

- If we understand a strong class bias in voting turnout, the poor and less well educated neglecting the polls, we might expect that there would be an unrealized opportunity for class-based parties to mobilize votes and win elections.

- If politics were organized mainly along a single ideological liberal-conservative dimension and voters choose the party "closest" to their own preferences, then we understand that parties and candidates (and ultimately public policies) will converge on the centrist median voter position.

- If ideology (or what passes for political philosophy) were mere pap in the public's mind, then candidates would understand that developing ideological argument—developing overarching symbolic justifications—would be a waste of time and would refrain from such discussion.

Of course, scientific observation shows all these propositions to be far off the mark. The public does pay attention to public debate and policy-making, and politicians take great pains to please the general public. The relatively minor class-based differences in turnout are hardly the stuff of incipient partisan realignment, though they may be important from time to time. U.S. politics are largely multidimensional, and it is not at all clear that voters prefer muddled centrism to clearly distinctive policy advocacy. And the symbolism of political philosophy continues to play a part in both elite debate and in electoral campaigns.

To be sure, we genuinely need to know much more than we do. While each of these simple propositions is demonstrably false on its own terms, each does contain some truth. And more than that, the discipline is in the process of developing richer ideas about how mass politics is structured. The current agenda includes:

The nature of public opinion itself.   To what extent do people hold meaningful political views? Are there overarching principles that organize political thinking? If so, what are they?

Information processing.   How do people incorporate new information? What do people retain of the information they encounter? How does the typical citizen use new information in making political judgments?

Group and party identification.   What does it mean to identify with a group or political party? How does identification shape political behavior?

Linkage mechanisms.   What sorts of linkage mechanisms translate public judgments into a force in elite politics? Do those mechanisms produce stable connections between mass and elite, or do the connections vary meaningfully? How much should elites be guided by mass publics? Are elites willing to ignore short-term mass preferences in the interest of what those elites perceive to be long-term mass preferences?

Democratic capacity.   Are the known limitations of mass publics as decision makers readily overcome when people are systematically exposed to more information and discussion? What type of decisions would a more informed and engaged citizenry produce?

This book is about electoral democracy in the United States, with a special emphasis on the stable, regularized, institutionalized features of the connections between ordinary citizens and elite policy-making. In the essays in this volume, the authors push our boundaries of understanding and invite a more rigorous form of theorizing about the potentialities of democratic government.

Individual Psychology and Electoral Democracy

The first four chapters in the book deal with the factors that shape citizens' thinking about politics. The first chapter, written by Donald R. Kinder, considers the question of how people organize their political attitudes. When Converse showed that most citizens do not organize their attitudes along a liberal-conservative continuum, he left open the question of how—or even whether—people organize their political thoughts and feelings. Converse's original answer stressed the great heterogeneity of the electorate—some people do follow a well-organized and sophisticated liberal-conservative view of politics, while others appear to give virtually no systematic thought whatsoever to politics. For the bulk of the electorate, some mechanisms existed, but they were looser and more oriented toward relevant groups than toward fundamental political principles.

This reliance on feelings toward groups is Kinder's starting point as he considers the factors that shape current thinking about politics. Kinder suggests a coherent and powerful explanation for how citizens organize their political thoughts: they use ethnocentrism—or ethnic identification—to provide a pervasive orientation toward matters that range well beyond the politics of race or ethnicity itself. His conclusions, however, should give pause because they surely buttress the worries of democracy's doubters: all over the world, the politics of ethnic division have proven enormously appealing to ambitious politicians and have produced unmitigated human disaster. Kinder's work should prove both crucial and controversial because it raises fundamental normative questions about the disturbing character of democratic decision making.

The next chapter, written by Larry M. Bartels, picks up a different piece of the intricate question of how masses think about politics and what this means for democratic governance. Bartels returns to the fundamental question of attitude stability and instability and addresses in a remarkably direct way the question of how effectively mass publics can fulfill their role as self-governors. The chapter is deeply rooted in the contemporary psychological literature as well as in modern theories of social choice. While disagreeing with the commonplace notion that citizen attitudes are nonsense, he shows clearly that having meaningful attitudes is not the same as having meaningful preferences and thus that meaningful attitudes are not enough to provide the foundation for democratic government. At root, this argument calls for a much more sophisticated theory about how the public governs itself—and commands the attention of democratic theorists of all stripes. Needless to say, Bartels's contention should provoke a serious reaction.

Together, the Kinder and Bartels chapters provide a picture of how individual psychology and mass attitudes interact to help shape democratic politics in the United States. Their work here is part of a general renaissance of interest in how citizens' fundamental behavior informs our judgments of democracy.

The next two chapters provide broad overviews of important areas of research. Herbert F. Weisberg and Steven H. Greene examine partisanship, and Marco R. Steenbergen and Milton Lodge examine how citizens evaluate political objects such as candidates and parties.

In making sense of mass voting behavior, party identification has been a critical concept—by many accounts *the* critical concept. In some ways, parties are just another group, but they are very specialized groups. They exist to compete for office.

Parties serve as linchpins for democratic politics in all advanced industrial democracies. In some systems, partisanship—the idea of identifying with a party—is very difficult to separate from electoral choice because people vote for a party. In the United States, with its multiple elections and candidate-centered campaigns, partisanship can be quite distinct from any particular vote decision. Partisanship is among the most durable of political attitudes in the United States. Unlike specific issue preferences or even ideology, a person's partisanship tends to hold over fairly lengthy time periods (Converse 1976; Converse and Markus 1979).

Weisberg and Greene put the concept of party identification into the context of contemporary social psychology, updating the intellectual bases for the concept that originated in the social psychology of a half century ago. They provide a comprehensive review of the literature and suggest promising paths along which new research might follow. The chapter is a natural starting point for students of electoral politics interested in partisanship and a major reference for scholars more generally.

In studying the political behavior of electorates, we need to move beyond group or party orientations. By any standard, it is critical to know how citizens process information and make political judgments. When evaluating candidates such as George Bush, Bill Clinton, and Al Gore, how do voters use the information they encounter? Understanding the modes of political cognition will inform our fundamental views about electoral democracy.

Consider two different cognitive styles: "memory-based" and "on-line" information processing. When people using the memory-based style encounter information, they store the information in memory, to be used in forming evaluations about the candidates. Later, when talking politics or making voting decisions, these individuals call up the various specific bits of information and integrate them into the conversation or the political judgment. This, of course, is the sort of learning one ordinarily associates with schoolbooks and exams. Alternatively, when people using the on-line style encounter the same information, they use it to update immediately their judgments about the candidates—and then forget the specifics. At any later time, they can provide meaningful evaluations of the candidates but cannot reproduce the detailed information that went into those evaluations. Similar to share prices on Wall Street, the individuals' current evaluations reflect reasoned interactions with real information but appear free from the details that formed them.

This distinction is important for theory. While the voters with different cognitive styles might utilize the same information to come to a decision, on-line processors would *seem* a good deal less informed than memory-based processors. When interviewed by a researcher, on-line types are unable to connect their judgments with facts or arguments and appear to construct their views out of whole cloth, when in fact they have developed rich and meaningful evaluations. Thus, the apparent confusion and instability that political scientists often find in the electorate could be entirely misleading. It is clearly possible that citizens powerfully use political information in making their judgments while at the same time evince little residue of the specifics. If this were so, then we should be cautious about uncritically accepting the modern survey-based evidence that supports the Greek theorists' concerns. We should begin to reassess the conventional view of a woefully inadequate citizenry and begin to think anew about how the electorate's views anchor democratic government.

In part, this is an empirical question. Do voters more generally tend to be more on line or more memory based? To what information are voters generally sensitive? Do these factors vary by type of information and judgment? The chapter by Steenbergen and Lodge both summarizes and provides thoughtful insight on the ongoing and lively debate surrounding the question of human information processing of political information.

The first four chapters collectively provide a view of the current state of research in electoral politics from the standpoint of individual voter psychology. For any understanding of electoral democracy, this is the base from which all else builds. But we need to understand how individual voter psychology gets integrated into the social political system.

Decision Making

The next chapters deal with the voter as decision maker and suggest that the conventional image of a nonideological, centrist, and essentially passive electorate might well be worth reconsidering. From the standpoint of mass control of policy, the question of how issues affect evaluation and voter choice is central. The standard model that guides both professional and lay discussions of issue voting presumes that people select candidates who are close to them on the issues. This leads to the assumption that centrist candidates should be most successful.

Stuart Elaine Macdonald, George Rabinowitz, and Holly Brasher take issue with that view, arguing that a fundamentally different model more accurately reflects how voters evaluate candidates based on issues. The authors argue that citizens respond to the direction and intensity of candidate positions. Those candidates that fail to provide a clear sense of policy direction do not elicit issue-based responses and are liked and disliked equally by all voters. Rather than drawing centrist voters, centrist candidates are evaluated entirely on non-issue criteria. Successful issue-based candidacies require strong issue stands where the direction of the stance is supported by the majority of the electorate.

Among recent politicians, Bill Clinton and John McCain behaved in ways that fit the precepts of the directional model, while Ross Perot more closely fits the proximity model. Macdonald, Rabinowitz, and Brasher compare and then apply the directional and proximity theories in the context of the 1996 U.S. presidential election. They find considerably stronger support for the directional model. The net implication of their work suggests that parties and candidates have little incentive to move to the political center on specific issues when seeking votes but do have strong incentives to be on the "correct"—that is, more popular—side of important issues.

Closely related to the view that issues are the key element linking politicians' policy decisions to the mass public's policy preferences is the view that ideology matters to choice. Elites tend to think and behave ideologically even if the mass public does not, so the ideological proclivities of elected leaders are important to the policies they are likely to enact. The seminal work on formal theory in the modern era, Anthony Downs's *An Economic Theory of Democracy* (1957), stressed the critical role of ideology as a shortcut for determining how parties were likely to behave when in office. While early survey research provided a strong caution against this simple ideological view of electoral politics, the work did not rule out a potentially potent role for ideology in elections.

Because elite discussion of politics occurs in an ideological frame, even marginally attentive voters are likely to learn the ideological labels and can invest them with positive or negative feelings. Thus, the symbols *liberal* and *conservative* can be important in determining voter behavior (Conover and Feldman

1981) without necessarily being connected to voters' attitudes on substantive issues. Further, while ideology is of mere modest import for most citizens, it is a serious matter for some. And when these ideologues disproportionately favor one side or the other, ideology can have a marked influence on aggregate electoral outcomes. Finally, the politics of ideology reflect not only voters' capacities and inclinations but also politicians' strategic decisions to imbue policymaking and political discourse with ideological symbolism. Examining the behavior of voters and politicians, Michael B. MacKuen, Robert S. Erikson, James A. Stimson, and Kathleen Knight document the recent rise of ideology in American electoral politics.

Almost all research on mass political decision making has focused on citizens' behavior. A somewhat different question is how citizens might behave if they were more fully informed and more thoughtful. Over the last decade there has been marked interest in the concept of deliberative polling, where representative groups of citizens are brought together to consider particular policy problems. This work has led naturally to speculation about what an ideal citizenry would be like—how sophisticated would it be, how widely would it participate, how much tolerance would it have? Would it be good at using the vote to express individual self-interest, or would it be more concerned with the "public good?" Would a more sophisticated and deliberative electorate be more or less likely to pursue politics of the Left or of the Right? Robert C. Luskin considers both the theoretical characteristics that might distinguish a more ideal public and the empirical evidence on how both sophistication and deliberation affect political choices. His chapter indicates that the political consequences are less clear than one might expect and suggests how difficult and how interesting is the exercise of drawing the implications of different institutionalizations in the mass public.

Electoral Democracy from a More Elite Perspective

If elections are more than symbolic events, electoral democracy needs to be an interactive process where the views and desires of the mass public meaningfully influence the behavior of political elites. In turn, the behavior of elites must influence the way the public feels about them. The presumed effectiveness of such mass-elite interactions motivates our concern with the character of public opinion and with the issue and ideological models of vote choice. The public's policy views and issue voting make a difference only if elites understand the genuine implications of people's expressed preferences, if they organize elite politics to reflect those preferences, and if they actually deliver what the public wants.

Michael W. Traugott considers a question that is very much at the heart of majoritarian democracy: Do voters feel that politicians should make decisions based on mass preferences as indicated by citizens in their responses to public opinion polls? This question could not have arisen in ancient Athens or even in early-twentieth-century America—the public opinion poll is a political institution new to our times. At its best, the scientific poll permits a much more precise and thus more meaningful connection between what the public wants and what elites can provide. However, the history of contemporary opinion polling, with all its peculiarities, suggests that the institution bears some watching. Traugott asks what motivates some voters to feel that politicians should be inclined to use polls and others to feel they should not.

This consideration of the role of political polls in democracy reflects the fundamental tension between majoritarian and elite-controlled democracy that sparked debates about the design of the U.S. Constitution and remains with us today. How much does the public itself play the desire for responsive government against the desire for responsible government? This implicit theme drives Traugott's analysis.

John Aldrich is keenly interested in change and equilibrium in the U.S. system. The fundamental linkage between mass and elite is typically thought to constitute a dynamic system in which a change on the mass side generates a reaction on the part of elites that then produces a change in the public. The cycle repeats itself as each side responds to the other. A concept that is usefully employed with regard to any dynamic system is that of equilibrium. The idea of equilibrium conveys a sense of dynamic tension, in that the system has a capacity to change, but all the pieces are currently in balance. This idea is explicitly formalized in game-theoretic treatments of social phenomena and is of importance for everyday understandings of politics.

Aldrich's chapter considers how the U.S. political system has evolved over the past fifty years, concentrating on the contrasts between equilibrium and disequilibrium. The period saw the remarkable transformation of the American South from a strongly Democratic area to a Republican-leaning region. During the same time frame, the racial landscape of the society was altered so that most African American citizens became free of explicit legally based discrimination. Aldrich's analysis focuses on changes at both the mass and elite levels, and he challenges some critical features of the standard elite-driven model of political change in the twentieth-century United States. His analysis probes both the factors that motivate change and the important role that disequilibrium plays in political systems. The implications of Aldrich's reconceptualization of American politics appear profound—we shall want to think more seriously about what generates stable and unstable political systems and, in truth, about whether political life constitutes a political system at all.

The concluding chapter by John Zaller takes a quite different turn on the question of elite motivation. For savvy politicians, the public opinion that matters is not that which rules today's opinion polls but instead that which will dominate tomorrow's election campaign. What is important is not *manifest* public opinion but *latent* public opinion. And that future opinion will reflect current policy decisions as political opponents frame them at election time. Following V. O. Key, Zaller focuses on politicians' concern about a foreseeable future, rather than an observed current, public opinion.

The mechanisms of latent opinion—the principles that guide how the public reacts to politicians and politicians lead the public—lie at the heart of democratic government. But they are exceedingly difficult to study because, in essence, latent public opinion is that which *might* have occurred had not politicians anticipated the public response. When in proper equilibrium, the mechanisms will produce outcomes in which the most serious power of public opinion never openly reveals itself. The public response that we do see arises from politicians' inevitable difficulties in anticipating the future and, more important, in pleasing contradictory public demands. But this response pales in comparison with what we might expect had politicians not done everything in their power to anticipate the course of public reactions.

In laying out the implications of politicians' anticipations, Zaller recognizes the imperfections of such a governing system. If voters are generally inattentive and make simplistic judgments—often wanting to have their cake and eat it too—they provide only clumsy guidance for policymakers. Yet these responses motivate politicians to perform to the public's tastes. If the latent-opinion system represents an inexact management tool, it *is* a management tool that constantly forces those in government to seek ways to satisfy the public's strongest demands. And it is an understanding of democracy's powers and limits that is the target of Zaller's essay.

Final Comment

Virtually no serious student of mass electorates has been satisfied with the quality of citizen engagement. Yet all successful modern industrial societies have been democratic. And from a humanistic perspective, there is much to be said for a form of government in which citizens have an explicit say in determining the leaders and policies under which they live. Hence, both historical success and humanistic appeal provide good grounds for having faith in democracy.

But faith is a poor substitute for knowledge. Compared to the full range of human history, our practical experience with democracies and the problems of governing large complex societies is still in its early stages. Much remains to be learned about what is real, systematic, and consequential, and what is not. The quality and durability of electoral democracy as a political form ultimately will rest on our collective ability to appreciate and protect its strengths while understanding and improving upon its weaknesses. The chapters in this book are directed toward that end.

REFERENCES

Bryce, J. 1899. *The American Commonwealth.* 2 vols. New York: Macmillan.
Conover, Pamela Johnston, and Stanley Feldman. 1981. The Origins and Meaning of Liberal-Conservative Self-Identifications. *American Journal of Political Science* 25:617–45.
Converse, Philip E. 1964. The Nature of Belief Systems in Mass Publics. In David Apter, ed., *Ideology and Discontent.* New York: Free Press of Glencoe.
———. 1975. Public Opinion and Voting Behavior. In Fred Greenstein and Nelson Polsby, eds., *Handbook of Political Science,* vol. 4. Reading, Mass.: Addison-Wesley.
———. 1976. *The Dynamics of Party Support: Cohort-Analyzing Party Identification.* Beverly Hills, Calif.: Sage.
Converse, Philip E., and Gregory B. Markus. 1979. *Plus ça Change*. . . The New CPS Election Study Panel. *American Political Science Review* 73:32–49.
Downs, Anthony. 1957. *An Economic Theory of Democracy.* New York: Addison, Wesley, and Longman.
Lippmann, Walter. 1965 (1922). *Public Opinion.* New York: Free Press.

1
Belief Systems after Converse

Donald R. Kinder

The Question of Capacity

Whether common people are capable of offering sensible advice on affairs of state is both an ancient and timely question, and the answers provided by thoughtful analysts have not always been friendly to democratic aspirations. Plato, to take one notable example, was sure that the citizens of Athens possessed neither the experience nor the knowledge required for sound and independent judgment. Democracy, in his view, was dangerous (*The Republic*, 375, 376). Closer to our own time and place we find Walter Lippmann's thoroughgoing skepticism toward democratic possibilities, expressed first in *Public Opinion* (1922) and then, carried out to its logical and sour conclusion a few years later, in *The Phantom Public* (1925). Lippmann suggested that the ordinary person who wants to be a virtuous citizen was like a fat man who wishes to become a ballet dancer (1925, 39). Or consider Schumpeter's famous assault on what he called the "classical doctrine" of democracy. In the end, Schumpeter concluded, "the electoral mass is incapable of action other than a stampede" (1942, 282).

For the most part, these arguments were expressed without benefit of systematic evidence. Schumpeter was right to say that in deciding whether the conditions for democracy are met requires "laborious appraisal of a maze of conflicting evidence" (1942, 254), but he did not undertake such an analysis himself. To be fair, in Schumpeter's time, there was not all that much evidence to analyze.

Which brings us to Philip Converse and his celebrated—or notorious—but certainly influential analysis of belief systems in mass publics. After poring over national surveys carried out in 1956, 1958, and 1960, Converse concluded that most Americans are innocent of ideology, ill prepared, and perhaps even incapable of following (much less actually participating in) discussions about the direction government should take. My purpose here is to pay a brief return visit to this famous article and the huge commotion it stirred up and to excavate what I take to be the largely neglected and mostly affirmative lesson of Converse's original analysis. And then, in the heart of the chapter, I trace out the implications of this lesson in my own research. I begin with Converse and the role of the federal government in the regulation of electric power in the Eisenhower years and end with bold claims about U.S. ethnocentrism at the dawn of the twenty-first century. My burden is to persuade you that the beginning of the chapter and the end actually belong together or, put another way, that critics of my work should actually direct their fire at Converse. By the argument offered here, the directions I have taken and the mistakes I have made are at least partly his fault.[1]

Belief Systems according to Converse

Converse's analysis begins with information. More precisely, it begins with *differences* in information: the "staggering" differences that characterize the distribution of political information within modern societies, running from "vast treasuries of well-organized information among elites interested in the subject to fragments that could virtually be measured in a few 'bits' in the technical sense" (1964, 212). Converse's primary purpose is to convince us that the consequences for the quality of political reasoning of such informational differences are both underappreciated and profound. In particular, as we move from a thin stratum of political elites at the apex of society down to the grassroots, Converse argues that two striking transformations take place:

> First, the contextual grasp of "standard" political belief systems fades out very rapidly, almost before one has passed beyond the 10% of the American population that in the 1950s had completed standard college training. Increasingly, simpler forms of information about "what goes with what" (or even information about the simple identity of objects) turn up missing. The net result, as one moves downward, is that constraint declines across the universe of idea-elements, and that the range of relevant belief systems becomes narrower and narrower. Instead of a few wide-ranging belief systems that organize large amounts of specific information, one would expect to find a proliferation of clusters of ideas among which little constraint is felt, even, quite often, in instances of sheer logical constraint.
>
> [And second,] the character of the objects that are central in a belief system undergoes systematic change. These objects shift from the remote, generic, and abstract to the increasingly simple, concrete, or "close to home." Where potential political objects are concerned, this progression tends to be from abstract "ideological" principles to the more obviously recognizable social groupings or charismatic leaders and finally to such objects of immediate experience as family, job, and immediate associates. (1964, 213)

Together, these two transformations would seem to pose a strong challenge to democratic hopes. In Converse's analysis, the fragmentation and concretization that characterize everyday political thinking "are not a pathology limited to a thin and disorganized bottom layer of the *lumpenproletariat;* they are immediately relevant in understanding the bulk of mass political behavior" (1964, 213).

Converse came to his melancholy conclusions in part because of Americans' unfamiliarity with ideological concepts. Citizens who seemed to rely on a relatively abstract and far-reaching conceptual dimension such as liberalism or conservatism when they commented on what they liked and disliked about the major parties and candidates comprised, according to Converse's classification, less than 3 percent of the public. Near-ideologues, citizens who made use of abstract concepts but appeared neither to rely on them heavily nor to understand them very well, made up just another tenth of the sample. Thus the great majority of Americans—close to 90 percent—showed no taste for the abstract concepts that seem a standard part of political analysis.

Unfamiliarity with ideological terms could reflect naïveté or, less significantly, difficulties in the articulation of ideological ideas. Perhaps many people simply cannot enunciate the principles that in fact inform their beliefs. With this possibility in mind, Converse calculated correlations between opinions on topical issues separately for each of two groups, both interviewed in 1958: a national cross-section of the general public and a smaller group made up of candidates for the U.S. House of Representatives. Both groups were asked their opinions on pressing domestic and foreign policy issues—such matters as aid to education, military support for countries menaced by communist aggression, and the like. Candidates' positions toward these problems were much more consistent than were the positions expressed by the general public. Indeed, among the public, there was little consistency at all. While candidates tended to be either liberal or conservative, citizens tended to scatter all over the (ideological) place.

Not only did opinions on matters of policy appear unconnected to one another, they also seemed to wobble back and forth randomly over time. Eight of the policy questions included in the 1958 national survey were posed to the same people two years earlier, in the 1956 survey, as well as two years later, in 1960. Although there were virtually no aggregate shifts in opinion on any of these issues across this period, and despite precautions taken to discourage superficial replies, Converse found a great deal of instability at the individual level. On average, less than two-thirds of the public came down on the same side of a policy controversy over a two-year period, where half would be expected to do so by chance alone. Furthermore, a close inspection of the dynamics of this considerable reshuffling led Converse to suggest that on any particular issue, the public could be separated into one of two groups: the first

made up of citizens who possess genuine opinions and hold onto them tena-
ciously, the second composed of citizens who are quite indifferent to the issue
and when pressed, either confess their ignorance outright or out of embarrassment or misplaced civic obligation invent an attitude on the spot—not a real
attitude but a "nonattitude" (Converse 1970). The democratically disheartening conclusion of this analysis is that those citizens belonging to the first
group—known collectively as an "issue public"—are often substantially outnumbered by those belonging to the second. Nonattitudes are more common
than the real thing.

As we know, it did not take long for Converse's powerfully argued and forceful conclusions to provoke a huge commotion. For a time—quite a long time—
it seemed that the commotion would never end. Way back in 1982, at the annual
meeting of the American Political Science Association in Denver, I presented a
paper under the title "Enough Already about Ideology."[2] It had no effect: the
torrent of papers and chapters and books continued without slackening.

Perhaps the most compelling line of criticism directed at "The Nature of
Belief Systems" (or so it seemed for a time) was that Converse had ignored politics, that his analysis had paid too little attention to the nature of campaigns
and public debate. Under this view, the sophistication of citizens' understanding of politics mirrors the sophistication of the public debate they witness. Provide Americans with a more thoughtful and philosophical politics, so ran the
argument, and they are perfectly capable of responding in kind.

On this point, the critics certainly had time on their side. Converse's conclusions surely reflected in part the comparatively tranquil Eisenhower years, a
period of political recovery from the intense ideological debates of the New
Deal and from the collective trauma of depression and war. The original claim
surely must be modified given the events that have subsequently shattered
national tranquillity.[3]

Not really. A full account of the evidence relevant to this point would be
long and complicated, and I have here neither the space nor the heart to plow
through all the details.[4] Suffice it to say that Converse's original claim of ideological naïveté stands up quite well, both to detailed reanalysis and to political
change. Indeed, in some respects, the claim is strengthened. *Despite* the bois-
terous events and ideological debates that have occasionally visited U.S. politics
since 1960, most citizens continue to glance at the political world bewildered by
ideological concepts, lacking a consistent outlook on public policy, in possession of genuine opinions on only a few issues, and knowing precious little.[5]

Groupcentrism ("Social Groupings as Central Objects in Belief Systems")

In portraying Converse's analysis as a relentless and effective attack on the idea
that citizens in modern mass societies think about politics in ideologically

sophisticated ways, I have overlooked, as many have, the sunny side of Converse. Halfway through his devastating assault, Converse paused to speculate what citizens might be up to, given that ideological reasoning was beyond their capacity and interest. The result was a five-page sketch of "the role that visible social groupings come to play as objects of high centrality in the belief systems of the less well informed" (1964, 234). Building on reference-group theory's principal insight—that people "frequently orient themselves to groups other than their own" (Merton and Rossi 1968, 35)—Converse suggested that citizens organize their opinions on policy according to the sentiments they feel toward the social groupings that such policies seem to benefit or harm.

Converse began this argument by inviting us to imagine a set of policies formulated to emphasize a highly visible and familiar social grouping: in this case, and in the vernacular of the times, "Negroes." Such policies were in many respects diverse, but they shared one feature in common. Each could be read as advancing or impairing the interests of Negroes. As in:

Negroes should be kept out of professional athletics.

The government should see to it that Negroes get fair treatment in jobs and housing.

Even though it may hurt the position of the Negro in the South, state governments should be able to decide who can vote and who cannot.

Converse argued that for many people, it is the social group, not abstract arguments over states' rights or federal responsibilities, that looms large in these various policy proposals. Because abstractions of this sort "take on meaning only with a good deal of political information and understanding, the attitude items given would tend to boil down for many respondents to the same single question: 'Are you sympathetic to Negroes as a group, are you indifferent to them, or do you dislike them?'" (235).

In this thought experiment, Converse was using race to make a general point about the potential of social groupings to organize belief systems. The "advantage" of race in this respect is that the markers for group membership are highly visible, "in the skin," so to speak. But Converse mentioned religion, social class, and nationality as well as race and offered the 1960 presidential campaign and John Kennedy's Catholicism as a case in point. In short, Converse argued that because ideological principles are too abstract and too demanding, citizens organize their political thinking around visible social groupings. In this way, they simplify complex and technical questions of public policy by turning them into judgments on the moral qualifications of the groups involved.

If the evidence relevant to this claim was fragmentary some thirty-five years ago, it is now abundant and overwhelmingly positive, and so Converse's spec-

ulation seems, to me at least, unassailable.[6] Public opinion is shaped in powerful ways by the feelings citizens harbor toward the social groups they see as the
principal beneficiaries (or victims) of the policy. We can see this in opinion
toward affirmative action and school integration (e.g., Kinder and Sanders
1996; Sears, Hensler, and Speer 1979; Sniderman, Brody, and Kuklinski 1984);
spending on welfare programs (e.g., Feldman 1983; Gilens 1999); foreign policy
(e.g., Bartels 1992; Hurwitz and Peffley 1987); government action against AIDS
(e.g., Price and Hsu 1992); immigration (e.g., Citrin, Reingold, and Green 1990;
Pettigrew and Meertens 1995), and more. Group sentiment is not the only thing
driving opinion in these various policy disputes, but it is always present, and of
all the diverse ingredients that make up opinion, it is often the most powerful.

My own research on the politics of race could be placed here as well. It adds
to the case for groupcentrism by concentrating on racism, a particularly persistent and pernicious form of groupcentrism. Over the years I have found racial
prejudice to play an important and expansive role in white Americans' political judgments and choices (Kinder 2003; Kinder and Mendelberg 2002; Kinder
and Sanders 1996; Kinder and Sears 1981). On equal opportunity in employment, school desegregation, federal programs of assistance, and affirmative
action at work and at school, racially prejudiced whites line up on one side and
racially sympathetic whites line up on the other. To be sure, racism is not the
only thing that matters for opinion on such issues. Interests make a difference
(especially the harms and benefits at stake for groups) and so do political values such as equality and limited government. Nor is the effect of racism fixed
and automatic: its prominence in white opinion depends partly on social conditions (Kinder and Mendelberg 1995) and especially on political circumstances, on how issues and campaigns are formulated and framed (Kinder,
Berinsky, and Winter 1998; Kinder and Sanders 1996). But all things considered, for white opinion on matters of race, racism remains the single most
important factor.

With these results in mind, you could say that the U.S. political system effectively converted Converse's thought experiment of forty years ago into a real
one. Over this period, Americans have been confronted with a series of actual
policy questions formulated in such a way as to emphasize a highly visible and
familiar social group—black Americans—with the questions covering equal
access to public accommodations, the right to vote, protection from discrimination, the integration of schools and neighborhoods, poverty and economic
inequality, affirmative action, political representation, and welfare reform,
among others. And with respect to this real experiment in public policy, my
results confirm Converse's speculation. On policies having to do with race,
groupcentrism prevails.

In some ways the most striking result in this work for me is the intrusion of
racism on opinions that on their face are not about race at all. It is perhaps not

that surprising to find racism an important cause of white opinion on such policies as affirmative action or school integration. More surprising is that racism also figures prominently in white Americans' views on welfare, capital punishment, sexual harassment, gay rights, immigration, spending on defense, and others. This result—the long reach of racism—recalls another, reported fifty years ago by Daniel Levinson and his colleagues in *The Authoritarian Personality* (Adorno et al. 1950). Levinson discovered that antisemitism was just one aspect of a person's broader outlook on society and politics. Fear and contempt for Jews, it turned out, was often accompanied by fear and contempt directed at blacks, criminals, Japanese Americans, conscientious objectors, immigrants, and "foreign ideas." To this wide-ranging syndrome of resentments Levinson gave the name *ethnocentrism*. In the next section, I argue for ethnocentrism's rehabilitation, to spell out the reasons why we need the idea of ethnocentrism to understand U.S. politics today.

Ethnocentrism

The term *ethnocentrism* was actually invented not by Daniel Levinson for use in the study of antisemitism but some fifty years before, at the turn of the century, by William Graham Sumner, a professor of political and social science at Yale, a distinguished scholar, and for a time, an ardent and influential social Darwinist. In his academic pursuits, Sumner believed passionately in the possibility of a comprehensive science of society and equally passionately that he was the one to provide it. He launched his audacious project with an essay on social norms. He intended it to be the first chapter in his comprehensive analysis, but when it grew past two hundred thousand words, Sumner surrendered to the advice of his friends and permitted it to be published separately. It appeared in 1906 under the imposing title: *Folkways. A Study of the Sociological Importance of Usages, Manners, Customs, Mores, and Morals.*[7]

Sumner created the idea of ethnocentrism to describe what he took to be a universal condition: namely, that members of human groups are convinced that their way of doing things—their folkways—are superior to the way things are done elsewhere. Ethnocentrism, as Sumner put it, is the

> technical name for this view of things in which one's own group is the center of everything.... Each group nourishes its own pride and vanity, boasts itself superior, exalts its own divinities, and looks with contempt on outsiders. Each group thinks its own folkways the only right ones, and if it observes that other groups have other folkways, these excite its scorn. (1906, 12)

For proof of ethnocentrism's ubiquity, Sumner cited Euripides, common knowledge, and a dozen or so ethnographies supplied by the anthropology of the day. From *Folkways* we learn that the Greenland Eskimo believe that Europeans appeared on the Eskimo homeland to be taught the good manners that the newcomers so conspicuously lacked, that the Mbayas of South America are instructed by divine authority to take their neighbors' wives and property, that the Chinese know that men of distinction come only from their own grand and glorious Middle Kingdom, and so on. More recent and systematic surveys merely fortify Sumner's original and disheartening point. When referring to outsiders, humans seem all too prepared to resort to terms of contempt and abomination. Around the world, in-group favoritism prevails (Brewer and Brown 1998; Brewer and Campbell 1976; Campbell and LeVine 1961; Sumner, Keller, and Davie 1927; Tajfel et al. 1971).[8]

So impressive is the generality of this inclination to venerate one's own and disparage outsiders that its origins are commonly ascribed to equally general conditions: the ubiquity of group conflict (e.g., Coser 1956), the evolutionary advantages of group solidarity (e.g., Campbell 1965), or the primitive and perhaps universal psychological need for positive identity (e.g., Tajfel 1981).

These arguments are fascinating, but my interest is less in ethnocentrism as a general habit and more in the possibility that some people are more ethnocentric than others—reliably and consistently so—and that such differences have consequences for how and what people think about politics. Ethnocentrism in this sense is all but invisible in modern political analysis, and it is especially hard to find in empirical studies of U.S. public opinion of the sort that I will describe shortly. I think this is a mistake, though I have not yet accumulated sufficient evidence to be certain. The project is under way, but not too far under way, and in this connection we should remember that in the social sciences, as someone once said, there are many departures but few arrivals.

My definition of ethnocentrism draws heavily on the writings of Daniel Levinson (1949; Adorno et al. 1950). Like Levinson, I take ethnocentrism to be an ideological system regarding groups and group relations. What does it mean to say that ethnocentrism is an ideological system? I mean first of all that ethnocentrism has considerable range: it is an ideological system about group relations in general, not an attitude toward one group in particular. Second, I mean that the beliefs that comprise ethnocentrism are well-organized, interconnected pieces of the same system: ethnocentrism is a coherent point of view. Third, by referring to ethnocentrism as an ideological system I mean to imply its stability: ethnocentrism is a habit, a hard-to-change perspective on the social world. Fourth and finally, like ideological systems generally, ethnocentrism is neither neutral nor free of emotion: the foundational elements that make up ethnocentrism are deeply evaluative and highly charged beliefs about social groups—that Jews are conniving, say, or that blacks are lazy.

Conceived of in this way, a primary and distinguishing feature of ethnocentrism is its generality. While prejudice is hostility directed at a specific group, ethnocentrism refers to a "relatively consistent frame of mind concerning 'aliens' generally" (Adorno et al. 1950, 102). Ethnocentrism, in contrast to prejudice, "has to do not only with numerous groups toward which the individual has hostile opinions and attitudes but, equally important, with groups toward which he is positively disposed." Thus when we turn our attention from racism or antisemitism or any other particular group animosity on the one hand to ethnocentrism on the other, we encounter, as Levinson once wrote, the "problem of prejudice, broadly conceived" (1949, 19).

Does ethnocentrism actually exist? Levinson was certain the answer was yes. He and his colleagues began their research in the early 1940s as an investigation of antisemitic attitudes in the United States, mindful of the horrific events unfolding in Europe. To measure such attitudes, Levinson drew on the writings of notorious antisemites and, as he put it, "everyday American antisemitism." The final version of the antisemitism scale includes such questions as:

> *Persecution of the Jews would be largely eliminated if the Jews would make really sincere efforts to rid themselves of their harmful and offensive faults.*
>
> *The trouble with letting Jews into a nice neighborhood is that they gradually give it a typical Jewish atmosphere.*

In composing these questions, Levinson was trying to avoid flagrant antisemitism, to soften and partially disguise antisemitic feelings by adding qualifying phrases and references to democratic ideals. Levinson and his associates then put these questions and others like them to samples of college students, schoolteachers, nurses, psychiatric patients, Kiwanis club members, veterans, and union members, among others. The questions are quite diverse—they roam over considerable territory and bring up a variety of conceivable objections to Jews—but people answer them consistently, as if they were about one thing only. Levinson concluded from such consistency that "antisemitism is best conceived psychologically not as a specific aversion but as an ideology, a general way of thinking about Jews and Jewish-Gentile interaction" (Adorno et al. 1950, 92).

Levinson and his colleagues next wanted to see whether antisemitism was linked with other animosities, whether it might not be one aspect of a broader outlook on family, society, and politics. In other words, the researchers shifted their focus from antisemitism to ethnocentrism. And to investigate ethnocentrism, Levinson developed a new set of questions, written once again to soft-pedal hostility and ranging over a wide array of targets: blacks, Japanese Americans, Filipinos, criminals, the insane, European refugees, even "foreign ideas." Remarkably enough, all these elements seemed to belong to the same system. That is, Americans who rejected "alien" ideas were (more or less) the same people who insisted that blacks be kept in their place, who questioned the loyalty of Japanese Americans, who were afraid of being contaminated by Jews, and so on. The generality of hostility in these materials is extraordinary.[9]

When *The Authoritarian Personality* was published, it was greeted with widespread acclaim and then, in the space of a few years, buried under an avalanche of criticism.[10] Two complaints did most of the damage. First, because of limitations of funding, Levinson and his colleagues were forced to rely on volunteers for their studies, and they accomplished this by working through formal organizations. The result was a sample that was disproportionately middle class and socially active—and therefore, perhaps, more likely to show the coherence of ideas about social groups and politics that was the study's central finding. Second and more damaging was the criticism that the truly impressive figures Levinson and his colleagues report on the consistency of social attitudes are inflated, for the correlations are partly a product of the tendency for people to agree to assertions irrespective of their content. We know this tendency today as the acquiescence response set, and its effects are surprisingly powerful (Altemeyer 1981).

So is there really such a thing as the ethnocentric turn of mind? In the end, Levinson and his colleagues cannot say. The critics were right to point out the study's defects, and they were persuasive. But it is important to keep in mind that they established only that *The Authoritarian Personality* failed to prove its conclusions, not that its conclusions were incorrect. This is an important distinction, one that seems to have been missed in the widespread and mostly well deserved battering the study received.

If it was left to others to make the case for this aspect of ethnocentrism, it seems to me that they have now made it. With measures corrected against the intrusions of response set, for samples drawn both inside and outside the United States, and for elites as well as ordinary citizens, the basic ethnocentrism result seems to hold. Much as Levinson and his colleagues concluded more than fifty years ago, disdain for any particular group appears to be part of a broader ideological system, one that finds and denigrates aliens and adversaries everywhere (e.g., Altemeyer 1981, 1996; McFarland, Ageyev, and Abalakina 1993).

We find this to be true in our own work as well (Kam and Kinder 1999; Kinder and Deane 1997; Kinder, Kam, and Deane 2000). For both theoretical and practical reasons, we have chosen to measure ethnocentrism through stereotypes. Stereotypes are beliefs that a person may hold or reject pertaining to the characteristic features of some group (e.g., Allport 1954; Stangor and Lange 1994). In contemporary cognitive psychology, stereotypes are treated as natural categories and stereotyping as a commonplace manifestation of the ubiquitous human process of categorization (e.g., Fiske 1998). As such, stereotypes are, we say, the right cognitive "container" for ethnocentrism: ethnocentrism is represented in the mind through stereotypes.

To measure ethnocentrism expressed in terms of stereotypes, we have drawn on a battery of questions originally developed by the National Opinion Research Center at the University of Chicago for use in its General Social Survey. Slightly modified, this measure was included in the 1992 and 1996 National Election Studies (NES), and it has provided the primary measure of ethnocentrism for our analysis so far. Here is the core question, lifted directly from the 1992 NES:

> Now I have some questions about different groups in our society. I'm going to show you a seven-point scale on which the characteristics of people in a group can be rated. In the first statement a score of 1 means that you think almost all of the people in that group are "hard-working." A score of 7 means that you think almost all of the people in the group are "lazy." A score of 4 means that you think the group is not towards one end or the other, and of course you may choose any number in between that comes closest to where you think people in the group stand.
>
> Where would you rate whites in general on this scale?

After being asked to judge whites on this score, respondents were then asked to make the same judgment, this time about blacks, Asian Americans, and Hispanic Americans, in turn. Then the same procedure was repeated with two other dimensions, first for "unintelligent versus intelligent" and then for "violent versus peaceful."

The aim of these questions is to assess the extent to which Americans subscribe to stereotyped representations of the moral character and intellectual capacity of various social groups. From our point of view, this concentration is apt on two grounds: first because such traits are central features of stereotypes (e.g., Fiske 1998; Stangor and Lange 1994), and second because ethnocentric claims of in-group superiority are commonly expressed precisely in such terms: in-groups are generally smarter, more industrious, more trustworthy and so on than are out-groups (Brewer and Campbell 1976; Levinson 1949).[11]

These questions are formatted so that people can express favoritism for their own group without flagrantly violating norms of fairness. Thus, for example, white Americans who believe that blacks are less intelligent on average then whites can say so indirectly, in a sequence of separated judgments, without ever having to subscribe explicitly to the invidious comparison. In addition to this practical advantage, measuring ethnocentrism through social comparison is also appropriate on theoretical grounds. Ethnocentrism requires consideration of in-groups and out-groups, and difference scores do just that.

With this in mind, to measure ethnocentrism, we first divided our national samples into three groups: blacks, Hispanics, and (non-Hispanic) whites.[12] Then for each group taken separately, we computed an average difference score, weighting equally each of the nine comparisons (3 out-groups × 3 attributes). Consistent with the expectation that ethnocentrism is an ideological system, this procedure yields a highly reliable scale.[13] In principle, the scale ranges from –1 to +1, where –1 means that Americans regard out-groups to be superior in every respect to their own group; +1 means that Americans regard out-groups to be inferior in every respect to their own group. This means that in a society free of ethnocentrism, our scale should be distributed in a tight band around 0, signifying that Americans regard out-groups and their own group to be (on average) indistinguishable.

In practice this is not what we find. Instead, most Americans display some ethnocentrism. The distribution of the ethnocentrism scale is centered not at zero. Rather, it is displaced in the ethnocentric direction, at +0.10. In percentage terms, a small number of Americans end up on the nonethnocentric side of the neutral point, and many land right on or close to it, but most Americans are to be found on the positive side of neutrality, in the region of ethnocentrism. Extreme ethnocentrism is rare, but in mild form, it is pervasive, much as Sumner would have anticipated.

Ethnocentrism and Public Opinion

The mere existence of ethnocentrism of course says nothing one way or the other about its political importance. Ethnocentrism might be a psychological curiosity, unconnected to the wider world of public life. My last bit of business here is to convince you otherwise, that ethnocentrism is politically consequential. I'll try to do so by providing a quick tour of two cases where our empirical analysis is furthest along: the first concerns immigration policy, while the second takes up war in the Persian Gulf.

Ethnocentrism and the Golden Door

The overwhelming majority of Americans come from some other place: Europe, Canada, the Middle East, Latin America, the Caribbean, the Indian subcontinent, Southeast Asia, Africa. No other country has been settled by such a variety of peoples. To the impoverished and persecuted around the world, the United States has been the "golden door," an opening to a prosperous, emancipated, and altogether better life.

Those in flight from poverty and violence are not always invited in, of course. At the beginning of the twentieth century, huge numbers of southern and eastern Europeans seeking refuge in the United States set off a flagrantly nativist reaction (Higham 1988). For many U.S. citizens at the time, immigration seemed to threaten the end of the American nation. One response was the Immigration Act of 1924, which imposed sharp limits on immigrants from outside the Western Hemisphere. The new law deliberately favored British and northern Europeans; it was, as the *Los Angeles Times* announced at the time and evidently without irony, a "Nordic Victory" (Mills 1994, 15).

By the end of the twentieth century, immigration had returned to the nation's political agenda, serving as a focal point for campaigns, state and national legislation, court cases, and everyday political discussions. During the 1980s, more than nine million people came to the United States, in raw numbers the largest migration in the country's history. The vast majority came from Latin America and Asia, and many entered the country illegally (Espenshade 1995). How do Americans think about this increasingly central and contentious issue? What role, if any, does ethnocentrism play in U.S. opinion on immigration?

To find out, Cindy Kam, Claudia Deane, and I have analyzed data supplied primarily by the 1992 and 1996 National Election Studies (Kinder and Deane 1997; Kinder, Kam, and Deane 2000). The comparative advantage of the 1992 NES for present purposes is that it included an extensive set of opinion questions on immigration, a reflection of the issue's return to political prominence. Answers to these various questions, summarized in table 1.1, display a U.S. public that is generally quite tough-minded in its views on immigration. Many more Americans believe that the number of immigrants admitted to the country should be decreased than say that immigration should be increased. Likewise, most say that legal immigrants should have to wait for government services after they arrive. Finally, Americans are generally more impressed with the negative consequences of immigration than the positive: on balance, they deny that Hispanic or Asian immigrants have anything to add to U.S. culture, worry that immigrant demand on public services will drive up taxes, and believe that immigrants will take jobs away from Americans already here.

If immigration is generally unpopular with the U.S. people, it is more unpopular in some quarters than in others. Why? How should variation in opinion on immigration be explained?

By ethnocentrism, perhaps. To see if this is so, we used the measure described in the preceding section of the chapter, based on stereotyped characterizations of racial and ethnic groups. To make our empirical results credible, our analysis takes into account explanations in addition to ethnocentrism, notably: (1) *Parochialism,* the notion that hostility directed at immigrants is partly a reflection of an unenlightened perspective on the wider world, measured by education and political knowledge (Citrin et al. 1990; Espenshade and Calhoun 1993; Quillian 1995; Simon and Alexander 1993). (2) *Perceptions of threat,* the claim, drawn from realistic group-conflict theory, that hostility and, by implication, opposition to immigration, are rooted primarily in the perception of threat (e.g., Blumer 1958; Coser 1956; Sherif and Sherif 1953; Sumner 1906). We represent threat in three different ways: working in low-wage, low-skill occupations, under the assumption that such workers are the most vul-

TABLE 1.1 American Opinion on Immigration

Immigration levels
Do you think the number of immigrants from foreign countries who are permitted to come to the United States to live should be increased a little, increased a lot, decreased a little, decreased a lot, or left the same as it is now?

Increased a lot	2.6%
Increased a little	5.3
Same as now	43.1
Decreased a little	25.9
Decreased a lot	23.2

Government Benefits for Immigrants
Do you think that immigrants who come to the United States should be eligible as soon as they come here for government services such as Medicaid, food stamps, and welfare, or should they have to be here for a year or more?

Eligible immediately	20.3
Wait a year or more	79.7

Consequences of Immigration
Many different groups of people have come to the United States at different times in our history. In recent years, the population of the United States has been changing to include many more people of Hispanic and Asian background. I'm going to read a list of things that people say may happen because of the growing number of Hispanic people in the United States. For each of these things, please say how likely it is to happen.

How likely is it that the growing number of Hispanics will improve our culture with new ideas and customs?

Extremely likely	3.0
Very likely	13.0
Somewhat likely	49.2
Not at all likely	34.8

(How likely is it) to cause higher taxes due to more demands for public services?

Extremely likely	19.6
Very likely	37.3
Somewhat likely	35.7
Not at all likely	7.4

(How likely is it) to take jobs away from people already here?

Extremely likely	20.3
Very likely	29.3
Somewhat likely	37.7
Not at all likely	12.6

How likely is it that the growing number of Asians will improve our culture with new ideas and customs?

Extremely likely	4.3
Very likely	17.0
Somewhat likely	53.2
Not at all likely	25.4

(How likely is it) to cause higher taxes due to more demands for public services?

Extremely likely	11.3
Very likely	27.3
Somewhat likely	43.3
Not at all likely	18.0

(How likely is it) to take jobs away from people already here?

Extremely likely	18.9
Very likely	30.8
Somewhat likely	37.5
Not at all likely	12.8

Source: 1992 National Election Study.
Note: Respondents who answered "don't know" to a particular question (never more than 3% of the sample) are excluded. Number of cases is 2,175.

nerable to economic competition from today's immigrants (Abowd and Freeman 1991; Borjas and Freeman 1992); living in states with large proportions of Hispanics and Asians, with the expectation that opinions on immigration will harden as the proportion of immigrants living in their states increases; and receiving federal assistance—specifically food stamps, AFDC, and Medicaid—anticipating that those most dependent on such programs may feel most threatened and so be most prepared to reduce the numbers of immigrants and to withhold benefits from those already arrived. (3) *Apprehensions about change in society's moral standards,* on the idea that immigration is opposed primarily by those most upset at the prospect of social change and moral contamination (Adorno et al. 1950). (4) *Faith in the capacity of the U.S. economy,* on the idea that generous opinions on immigration are more likely when the future seems bright, when the economy appears capable of assimilating new arrivals. And (5) *Commitment to political principles,* on the idea that Americans come to their opinions on immigration as they do on other topics, that is, by deciding whether a particular policy matches or violates their principles (Feldman 1988; Feldman and Zaller 1992; Kinder and Sanders 1996), represented here by two core ideas in particular: equal opportunity and limited government.[14]

The effects of ethnocentrism on U.S. immigration opinion, with all these alternative explanations taken into account, are summarized in table 1.2. Given the form taken by the measures of immigration opinion, we relied on ordered probit for statistical estimation. For convenience of interpretation, we coded all our measures of opinion on immigration onto the 0–1 interval, with 1 representing the "generous" position.[15]

The coefficient estimates arrayed in the first row of table 1.2 indicate that Americans' views on immigration are indeed determined in an important way by ethnocentrism. According to these results, ethnocentrism predisposes Americans to believe that immigration should be cut back; that immigrants

TABLE I.2. Effects of Ethnocentrism on Americans' Opinion toward Immigration

	Levels of Immigration	Assistance to Immigrants	Hispanic Immigrants' Impact on:			Asian Immigrants' Impact on:		
			Culture	Taxes	Jobs	Culture	Taxes	Jobs
Ethnocentrism	-.857*** (.168)	-1.013*** (.249)	-1.397*** (.180)	-1.086*** (.168)	-1.122*** (.169)	-1.396*** (.176)	-1.068*** (.166)	-.813*** (.167)
Moral traditionalism	-.736*** (.148)	.320 (.199)	-.642*** (.151)	-.975*** (.147)	-.742*** (.146)	-.351** (.148)	-.616*** (.147)	-.737*** (.145)
Political awareness	.304*** (.119)	.426*** (.163)	.121 (.123)	.193 (.119)	.620*** (.119)	.550*** (.122)	.657*** (.119)	.498*** (.118)
Education	.246** (.125)	.112 (.170)	.028 (.129)	.098 (.124)	.290** (.124)	.214* (.127)	.324*** (.124)	.326*** (.123)
Occupation: low	.040 (.078)	.211** (.108)	.095 (.081)	-.007 (.077)	-.090 (.077)	-.021 (.079)	-.012 (.077)	.031 (.077)
Occupation: high	.006 (.089)	.202* (.121)	.060 (.092)	.067 (.089)	.034 (.089)	-.070 (.091)	.025 (.089)	-.022 (.088)
Out of labor market	.215*** (.083)	.094 (.117)	.301*** (.086)	-.083 (.082)	.014 (.082)	.221*** (.084)	.016 (.082)	.134* (.082)
Proportion Hispanic and Asian in state (log)	-.014 (.026)	.014 (.035)	.041 (.027)	-.038 (.026)	.084*** (.026)	-.016 (.027)	.042 (.026)	.074*** (.026)
Dependence on government programs	.091 (.131)	.761*** (.165)	.419*** (.133)	-.058 (.130)	-.071 (.130)	.231* (.133)	-.135 (.130)	-.199 (.130)
Retrospective economic assessments	.553*** (.158)	.588*** (.214)	.036 (.162)	.505*** (.157)	.659*** (.157)	.041 (.160)	.645*** (.157)	.712*** (.156)
Egalitarianism	.473*** (.151)	1.092*** (.205)	.654*** (.156)	.412*** (.150)	.278* (.149)	.384** (.153)	.256* (.150)	.012 (.149)

Limited government	.022	-.177	.033	.025	.112	.019	.254***	.072
	(.081)	(.111)	(.083)	(.081)	(.080)	(.082)	(.081)	(.080)
δ_1	-.503	2.15	-.442	-.982	-.959	-.335	-1.01	-1.02
δ_2	.247		1.07	.070	-.053	1.21	-.027	-.118
δ_3	1.77		2.03	1.44	1.21	2.13	1.30	1.08
δ_4	2.38							
n	1,695	1,666	1,721	1,716	1,720	1,719	1,715	1,722
Log-likelihood	-2,119.45	-815.33	-1,761.16	-2,056.76	-2,120.41	-1,851.61	-2,053.96	-2,171.00
χ^2_{12}	141.05	121.14	191.05	185.34	276.92	173.86	268.28	189.77

Source: 1992 National Election Study.

Note: Table entry is the ordered probit regression coefficient, with standard errors in parentheses. Each column is a separate equation.

*$p < .10$; **$p < .05$; ***$p < .01$.

should wait, perhaps indefinitely, for government benefits; that immigrants raise taxes, displace workers, and (especially) contribute nothing to U.S. culture. The effect of ethnocentrism easily surpasses statistical significance in every case.

As important as ethnocentrism is for opinion on immigration, it is of course not the whole story. Table 1.2 shows that several of the plausible explanations that we included in our analysis matter as well. U.S. opinion on immigration is a reflection of not one thing but many things: ethnocentrism, to be sure, but also ignorance, worry about decline in moral standards, faith in the capacity of the U.S. economy, and commitment to the ideal of equal opportunity. But if ethnocentrism is not the only force behind opinion on immigration, it is a strong and consistent one, rivaling or exceeding in power any other explanation that we considered.

This power of ethnocentrism for immigration opinion can be seen more clearly in graphical form. Effect size is difficult to read directly from probit coefficients, so we used the estimates reported in table 1.2 to generate predicted scores on immigration opinion, presenting them in figure 1.1, for each of four representative instances: whether immigration should be increased or curtailed, whether or not immigrants should have to wait for government benefits, the likelihood that Hispanic immigrants will take jobs away from people already here, and the likelihood that Asian immigrants will drive up taxes.[16]

Figure 1.1 shows that opposition to immigration policy rises steeply with increases in ethnocentrism. Consider perhaps the most basic question of all, whether levels of immigration should be altered or kept the same. Our results indicate that across the range of ethnocentrism found in the U.S. public today (that is, from roughly –.2 to .5), the likelihood that an otherwise average American would support cuts in immigration increases from about 40 percent to nearly 70 percent. The other graphs set out in figure 1.1 tell essentially the same story.

In short, if ethnocentrism is not the only force behind U.S. opinion on immigration, it is a strong and consistent one. One could fairly say, with these results in hand, that public opinion on immigration derives in an important way from prejudice, broadly conceived.[17]

Ethnocentrism and Desert Storm

On 2 August 1990, at Saddam Hussein's command, Iraqi troops poured across the country's border with Kuwait and quickly seized control of its vital centers. In less than a week, Hussein was able to announce to the world that Kuwait belonged—or in the formulation he preferred, had rightfully been returned—to Iraq. President Bush immediately denounced the invasion, referring to it as a form of "naked aggression." The president pledged U.S. participation in an

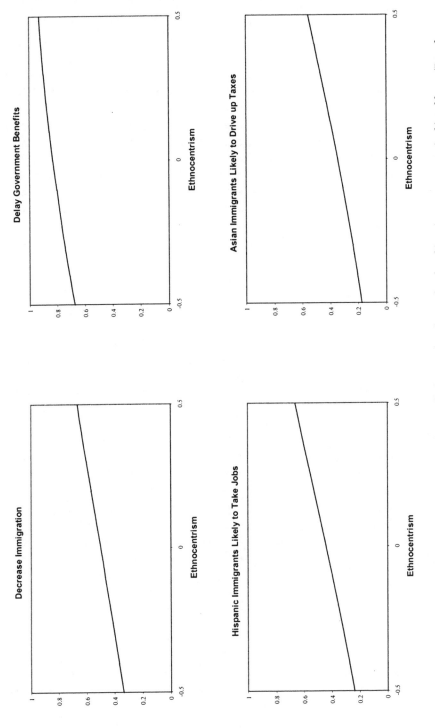

Fig. 1.1. Ethnocentrism predicts opposition to immigration. Predictions are based on ordered probit estimates as summarized in table 1.2. (Data from 1992 National Election Study.)

economic blockade of Iraq, dispatched U.S. warships to the Persian Gulf, and, several days later, announced that he was sending troops to Saudi Arabia to defend against potential Iraqi incursions there. Early in November, without clear evidence that the economic sanctions were working and apprehensive that the international coalition enforcing the economic blockade might unravel, Bush began to lay the groundwork for a military offensive. Following the midterm congressional elections, the president announced a substantial increase in the U.S. military presence in the Middle East. By the end of the month, Bush succeeded in persuading the United Nations Security Council to authorize force against Hussein's troops unless they withdrew from Kuwait by 15 January. On the home front, meanwhile, Bush's impatience with economic sanctions and his escalation of the military option provoked alarm and criticism from Democrats in Congress. Hearings began, followed by a contentious floor debate. As the 15 January deadline approached, Congress voted, largely along partisan lines, to authorize the use of force. Promising that victory would establish "a new world order," the president declared as the deadline expired that "the world could wait no longer." On 16 January, with no sign of Iraqi withdrawal, U.S. forces entered the war, first through a devastating aerial bombardment and then, five weeks later, through a massive ground assault. Iraqi troops broke and ran. In short order, a cease-fire was announced, sovereignty was restored to Kuwait, and victory was declared. By the end of February, from the point of view of most Americans, the Persian Gulf War had passed into history (Mueller 1994).

In a pair of previous papers, Lisa D'Ambrosio and I (Kinder 1993; Kinder and D'Ambrosio 1998) analyzed U.S. reaction to the Persian Gulf War, paying special attention to emotion. Our primary purpose was to use this episode to clarify the nature and demonstrate the importance of emotion for political life. My object here is to show that the emotional reactions that Americans experienced as the war unfolded can be accounted for, in part, by ethnocentrism.

To do so, I draw on evidence provided by the well-timed 1990–91–92 NES Panel Study. As part of NES's continuing study of congressional elections, personal interviews were completed with a national probability sample of two thousand U.S. citizens of voting age immediately following the 1990 national midterm elections. Most were questioned after President Bush announced increases in troop strength in the Middle East and before the congressional debate over the authorization of force. Nearly fourteen hundred of these same respondents were then reinterviewed in June and July 1991, after the welcome home victory parades and as the dust of Desert Storm had begun to settle, and then again in the fall of 1992, both before and after the national elections. Roughly midway through the summer 1991 interview, respondents were asked to recollect their emotional reactions to the war:

We are interested in the feelings you might have had during the Persian Gulf War—not the feelings you have now, but how you felt then, during the war. During the war, did you ever feel:

proud?
upset?
sympathy for the Iraqi people?
worried that the fighting might spread?
angry at Saddam Hussein?
disgusted at the killing?
afraid for American troops?

When respondents indicated that they had felt a particular emotion, they were asked in a follow-up question about whether they had felt it strongly.

This inventory corresponds quite well to what psychologists call basic emotions. Basic emotions emerge early in life, show up in all cultures, and, perhaps most important, represent adaptations that have evolved to prepare the human species to cope with a set of fundamental life tasks—"universal predicaments"—that have recurred innumerable times in evolutionary history: fighting, falling in love, escaping predators, confronting sexual infidelity (Damasio 1994; Ekman 1992; Lazarus 1991). Emotions, defined this way, are a common feature of everyday experience and, as table 1.3 shows, common as well in the U.S. public's reaction to the Gulf War.

Indeed, one could say that table 1.3 is overrun with emotion. For example, an overwhelming majority of Americans reported experiencing intense anger at Saddam Hussein, and nearly half reported strong feelings of sympathy for the Iraqi people. Such results speak to the richness of emotional response to the war. More than half those interviewed (58.5 percent) reported at least six discrete emotional reactions to the war, and of the 1,385 Americans questioned in the summer of 1991, exactly 1 admitted to no emotional experience whatever.

TABLE 1.3. Americans' Emotional Reactions to the 1991 Persian Gulf War

	Yes	Yes and Strong
During the war, did you ever feel:		
Proud	72.8%	59.6%
Upset	75.6	60.9
Worried that the fighting might spread	67.6	50.5
Disgusted at the killing	84.8	74.8
Afraid for U.S. troops	87.4	78.4
Sympathy for the Iraqi people	74.8	47.6
Angry at Saddam Hussein	92.4	86.5

Source: 1990–92 National Election Study.

The findings shown in table 1.3 suggest a contrast between the distribution of emotion in mass publics on the one hand and the distribution of information on the other. Regarding information, Converse once offered the aphorism: "low mean, high variance" (1990, 372). By this he meant that the average citizen knows remarkably little about politics but that the range of information among citizens is remarkable, too, from citizens who know virtually nothing to those who know practically everything. Rather the reverse seems to hold for political emotion: for emotion, the formula seems to be high mean, low variance.

In our previous papers, we have shown that emotional reactions to the Gulf War were not just common but consequential. When U.S. forces entered the war in mid-January, public support for President Bush and his policies shot skyward. Our findings suggest that these dramatic changes in public opinion can be traced back at least in part to emotion. That is, citizens treat their emotional experience as informative (Schwarz 1992). Thus, for example,

- Americans who reported that they had experienced *pride* as the war was being fought became more favorable in their view of the President's performance and more certain that the United States had done the right thing in sending troops to the Persian Gulf, while those who said they had been *upset* by the war moved in the opposite direction.
- Americans who reported that they had experienced *anger* at Saddam Hussein were more inclined to say that U.S. forces should have continued into Baghdad to remove him from power.
- Americans whose emotional experience included *sympathy* for the Iraqi people tended to think that the United States did not act quickly enough in providing assistance to the Kurds.

The question for present purposes is the extent to which these politically consequential emotional reactions to the war can be accounted for by ethnocentrism.[18]

The answer appears in table 1.4. For the purpose of this analysis, ethnocentrism is measured exactly as in our analysis of U.S. opinion toward immigration. The table is partitioned into seven columns, one for each of the emotions. Each equation also includes, for purposes of statistical control, measures of gender, age, attention paid to public affairs, and information about politics. The estimates presented in table 1.4 come, once again, from an ordered probit analysis, with all variables coded for convenience onto the 0–1 interval.

The main business of table 1.4 is to reveal whether a connection exists between ethnocentrism and emotion. As in the case of immigration, we are once again not disappointed. Ethnocentrism does indeed predict Americans' emotional reactions to the Persian Gulf War (see the coefficients arrayed in the first row of the table). Ethnocentrism is not the only relevant factor, of course.

Table 1.4 also reveals that, as expected, women were consistently more likely to report emotional experience than men and that attention to public affairs accentuated emotional response to war, while information more often moderated it. But taking these effects into account, ethnocentrism contributed independently to emotion. Moreover, the effects of ethnocentrism show up most visibly just where they should, on emotions that reinforce in-group solidarity or heighten hostility toward the out-group. Thus ethnocentrically inclined Americans were more likely to experience pride in the U.S. triumph, less likely to report being upset by the war, more apt to feel anger toward Hussein, and less likely to experience sympathy for the Iraqi people.

These results can be seen more clearly in figure 1.2, where we translate the probit results on emotion into graphical form, just as we did earlier for the case of immigration. Figure 1.2 presents curves summarizing the likelihood that average Americans will (strongly) experience a particular emotion solely as a function of differences in ethnocentrism. As shown there, pride, upset, anger, and sympathy—all of which exercise politically consequential effects on Americans' views of President Bush and his policies—are all systematically and quite powerfully determined by ethnocentrism.

That ethnocentrism figures so prominently in the U.S. public's reaction to the Persian Gulf War may not be that surprising. If we are to find evidence of ethno-

TABLE 1.4. Effects of Ethnocentrism on Americans' Emotional Reactions to the 1991 Persian Gulf War

	Proud	Upset	Worried	Disgusted	Afraid	Sympathetic	Angry
Ethnocentrism	1.090***	−.636**	−.278	−.636**	.070	−.712***	2.421***
	(.269)	(.258)	(.251)	(.294)	(.303)	(.242)	(.501)
Female	−.207**	.812***	.451***	.839***	.535***	.416***	.380***
	(.092)	(.094)	(.088)	(.105)	(.105)	(.086)	(.126)
Age	−.339	−.501**	−.328	.734***	−.338	.417**	−.299
	(.218)	(.219)	(.209)	(.253)	(.244)	(.203)	(.303)
Attention	.777***	.257	.409*	.531**	.523**	.208	.934***
	(.218)	(.222)	(.210)	(.242)	(.245)	(.204)	(.294)
Information	−.362	.019	−.527**	−.686**	−.744***	.525**	−.473
	(.245)	(.249)	(.238)	(.278)	(.283)	(.233)	(.330)
δ_1	−.466	−.420	−.350	−.499	−1.05	−.082	−1.01
δ_2	−.090	.034	.118	−.083	−.630	.696	−.619
n	770	771	773	765	771	772	771
Log-likelihood	−694.18	−675.15	−767.65	−521.83	−506.26	−798.77	−324.14
χ_5^2	32.94	84.23	37.72	98.38	42.51	41.57	53.53

Source: 1990–92 National Election Study.

Note: Table entry is the ordered probit regression coefficient, with standard errors in parentheses. Each column is a separate equation.

*$p < .10$; **$p < .05$; ***$p < .01$.

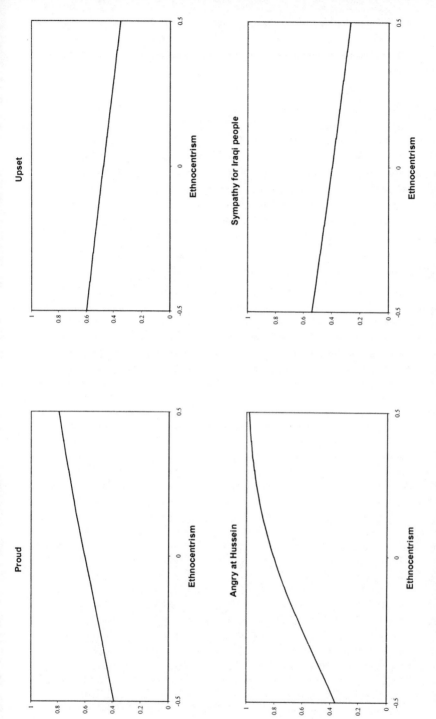

Fig. 1.2. Ethnocentrism predicts emotional reactions to the Gulf War. Predictions are based on ordered probit estimates as summarized in table 1.4. (Data from 1990–91–92 National Election Study.)

centrism anywhere, we should find it most abundantly in the case of war. True enough, but keep in mind that ethnocentrism in our analysis is measured with reference entirely to social groups in *America:* white Americans, black Americans, Hispanic Americans, and Asian Americans. Those Americans who regard their own racial or ethnic groups to be superior to other U.S. racial and ethnic groups were especially angry at Saddam Hussein and especially indifferent to the suffering of the Iraqi people. What is informative about these results, what adds to the case for ethnocentrism, is that emotional reactions to the war were determined not by aversion to Arabs and Iraqis but by prejudice, broadly conceived.

Conclusions and Implications

By most standards, Americans are remarkably affluent, well educated, and virtually swimming in information about the wider world of politics. Yet despite these advantages, most Americans glance at the political world bewildered by ideological concepts, without a consistent outlook on public policy, holding real opinions on just a handful of issues, and knowing precious little about the vicissitudes of political life. So it was, according to Converse, in the Eisenhower years, and so, by and large, I've suggested here, it remains today.

Rather than dwell on the negative in Converse's brilliant analysis—the failure of most Americans to reason about politics in ideologically sophisticated and informationally rich ways—here I have tried to accentuate the positive, to emphasize and amplify Converse's affirmative suggestion about how Americans might think about politics. If ideological principles are too abstract and too demanding, many Americans will organize their opinions around visible social groupings, simplifying complex questions of public policy by turning them into judgments on the deservingness of the groups involved. The evidence on groupcentrism available to Converse as he was dissecting U.S. belief systems some forty years ago was fragmentary; today it is overwhelming.

Not content to let things rest there, in the final part of my chapter I took Converse's suggestion much further than he intended and ended up calling, perhaps surprisingly, for the rehabilitation of ethnocentrism: not that we should have more ethnocentrism in politics, but that we should have more ethnocentrism in political analysis. *The Authoritarian Personality,* I suggested, was on to something, and to clarify what that something was I offered two empirical demonstrations: one concerning attitudes toward immigration, the other on support for war. In both cases, ethnocentrism emerged as a principal determinant of opinion.[19]

Two empirical demonstrations are better than one, of course, but the argument for ethnocentrism requires more. If ethnocentrism is a general ideological system—if it is prejudice, broadly conceived—then its effects must show up in lots of places, not just one or two. With this requirement in mind, we have begun to extend our analysis of ethnocentrism into additional domains—welfare, social insurance, crime, language (Gross and Kinder 2000; Kam and Kinder 1999; Kinder, Kam, and Deane 2000)—and we are planning still more (religion, race, gender and sexuality).

Here at the close of the chapter, I want to touch briefly on two questions. First, if ethnocentrism is as significant as I have suggested, then what conditions activate ethnocentrism, turn ethnocentrism from a mere human habit into a political force? Second, what does the rehabilitation of ethnocentrism imply for Converse's conclusion, which is where we began, that Americans are, by and large, innocent of ideology?

Activating Ethnocentrism

Higham may be correct when he writes that "no age or society seems wholly free from unfavorable opinions on outsiders" (1988, 3); he is certainly right about contemporary U.S. society. But the presence of ethnocentrism among Americans is not the same as the presence of ethnocentrism in our politics. Ethnocentrism not only bubbles up from below but is shaped and activated from above. The expression of ethnocentrism in politics depends substantially on the activities of elites—elected officials, members of the press, parties and interest groups, who influence which issues come to prominence and how such issues are framed.

In advancing this claim I am borrowing one last time from someone named Converse. Groupcentrism, Converse suggested, provides a powerful logic for public opinion, but he was quick to add that there was nothing inevitable or universal about it. Groupcentrism requires that citizens see for themselves a connection between some political dispute on the one hand and some visible social grouping on the other. That is, to get groupcentrism up and running, citizens must, as Converse put it, "be endowed with some cognitions of the group as an entity and with some interstitial 'linking' information indicating why a given party or policy is relevant to the group. Neither of these forms of information can be taken for granted" (1964, 236–37). Thus groupcentrism and, by extension, ethnocentrism depend on information, and so both can be short-circuited by the kinds of informational shortcomings that students of public opinion run into regularly.

These gaps in public understanding are of course partly a product of the limited attention and modest skills that citizens typically bring to politics. We see this vividly in our own analysis, and in just the way that Converse would expect. In particular, we frequently find interactions between ethnocentrism and political information. The effects of ethnocentrism are strongest among the best-informed citizens. Among the least informed, the effects of ethnocentrism are weakest, often disappearing entirely.

The extent to which citizens possess the requisite underlying information also depends on what is happening in politics. Ethnocentrism, I'm suggesting, will be a more or less prominent feature of U.S. public opinion depending on the particular constellation of issues temporarily holding center stage. Immigration lends itself to ethnocentrism in a way that health care reform does not. Moreover, political issues are multifaceted; they are always, as Verba and his colleagues put it, "many issues at once" (1987, 94). A proposal to increase federal spending on finding a cure for AIDS might be framed in any number of ways: as the right response to a lethal disease; as a diversion of resources away from more pressing health needs; or as squandering money and attention on homosexuals and drug abusers. Ethnocentrism seems much more likely to be activated by the last frame than by the first two. Thus, even if ethnocentrism is pervasive, there is nothing inevitable about ethnocentric politics: the place of ethnocentrism in political life depends on how citizens understand the issues and events of their time, and this, in turn, depends on how those issues and events are framed (Kinder and Sanders 1990, 1996; Nelson and Kinder 1996).

Back to Belief Systems

In "The Nature of Belief Systems in Mass Publics," Converse dealt a permanent and fatal blow to the proposition that Americans reason about politics in ideologically sophisticated ways. To Converse, Americans appeared quite "innocent" of ideology. Innocent of ideology, yes, but not innocent altogether.

One recent and instructive turn in the quantitative study of public opinion has been to take up public opinion one instance at a time: opinion in a particular domain on a specific topic. By abandoning the analysis of belief *systems,* such analysis is necessarily less panoramic and sweeping than what Converse provided. Here I have in mind research on the willingness of Americans to extend political rights to groups they despise (e.g., Sullivan, Pierson, and Marcus 1982), views on relations with the Soviet Union (Bartels 1992), opinions on policies intended to reduce poverty and economic inequality (Bobo and Kluegel 1993), affirmative action (Bobo and Smith 1994; Kinder and Sanders 1996), welfare reform (Gilens 1999), or the work I have briefly described here on immigration and war. In each of these quite different domains, analysts have succeeded in uncovering a relatively sturdy foundation for opinion. Not nonattitudes but real opinions seem to be on display, reasonably well embedded in a set of relevant political and social considerations. Such findings suggest a structure and intelligibility to public opinion rather greater than Converse's original analysis implied and so suggest a more widespread competence in public affairs than where things were left in 1964.

But structure and intelligibility ain't everything. It seems to me that the ideas and sentiments that are providing the intelligibility and structure are often democratically disheartening. For example, the reluctance to extend rights to others has its roots partly in personal distress and insecurity—the "psychological burden of freedom," as Lane (1962, 26) once put it. An important ingredient in whites' opposition to affirmative action programs and support for welfare reform—probably the most important ingredient—is racism (Gilens 1999; Kinder and Sanders 1996). And, of course, an additional and perfect case in point is provided by ethnocentrism. Here I've tried to suggest that there is something real and systematic behind opposition to more generous immigration policies and support for military intervention, and that something is ethnocentrism. Like the ideological principles that Converse looked for but could not find, groupcentrism and ethnocentrism hold out the promise of a general solution to the puzzle of public opinion, but not necessarily an inspiring one. That public opinion is real and that it is organized in systematic and knowable ways does not necessarily make it, or the policies that it influences, enlightened.

NOTES

I am grateful to Cindy Kam for her help in the analysis and presentation of empirical results here.

1. Years ago, stumbling through graduate school, I came upon a paper by someone named Converse. Reading "The Nature of Belief Systems in Mass Publics" was astonishing and exhilarating, as high-octane an intellectual experience as I could want. The power and reach of the analysis on display drew me into Converse's line of work—not that I could do what he did, but what he did could be an ambitious and honorable calling.

During this period I was reading Converse voraciously, but I had not yet met him, never even glimpsed him. I imagined him vividly, however. In my mind, he was a huge figure, with a gigantic head.

That turned out to be wrong. But in an important way my mind's eye had it exactly right: Converse was and remains a towering intellectual figure. I am delighted to have this opportunity to register my abiding admiration for his work.

2. Conceding defeat, this paper was published with the yawny title "Diversity and Complexity in American Public Opinion" (Kinder 1983).

3. Converse himself partly conceded this point (1975)—and in so doing, I believe, conceded too much (Kinder 1983).

4. For more than you are likely to want to know on this topic, see Kinder 1983, 1998.

5. This "review" of mine, in so far as it is a review at all, has passed over all kinds of interesting arguments and results—as it must, in the interests of space. One line of work I cannot ignore entirely, however, is that which takes off from the nonattitude thesis, perhaps the most devastating element in Converse's original indictment. If Converse is right here, then when it comes to politics, people simply don't know what they want. "Democratic theory," as Achen put it, "loses its starting point" (1975, 1227).

As Converse argued, unstable opinions are a direct sign of the casual and shallow character of much everyday political thinking. But the recent rise to prominence of such issues as abortion and affirmative action suggests that issue publics need not be confined to small splinters of the general public. When policy proposals become entangled in moral, racial, and religious feelings, the nonattitude problem may diminish quite dramatically (e.g., Converse and Markus 1979; Feldman 1989). Moreover, unstable opinions are partly a product of the imperfect way we put questions to citizens (Achen 1975; Krosnick and Berent 1993) and partly a reflection of elites failing to provide frames that would help citizens find their way to real opinions (e.g., Chong 1993; Kinder and Sanders 1996; Zaller and Feldman 1992). Improve the questions, induce elites to provide a clarifying debate, and real attitudes will increase. Taken all around, the problem posed by nonattitudes seems to be a bit more remediable than Converse's analysis originally implied.

6. Converse could cite only a few fragments of evidence from his own analysis on this point. One was that the association between opinions on fair play for black Americans in employment and housing, on the one hand, and opinions on whether the government in Washington should ensure that white and black children attend school together, on the other, was conspicuously large. Not only was this association larger than any other correlation in the entire mass public matrix, it was also larger than the corresponding correlation found among elites—the only such decisive reversal Converse came across in all his analysis. Another bit of supporting evidence was that the opinions of Americans on issues of race were much more stable over time than were opinions on matters of public policy generally: that is, such opinions were less subject to the charge that they were really nonattitudes.

In this empirically impoverished condition, Converse might have chosen to remind us of a smashing result presented earlier in his paper (and earlier still in Campbell et al. 1960), perhaps the major positive finding to emerge from the otherwise futile quest for the ideological foundations of U.S. public opinion: when Americans are asked to evaluate political parties and presidential candidates, respondents refer mostly to social groups. In Converse's (1964) original classification, some 42 percent did so, typically by naming benefits and deprivations that parties and candidates had visited on social groupings in the past or might deliver in the future.

Converse may have been reluctant to cite this evidence because the "group benefits" result mixes together citizens who favor or oppose a party or candidate because of what they did or might do to their *own* groups with those who favor or oppose a party or candidate because of what they did or might do to their *reference* groups (see Converse 1964, 216). Converse had only the latter in mind when he wrote of social groupings as central objects in belief systems.

7. The comprehensive sociology was completed by Sumner's associates following his death and published in four volumes by Yale University Press (Sumner, Keller, and Davie 1927).

8. This literature is persuasive, as far as it goes, but what is missing here, perhaps surprisingly, is systematic evidence on in-group favoritism among naturally occurring groups in postindustrial stratified societies such as the United States. Part of what we have accomplished in our ongoing research on ethnocentrism has been to fill this gap. I'll refer to some of these results later in the chapter.

9. As their work proceeded, Levinson and his associates became convinced that

ethnocentric ideology could be explained only by invoking the idea of personality, that antisemitism and ethnocentrism are themselves expressions of a deeper psychological coherence. Underneath ethnocentric ideology, they tried to show, was the authoritarian personality. I am not so interested in this part of their story, and in any case, I am persuaded much less by it. Other explanations for ethnocentrism—provided by realistic group-conflict theory (Coser 1956; Olzak 1992; Sumner 1906) or by social-identity theory (Tajfel 1981)—also are not entirely persuasive. The underlying causes of ethnocentrism remain elusive (Kinder 1999, chap. 2).

10. Especially devastating were the essays collected in Christie and Jahoda 1954, particularly Hyman and Sheatsley's masterful critique. More generally, my reading of *The Authoritarian Personality* draws on Altemeyer 1981; Christie 1954; and most of all, Brown 1965, chap. 1. Brown's work remains to this day the most insightful discussion of the study itself, the methodological hue and cry that it incited, and what remained to take seriously after the controversy passed.

11. Our measure of ethnocentrism takes in-groups and out-groups to be defined by race and ethnicity. Depending on the issues at stake, these boundary lines might be defined in many other ways: by family, neighborhood, sexual orientation, occupation, class, religion, national community, and more. Our work is beginning to explore some of these alternative possibilities.

12. We would have liked to examine the reactions of Asian Americans as well, but the National Election Study does not supply enough cases to support even the most rudimentary analysis. For related reasons, any results for Hispanics should be read cautiously. *Hispanic* is a generic category, convenient for some administrative purposes, perhaps, but concealing enormous diversity (see, e.g., Portes and Truelove 1987).

13. Cronbach's *alpha* for the composite scale of ethnocentrism is .88 for whites, .74 for blacks, and .68 for Hispanics.

14. For details on measurement, see Kinder, Kam, and Deane 2000.

15. All other right-hand-side variables are coded on the 0–1 interval as well, with one exception: the proportion of each state's population accounted for by Hispanics and Asians (logged), which ranges from 4.71 (West Virginia) to 1.04 (California).

16. These computations assume individuals who, apart from their scores on the ethnocentrism scale, are typical of the population as a whole: high school educated, employed in a middling occupation, and average on all other predictor variables.

17. The effects of ethnocentrism on display in table 1.2 and figure 1.1 are not only sizable but robust. They show up under various alternative specifications, with different measures of ethnocentrism, and in the 1996 NES data as well as in 1992. Details on all this and more are spelled out in Kinder, Kam, and Deane 2000.

18. Emotion influenced Americans' assessments of President Bush and his policies in another way as well: the experience of anxiety induced Americans to take the war more seriously than they otherwise would, thus elevating the importance of the war's outcome for the president's reputation and popularity (Kinder and D'Ambrosio 1998; this result is consistent with those reported by Marcus and MacKuen 1993, as set in the context of U.S. presidential campaigns).

19. The results on ethnocentrism I've presented here are "on average effects." But of course there is no reason to think that the same effect should describe everyone, that ethnocentrism should be equally important for all Americans. An important feature of our analysis has been to look for evidence of the variable impact of ethnocentrism, and

although I do not have the space to provide a general review of these results, one finding does bear mentioning. We find strong and consistent suggestions that ethnocentrism matters more for whites than it does for blacks or Hispanics. Whites are more likely to show in-group favoritism; their rejection of out-groups is more consistent; and these attitudes, which together comprise the ideological system that is ethnocentrism, much more successfully predict whites' views on immigration and on war. These findings generally conform to Tajfel's (1981) suggestion that ethnocentrism appeals primarily to members of dominant groups. For those occupying positions of wealth, privilege, and power, ethnocentrism provides a powerful defense of the status quo. Things are as they should be; virtue has been rewarded. Meanwhile, groups at the bottom of society have a more difficult time convincing even themselves of their superiority.

REFERENCES

Abowd, John M., and Richard B. Freeman, eds. 1991. *Immigration, Trade, and the Labor Market.* Chicago: University of Chicago Press.

Achen, Christopher H. 1975. Mass Political Attitudes and the Survey Response. *American Political Science Review* 69:1218–31.

Adorno, T. W., Else Frenkel-Brunswik, D. J. Levinson, and R. N. Sanford. 1950. *The Authoritarian Personality.* New York: Harper.

Allport, Gordon W. 1954. *The Nature of Prejudice.* Reading, Mass.: Addison-Wesley.

Altemeyer, Bob. 1981. *Right-Wing Authoritarianism.* Winnipeg: University of Manitoba Press.

————. 1996. *The Authoritarian Specter.* Cambridge: Harvard University Press.

Bartels, Larry. 1992. The American Public's Defense Spending Preferences in the Post–Cold War Era. *Public Opinion Quarterly* 58:479–508.

Blumer, Herbert. 1958. Race Prejudice as a Sense of Group Position. *Pacific Sociological Review* 1:3–7.

Bobo, Lawrence, and James R. Kleugel. 1993. Opposition to Race Targeting: Self-Interest, Stratification Ideology, or Racial Attitudes? *American Sociological Review* 58:443–64.

Bobo, Lawrence, and Ryan A. Smith. 1994. Antipoverty Policy, Affirmative Action, and Racial Attitudes. In S. Danziger, G. D. Sandefur, and D. H. Weinberg, eds., *Confronting Poverty: Prescriptions for Change.* Cambridge: Harvard University Press.

Borjas, George J., and Richard B. Freeman, eds. 1992. *Immigration and the Work Force.* Chicago: University of Chicago Press.

Brewer, Marilyn B., and Rupert J. Brown. 1998. Intergroup Relations. In Daniel Gilbert, Susan Fiske, and Gardner Lindzey, eds., *Handbook of Social Psychology,* 4th ed. Boston: McGraw-Hill.

Brewer, Marilyn B., and Donald T. Campbell. 1976. *Ethnocentrism and Intergroup Attitudes.* New York: Wiley.

Brown, Roger. 1965. *Social Psychology.* New York: Free Press.

Campbell, Angus, Philip E. Converse, Warren E. Miller, and Donald E. Stokes. 1960. *The American Voter.* New York: Wiley.

Campbell, Donald T. 1965. Ethnocentric and Other Altruistic Motives. In D. Levine, ed., *Nebraska Symposium on Motivation.* Lincoln: University of Nebraska Press.

Campbell, Donald T., and Robert A. LeVine. 1961. A Proposal for Cooperative Cross-Cultural Research on Ethnocentrism. *Journal of Conflict Resolution* 5:82–108.

Chong, Dennis. 1993. How People Think, Reason, and Feel about Rights and Liberties. *American Journal of Political Science* 37:867–99.

Christie, Richard. 1954. Authoritarianism Re-Examined. In Richard Christie and Marie Jahoda, eds., *Studies in the Scope and Method of "The Authoritarian Personality."* New York: Free Press.

Christie, Richard, and Marie Jahoda, eds. 1954. *Studies in the Scope and Method of "The Authoritarian Personality."* New York: Free Press.

Citrin, Jack, Beth Reingold, and Donald P. Green. 1990. American Identity and the Politics of Ethnic Change. *Journal of Politics* 52:1124–54.

Citrin, Jack, Beth Reingold, Evelyn Walters, and Donald P. Green. 1990. The "Official English" Movement and the Symbolic Politics of Language in the United States. *Western Political Quarterly* 43:535–59.

Converse, Philip E. 1964. The Nature of Belief Systems in Mass Publics. In D. E. Apter, ed., *Ideology and Discontent.* New York: Free Press.

———. 1970. Attitudes and Non-Attitudes: Continuation of a Dialogue. In Edward R. Tufte, ed., *Analysis of Social Problems.* Reading, Mass.: Addison-Wesley.

———. 1975. Public Opinion and Voting Behavior. In Fred I. Greenstein and Nelson W. Polsby, eds., *Handbook of Political Science.* Reading, Mass.: Addison-Wesley.

———. 1990. Popular Representation and the Distribution of Information. In John A. Ferejohn and James H. Kuklinski, eds., *Information and Democratic Processes.* Urbana: University of Illinois Press.

Converse, Philip E., and Gregory B. Markus. 1979. *Plus ça Change* . . . The New CPS Election Study Panel. *American Political Science Review* 73:32–49.

Coser, Lewis A. 1956. *The Functions of Social Conflict.* Glencoe, Ill.: Free Press.

Damasio, Antonio R. 1994. *Emotion, Reason, and the Human Brain.* New York: Putnam.

Ekman, Paul. 1992. An Argument for Basic Emotions. *Cognition and Emotion* 6:169–200.

Espenshade, Thomas J. 1995. Unauthorized Immigration to the United States. *Annual Review of Sociology* 21:195–216.

Espenshade, Thomas J., and Charles A. Calhoun. 1993. An Analysis of Public Opinion toward Undocumented Immigration. *Population Research and Policy Review* 12:189–224.

Feldman, Stanley. 1983. Economic Individualism and American Public Opinion. *American Politics Quarterly* 11:3–29.

———. 1988. Structure and Consistency in Public Opinion: The Role of Core Beliefs and Values. *American Journal of Political Science* 32:416–40.

———. 1989. Measuring Issue Preferences: The Problem of Response Instability. In James A. Stimson, ed., *Political Analysis,* vol. 1. Ann Arbor: University of Michigan Press.

Feldman, Stanley, and John Zaller. 1992. The Political Culture of Ambivalence: Ideological Responses to the Welfare State. *American Journal of Political Science* 36:268–307.

Fiske, Susan T. 1998. Stereotyping, Prejudice, and Discrimination. In Daniel Gilbert, Susan Fiske, and Gardner Lindzey, eds., *Handbook of Social Psychology,* 4th ed. Boston: McGraw-Hill.

Gilens, Martin. 1999. *Why Americans Hate Welfare.* Chicago: University of Chicago Press.

Gross, Kimberly, and Donald R. Kinder. 2000. Ethnocentrism Revisited: Explaining American Opinion on Crime and Punishment. Paper presented at the annual meeting of the American Political Science Association, Washington, D.C.

Higham, John. 1988. *Strangers in the Land. Patterns of American Nativism, 1860–1925.* 2d ed. New Brunswick, N.J.: Rutgers University Press.

Hurwitz, Jon, and Mark A. Peffley. 1987. How Are Foreign Policy Attitudes Structured? *American Political Science Review* 81:1099–1120.

Hyman, Herbert, and Paul B. Sheatsley. 1954. The Authoritarian Personality: A Methodological Critique. In Richard Christie and Marie Johoda, eds., *Studies in the Scope and Method of "The Authoritarian Personality."* New York: Free Press.

Kam, Cindy D., and Donald R. Kinder. 1999. Ethnocentrism Revisited: Public Opinion and the American Welfare State. Paper presented at the annual meeting of the American Political Science Association, Atlanta.

Kinder, Donald R. 1983. Diversity and Complexity in American Public Opinion. In Ada Finifter, ed., *Political Science. The State of the Discipline.* Washington, D.C.: American Political Science Association.

———. 1993. Reason and Emotion in American Political Life. In Ellen Langer and Roger Schank, eds., *Reason and Choice in Social Behavior.* Hillsdale, N.J.: Lawrence Erlbaum.

———. 1998. Opinion and Action in the Realm of Politics. In Daniel Gilbert, Susan Fiske, and Gardner Lindzey, eds., *Handbook of Social Psychology,* 4th ed. Boston: McGraw-Hill.

———. 1999. Aliens and Enemies. The Return of Ethnocentrism to American Political Life. Unpublished manuscript, Department of Political Science, University of Michigan.

———. 2003. Myrdal's Prediction. Prejudice versus Principles in American Political Life. Unpublished manuscript, Department of Political Science, University of Michigan.

Kinder, Donald R., Adam Berinsky, and Nicholas Winter. 1998. Racism's End? Stability and Change in White Americans' Opinions on Matters of Race. Paper presented at the annual meeting of the American Political Science Association, Boston.

Kinder, Donald R., and Lisa D'Ambrosio. 1998. War, Emotion, and Public Opinion. Unpublished manuscript, Department of Political Science, University of Michigan.

Kinder, Donald R., and Claudia Deane. 1997. Closing the Golden Door? Exploring the Foundations of American Opposition to Immigration. Paper presented at the annual meeting of the Midwest Political Science Association, Chicago.

Kinder, Donald R., Cindy D. Kam, and Claudia Deane. 2000. Ethnocentrism and the Golden Door. Unpublished manuscript, Department of Political Science, University of Michigan.

Kinder, Donald R., and Tali Mendelberg. 1995. Cracks in American Apartheid: The Political Impact of Prejudice among Desegregated Whites. *Journal of Politics* 57:401–24.

———. 2000. Individualism Reconsidered: Principles and Prejudice in Contemporary American Opinion. In David O. Sears, James Sidanius, and Lawrence Bobo, eds., *Racialized Politics: The Debate about Racism in America.* Chicago: University of Chicago Press.

Kinder, Donald R., and Lynn M. Sanders. 1990. Mimicking Political Debate with Survey Questions: The Case of White Opinion on Affirmative Action for Blacks. *Social Cognition* 8:73–103.

———. 1996. *Divided by Color: Racial Politics and Democratic Ideals.* Chicago: University of Chicago Press.

Kinder, Donald R., and David O. Sears. 1981. Prejudice and Politics: Symbolic Racism versus Racial Threats to the Good Life. *Journal of Personality and Social Psychology* 40:414–31.

Krosnick, Jon A., and Mathew K. Berent. 1993. Comparisons of Party Identification and Policy Preferences: The Impact of Survey Question Format. *American Journal of Political Science* 37:941–64.

Lane, Robert E. 1962. *Political Ideology.* New York: Free Press.

Lazarus, Richard S. 1991. *Emotion and Adaptation.* New York: Oxford University Press.

Levinson, Daniel J. 1949. An Approach to the Theory and Measurement of Ethnocentric Ideology. *Journal of Psychology* 28:19–39.

Lippmann, Walter. 1922. *Public Opinion.* New York: Macmillan.

———. 1925. *The Phantom Public.* New York: Harcourt, Brace.

Marcus, George E., and Michael B. MacKuen. 1993. Anxiety, Enthusiasm, and the Vote: The Emotional Underpinnings of Learning and Involvement during Presidential Campaigns. *American Political Science Review* 87:672–85.

McFarland, Sam, Vladimir Ageyev, and Marina Abalakina. 1993. The Authoritarian Personality in the United States and the Former Soviet Union: Comparative Studies. In William F. Stone and Richard Christie, eds., *Strength and Weakness. The Authoritarian Personality Today.* New York: Springer-Verlag.

Merton, Robert K., and Alice Kitt Rossi. 1968. Contributions to the Theory of Reference Group Behavior. In Herbert Hyman and Eleanor Singer, eds., *Readings in Reference Group Theory and Research.* New York: Free Press.

Mills, Nicolaus, ed. 1994. *Arguing Immigration.* New York: Simon and Schuster.

Mueller, John E. 1994. *Policy and Opinion in the Gulf War.* Chicago: University of Chicago Press.

Nelson, Thomas E., and Donald R. Kinder. 1996. Issue Frames and Group-Centrism in American Public Opinion. *Journal of Politics* 58:1055–78.

Olzak, Susan. 1992. *The Dynamics of Ethnic Competition and Conflict.* Stanford, Calif.: Stanford University Press.

Pettigrew, Thomas F., and R. W. Meertens. 1995. Subtle and Blatant Prejudice in Western Europe. *European Journal of Social Psychology* 25:57–75.

Portes, Alejandro, and Cynthia Truelove. 1987. Making Sense of Diversity: Recent Research on Hispanic Minorities in the United States. *Annual Review of Sociology* 13:359–85.

Price, Vincent, and M. L. Hsu. 1992. Public Opinion about AIDS: The Role of Misinformation and Attitudes toward Homosexuality. *Public Opinion Quarterly* 56:29–52.

Quillian, Lincoln. 1995. Prejudice as a Response to Perceived Group Threat: Population Composition and Anti-Immigrant and Racial Prejudice in Europe. *American Sociological Review* 60:586–611.

Schumpeter, Joseph A. 1942. *Capitalism, Socialism, and Democracy.* New York: Harper and Brothers.

Schwarz, Norbert. 1992. Feelings as Information. In E. Tory Higgins and Richard M. Sorrentino, eds., *Handbook of Motivation and Cognition,* vol. 2. New York: Guilford Press.

Sears, David O., Carl P. Hensler, and Leslie K. Speer. 1979. Whites' Opposition to Busing: Self-Interest or Symbolic Politics? *American Political Science Review* 73:369–84.

Sherif, Muzafer, and Carolyn W. Sherif. 1953. *Groups in Harmony and Tension*. New York: Harper.

Simon, R. J., and S. H. Alexander. 1993. *The Ambivalent Welcome: Print Media, Public Opinion, and Immigration*. Westport, Conn.: Praeger.

Sniderman, Paul M., Richard A. Brody, and James H. Kuklinski. 1984. Policy Reasoning and Political Values: The Problem of Racial Equality. *American Journal of Political Science* 28:75–94.

Stangor, Charles, and James E. Lange. 1994. Mental Representations on Social Groups: Advances in Understanding Stereotypes and Stereotyping. *Advances in Experimental Social Psychology* 26:357–416.

Sullivan, John L., James E. Piereson, and George E. Marcus. 1982. *Political Tolerance and American Democracy*. Chicago: University of Chicago Press.

Sumner, William Graham. 1906. *Folkways: A Study of the Sociological Importance of Usages, Manners, Customs, Mores, and Morals*. Boston: Athenaeum.

Sumner, William Graham, A. G. Keller, and M. R. Davie. 1927. *The Science of Society*. New Haven: Yale University Press.

Tajfel, Henri. 1981. *Social Identity and Intergroup Relations*. Cambridge: Cambridge University Press.

Tajfel, Henri, M. G. Billig, R. P. Bundy, and C. Flament. 1971. Social Categorization and Intergroup Behavior. *European Journal of Social Psychology* 1:149–78.

Verba, Sidney, Steven Kelman, Gary R. Orren, Ichiro Miyake, Jojo Watanuki, Ikuo Kabashima, and G. Donald Ferree Jr. 1987. *Elites and the Idea of Equality*. Cambridge: Harvard University Press.

Zaller, John, and Stanley Feldman. 1992. A Simple Theory of the Survey Response: Answering Questions versus Revealing Preferences. *American Journal of Political Science* 36:579–618.

2

Democracy with Attitudes

Larry M. Bartels

Psychological research on the nature of attitudes has informed a good deal of recent empirical work in political science. However, the implications of this research for normative theories of democracy have received much less attention. In this essay I seek to highlight some aspects of contemporary psychological understanding that bear on the nature of public opinion, and I explore in some detail the challenges they pose to traditional conceptions of how policy decisions might be justified on democratic grounds.

The seminal research of Philip Converse—most notably his work of the early 1960s published in the classic essays on "The Nature of Belief Systems in Mass Publics" (1964) and "Attitudes and Non-Attitudes: Continuation of a Dialogue" (1970)—provides an obvious and important starting point for my analysis. Converse's brilliant empirical research seems to me to have punched a significant hole in conventional, romanticized accounts of the popular underpinnings of democracy. A great deal of additional research—alas, less brilliant, even though some of it ranks with the best political science produced in the generation since Converse wrote—has been devoted to rejecting, reiterating, or recasting his claims. The end result, at least as I score it, has been to leave Converse's empirical position fundamentally intact—and his "stiff challenge to democratic hopes" (as Kinder calls it in his contribution to this volume) still substantially unaddressed.[1] Thus, I attempt here to renew the challenge, with some updating and sharpening to reflect significant empirical and theoretical developments that seem to me to have made it even more daunting than in Converse's original formulation.

In particular, what Converse described as a problem of "non-attitudes" will be treated here as a problem of "attitudes." I shall not want or need to assert, as Converse did, that many citizens "do not have meaningful beliefs, even on issues that have formed the basis for intense political controversy among elites for substantial periods of time" (1964, 245). Instead, I shall argue that citizens

48

have "meaningful beliefs" but that those beliefs are not sufficiently complete and coherent to serve as a satisfactory starting point for democratic theory, at least as it is conventionally understood. To summarize in a phrase, citizens have *attitudes* but not *preferences*.

The first third of my essay elaborates the distinction between attitudes and preferences, highlighting the extent to which the theories and evidence provided by contemporary psychologists and scholars of public opinion have rendered problematic the most fundamental assumptions of economists and liberal democratic theorists. The second section provides a variety of examples of how the fluidity and contingency of attitudes can produce "framing effects," in which seemingly arbitrary variations in choice format or context produce contradictory expressions of popular will. The last third of my essay explores the implications of these phenomena for normative theories of democracy, arguing that political scientists and political philosophers together will have to develop a richer, more subtle justification than they have so far for what I refer to here as "democracy with attitudes."

Attitudes, Not Preferences

The major premise of my argument is that citizens should be thought of as having *attitudes* rather than *preferences*. The significance of this distinction between attitudes and preferences has been stressed most forcefully by the psychologists Daniel Kahneman and Amos Tversky, who have used it to challenge the behavioral assumptions underlying conventional economic theory (e.g., Tversky and Kahneman 1986; Tversky 1996) and to criticize specific policy-making procedures based on those assumptions (Kahneman and Knetsch 1992; Kahneman, Ritov and Schkade 2000; Kahneman and Ritov n.d.). My aim here is to extend Kahneman and Tversky's critique to the broader realm of politics—and to emphasize specifically its significance for normative theories of democracy.

In this section I briefly specify the characteristics of preferences as they have been understood in liberal political theory. Given the common intellectual origins of liberal political theory and liberal economic theory, it should not be surprising that their fundamental assumptions are, in the respects most relevant here, quite similar. I then argue that *attitudes* as understood by psychologists and public opinion researchers have rather different characteristics from those attributed to *preferences*. Here, recent work on political opinions nicely parallels and reinforces the work of cognitive and social psychologists. In particular, I argue that the "catalogue of horrors" (Zaller 1992, 29) uncovered by public opinion researchers studying attitude structure and response stability in the wake of Converse's (1964) pioneering analysis reflects precisely the ways in which attitudes differ from preferences.

In politics, as in other realms, responses to questions in opinion surveys and experiments—and referenda—are constructed from a disparate assortment of more or less relevant "considerations" (Zaller 1992), including bits and pieces of information, prototypes, symbols, slogans, and prejudices. The psychological mechanisms underlying attitude construction generate a variety of systematic and predictable violations of familiar axioms of preference consistency and stability, including preference reversals, question-ordering effects, anchoring effects, and inconsistencies in responses involving magnitudes or probabilities. But the important, often-overlooked point is that these phenomena are not mere curiosities of opinion measurement; they are challenges to the most fundamental assumptions of democratic theory. Without preferences, I will argue, democratic theory—at least in its most familiar liberal guise—"loses its starting point" (Achen 1975, 1227).

Preferences as the Basis of Liberal Democratic Theory

Preferences lie close to the heart of liberal democratic theory. That fact is evident from the first page of Robert Dahl's classic study, *Polyarchy*, which stipulated that "a key characteristic of a democracy is the continued responsiveness of the government to the preferences of its citizens, considered as political equals" (1971, 1). In the same vein, David Miller argued, "In the liberal view, the aim of democracy is to aggregate individual preferences into a collective choice in as fair and efficient a way as possible" (1992, 55).

Miller went on to acknowledge in a footnote that "[s]ome liberals may protest at this appropriation of the term" for an interpretation that "only fastens upon one strand of liberalism—the importance it attaches to individual preferences and their expression," but he argued that that strand "prevails in contemporary liberal societies, where democracy is predominantly understood as involving the aggregation of independently formed preferences" (1992, 55). I, too, shall focus on this single, centrally important strand of liberal democratic theory, exploring the implications of recent research on the nature of attitudes for preference-based theories of democracy.

Most liberal democratic theorists, including Dahl and Miller in the passages just quoted, assume as a matter of course that citizens do, in fact, have definite preferences and that the primary problem of democracy is to assure that a government will respond appropriately to those preferences. A more cautious, if less magisterial, view was propounded a half century earlier by noted political philosopher H. L. Mencken, who characterized democracy as "the theory that the common people know what they want, and deserve to get it good and hard" (quoted by Mueller 1992, 984). Here, the notion that "the common people know what they want" is an explicit part of the theory, on a par with the notion that they "deserve to get it good and hard," rather than being (as in Dahl's and

Miller's and many other formulations) an unstated, presumably unproblematic, background assumption.

Not surprisingly, the assumption that citizens have definite preferences is made even more explicit in formal, deductive or quasi-deductive versions of liberal democratic theory. The first substantive chapter of Kenneth Arrow's classic work, *Social Choice and Individual Values,* is titled "The Nature of Preference and Choice" and specifies that

> the chooser considers in turn all possible pairs of alternatives, say *x* and *y*, and for each such pair he makes one and only one of three decisions: *x* is preferred to *y*, *x* is indifferent to *y*, or *y* is preferred to *x*. The decisions made for different pairs are assumed to be consistent with each other, so, for example, if *x* is preferred to *y* and *y* to *z*, then *x* is preferred to *z*. (1951, 12)[2]

What, exactly, does this assumption of rational consistency entail? Perhaps most fundamentally, that for any given chooser there is a definite, one-to-one mapping between pairs of alternatives and preferences. If I prefer *x* over *y*, there cannot be some different, equally valid sense in which I prefer *y* over *x*.[3] My preference for *x* over *y* may be contingent on particular features of the world, such as my upbringing or income level. It may be based on incomplete information regarding some or all of the consequences of *x* and *y*. I may find myself tomorrow preferring *y* over *x*. But for now, my preference for *x* over *y* is somehow intrinsic both to me and to the objective states of the world represented by the specified alternatives.[4]

Tversky and Kahneman (1986) used the term *invariance* to highlight the assumption that preferences do not depend on arbitrary features of the context, formulation, or procedure used to elicit those preferences, and Arrow (1982) used the term *extensionality* for a closely related idea. This is the fundamental, often unstated assumption about the nature of preferences that seems to be rendered deeply problematic by psychological research on the nature of attitudes.

What happens if we attempt to do without the assumption that preferences are consistently associated with objective states of the world? What if we recognize preference expressions as inherently dependent on how we think and talk about the relevant alternatives? For social scientists, I will argue, the result may be a very fruitful complication; for normative theorists of democracy, however, the resulting complication is likely to be far more troublesome.

How Attitudes Differ from Preferences

What is an "attitude"? As with many fundamental scientific concepts, scholars have proposed a bewildering array of overlapping definitions; however, the core notion is nicely captured by Eagly and Chaiken's definition of an attitude as "a psychological tendency that is expressed by evaluating a particular entity with some degree of favor or disfavor" (1998, 1). One useful aspect of this definition is that it refers to a "psychological tendency" rather than to a fixed characteristic; another is that it distinguishes between this "tendency" and its particular expression; yet another is that it emphasizes a favorable or unfavorable evaluation as the defining feature of an attitude.

It is worth noting, however, that Eagly and Chaiken's definition leaves unspecified the nature of the "particular entity" that is the object of this favorable or unfavorable evaluation. In relatively simple cases, this "particular entity" may be unproblematic; to say that I like raspberry ice or even Monet's *Bordighera* seems clear enough. But what does it mean to say that I like the Count Basie Band or New York City? These cases are more complex, not only because summary labels are being applied to disparate concrete stimuli but also because my attitude toward New York City—real as it is—cannot be derived in any straightforward way from my attitudes toward each of the disparate concrete stimuli evoked by that summary label (Metropolitan Museum plus Central Park minus Penn Station plus Greenwich Village, and so on).

Kahneman, Ritov, and Schkade's (2000) discussion of a typical stimulus in an environmental policy problem nicely highlights some of these complexities. What, they asked, is the relevant psychological entity in a scenario involving twenty thousand migrating birds drowning in uncovered oil ponds? Employing the general psychological principle of "valuation by prototype," they argued that attitudes toward this problem are likely to be derived from "a mental representation of a prototypical incident, perhaps an image of an exhausted bird, its feathers soaked in black oil, unable to escape. The hypothesis of valuation by prototype asserts that the affective value of this image will dominate expressions of the attitude to the problem," while "the number of bird deaths will have little effect" (Kahnerman, Ritov, and Schkade 2000, 652).

This general psychological principle has a variety of important implications for the problem of eliciting public judgments regarding issues of public policy. First, if the "complexity of a response" depends on "the number of variables that are logically and psychologically relevant to it" (Kahneman and Ritov n.d., 11), then issues of public policy are likely to evoke complex responses indeed, with a good deal of scope for response variability over time and across contexts as various relevant prototypes happen to be made salient. Whereas a simple hypothetical scenario involving twenty thousand birds drowning in oil is likely to evoke a single prototype—an individual bird drowning in oil—any real policy issue may evoke a wide variety of "logically and psychologically relevant" prototypes, and thus it may produce a wide variety of associated emotional reactions.

This account of the nature of attitudes will sound quite familiar to anyone conversant with recent scholarship in the field of public opinion and political psychology, thanks in large part to the forceful advocacy of John Zaller (1992). Zaller proposed a model in which responses to opinion surveys are generated by canvasing more or less carefully a stock of potentially relevant *considerations* corresponding to Kahneman and Ritov's "logically and psychologically relevant" variables. In this model, cognitive limitations and the demands of the opinion survey as a social interaction typically produce "top of the head" responses based on "considerations that are immediately salient or accessible" (Zaller 1992, 49). The vagaries of the process by which relevant considerations are canvased to construct a response to any given question may account for a variety of peculiarities in observed response patterns, including unstable responses, preference reversals, question-ordering effects, and anchoring effects.

This account of the psychological nature of attitudes also sheds some light on a variety of familiar inconsistencies in responses involving magnitudes or probabilities, since these quantities are by their nature abstract rather than concrete and specific. Lacking a preconstructed attitude toward twenty thousand migrating birds drowning in oil, I may use the salient prototype of a single bird drowning in oil as the primary ingredient in constructing my response. I know I should feel worse about twenty thousand drowning birds than about one drowning bird, but since my imagination cannot make twenty thousand drowning birds concrete and specific, my response is likely to be insufficiently sensitive to the scale of the problem.

A variety of analysts (Kahneman and Knetsch 1992; Baron 1997) have shown that value judgments "are often remarkably insensitive to quantity or scope of the good provided" (Baron 1997, 74). For example, between-subject comparisons might reveal a willingness to pay only 20 percent more to prevent twelve traffic injuries for every one hundred thousand drivers than to prevent four injuries for every one hundred thousand drivers (Jones-Lee, Loomes, and Philips 1995) or only 34 percent more to preserve fifty-seven wilderness areas than to preserve one wilderness area (McFadden 1994). Responses of this sort are hard to take seriously as manifestations of genuine public preferences but are easy to interpret as expressions of attitudes generated primarily from emotional reactions to salient prototypes (such as a mental image of a single injured motorist or a single pristine wilderness area).

The phenomenon of insensitivity to scope has loomed large in discussions of contingent-valuation methods, which attempt systematically to measure public "willingness to pay" for nonmarket goods. A panel of leading scholars commissioned by a federal agency to evaluate contingent-valuation methods cited insensitivity to scope as a major hurdle that credible contingent-valuation studies must overcome (National Oceanographic and Atmospheric Administration 1993). While some analysts (especially economists) seem relatively opti-mistic about the possibility of overcoming that hurdle, many others (especially psychologists) are less sanguine.

Much of this debate has focused on specific features of contingent-valuation methods, such as the distinction between asking respondents how much they would be willing to pay for a specified public good and asking them in referen-dum fashion whether they would be willing to pay a specified amount. How-ever, for my purposes here, the important point is that insensitivity to scope in contingent-valuation surveys is a manifestation of the fact that citizens do not have well-defined preferences of the sort that would allow them to provide consistent, logically defensible responses to concrete questions about these and other public policy issues. In the words of Kahneman and Ritov,

> respondents are inadequately sensitive to scope in CV [contingent-valua-tion] surveys because WTP [willingness to pay] is an expression of attitude, and attitudes tend to be dominated by the evaluation of representative exem-plars. Evaluation by exemplars and the resulting difficulties in the processing of extensional information are manifestations of a psychological principle that has considerable generality. It would be naive to expect psychological laws to be negated by procedural fiddling. (n.d., 16)

Why Not Preferences

How do we *know* that the "psychological laws" asserted by Kahneman and Ritov cannot be "negated by procedural fiddling" and that *attitudes* cannot attain the completeness and consistency required of *preferences?* Are the limita-tions of human judgment outlined in the preceding pages really so general? Two considerations suggest to me that they are—and, indeed, may help to explain why psychological laws take the form they do.

I mention these considerations briefly here, and with some trepidation, since they arise from fields of scientific research even further outside my own narrow area of expertise than those I have been considering thus far. Neverthe-less, if my tenuous grasp of these considerations is not wholly incorrect, they provide significant additional support for my argument that a realistic demo-cratic theory must be built on a foundation of attitudes, not preferences.

The first of these considerations involves the relationship between language on one hand and thought and communication on the other. That relationship has, of course, been the subject of a great deal of research by linguists and cog-nitive scientists.[5] However, what I wish to stress here is the narrower but more immediately relevant insight of an economist, Ariel Rubinstein, regarding the potential importance of language as a *limitation* on the formulation and expression of preferences. In Rubinstein's words, when a decision maker is involved in an intentional choice, he, using his daily language, *describes* the choice to himself or to agents who operate on his behalf. Thus, "My first priority is to get as many guns as possible and only secondarily do I worry about increasing the quantity of food" is a natural description of a preference relation. "I spend 35% of my income on food and 65% on guns" is a natural description of a rule of behavior, one consistent with maximizing some Cobb-Douglas utility function. On the other hand, the function $(\log (x_1 + 1))x_2$ is a standard utility function that is expressed by a simple mathematical formula, but I do not know about any rule of behavior stated in everyday language which corresponds to this utility function.

When a decision maker is a collective (recall that decision makers in economics are often families, groups or organizations), the presumption that preferences are definable makes even more sense. In that case, a decision rule must be stated in words in order to be communicated among the individuals in the collective, in the deliberation and the implementation stages. (1998, 554)

We should, I think, take seriously the possibility that natural language imposes significant restrictions on our ability to describe and deliberate about alternative policy outcomes, either within our own minds or with other people. But in that case, the difficulty of specifying a preference ordering that is both complete and coherent *and* susceptible of being stated in words seems daunting indeed.

The other, perhaps even more basic, objection to the assumption that citizens have preferences stems from the architecture of the brain, which seems well suited to facilitating distributed processing of the sort that we might expect to generate *considerations* but very ill suited to integrating those considerations in any way that might be expected to generate complete and coherent *preferences*. This structural decentralization extends even to such basic perceptual activities as vision, which apparently rely much more on efficient but fragmentary monitoring than on coherent integration. According to a recent summary,

the visual system is not even attempting to build a rich, detailed model of the current scene but is instead geared to using frequent saccades to retrieve information *as and when it is needed* for some specific problem-solving purpose. . . . One explanation of our subjective impression of forming a rich inner representation of the whole scene is that we are prone to this illusion because we are able to perform fast saccades, retrieving information as and when required. (Clark 1998, 263–64)

Clark's account of visual perception could hardly sound more familiar to anyone conversant with recent research on the nature of attitudes. If "our subjective impression of forming a rich inner representation of the whole scene" is an "illusion" of visual perception produced by "retrieving information as and when required" from different parts of the brain, how can we doubt that our subjective impression of forming complete, coherent preferences regarding alternative public policies is equally illusory?

The problem is not, as Converse's (1970) "non-attitudes" terminology might suggest, that there is "no there there." Rather, it is that the structure of attitudes—and, at a deeper level, the cognitive mechanisms by which they are constructed and expressed—do not happen to endow attitude expressions with the nice properties of global coherence and consistency that would allow them to play the role of preferences in existing versions of liberal democratic theory. The middle ground between *nonattitudes* on one hand and *preferences* on the other is broad indeed—and it seems to be where the action is.

The Importance of Framing

Is the distinction stressed here between preferences and attitudes merely a theoretical nicety, or does it have real political implications? In this section I argue that the context dependency of attitudes may create significant problems for any attempt to discern public preferences on issues of public policy. I do this by providing examples of what are often referred to, following Tversky and Kahneman (1982), as "framing effects"—situations in which alternative ways of posing a policy issue produce distinctly different public responses. Framing effects are hard to accommodate within a theory built on the assumption that citizens have definite preferences to be elicited, but they are easy to reconcile with the alternative view that any given question may tap a variety of more or less relevant attitudes.

Many of my examples of framing effects are drawn from experimental work on question wording and question ordering. Survey researchers have been generating such examples for more than half a century but have only recently (in the work of Tourangeau and Rasinski 1988; Wilson and Hodges 1991; Zaller 1992; Zaller and Feldman 1992) begun to explore the theoretical significance of question-wording and question-ordering effects. From my point of view, these effects provide examples of the more general context dependency of attitudes—and thus of the potential political significance of the distinction I have drawn between attitudes and preferences.

Different Frames, Different Considerations

I begin with what seems to me to be the simplest type of framing effect: a difference in response produced by prompting consideration of some additional aspect of an issue that might otherwise be ignored. This sort of effect can be generated especially simply (by asking the same question of comparable groups of respondents with and without an additional statement or question prompting attention to the additional consideration), and it can be interpreted especially simply (as reflecting the difference between Zaller's [1992] "top of the head" opinions in which the additional consideration may play no role and more considered opinions in which it does).

An example of one such framing effect is provided by Kahneman, Ritov, and Schkade's (2000) study of public ratings of the importance of various problems. Subjects were presented with a relatively vivid environmental problem involving cyanide fishing in coral reefs around Asia and a relatively arcane public health problem involving a documented increase in multiple myeloma (a disease of the bone marrow) among elderly people. When judged independently (by different but comparable groups of subjects), the mean importance rating for the problem involving coral reefs (3.78 on a 0–6 scale) was significantly higher than for the problem of myeloma (3.24). However, when each group of subjects rated the importance of the second problem after having seen the first, the mean importance attributed to coral reefs declined slightly (from 3.78 to 3.62) while the mean importance attributed to myeloma increased substantially (from 3.24 to 4.26). Kahneman, Ritov, and Schkade's interpretation of these results is that "the difference between the categories of ecological and human problems is only salient when the issues are directly compared, not when they are valued in isolation" (2000, 658).

Hyman and Sheatsley (1950) reported a similar contextual effect in attitudes toward letting Communist newspaper reporters work in the United States. Half of a national sample was asked, "Do you think the United States should let communist newspaper reporters from other countries come in here and send back to their papers the news as they see it?": 36 percent said yes. The other half of the sample was asked the same question, but it was preceded by a question asking whether "a Communist country like Russia should let American newspaper reporters come in and send back to America the news as they see it?" In this second group, 90 percent agreed that American reporters should be allowed in Russia, and 73 percent—twice as many as in the first group—said that communist reporters should be allowed to work in the United States. As Schuman and Presser noted, "The obvious interpretation is that when either question is asked first, many respondents answer in terms of pro-American or anti-Communist sentiments, but when the second question is asked a norm of reciprocity is immediately made salient and a substantial number of respondents feel bound to follow that norm and provide an answer that is consistent with their previous response" (1981, 28).[6]

What are we to make of examples like these? Let us imagine for a moment that a referendum was proposed to settle the question of whether communist reporters should be allowed to work in the United States. Would the appropriate reflection of public sentiment with respect to this issue be the 36 percent support for the proposal considered alone or the 73 percent support for the proposal after the norm of reciprocity has been stimulated? I suspect that most observers would consider the latter result more legitimate, on the view that it incorporates at least one additional consideration that citizens should consider relevant—and *do* consider relevant when it is brought to their attention. But in that case, would a context that stimulated still other considerations be even more appropriate? *Which* others? Given the practical impossibility of stimulating *every* consideration that is logically relevant (or might be considered relevant by someone), how might we judge whether one set of considerations is better than another?

The question of how to evaluate alternative question frames from the standpoint of democratic theory arises even more clearly for another type of framing effect, in which one frame is not merely an elaboration of another but different in kind. In that case, the natural intuition that more is better than less is clearly an insufficient normative guide, since either frame may ignore some potentially relevant considerations that the other evokes. One possibility might be to construct a metaframe combining both alternative perspectives, but, as we will see, that approach is not always feasible even if it would often be desirable.

Some of the most striking framing effects on record come from question-wording experiments conducted as part of the 1984, 1985, and 1986 General Social Surveys (Smith 1987; Rasinski 1989). Respondents in these surveys were asked whether "we" are spending "too much, too little, or about the right amount" on each of a variety of government programs. Separate random subsamples evaluated essentially similar sets of programs but with more or less subtle differences in how each program was denoted.

Some of the resulting differences in responses may reflect genuine, albeit subtle, differences in the substance of the alternative questions. For example, the proportion of the public saying too little was being spent on "dealing with drug addiction" may have exceeded the corresponding percentage for "drug rehabilitation" (by an average of 9 percentage points in the three separate surveys) because some respondents who did not want more money spent on "rehabilitation" *did* want more money spent on other approaches to "dealing with drug addiction," such as crop eradication, crackdowns on smuggling, or incarceration of drug dealers or drug users.

In other cases, differences in responses seem attributable to differences in the factual premises incorporated in the question wording. For example, the proportion of the public saying too little was being spent on "halting the rising crime rate" exceeded the corresponding proportion for "law enforcement"—with no stipulation of a "rising crime rate"—by from 10 to 14 percentage points.[7] Similarly, the proportion saying that too little was being spent on "solving problems of big cities" exceeded the corresponding proportion for "assistance to big cities"—with no stipulation of "problems" or of "solving" those problems—by from 25 to 31 percentage points (Rasinski 1989, 391, 393).

In one sense, these examples seem roughly analogous to the effects of evoking additional considerations documented earlier: respondents seem to be swayed by considerations (either of existing crisis or of program effectiveness) that are evoked by one version of the question but not by the other. However, the normative status of the additional considerations seems less clear in these cases than in the case of communist reporters. Is "solving problems" in fact what these programs would be doing? The resolution of this linguistic quibble about appropriate question framing seems to require a prior resolution of the very same substantive controversy the question is intended to address! In my view, at least, there is no hope of settling on any "neutral" way of posing such questions for democratic deliberation.

One final example from the General Social Surveys seems to raise even more difficult normative issues. While 20 to 25 percent of the respondents in each year said that too little was being spent on "welfare," 63 to 65 percent said that too little was being spent on "assistance to the poor" (Rasinski 1989, 391). This effect not only is spectacularly large but also is very hard to account for in any straightforward logical terms. "Welfare" clearly has deeply unpopular connotations for significant segments of the U.S. public and stimulates rather different mental images (or, to revert to the technical language of the preceding section, "schematic exemplars") than does "assistance to the poor."[8] The important point here is that these very different mental images are attached to the *same* set of programs and policies; any effort to make subtle distinctions of substance between "welfare" and "assistance to the poor" seems fruitlessly tendentious. Nevertheless, one frame suggests that a substantial majority of the public supports spending more on those programs and policies, while the other—equally legitimate on its face—suggests that they are deeply unpopular. What can a democratic theory of preferences make of this perplexing situation?

The conceptual problem raised clearly and acutely by the disparity in opinion toward "welfare" and "assistance to the poor" in these question-wording experiments is raised less obviously by a considerable variety of nonexperimental comparisons of alternative question wordings. For example, Mueller cataloged responses to various survey questions regarding support for the Korean War and found that "support for the war was clearly tied to the anti-Communist spirit in America at the time. To generate a kind of war fever, one merely had to toss the words, 'Communist invasion,' into the discussion" (1973, 48). Thus, in one poll conducted in September 1953, 64 percent of the public agreed that "the United States did the right thing in sending troops to stop the Communist invasion," while in another poll conducted two months later only 38 percent thought "we did the right thing in getting into the fighting in Korea."[9]

Same Questions, Different Answers

The preceding pages provide a variety of examples in which elaborating or modifying the framing of a question produces markedly different responses, even though the substantive issue underlying the alternative frames is unchanged. In an important sense, all of these examples provide evidence against the notion that citizens have fixed preferences regarding the underlying substantive issues. As Zaller wrote of Mueller's Korean War example,

> The counterargument to this conclusion—that different questions were involved and should therefore be expected to produce different answers even if people did have preexisting opinions—does not seem to me credible. The issue that people were addressing—the appropriateness of the U.S. response to an invasion of South Korea by the Communist government of North Korea—was the same whether or not the survey question used the critical phrase "Communist invasion." Thus, anyone who had a fixed opinion on the war should have been able to express it whether communism was mentioned or not. (1992, 34)

Zaller went on to cite an even purer, albeit artificial, example of divergent responses to substantively identical questions in Tversky and Kahneman's (1982) comparison of policy options framed alternatively in terms of gains or losses. One group of college students was asked,

> Imagine the U.S. is preparing for the outbreak of an unusual Asian disease, which is expected to kill 600 people. Two alternative programs have been proposed. Assume that the exact scientific estimates of the consequences of the programs are as follows:
>
>   If program A is adopted, 200 people will be saved.
>   If program B is adopted, there is a one-third probability that 600 people will be saved, and a two-thirds probability that no people will be saved.
>
> Which of these two programs do you favor?

Faced with this choice, 72 percent chose the certain gain associated with program A over the uncertain gain associated with program B. However, when a similar group of students was presented with exactly the same choice described in different terms, only 22 percent chose the certain loss associated with program C in which "400 people will die" over the uncertain loss associated with program D in which "there is a one-third probability that nobody will die, and a two-thirds probability that 600 people will die." Zaller concluded that "differences in the wording of questions can determine how people think about and hence respond to issues even when, as here, the denotative meanings of the competing wordings are exactly the same" (1992, 34).

Another striking example of the significance of how choices are framed is provided by Pruitt's (1970) research comparing the behavior of experimental subjects in two different versions of a bilateral repeated Prisoner's Dilemma game. In one version of the game, subjects were presented with the conventional *bimatrix form* in figure 2.1, in which each player's payoffs in each round of the game are indicated as a function of both players' choices between their alternative strategies *A* and *B*. In the other experimental condition, each subject was presented with the choice represented by the *decomposed form* of the game shown in figure 2.2 and told that the other player would simultaneously face a parallel choice.

It is not hard to see that the alternative game forms presented in figures 2.1 and 2.2 are completely equivalent, both in the choices faced by each player and in the payoffs resulting from those choices. Nevertheless, Pruitt's subjects were much more likely to choose the "cooperative" strategy *A* in the decomposed form of the game shown in figure 2.2 than in the conventional bimatrix form of the game shown in figure 2.1. Selten's interpretation of this finding is that the decomposed form of the game "makes it easy to recognize choice *A* as a friendly act" (1998, 418). Alternatively, the bimatrix form may heighten the salience of the most unequal outcomes (0, 4) and (4, 0), inducing each player to avoid getting the "sucker's payoff." Whatever the appropriate psychological interpretation may be, it is clear that Pruitt's result "cannot be explained by any theory which exclusively focuses on the relationship between behaviour and payoff" (Selten 1998, 418). Here, once again, the context of choice has a crucial impact on the outcome.

What should a democratic theorist make of this context dependence? How might either context—or either outcome—be judged more appropriate than the other?

Lest the Asian disease and Prisoner's Dilemma examples seem too contrived to be seriously unsettling, it is worth noting that qualitatively similar effects also arise in more naturalistic settings that are still a good deal less complex than the Korean War or welfare examples. For example, most people would probably acknowledge that "forbidding" an action is substantively equivalent to "not allowing" it. However, Schuman and Presser have noted that in three separate split-sample experiments conducted in the mid-1970s, from 44 to 48 percent of the American public would "not allow" a communist to give a speech, while only about half as many would "forbid" him or her from doing so (1981, 277).[10] Once again, substantively identical questions produce markedly different results. Which of these results reflect the public's "true" opinion about the underlying policy? I can suggest no sensible way to answer that question.

		Player 2's choice	
		A	*B*
Player 1's choice	*A*	(3, 3)	(0, 4)
	B	(4, 0)	(1, 1)

Fig. 2.1.   **Prisoner's dilemma game in bimatrix form** (showing payoffs for [Player 1, Player 2] as a function of both players' choices).

		Payoff resulting	
		for me	for him
Player 1's choice	*A*	0	3
	B	1	0

Fig. 2.2.   **Prisoner's dilemma game in decomposed form** (showing payoffs resulting from Player 1's choice).

The Ubiquity and Political Significance of Framing Effects

I interpret the variety of framing effects cited in the preceding pages as evidence for the thesis that citizens have attitudes rather than preferences. The contrasting patterns of responses I have documented in a variety of opinion surveys and experiments reflect real attitudes that are neither meaningless nor whimsical nor—at least in any common-language sense—irrational. However, neither are they the solid bedrock of fixed preferences that most liberal theorists of democracy (and their cousins, the economists) have taken as a starting point for their work.

How ubiquitous are these framing effects? Are the examples I have cited here simply carefully selected anomalies, or are they the tips of icebergs? There is good reason to be wary of overgeneralization, given the very wide variations in levels of information, motivation, cognitive capacity, and attitude constraint across individuals in any mass public—and in the sociology, salience, and complexity of various political issues and choice contexts. Conversely, if I am correct in believing that these framing effects reflect fundamental psychological limitations, they should appear with some frequency even in situations that seem ripe for the assumption that citizens have complete and consistent preferences regarding policy outcomes.

One common reaction to Converse's original work on the thinness, disorganization, and instability of mass opinion has been to challenge the extent to which it holds for times, places, populations, and questions beyond those actually studied by Converse. For example, Donald Kinder argues in his contribution to this volume,

> As Converse argued, unstable opinions are a direct sign of the casual and shallow character of much everyday political thinking. But the recent rise to prominence of such issues as abortion and affirmative action suggests that issue publics need not be confined to small splinters of the general public. When policy proposals become entangled in moral, racial, and religious feelings, the nonattitude problem may diminish quite dramatically (e.g., Converse and Markus 1979; Feldman 1989). Moreover, unstable opinions are partly a product of the imperfect way we put questions to citizens (Achen 1975; Krosnick and Berent 1993) and partly a reflection of elites failing to provide frames that would help citizens find their way to real opinions (e.g., Chong 1993; Kinder and Sanders 1996; Zaller and Feldman 1992). Improve the questions, induce elites to provide a clarifying debate, and real attitudes will increase. Taken all around, the problem posed by nonattitudes seems to be a bit more remediable than Converse's analysis originally implied.

I suspect that Kinder's assessment is widely held: the common view of political scientists seems to be that the signs of "casual and shallow" thinking that Converse took as evidence of non-attitudes may characterize some of the people some of the time, or even most of the people most of the time, but are by no means endemic. My own reading of the evidence is more pessimistic. At least if "attitudes" are taken to mean logically consistent summary evaluations of any conceivable political object—evaluations that could form the basis for "preferences" in Arrow's sense—then it seems clear to me that even splendidly well informed, attentive citizens will routinely flunk the test.

Empirical analysis provides little basis for supposing that even well-informed, well-thought-out opinions are likely to be immune from framing effects, insensitivity to magnitude, and other manifestations of context dependence. Thus, for example, Converse recorded his surprise at discovering only "trifling" differences in attitude stability between highly educated and less well educated citizens (1975, 103–4). The magnitude of the question-wording effect in Schuman and Presser's (1981) study of "forbidding" or "not allowing" a communist to give a speech diminished with formal education but did not disappear even among those with college degrees.[11] In a study of alternative ways of framing the issue of affirmative action (Kinder and Sanders 1990, 91), less-informed survey respondents were "more susceptible" than their better-informed counterparts to some but not all of the framing effects examined. The electoral choices of well-informed respondents appear to be more sensitive than those of less-informed respondents to some aspects of their "social location" but less sensitive to others (Bartels 1996).

Much more empirical research along these lines is no doubt warranted. But the evidence already in hand provides rather modest grounds for imagining that the context dependence of political attitudes described here is simply a result of ignorance, inattention, or bias, to be remedied by more careful thought or unfettered deliberation. For the moment, at least, it seems to me that we must probably accede to Kahneman, Ritov, and Schkade's conclusion that the context dependence of preferences is "an unavoidable consequence of basic cognitive and evaluative processes. It is not a result of defective procedures" (2000, 660).

This point may be dramatized by drawing examples and evidence from precisely the two issue areas—abortion and affirmative action—that Kinder (and others) have suggested as prime exceptions to the "casual and shallow character of much everyday political thinking." The vagaries of public opinion evident even in these realms of unusual salience and concreteness seem to me to support Converse's felicitous (if somewhat facetious) assertion that "what needs repair is not the item[s] but the people" (1970, 176).

Some of the complexities running beneath the surface of public opinion on the issue of abortion are suggested by Freedman and Goldstein's (1998) analysis of responses to two questions on the topic in American National Election Study (NES) surveys. In response to the NES's usual general question about abortion, asked in 1996, about 40 percent of the eventual respondents in the 1997 NES Pilot Study said that "By law, a woman should always be able to obtain an abortion as a matter of personal choice." However, in response to a separate Pilot Study question, 39 percent of these respondents favored "a proposed law to ban certain types of late-term abortions, sometimes called partial birth abortions."[12] That is, a substantial fraction of those who believed that abortions should "always" be permitted "as a matter of personal choice" also believed that "partial birth abortions" should be banned. While it is certainly possible to render these two positions logically consistent (for example, by stipulating the availability of some practical alternative to "partial birth abortions" in those situations where they are currently being chosen), it seems more straightforward simply to acknowledge that, when it comes to public opinion, "always" never means always.

Perhaps, as Kinder asserts, complexities like these could be cleared up

through more careful question writing or more effective political socialization—"Improve the questions, induce elites to provide a clarifying debate, and
real attitudes will increase." But if *attitudes* imply complete and coherent *preferences* of the sort required by conventional liberal democratic theory, I think
not. As Kinder's own reference to the unusual "prominence" of the abortion
issue suggests, political elites have had about as much chance to "provide a
clarifying debate" on this issue as on any topic currently before the U.S. public—without succeeding, at least by the evidence of Freedman and Goldstein,
in producing any clear reconciliation of the powerfully competing values at
stake.[13]

Nor is it obvious how one would "clarify" preferences regarding abortion
policy through "careful question writing." Some of the ambiguities inherent in
such attempts at clarification are suggested by another analysis from the 1997
NES Pilot Study, this one comparing alternative ways of referring to the actors
on each side of the abortion debate (Sapiro 1998). Half the Pilot Study respondents were asked to rate "opponents of abortion" and "supporters of abortion"
on a one hundred–point "feeling thermometer"; the other half were asked to
rate "pro-life people" and "pro-choice people."

It seems fruitless to deny that these are, in essence, alternative ways of tap-
ping exactly the same substantive attitudes. Nevertheless, they produced
significantly different results, with *both* "pro-life" and "pro-choice" people
receiving much more favorable ratings than abortion "opponents" or "supporters," respectively. Both differences appeared consistently among men and
women, among more and less politically aware respondents, and among those
who were themselves opponents and supporters of abortion.[14] While these differences testify to the success of the rhetorical strategies adopted by abortion
supporters and abortion opponents in labeling themselves as "pro-choice" and
"pro-life," respectively, they do nothing to justify one's faith in the reality of
public attitudes toward abortion supporters or opponents independent of the
particular words that happen to be used to denote them.

Of course, one might still object that questions in opinion surveys are a far
cry from real political decisions, and that peculiar responses to survey questions even about an issue as salient and fundamental as abortion have little
genuine relevance for democratic theory. That objection seems to me to be
misguided in both its aspects. For one thing, while most consequential decisions in actual democracies are made by representatives and not directly by citizens in policy referenda, theories of representation are almost invariably
grounded in analogous choices of policies by representatives, or of representatives by citizens, or both (Pitkin 1967; Manin 1997); thus, as long as we continue
to evaluate democracy in terms of the correspondence between citizens' preferences and policy outcomes, all of the same theoretical problems will simply

reappear when we attempt to specify what kind of representation is most democratic. Moreover, even if the specific formats and substantive content of the questions in some of the examples I have recited bear little superficial resemblance to the questions put to citizens in policy referenda or to representatives in the legislative arena, there is no reason to suppose that the same conceptual problems do not arise in posing "real" political issues.

The practical reality of the conceptual problems considered here is illustrated in semicomical form by a recent procedural controversy in Missouri. The Missouri Supreme Court ordered the removal from referendum ballots of a fiscal summary prepared by a legislative committee estimating that Amendment 9 would cost the state forty thousand dollars per year to implement; the amendment stipulated that election ballots should include the phrase "DISREGARDED VOTERS' INSTRUCTIONS ON TERM LIMITS" in capital letters next to the names of congressional candidates who did not support a specific federal constitutional amendment (Wolfe 1996).[15] Would the committee's fiscal note have provided a more appropriate frame for citizens' consideration of this referendum measure? For that matter, would the proposed ballot language have provided a more appropriate frame for citizens' consideration of congressional candidates? Should a referendum to set a higher minimum wage include a fiscal note indicating that "Revenue loss due to job loss may be significant?"[16]

A rather less frivolous example of the same practical dilemma arose in a recent referendum on the abolition of affirmative action programs in Houston. According to a *New York Times* report,

> the fundamental truth that seems to have emerged from the debate here is that the future of affirmative action may depend more than anything else on the language in which it is framed.
>
> The vote Tuesday came only after a tumultuous debate in the City Council over the wording of the measure. Rather than being asked whether they wanted to ban discrimination and "preferential treatment," to which voters said a clear "yes" in California last year and to which polls showed Houston voters would also say yes, residents were instead asked whether they wished specifically to ban affirmative action in city contracting and hiring.
>
> The legal effect was the same under either wording, but to this revised question they answered "no," by 55 percent to 45 percent. . . .
>
> Affirmative-action proponents around the nation hailed not just the result of Houston's vote, but the phrasing of the referendum as a straight up-or-down call on affirmative action, and they said that is the way the question should be put to voters elsewhere.
>
> Its opponents, meanwhile, who are already in court challenging the City Council's broad rewording as illegal, denounced it as a heavy-handed way of obscuring the principles that were really at stake. (Verhovek 1997)

Who is to decide what principles are "really at stake" in a policy choice like the one at issue in Houston? If we accept, at least for the sake of argument, that a referendum using the original wording "taken almost directly from the Civil Rights Act of 1964" (Verhovek 1997) would have passed, as most observers seem to have believed, would that result have been more or less legitimate than the actual result?

These questions are of a piece with the questions I have raised based on the theoretical and experimental work of psychologists and public opinion researchers. Political elites who pose referendum questions must frame complex, difficult political issues in specific, concrete language. If citizens had definite, preexisting preferences regarding the underlying issues, any reasonable choice of language might elicit those preferences equally well. But democracy with attitudes is more complicated and more controversial.

Democracy without Preferences

Can we have a viable theory of democracy based on the assumption that citizens have attitudes rather than preferences? What might such a theory look like?

A Rhetorical Free-for-All?

One possible reaction to the evidence of framing effects presented here is simply to acknowledge that framing issues is an important aspect of political contestation in a democracy. As Gamson and Modigliani put it,

> Every public issue is contested in a symbolic arena. Advocates of one or another persuasion attempt to give their own meaning to the issue and to events that may affect its outcome. Their weapons are metaphors, catchphrases, and other condensing symbols that frame the issue in a particular fashion. (1987, 143)

A variety of political scientists have echoed Gamson and Modigliani's point in a variety of ways. For example, Kinder and Sanders argued that "the opinions expressed by the public on political issues should be understood not as the revelation of fixed inner states but as the result of a question-answering process, one that mimics the dialogue surrounding controversial political issues" (1990, 99).[17] Iyengar interpreted his demonstration of framing effects arising from television news coverage as "further confirmation of the inherently circumstantial nature of human judgment" (1991, 130). Johnston and his colleagues acknowledged "the image of the electorate which dominates popular discussion of mass politics: the people as a free-standing body, with its own indomitable collective opinion," but they went on to argue for a broader view of the electoral process encompassing not only "how voters choose" but also "how parties and leaders shape the alternatives from which the choice is made" (1992, 3).

To their credit, these and other scholars have followed through on their observations by carrying out detailed empirical studies of how political elites attempt to frame controversial political issues and of how those efforts influence policy outcomes. I have no doubt that political scientists in the years to come will learn a great deal more about strategies of framing—and about when and why some of those strategies work better than others.

Unfortunately, even very successful empirical research along these lines may be of quite limited use to democratic theorists unless it can be connected to some coherent normative account of what makes one frame more appropriate than another as a basis for democratic choice. In the absence of such a coherent normative account, political debate and policy choice can only be thought of as a rhetorical free-for-all, a practical art in which—at best—the ends justify the means.[18]

Of course, it is possible simply to equate the relative normative legitimacy of competing frames with their observed success in the political arena. This approach has the practical virtue of allowing empirical research on framing strategies and their consequences to serve double duty as a basis for normative theorizing. It also neatly exploits the traditional faith of liberal theorists in the virtues of free and unfettered political debate.[19]

The primary problem with this solution by definition is that its appeal seems to depend heavily on citizens' ability to judge which frame is most appropriate for a given issue. Not only must competing political elites offer an "appropriate" selection of competing frames, but citizens must be able to pick and choose among those competing frames in "appropriate" ways.[20] Citizens must have consistent preferences regarding how issues should be framed to rescue us from the embarrassing fact that they do not have consistent preferences regarding the issues themselves!

Consider, for example, the role of framing in Johnston et al.'s (1992) analysis of the 1988 Canadian election campaign. In the course of their seven-week election study, Johnston and his colleagues reminded half their survey sample that "Canada has reached a free trade agreement with the United States" and asked the respondents whether they supported or opposed that agreement. Respondents in the other half of the sample were asked the same question but with the phrase "the Mulroney government" substituted for "Canada."

Associating the trade deal with the prime minister rather than with "Canada" reduced support for it by about 10 percentage points in the early part of the 1988 campaign.[21] However, this difference as a result of question wording dissipated later in the campaign—especially after a highly publicized debate among the candidates in which Mulroney's Liberal opponent, John Turner, criticized the prime minister's negotiation of the Free Trade Agreement with the memorable phrase "I happen to believe that you have sold us out." As Johnston et al. put it,

> The existence of an impact from the experiment before the debates indicated the potential for discrediting the FTA by linking it to Brian Mulroney. The disappearance of this effect after the debates indicated that the potential was realized in the campaign—distrust of Brian Mulroney was now biting in the electorate at large. We had implanted uncertainty about the agent in the "Mulroney" treatment group. After the debates this treatment had little further impact: all respondents—even those assigned to the "Canada" treatment—now came to us with Mulroney-related doubts about the FTA already in place. We no longer needed to remind them of the linkage between the prime minister and the FTA; John Turner's accusation that Brian Mulroney had sold us out did the job for us. (1992, 151–52)

Johnston and his colleagues' analysis seems to provide convincing evidence that the "Mulroney" frame won out over the "Canada" frame in the actual political debate surrounding the Free Trade Agreement in the 1988 campaign. But does that mean that attitudes toward the "Mulroney" agreement were somehow more genuine or more worthy of political consideration than attitudes toward the "Canada" agreement? Or that ordinary Canadians consciously judged the "Mulroney" frame to be more appropriate? If John Turner had happened to be a less resourceful political debater, would attitudes toward the "Mulroney" agreement have been less deserving of respect? Objectively, the agreement was *both* Mulroney's agreement and Canada's agreement. But the relative weight attached to those two competing perspectives in the course of the campaign seems to reflect accidental features of the political context rather than their relative intrinsic appropriateness. A successful *normative* theory of framing will, I believe, require some sturdier moral basis than empirical research alone can provide.

May the Best Frame Win?

If political attitudes are context dependent, as the various examples of framing effects rehearsed here strongly imply, it seems clear that any adequate normative theory of democracy based on those attitudes will require a normative theory of political contexts. My aim in this section is not, alas, to propose a workable normative theory of political contexts but simply to suggest some of the directions that such a theory might take—and some of the difficulties that such a project will encounter.

Zaller's (1992) notion that attitude expressions reflect some readily accessible sample from a universe of relevant considerations suggests one potentially useful normative standard: frames that evoke larger samples of the universe of considerations relevant to the issue at hand are more appropriate than those that evoke smaller samples. I have already suggested this as a potentially appealing benchmark for evaluating situations in which framing effects are produced by introducing additional considerations into an otherwise identical context. For example, this is the logic by which policy choices regarding the treatment of communist reporters in the United States might be considered more legitimate when considerations of reciprocity are made salient than when they are not, or judgments regarding the importance of cyanide fishing in coral reefs considered more legitimate when human health problems are introduced as a basis for comparison than when they are not.

One important practical difficulty in applying this proposed normative standard is that the "universe of considerations relevant to the issue at hand" can seldom be clearly specified. It seems easy to agree that a norm of reciprocity is "relevant" to judgments regarding appropriate treatment of communist reporters in the United States, but it is less obvious that the fate of multiple myeloma patients is "relevant" to judgments regarding the importance of coral reefs around Asia—unless we are willing to accept that the universe of potentially relevant considerations for any problem of interest is, effectively, infinitely large.

Moreover, it seems risky to assume as a matter of principle that more is necessarily better—that evoking additional considerations will produce a judgment that better approximates a citizen's "true preference." If these additional considerations are in some sense unrepresentative of the entire universe of relevant considerations, they may bias judgments in more or less arbitrary ways. A judgment based on reciprocity may not be appropriate if it ignores many other relevant considerations implying the opposite policy conclusion. The connotations evoked by the words *welfare* or *communist invasion* may be relevant to judgments involving those issues, but these connotations may achieve much more salience than they deserve in light of the whole range of relevant considerations that might be brought to bear on those issues.

Thus, it seems that we must amend our proposed normative standard: frames that evoke larger and more representative samples of the universe of considerations relevant to the issue at hand are more appropriate than those that evoke smaller and less representative samples.[22] Unfortunately, this amended standard seems impossible to apply in practice, since determining that one frame evokes a "more representative" sample of the relevant universe of considerations than another requires (at least in principle) that we be able to enumerate and weigh those considerations. Neither Zaller nor any other analyst of political attitudes has proposed a concrete model specifying what a universe of potentially relevant considerations is supposed to consist of or how it is supposed to be sampled from.[23]

In much the same way, survey methodologists sensitive to the prevalence of question-wording effects sometimes recommend "neutral" question wording or counterarguments within the text of a question to ensure "balance," but these authors seldom provide any clear advice about how to calibrate "balance" or "neutrality" except, perhaps, by reference to some known distribution of existing opinion—an obviously circular solution. As Schuman and Presser nicely put it, "counterarguments tend to create new questions, not simply more balanced versions of previous questions" (1981, 200).

If more considerations are not necessarily better—and if we are unwilling to accept the observed success of competing frames as a reliable indicator of their normative legitimacy—what other sort of normative standard might be compelling? Some political philosophers have attached legitimacy not directly to competing frames or the outcomes they imply but to the deliberative procedures producing those outcomes. If real political debate is marred by a variety of important flaws, perhaps we can find (or imagine) less flawed procedures and infer that they produce (or would produce) less flawed outcomes.

This approach comes in two superficially distinct but logically similar flavors—a "negative" version positing the (actual or hypothetical) minimization of negative features of the political process and a "positive" version positing the (actual or hypothetical) maximization of positive features of the political process. Rawls's (1971) "original position"—in which reasoning about justice is conducted behind a "veil of ignorance," without reference to personal stakes—is an influential example of a negative ideal. Habermas's (1982) "ideal speech situation"—in which unlimited free discussion among political equals is supposed to produce a rational consensus—is a prototypical positive standard; Dahl's (1989) notion of "enlightened understanding" has much the same flavor.

Fishkin proposed and has subsequently implemented a more practical version of the same positive deliberative ideal. His "deliberative opinion poll" brings random samples of ordinary citizens together to study and discuss important political issues. The views expressed by these representative citizens after they have studied and deliberated are taken to reflect "what the public *would* think, if it had a more adequate chance to think about the questions at issue" (Fishkin 1991, 1). Of course, one is tempted to wonder how adequately a few days of democracy camp can approximate the abstract glories of Habermas's ideal speech situation, especially when someone with his or her own political views must assemble the study materials and hire and train the "facilitators" who moderate the collective deliberation. Nevertheless, the intuition that informed, deliberative opinions are more worthy of respect than top-of-the-head survey responses seems in principle to be compelling.[24]

A more fundamental question is whether this or any other procedural standard points us toward a resolution of the various paradoxes and uncertainties raised by the characterization of attitudes summarized here. Would Habermas's ideal speech situation make concrete the suffering of twenty thousand birds drowning in oil or synthesize the myriad charms and irritations of New York City? Can better deliberative procedures reconcile conflicting attitudes toward "welfare" and "assistance to the poor," much less "forbidding" and "not allowing"?

The hopeful assertions of democratic theorists regarding the positive effects of deliberation (for example, Fishkin 1991; Miller 1992; Benhabib 1996; Gutmann and Thompson 1996) are seldom supported by systematic empirical evidence, and when real political processes are used as examples, the standards by which they are judged are typically much less demanding than would be required to resolve specific political disputes like the one surrounding the framing of Houston's referendum on affirmative action. For example, Gutmann and Thompson concluded that "[s]ome citizens already make remarkably good use of the limited opportunities for deliberation that exist. Deliberation may not have produced the best possible solution to health care priorities in Oregon or environmental risks in Tacoma, but its results were probably no worse than less deliberative means would have achieved, and they surely advanced public understanding further" (1996, 359).

Analysts of actual political deliberation have, perhaps not surprisingly, painted a less rosy portrait than philosophers of deliberative democracy. Real New England town meetings apparently involve a good deal of false unanimity, with most important decisions settled in advance through informal networks reflecting preexisting inequalities in social status and political power (Mansbridge 1983). The atmosphere of public-spiritedness and mutual respect central to theorists' accounts of democratic deliberation may be difficult or impossible to achieve in real societies burdened by sexism, racism, and fundamental cultural schisms (Sanders 1997; Mendelberg and Oleske 1996).

However that may be, the more important point here is that theorists of deliberative democracy have done very little to specify how deliberation might be organized to overcome the defects of particular political contexts or to assess the relative democratic legitimacy of alternative issue frames. For example, Gutmann and Thompson's five "constitutional principles of a deliberative democracy" include three "conditions that regulate deliberation" ("reciprocity," "publicity," and "accountability") and two "key components of the content of deliberation" ("liberty" and "opportunity") (1996, 199). It is hard to see how principles at this level of generality could reliably resolve specific disputes about the relative appropriateness of alternative choice contexts of the sort considered here.

In some cases, Gutmann and Thompson's substantive principles might be taken to imply specific policy results more or less directly, regardless of the choice contexts or procedures that would be necessary to produce those outcomes from any "democratic" political process. But given the scope for political bias in reasoning of this sort from very general principles to specific policy conclusions, such derivations are unlikely to be reliable—whether or not they should be considered "democratic." For example, it is not hard to imagine partisans on both sides of the affirmative action debate in Houston arguing that Gutmann and Thompson's substantive principles of "liberty" and "opportunity" entail precisely their own preferred policy outcomes. However the philosophers might adjudicate such an argument, the rest of us may wish for a theory of democracy in which the theorists' thumbs weigh less heavily on the scales.

Of course, in a literal sense, democratic theorists might still insist on choosing between alternative issue frames on strictly procedural grounds. For example, one might argue that the proponents of abolishing affirmative action in Houston were entitled to their preferred question wording, since they had duly submitted the twenty thousand signatures required by law to get their proposition on the ballot. Alternatively, one might argue that the Houston City Council, as a broadly representative body, was better suited to make what was clearly a politically sensitive decision about the appropriate wording of this ballot measure. As a purely legal matter, one or the other of these two views must, presumably, prevail in the end. However, from the standpoint of democratic theory neither seems really satisfactory, since in either case there is strong reason to believe that a different, more or less equally legitimate procedure would have produced diametrically opposite results.

A Concluding Analogy

The implications for normative political theory of recent work on the nature of attitudes seem comparable in important respects to the implications of Arrow's (1951) landmark work on the logical problems of preference aggregation. Arrow demonstrated with mathematical rigor that what many democratic theorists seemed to want—a procedure for "adding up" coherent individual preferences to arrive at a coherent "collective preference"—was simply, logically, unattainable. One commentator referred rather melodramatically to Arrow's theorem and related theoretical work as

> a gigantic cavern into which fall almost all of our ideas about social actions. Almost anything . . . anyone has ever said about what society wants or should get is threatened with internal inconsistency. It is as though people have been talking for years about a thing that cannot, in *principle*, exist, and a major effort is needed to see what objectively remains from the conversations. (Plott 1976, 511–12)

Subsequent work by political scientists (Shepsle 1979; Riker 1980; Calvert 1995) has taken Arrow's result as a spur to specify and explain how specific political institutions shape collective choices in the absence of any equilibrium derivable directly from individual preferences. For example, committee specialization, germaneness rules, and conference procedures in legislatures may simplify policy choices sufficiently to assure the existence of stable equilibria even in settings where distributions of "pure preferences" would otherwise make any outcome potentially susceptible to being overturned through agenda manipulation and multidimensional logrolling.

From the perspective of empirical political science, these developments have been stimulating and fruitful. However, they have done little or nothing to fill the gaping hole in normative political theory identified by Plott. If collective choices depend crucially on the detailed working of political institutions, how should political institutions themselves be evaluated? So far, democratic theory has produced no satisfactory answer to that key question.[25]

While nothing in the scholarly literature on attitudes has the theoretical elegance of Arrow's theorem, the intellectual problem posed by that literature is, I believe, similar both in kind and in magnitude to the problem posed by Arrow's work. The realization that collective outcomes could not be interpreted simply as an unproblematic "adding up" of individual preferences has spurred a fruitful flurry of empirical work on how political institutions structure those outcomes—but no satisfactory normative theory of how they *should* do so. In much the same way, the realization that attitude expressions are powerfully (and, in my view, intrinsically and unavoidably) context dependent has begun to spur a fruitful flurry of empirical work on how political issues are framed—but no satisfactory normative theory of how they *should* be framed.

In both cases, a successful normative resolution may require a style of theorizing unfamiliar to political philosophers and political scientists alike. While such theorizing may be inspired and informed by relevant empirical work, its core feature will probably be a more subtle specification of the moral grounds on which one political context or institution might be deemed superior to another. It will not be sufficient to evaluate contexts or institutions by reference to their success or failure in reflecting citizens' preferences, since that is merely to beg the question.

In both cases, the most obvious alternative to theoretical progress is a much-diluted version of democratic theory along the general lines proposed by Riker, who argued that "popular rule" is impossible but that citizens can exercise "an intermittent, sometimes random, even perverse, popular veto" on the machinations of political elites (1982, 244).[26] If that sort of democracy is the best we can hope for, we had better reconcile ourselves to the fact. Conversely, if we insist on believing that democracy can provide some attractive and consistent normative basis for evaluating policy outcomes, we had better figure out more clearly what we are talking about.

NOTES

This essay is a by-product of collaborative work with Daniel Kahneman and Kristine Kuhn. I am grateful to them for much insight and instruction, but I absolve them of any responsibility for my arguments or conclusions. An earlier version of the analysis was presented in colloquia at Harvard, Princeton, and Columbia, and I thank the participants on those occasions for stimulating questions and reactions. I also thank Christopher Achen, Dana Ansel, Adam Berinsky, Amy Gutmann, Stephen Holmes, Donald Kinder, Dan Kryder, Tali Mendelberg, Thomas Romer, and John Zaller for especially helpful comments and advice and Dean Michael Rothschild of the Woodrow Wilson School for generous financial support.

1. This is, obviously, a very simple summary of a long and complex scientific debate. Donald Kinder's contribution to this volume provides a somewhat more detailed account of Converse's findings and subsequent research in the field, as well as an assessment of the outcome that is somewhat less one sided than mine and perhaps more representative of general scholarly judgment. Indeed, in some respects my position is probably more "Con(tro)versial" even than Converse's—compare, for example, Converse 1990 with Bartels 1996.

2. In an aside, Arrow noted, "Many writers have felt that the assumption of rationality, in the sense of a one-dimensional ordering of all possible alternatives, is absolutely necessary for economic theorizing," but he also argued, "There seems to be no logical necessity for this viewpoint; we could just as well build up our economic theory on other assumptions as to the structure of choice functions if the facts seemed to call for it. The work of the institutionalist school may be regarded in part as such an attempt, though no systematic treatment has emerged" (1951, 21). Fifty years later, economists seem to have made little further progress in this regard; while a more flexible theory may be possible in principle, no "systematic treatment" along the lines Arrow suggested is actually in sight.

3. Of course, I may prefer *x* over *y* as a prospective political leader but *y* over *x* as a prospective dinner companion. This is not a case of inconsistent preferences but of consistent preferences in two distinct realms that require separate analysis.

4. One way of expressing this assumption is by associating definite quantities of "utility" with each alternative and stipulating that *x* is preferred to *y* if and only if the utility associated with *x* exceeds the utility associated with *y*. For present purposes, however, there is no obvious benefit—and some loss of intuition—in recasting the problem of "preferences" as a problem of "utilities."

5. I have found Lakoff's (1987) summary of some of this research especially clear and stimulating.

6. Schuman and Presser (1981, 29) replicated Hyman and Sheatsley's experiment in 1980. The level of support for communist reporters was a good deal higher than in 1948 in the baseline condition (55 percent compared 36 percent), but priming the norm of reciprocity still increased that support substantially (from 55 percent to 75 percent).

7. Alternatively, but in my view less plausibly, this difference also might be attributable to a genuine difference in the substance of the two questions, with some respon-

dents wanting to spend more on approaches to crime other than law enforcement, such as social programs in crime-ridden neighborhoods.

8. Gilens (1999) and Ansel (1997, chap. 3) provide nuanced analyses of public attitudes toward welfare.

9. This disparity does not seem to reflect changes in underlying attitudes toward the war in the intervening two months, since a previous administration of the "getting into the fighting" question in August registered only 27 percent support. Mueller (1973) provided a detailed analysis of these and other nonexperimental comparisons involving a variety of survey questions repeated periodically throughout the course of the war. Mueller (1994) provided an even more detailed analysis of public opinion in the Gulf War, arguing at one point that "28 percent was willing to go to war, 46 percent was willing to engage in combat, and 65 percent was willing to use military force—that is, one could as easily argue that the doves outnumbered hawks by two to one as the reverse" (30).

10. Schuman and Presser's (1981) results using data from the mid-1970s replicated the results of a similar experiment conducted in 1940 (Rugg 1941) that indicated a much higher overall level of opposition to free speech by communists but a quite similar difference of 21 percentage points between the "forbid" and "not allow" question wordings.

11. The percentages unwilling to "allow" free speech by communists were 68 among those with grade-school educations and 20 percent among those with college degrees, while the corresponding percentages willing to "forbid" free speech by communists were 40 percent and 13 percent, respectively. Thus the absolute effect of the question-wording difference was substantially smaller among the college educated, but the *relative* reduction in support for "forbidding" free speech by communists was on the order of 40 percent in both groups (Schuman and Presser 1981, 279).

12. Forty-nine percent of these pro-choice respondents opposed a ban on partial birth abortions, while the remaining 12 percent said they didn't know whether they favored or opposed such a ban.

13. Alvarez and Brehm attempted to analyze public "ambivalence" about abortion by applying heteroskedastic probit models to a variety of specific policy questions. They concluded that "the attitudes of American citizens toward abortion policy are rooted in conflicting core beliefs" (1995, 1076).

14. The average magnitude of the differences in ratings between the alternative frames was nine points on the one hundred–point feeling thermometer. The average *t*-value for these differences in the twelve subgroup analyses involving men and women, more and less aware respondents, and abortion opponents and supporters was 3.0.

15. The court did not address the accuracy of the cost estimate but held that the legislative committee, as an advisory body to the Missouri General Assembly, had no constitutional authority to provide fiscal summaries in connection with ballot measures. A county clerk reported that "ballots were taken back to a printer for the sentence to be blocked out. Regular overprinting did not hide the words completely, so the ballots were overprinted again with 'a little squiggly design'" (Wolfe 1996).

16. The latter phrase was deleted by a Missouri circuit judge from a fiscal summary prepared by the same legislative committee, though the remainder of that fiscal summary was allowed to stand (Wolfe 1996).

17. Kinder and Sanders also emphasized the close analogy between survey responses

and other kinds of political decisions and the implication of that analogy for an appreciation of the political significance of framing effects in surveys: "those of us who design surveys find ourselves in roughly the same position as do those who hold and wield real power: public officials, editors and journalists, newsmakers of all sorts. Both choose how public issues are to be framed, and in both instances, the decisions seem to be consequential" (1990, 99).

18. One normative underpinning offered by Aristotle for his theory of civic discourse in *Rhetoric* seems to be of essentially this sort: "one should be able to argue persuasively on either side of a question, just as in the use of syllogisms, not that we may actually do both (for one should not persuade what is debased) but in order that it may not escape our notice what the real state of the case is and that we ourselves may be able to refute if another person uses speech unjustly" (Kennedy 1991, 34).

19. Not only liberal—Aristotle claimed in the same passage of *Rhetoric* that "the true and the just are by nature stronger than their opposites" and that "the underlying facts are not equally good in each case; but true and better ones are by nature always more productive of good syllogisms and, in a word, more persuasive" (Kennedy 1991, 34–35). Milton's similar assertion in *Areopagitica* ("Let her and falsehood grapple; who ever knew Truth put to the worse, in a free and open encounter?" [1973, 35]) is a more direct precursor of analogous arguments in many subsequent versions of liberal theory, such as John Stuart Mill's.

20. Zaller's parable of "Purple Land" provides one unhappily thin account of how this might work: "Even in cases of elite disagreement, in which each type of citizen mechanically followed the advice of his or her own type of politician or expert, there was no elite domination. For citizens could still be confident that, the more closely they looked into a subject, the more likely they would be to reach the same conclusion reached by the expert subcommunity sharing their own values" (1992, 314). How did the citizens of Purple Land decide in the first place which experts to mechanically follow? How did the experts translate their attitudes into policy conclusions? Zaller is silent on these points.

21. Johnston et al. speculated that the effect of the difference in question wording might have been even greater in earlier stages of the political debate: "much of the impact may have been absorbed by the time our fieldwork began, so intense over the summer had been the opposition's attempts to link the FTA to the prime minister" (1992, 151).

22. This revised criterion is underspecified as it stands, since it provides no rule for comparing a larger but less representative sample of considerations with a smaller but more representative sample. However, this problem does not seem insurmountable, since (if the other conceptual difficulties noted here could somehow be overcome) principles from sampling theory in statistics could presumably be used to specify an appropriate rule for weighing bias against incompleteness.

23. Zaller's "response axiom" stipulated that individuals "answer survey questions by averaging across the considerations that are immediately salient or accessible to them" (1992, 49), but the closest he came to specifying which considerations would be immediately salient or accessible was to assume that the "more recently a consideration has been called to mind or thought about, the less time it takes to retrieve that consideration or related considerations from memory and bring them to the top of the head for use" (1992, 48). What considerations are "related?" What is the logical or psycholog-

ical basis of these connections? What are the relative probabilities of sampling a more related but less recent consideration versus a less related but more recent one? Zaller's theory is not sufficiently detailed to suggest any clear answers to these questions. Boynton and Lodge (n.d.) offered a more detailed model along similar lines but with the relevant parameters fixed by assumption rather than derived from any normative theory of democracy.

24. I have proposed elsewhere (Bartels 1990, 1996) a quite different methodology for distilling "fully informed preferences" from survey responses on the basis of the observed relationship between information and preferences among respondents with similar social characteristics. This approach raises a different set of practical problems—most obviously, how do we measure information and how do we model the relationship between information and preferences? Despite these differences, the two approaches seem sufficiently similar in their underlying logic to be equally susceptible to the more general concerns raised here.

25. One of the very few democratic theorists to face the question directly (Miller 1992) suggested that deliberation might help to mitigate the force of the logical incoherence revealed by Arrow's theorem, either by generating widespread consensus about how to locate the various alternatives along a single dimension (or about how to separate the issue into independent unidimensional components) or by making it possible to identify instances in which collective decisions might legitimately be made using procedures that violate one or more of Arrow's conditions (such as the Borda count, which gives extra weight to intense preferences but may not select the single alternative—if there is one—preferred by a majority of citizens to every other alternative). However, Miller provided no empirical evidence in support of these assertions and no indication of how a theory of deliberative democracy might gauge the legitimacy of such effects if and when they do occur.

26. Mueller has pieced together a more extensive pedigree for a similarly minimalist view, referring to its adherents as democrats "of the Smith/Lincoln/Barnum/Forster/Churchill persuasion" (1992, 1002). British writer Sydney Smith made Mueller's list by arguing in the wake of the Napoleonic wars for "apathy, selfishness, common sense, arithmetic." Abraham Lincoln and P. T. Barnum both get partial credit for "You can't fool all the people all the time." E. M. Forster offered "two cheers for democracy" and anticipated Winston Churchill's observation that "democracy is the worst form of government except all those other forms that have been tried from time to time."

REFERENCES

Achen, Christopher H. 1975. Mass Political Attitudes and the Survey Response. *American Political Science Review* 69:1218–31.

Alvarez, R. Michael, and John Brehm. 1995. American Ambivalence towards Abortion Policy: Development of a Heteroskedastic Probit Model of Competing Values. *American Journal of Political Science* 39:1055–82.

Ansel, Dana Elizabeth. 1997. Poor Chances: The Working Poor Speak about Poverty and Opportunity. Ph.D. diss., Princeton University.

Arrow, Kenneth J. 1951. *Social Choice and Individual Values.* New Haven: Yale University Press.

———. 1982. Risk Perception in Psychology and Economics. *Economic Inquiry* 20:1–9.

Baron, Jonathan. 1997. Biases in Quantitative Measurement of Values for Public Decisions. *Psychological Bulletin* 122:72–88.

Bartels, Larry M. 1990. Public Opinion and Political Interests. Paper presented at the annual meeting of the Midwest Political Science Association, Chicago.

———. 1996. Uninformed Votes: Information Effects in Presidential Elections. *American Journal of Political Science* 40:194–230.

Benhabib, Seyla. 1996. Toward a Deliberative Model of Democratic Legitimacy. In Seyla Benhabib, ed., *Democracy and Difference: Contesting the Boundaries of the Political.* Princeton: Princeton University Press.

Boynton, G. R., and Milton Lodge. N.d. Hot Cognition: A Computational Model of Candidate Evaluation. Unpublished manuscript, University of Iowa and State University of New York—Stony Brook.

Calvert, Randall L. 1995. Rational Actors, Equilibrium, and Social Institutions. In Jack Knight and Itai Sened, eds., *Explaining Social Institutions.* Ann Arbor: University of Michigan Press.

Chong, Dennis. 1993. How People Think, Reason, and Feel about Rights and Liberties. *American Journal of Political Science* 37:867–99.

Clark, Andy. 1998. Where Brain, Body, and World Collide. *Daedalus* 127:257–80.

Converse, Philip E. 1964. The Nature of Belief Systems in Mass Publics. In David Apter, ed., *Ideology and Discontent.* New York: Free Press.

———. 1970. Attitudes and Non-Attitudes: Continuation of a Dialogue. In Edward R. Tufte, ed., *The Quantitative Analysis of Social Problems.* Reading, Mass.: Addison-Wesley.

———. 1975. Public Opinion and Voting Behavior. In Fred I. Greenstein and Nelson W. Polsby, eds., *Handbook of Political Science,* vol. 4. Reading, Mass.: Addison-Wesley.

———. 1990. Popular Representation and the Distribution of Information. In John A. Ferejohn and James H. Kuklinski, eds., *Information and Democratic Processes.* Urbana: University of Illinois Press.

Converse, Philip E., and Gregory B. Markus. 1979. *Plus ça Change* . . . The New CPS Election Study Panel. *American Political Science Review* 73:32–49.

Dahl, Robert A. 1971. *Polyarchy: Participation and Opposition.* New Haven: Yale University Press.

———. 1989. *Democracy and Its Critics.* New Haven: Yale University Press.

Eagly, Alice H., and Shelly Chaiken. 1998. Attitude Structure and Function. In D. T. Gilbert, S. T. Fiske, and G. Lindzey, eds., *The Handbook of Social Psychology,* 4th ed., vol. 1. New York: McGraw-Hill.

Feldman, Stanley. 1989. Measuring Issue Preferences: The Problem of Response Instability. In James A. Stimson, ed., *Political Analysis,* vol. 1. Ann Arbor: University of Michigan Press.

Fishkin, James S. 1991. *Democracy and Deliberation: New Directions for Democratic Reform.* New Haven: Yale University Press.

Freedman, Paul, and Ken Goldstein. 1998. Partial Birth Abortion Item, 1997 Pilot Study. Report to the Board of Overseers of the American National Election Studies.

Gamson, William, and Andre Modigliani. 1987. The Changing Culture of Affirmative Action. In R. D. Braungart, ed., *Research in Political Sociology,* vol. 3. Greenwich, Conn.: JAI Press.

Gilens, Martin. 1999. *Why Americans Hate Welfare: Race, Media, and the Politics of Antipoverty Policy.* Chicago: University of Chicago Press.

Gutmann, Amy, and Dennis Thompson. 1996. *Democracy and Disagreement.* Cambridge: Belknap Press of Harvard University Press.

Habermas, Jurgen. 1982. A Reply to My Critics. In John B. Thompson and David Held, eds., *Habermas: Critical Debates.* Cambridge: MIT Press.

Hyman, Herbert H., and Paul B. Sheatsley. 1950. The Current Status of American Public Opinion. In J. C. Payne, ed., *The Teaching of Contemporary Affairs.* New York: National Council of Social Studies.

Iyengar, Shanto. 1991. *Is Anyone Responsible? How Television Frames Political Issues.* Chicago: University of Chicago Press.

Johnston, Richard, André Blais, Henry E. Brady, and Jean Crête. 1992. *Letting the People Decide: Dynamics of a Canadian Election.* Montreal: McGill-Queen's University Press.

Jones-Lee, M. W., G. Loomes, and P. R. Philips. 1995. Valuing the Prevention of Non-Fatal Road Injuries: Contingent Valuation vs. Standard Gambles. *Oxford Economic Papers* 47:676.

Kahneman, Daniel, and J. L. Knetsch. 1992. Valuing Public Goods: The Purchase of Moral Satisfaction. *Journal of Environmental Economics and Management* 22:57–70.

Kahneman, Daniel, and Ilana Ritov. N.d. Attitude Theory, Dollars and the Environment: Bringing Psychology to Bear. Unpublished manuscript, Princeton University and Ben-Gurion University.

Kahneman, Daniel, Ilana Ritov, and David Schkade. 2000. Economic Preferences or Attitude Expressions? An Analysis of Dollar Responses to Public Issues. In Daniel Kahneman and Amos Tversky, eds., *Choices, Values, and Frames.* Cambridge: Cambridge University Press.

Kennedy, George A. 1991. *Aristotle: On Rhetoric: A Theory of Civic Discourse.* New York: Oxford University Press.

Kinder, Donald R., and Thomas E. Nelson. 1998. Democratic Debate and Real Opinions. In Nadya Terkildsen and F. Schnell, eds., *The Dynamics of Issue Framing: Elite Discourse and the Formation of Public Opinion.* Cambridge: Cambridge University Press.

Kinder, Donald R., and Lynn M. Sanders. 1990. Mimicking Political Debate with Survey Questions: The Case of White Opinion on Affirmative Action for Blacks. *Social Cognition* 8:73–103.

Krosnick, Jon A., and Matthew K. Berent. 1993. Comparisons of Party Identification and Policy Preferences: The Impact of Survey Question Format. *American Journal of Political Science* 37:941–64.

Lakoff, George. 1987. *Women, Fire, and Dangerous Things: What Categories Reveal about the Mind.* Chicago: University of Chicago Press.

Manin, Bernard. 1997. *The Principles of Representative Government.* Cambridge: Cambridge University Press.

Mansbridge, Jane J. 1983. *Beyond Adversary Democracy.* Chicago: University of Chicago Press.

McFadden, Daniel. 1994. Contingent Valuation and Social Choice. *American Journal of Agricultural Economics* 76:689–708.

Mendelberg, Tali, and John Oleske. 1996. Race and Deliberation. Unpublished manuscript, Department of Politics, Princeton University.

Miller, David. 1992. Social Choice and Deliberative Democracy. *Political Studies* 40:54–68.

Milton, John. 1973 (1644). *Areopagitica.* Cambridge, Eng.: Deighton, Bell.

Mueller, John E. 1973. *War, Presidents, and Public Opinion.* New York: Wiley.

———. 1992. Democracy and Ralph's Pretty Good Grocery: Elections, Equality, and the Minimal Human Being. *American Journal of Political Science* 36:983–1003.

———. 1994. *Policy and Opinion in the Gulf War.* Chicago: University of Chicago Press.

National Oceanographic and Atmospheric Administration. 1993. Report of the NOAA Panel on Contingent Valuation. *Federal Register* 58:4602–14.

Pitkin, Hanna Fenichel. 1967. *The Concept of Representation.* Berkeley: University of California Press.

Plott, Charles R. 1976. Axiomatic Social Choice Theory: An Overview and Interpretation. *American Journal of Political Science* 20:511–96.

Pruitt, D. G. 1970. Reward Structure of Cooperation: The Decomposed Prisoner's Dilemma Game. *Journal of Personality and Social Psychology* 7:21–27.

Rasinski, Kenneth A. 1989. The Effect of Question Wording on Public Support for Government Spending. *Public Opinion Quarterly* 53:388–94.

Rawls, John. 1971. *A Theory of Justice.* Cambridge: Belknap Press of Harvard University Press.

Riker, William H. 1980. Implications from the Disequilibrium of Majority Rule for the Study of Institutions. *American Political Science Review* 74:432–58.

———. 1982. *Liberalism against Populism: A Confrontation between the Theory of Democracy and the Theory of Social Choice.* San Francisco: Freeman.

Rubinstein, Ariel. 1998. Definable Preferences: An Example. *European Economic Review* 42:553–60.

Rugg, D. 1941. Experiments in Wording Questions: II. *Public Opinion Quarterly* 5:91–92.

Sanders, Lynn. 1997. Against Deliberation. *Political Theory* 25:347–77.

Sapiro, Virginia. 1998. Pro-Life People or Opponents of Abortion? Pro-Choice People or Supporters of Abortion? A Report on the NES 1997 Pilot Study. Report to the Board of Overseers of the American National Election Studies.

Schuman, Howard, and Stanley Presser. 1981. *Questions and Answers in Attitude Surveys: Experiments on Question Form, Wording, and Context.* New York: Academic Press.

Selten, Reinhard. 1998. Features of Experimentally Observed Bounded Rationality. *European Economic Review* 42:413–36.

Shepsle, Kenneth A. 1979. Institutional Arrangements and Equilibrium in Multidimensional Voting Models. *American Journal of Political Science* 23:27–59.

Smith, Thomas W. 1987. That Which We Call Welfare by Any Other Name Would Smell Sweeter: An Analysis of the Impact of Question Wording on Response Patterns. *Public Opinion Quarterly* 51:75–83.

Tourangeau, Roger, and Kenneth Rasinski. 1988. Cognitive Processes Underlying Context Effects in Attitude Measurement. *Psychological Bulletin* 103:299–314.

Tversky, Amos. 1996. Rational Theory and Constructive Choice. In Kenneth Arrow et al., eds., *The Rational Foundations of Economic Behavior.* New York: Macmillan.

Tversky, Amos, and Daniel Kahneman. 1982. The Framing of Decisions and the Psychology of Choice. In Robin Hogarth, ed., *Question Framing and Response Consistency.* San Francisco: Jossey-Bass.

———. 1986. Rational Choice and the Framing of Decisions. *Journal of Business* 59:251–78.

Verhovek, Sam Howe. 1997. Houston Voters Maintain Affirmative-Action Policy. *New York Times,* 6 November.

Wilson, Timothy, and Sarah Hodges. 1991. Attitudes as Temporary Constructs. In Abraham Tesser and L. Martin, eds., *The Construction of Social Judgment.* Hillsdale, N.J.: Erlbaum.

Wolfe, James F. 1996. Change in Ballot Wording Ordered. *Joplin (Missouri) Globe,* 19 October.

Zaller, John R. 1992. *The Nature and Origins of Mass Opinion.* Cambridge: Cambridge University Press.

Zaller, John, and Stanley Feldman. 1992. A Simple Theory of the Survey Response: Answering Questions versus Revealing Preferences. *American Journal of Political Science* 36:579–616.

3

The Political Psychology
of Party Identification

Herbert F. Weisberg and Steven H. Greene

Party identification is seen as the linchpin of our modern understanding of electoral democracy. The first article using this concept appeared in 1952, when Belknap and Campbell measured party identification with the simple question, "If a presidential election were being held today, do you think you would vote for the Democratic, Republican, or for some other party?" Respondents were grouped into four categories on the basis of their responses: Democratic, Republican, independent (if respondents indicated that their votes depend on the candidates), and don't know. This measurement of party identification did not last long. By the 1952 Survey Research Center national election study, the researchers switched to the now standard question, "Generally speaking, do you usually think of yourself as a Republican, a Democrat, an Independent, or what?" with follow-up questions designed to measure strength of partisanship and to coax independents to indicate the party to which they are closer.[1] This new measure was used in their write-up of the 1952 election (A. Campbell, Gurin, and Miller 1954) and, of course, in *The American Voter* (A. Campbell et al. 1960).[2]

   It is often useful to look back at the path not taken to see the advantages of the path that was taken. Belknap and Campbell admitted that their measure of party identification was "crude" (1952, 622), implying that the researchers were seeking—or had already found—a better measure. For one thing, the original measurement strategy was too short term, too tied to the vote decision itself. Yet not until a few years later did the University of Michigan researchers recognize that party-related attitudes should be seen as more enduring than candidate orientations or issue orientations (as related in W. Miller 1991, 238). What was more critical to the abandonment of one path for another was that the old wording was seen as not in line with social-psychological theories. Even Belknap and Campbell's original piece was very sensitive to the limitations of its use of vote intention as a measure of partisanship, appropriately recognizing that its vote-intention question does not measure the degree of identification with a party.

The Michigan model of the vote developed in the 1950s was based on social psychology. Minimally, this means that it was based on voters' attitudes rather than the concentration of the voters' social characteristics that underlies the earlier work by researchers at Columbia University (Lazarsfeld, Berelson, and Gaudet 1949; Berelson, Lazarsfeld, and McPhee 1954). Additionally, the party-identification concept underlying the now standard party-identification questions is based on the reference-group theory of the 1950s. Just as people identify with religious groups such as Catholics or Protestants, so people were seen as identifying with political groups such as Republicans or Democrats.

Several different understandings of party identification have been proposed in later years. Fiorina (1977, 1981) proposed a view of party identification as a "running tally" of past experiences with the parties, a view that fits in with the new interpretation of party identification as endogenous to the vote decision (Jackson 1975; Page and Jones 1979; Franklin and Jackson 1983). Achen (1989, 1992) has formalized this view of party identification as Bayesian updating of long-term party identification into current party identification (see also the information-theory perspective of C. Smith 1993). Additionally, party identification has often been interpreted as a low-information rational short-cut for obtaining more complete information about an election (Popkin 1991).

Such reinterpretation of the party-identification measure may seem to be too far a departure from its original basis in reference-group theory, but modern-day social psychology does not give much attention to the concept of reference groups.[3] Instead, intergroup relations is emphasized today, so the appropriate place to begin a reinvestigation of the social psychology of party identification is by reviewing the intergroup relations field. Attitude theory more generally has also evolved considerably since the 1950s, so the reinvestigation of the theoretical basis of party identification must also include a consideration of how attitudes are treated today in social psychology.

The party-identification concept has been explored much over the years. Its usefulness in providing a baseline "normal vote" expectation in elections was developed by Converse (1966). Converse also showed how partisan politicization follows fairly similar rules across national boundaries (Converse and Dupeux 1962; Converse 1969). The overtime dynamics of party identification are of particular importance, with Converse (1976) making one of the most important statements as to its strengthening with aging. When the relative importance of party identification and issues became a matter of debate, Markus and Converse (1979) showed that party identification was the dominant player (cf. Page and Jones 1979). In any event, it remains more stable than other attitudes (Converse and Markus 1979) and more long term than are other measures of partisanship (Converse and Pierce 1985). There certainly are debates about many theoretical and measurement issues relating to party identification, but the concept itself remains crucial to our contemporary understanding of voting behavior.

Whereas the measurement of the direction of partisanship by the standard party-identification question series is fairly uncontroversial, there have been challenges to how well that series measures two further components of partisanship: strength of identification and political independence. We will return to this topic later in this chapter. For the moment, though, it is appropriate to point out that the social-psychological implications of measuring the three components might be different—that is, different social-psychological theories might be appropriate for measuring partisan direction, strength, and independence.

This chapter has four purposes. First, the modern treatment of intergroup relations will be reviewed to show how contemporary approaches differ from the reference-group approach of the 1950s. Second, the modern treatment of attitudes will be surveyed for insights as to how party identification can be viewed more generally from an attitude theory perspective. Third, implications for our understanding and measurement of party identification will be discussed throughout.[4] Finally, the role of party identification in electoral democracy will be reexamined.

The Reference Group Theory Basis of Party Identification

The Early Michigan Use of Reference-Group Theory

Reference-group theory was at the core of the Michigan group's original writing about party identification. Their first article about party identification began by proclaiming that "the assumption that individual perceptions, evaluations, and behavior are determined in large part by the standard and values of the groups with which the person identifies has become accepted doctrine" (Belknap and Campbell 1952, 601). This article also recognized that strength of identification is an important concept: "Identification with a political party undoubtedly varies from a superficial preference for one or the other party to a strong sense of association with the symbols of the party, a feeling of group-belonging, and a high degree of involvement with party activities" (622). By *The Voter Decides* (A. Campbell, Gurin, and Miller 1954), the authors talk directly about political parties as groups. They explain that group belonging "may consist largely of a person's considering himself a member of the group—of identifying himself with it" (88). The two parties are viewed as serving as "standard-setting groups" for many Americans. As the authors summarize, "it is assumed that many people associate themselves psychologically with one or the other of the parties, and that this identification has predictable relationships with their perceptions, evaluations, and actions" (90).

In *The American Voter* (A. Campbell et al. 1960), the Michigan authors mention Key's use of the idea of "standing decisions" of voters to support one party or the other (120), but the book's theoretical development is clearly tied to the work of psychologists. The authors explicitly view the political party as a "group toward which the individual may develop an identification, positive or negative, of some degree of intensity" (122). Kurt Lewin's discussion is mentioned as viewing groups as real "if they have real effects" (296). *The American Voter* then paraphrases this by saying "groups are real because they are *psychologically* real, and thereby affect the way in which we behave" (296). This led to a discussion of reference groups: "groups can become reference points for the formation of attitudes and decisions about behavior; we speak then of *positive* and *negative reference groups*" (296).

The treatment of political independents in *The American Voter* is less directly tied to reference-group theory. The authors write, "we do not suppose that every person who describes himself as an Independent is indicating simply his lack of positive attraction to one of the parties. Some of these people undoubtedly are actually repelled by the parties or by partisanship itself and value their position as Independents. Certainly independence of party is an ideal of some currency in our society, and it seems likely that a portion of those who call themselves Independents are not merely reporting the absence of identification with one of the major parties" (A. Campbell et al. 1960, 123). This quotation does not use the term *group*, although the authors are invoking the same idea of positive and negative attraction that they used earlier in dealing with identification with party groups. The quotation suggests that some independents might not view either party as a positive reference group and that some might view both parties as negative reference groups. It is a matter of judgment whether this statement admits that for these independents, partisanship could be a negative reference group and independents could be a positive reference group.

The Intergroup Relations Field Today

The reference-group notion from social psychology may have been basic to the Michigan researchers' development of the party-identification concept during the 1950s, but it is not a common part of the parlance of modern social psychology. It is rarely mentioned in contemporary social psychology, whether because it is seen as standard, as old hat, or as overly simplistic. Yet groups remain important in social psychology, and Kinder refers to the "power and persistence of group-centrism in public opinion" (1998, 806). Indeed, intergroup relations is one of the liveliest areas in social psychology today. There is a considerable body of work on in-groups and out-groups and their roles in human behavior.[5] What is necessary is to incorporate this work into our contemporary understanding of party identification.

Reference-group theory developed out of such works as Hyman 1942, Merton 1957, and Hyman and Singer 1968. Much of this work was in the area of social comparison, with people being seen as comparing their outcomes with those of other groups. Social psychologists remain very interested in the process of categorization of people into groups. This work has both theoretical and applied aspects, with the applied aspects going into the areas of prejudice and of reducing intergroup conflicts. Reference-group theory, though, has largely been superseded by more wide-ranging social identity theories. Groups are still seen as meaningful reference points, but the focus is on the internalization of group-based attitudes.

The basic distinction in the intergroup relations field is between in-groups and out-groups, terms that Sumner (1906) originated, along with the claim that preferences for in-groups may be a universal human feeling. Two important psychological processes—exaggerating both intragroup similarities and intergroup differences—accompany this preference for in-groups (Brewer and Brown 1998, 558). As we shall subsequently see, any we-they group distinction can activate differential in-group–out-group responses (Tajfel 1970). Experimental results show that the terms *we* and *us* unconsciously activate positive emotions (Perdue et al. 1990). Accordingly, just referring to "Republicans" as *us* and "Democrats" as *them* can yield identification.

Theorists distinguish three sources of differential group-related responses: the positive consequences of in-group formation, the negative consequences of out-group differentiation, and the results of intergroup social competition. Studies find these three components to be "essentially independent" (Brewer and Brown 1998, 559). This distinction will be used to organize the following discussion of intergroup relations, with separate treatment of in-groups, group conflict, and out-groups.

In-Groups

We begin with the notion of an in-group, the conditions under which in-group associations form, and the reasons that people develop identifications with in-groups. Two critical sets of experiments led to current theorizing in the field. The first was the "robbers cave" experiments by Muzafer Sherif and associates (Sherif et al. 1954), in which the researchers created and then reduced hostility between two groups of young summer campers. This work led to questioning of the conditions that are necessary for in-group feelings to be formed. Tajfel and his colleagues at the University of Bristol (Tajfel et al. 1971) conducted further experiments in which the links between group members were designed to be minimal. For example, young people were divided into two groups randomly but were told that they had been grouped according to whether they overestimated or underestimated the number of dots in a picture, without the boys knowing who else was in their group. The people who were told they were overestimators favored their own group and discriminated against out-groups in a series of reward-allocation tasks, and the people who were told they were underestimators behaved similarly. The many subsequent studies of the topic have provided further understanding of this phenomenon, but the basic result still holds: in-group biases develop even in minimal group settings. This is often termed the *minimal group paradigm*. Categorizing people into groups leads to intergroup bias in favor of the in-group even under minimal conditions (Brewer 1979), and this can lead to negative treatment of the out-group, especially when competition is introduced.

The identification process. It is useful to point out that people can identify with a variety of groups. A person might consider herself a white, middle-aged Catholic American of Italian ancestry who wears glasses, has dark hair, is left-handed, and is a Democrat. Depending on the person and the social context, particular social identifications associated with these characteristics will be active. Some group identifications (e.g., gender and ethnicity) are more likely to be chronically accessible, whereas others may be made relevant by the situational environment (e.g., a sole white person in a room of African Americans), and others are rarely relevant as group characteristics (e.g., hair color and handedness). Donald Campbell (1958) referred to this process as *entitivity*—the extent to which the collective is seen as a unit.[6]

Why do people develop identifications with in-groups? Early explanations included a sociobiological view that people favor others who possess the same genes and a psychoanalytic position that focuses on identification with the group leader. Festinger's (1950) work assumed that people need to have their views confirmed by seeing that others in their reference groups share those views, though that is not necessarily part of current thinking on the topic. Other explanations of identification with in-groups emphasize motivation. For example, in-group identification might result from the feeling that one shares a common fate with one's in-group (Rabbie and Horwitz 1988) or from a need for self-enhancement by identifying with high-status groups. A particularly intriguing explanation is Brewer's (1991) optimal-distinctiveness theory, which hypothesizes that people have a need to achieve an optimal level of distinctiveness through a balance of feelings of group inclusion and differentiation. This explanation also implies that people may vary in the level of distinctiveness that is optimal for them.

Social identity theory. The concept being worked with here is *social identity*, the person's identity as part of groups, to be distinguished from the person's *personal identity*, the other part of a person's self-concept. Social identity theory developed as part of a rediscovery in Europe of the social and group parts of social psychology, but it has now become influential in the United States as well. As in Tajfel's experiments (Tajfel et al. 1971), social identity theory views categorization as producing social identity because the members are members of discrete groups, not because the in-group members perceive themselves as similar to or different from other people. Tajfel defines social identity as "that part of an individual's self concept which derives from his knowledge of his membership of a group (or groups) together with the value and emotional significance attached to the membership" (1978, 63). Tajfel's social identity theory holds that group membership and biased intergroup comparisons serve to bolster self-esteem. In Turner's more cognitively oriented "self-categorization theory" (Tajfel and Turner 1986), social identifications are categorizations of the self into groups that "depersonalize" the self, so that the self becomes an exemplar of a social category rather than a unique individual (Turner et al. 1987, 50; Brewer 1991, 476).

An underlying motivation assumed in Tajfel's social identity theory is that individuals want to maintain their self-esteem. Social groups vary in how they are evaluated, as judged through a social comparison process. Individuals seek to achieve positive social identity, based on social comparisons of their in-group with relevant out-groups. The basic hypothesis is that "pressures to evaluate one's own group positively through in-group/out-group comparisons lead social groups to attempt to differentiate themselves from each other" (Tajfel and Turner 1986, 16). Biased social comparisons favoring the in-group, which are part of one's self identity, thus serve to enhance self-esteem. Turner's self-categorization theory, in contrast, is strictly cognitive, holding that depersonalization of the self and consequent self-categorization as a group member underlie basic group processes. Both variants hold, however, that self-identification as a group member is a fundamental aspect of group relations leading to intergroup comparisons that favor the in-group.

Arthur Miller and Christopher Wlezien (1993) have already referred to recent work on social groups with respect to party identification but have done so more in the context of factor analysis of group thermometers to examine party-group connections than in terms of detailing the social-psychological theory. Social psychologists have noted the usefulness of social identity theory for understanding party identification (Hogg and Abrams 1988). Social identity theory has been applied most directly to party identification by Caroline Kelly (1988, 1989) in the British context, by Dominic Abrams (1994) in the Scottish context, and by Steven Greene (1999a, 1999b) in the U.S. context. Weisberg and Hasecke (1999) have provided a preliminary examination of strength of party identification in the United States from a social identity theory perspective.

It takes only a small extension of these ideas to speak of a person's *political identity*.[7] People can develop social identifications with political groups as part of their self-identities. The minimal-group paradigm implies that it should be very easy to develop identification with a party. Defining social identity in this way leads to interesting implications for party identification. Certainly, no formal membership institutions are necessary for a partisan social identification. Simply categorizing oneself politically as sympathetic to either party is likely enough to begin psychological group processes. The minimal-group paradigm suggests that any time politics is a salient environmental context, political party social identifications may be activated. Partisan conflict and partisan differentiation would thus seem to be a natural outgrowth of party identification. Furthermore, parties and candidates would seem to be advantaged by making parties salient *as political groups*. Understanding intergroup relations, however, requires moving past the in-group and examining group conflict as well as out-groups.

Group Conflict

Causes of group conflict.   The second component of contemporary work on intergroup relations is intergroup orientation. The major controversy on this topic is over the causes of intergroup competition and conflict. Tajfel's (1982) social identity theory suggests one process that could underlie this orientation. Group memberships affect people's self-esteem. People are thus motivated to be favorable to the group to which they belong or identify. The need for a positive social identity leads to a competitive intergroup orientation, which in turn can cause perceptual biases in favor of the in-group at the expense of the out-group.

By contrast, the realistic group-conflict theory approach (D. Campbell 1965) emphasizes competition for scarce resources as the source of intergroup conflict. Competition leads to conflicting interests, which in turn lead to social conflict. A side effect of this dynamic is greater identification with the in-group.

However, competition and conflict may be consequences rather than causes of group identification and in-group–out-group differentiation. Tajfel's minimal-group paradigm found intergroup rivalry without a conflict of interest between the groups (Tajfel et al. 1971). Further studies emphasize that this was in-group favoritism rather than discrimination against out-groups. That is, social categorization itself is sufficient to cause intergroup competition. Tajfel and Turner's (1986) social identity theory emphasizes competition for positive distinctiveness, enhancing the in-group's value.

Some other explanations of group conflict have been offered. Rabbie, Schot, and Visser (1989) emphasize interdependence as an explanation—members of an in-group feel that their self-interest depends on the decisions of other in-group members. Insko and Schopler (1987) argue in favor of a group schema explanation in which people do not trust out-groups because they have learned to expect that intergroup relations are competitive.

If these effects are evident in minimal group situations, it should not be surprising that they are prevalent in real group settings. Furthermore, these effects should be reinforced in real group settings as the person has prolonged identification with the relevant in-group. This is certainly the case with regard to political identity. Most people have lengthy identifications with their political party—or with independence—and this should make the effects even stronger than the minimal-group paradigm would suggest.

Effects of status differentials.   One further set of findings is relevant here. Differences in the status or power of groups can also affect intergroup orientations. Experimental results are both complicated and mixed. Higher-status groups have greater in-group bias (Mullen, Brown, and Smith 1992) but that effect depends on other factors being present, such as the relevance of the dimension of discrimination to the group status. Members of high-power groups discriminate against out-groups more than members of low-power groups (Sachdev and Bourhis 1987), even when the high-power group is a low-status group. Tajfel and Turner (1986) suggest that the status relationships are affected by three characteristics of the groups: the permeability of group boundaries (whether people can move from one group to the other), the stability of the status hierarchy, and the legitimacy of the distinctions. Unstable or illegitimate status differentials lead members of lower-status groups to stronger in-group bias (Brewer and Brown 1998, 571). Tajfel and Turner further describe three ways that lower-status in-groups deal with negative social identity: individual mobility (moving up to the higher-status out-group), finding new dimensions in which their in-group is more highly valued, or competing with higher-status out-groups. This suggests that there can be status differences between parties that will affect intergroup orientations. Kelly (1990) found this to be the case in Britain, where minority political group members had greater group social identification than did majority group members. However, there is also evidence in Britain of the lower social status classes voting for the party associated with the higher social class—known there as working-class Toryism (Butler and Stokes 1969)—which shows that lower-status in-groups sometimes have a weak sense of identification. This suggests the need for more study of the relationship between group status and voting in the context of social identity theory.

Out-Groups

The third component of intergroup relations is out-group hostility and prejudice. One point to emphasize is that research shows that in-group favoritism and negative attitudes toward out-groups may be independent of one another

(Brewer and Brown 1998). That is, a people with positive feelings toward the party with which they identify may or may not also have a negative attitude toward the other party. Beyond negative attitudes toward out-groups, however, a key bias is that out-group members are generally perceived to be more homogeneous than are in-group members. Out-group members are thought to resemble each other in terms of characteristics, attitudes, and behaviors. There are two main explanations of this out-group homogeneity effect. Quattrone (1986) focuses on people's limited contact with out-group members as opposed to their having many chances to observe the diversity of their in-group. Judd and Park (1988) instead emphasize memory processes. They argue that people find it easier to retrieve specific members of in-groups than out-groups, leading to perceptions of out-groups as homogeneous. It is only a short step from the out-group homogeneity effect to stereotyping of out-groups. Kelly's (1988, 1989) studies confirm the out-group homogeneity effect in the context of political parties in Great Britain in two of the very few applications of social identity theory to party identification.

The focus in the contemporary study of intergroup relations on attitudes toward out-groups as separate from attitudes toward the in-group has fairly obvious implications to the study of party identification. Liking one party need not mean disliking the other party. This argument fits a multidimensional conceptualization of partisanship, particularly one in which attitudes toward the Republican and Democratic Parties are treated as separate dimensions (Weisberg 1980; cf. Green and Citrin 1994). The view that attitudes toward in-groups and out-groups can be independent of one another suggests that systematic work would be useful to determine the conditions under which people have negative views toward the party with which they do not identify. The social psychology literature on group relations moves from here to ways of diminishing bias against out-groups, known more simply as reducing prejudice, but that direction is not of direct interest for the study of party identification.

Implications

The work on intergroup relations that has been summarized in this section certainly is quite different from the reference-group approach of the 1950s. It recognizes that identification with a group can occur even in minimal settings and that negative reactions to out-groups can occur under competitive conditions. From this perspective, it is not surprising that people develop party identifications when they discover that their family or that people like them are Republicans. Nor is it surprising that competitive elections lead to negative views of the opposite party.

There are several research questions that follow from this perspective. How much learning is required to establish positive views of a party? Under what circumstances do negative views of other parties get formed? The development of new democracies creates a laboratory in which topics such as these can be explored. How well does the usual seven-point scale capture social identification with a party? How does such identification impact ideology, voting, political interest, political activity, and other variables? What other factors are related to a partisan social identification? Are partisan comparisons solely a matter of favoring an in-party, or is out-party derogation also at work? All in all, this perspective provides an ambitious agenda for future research.

What about independence? Under what conditions would people view political independents as an in-group and partisans of both flavors as out-groups? If the media begin to emphasize negative news about both parties, will people move toward independence? If the media report that young people are predominately independent, does that make young people view independents as their in-group and partisans as the out-group? The theories described earlier seem to suggest that such effects are likely. Greene (2000) indeed found meaningful levels of in-group identification among political independents.

Dennis (1988) found four separate aspects of independence, two of which fit well with social identity theory. He terms the first form of independence *political autonomy,* by which he means a positive view of independence in terms of such values as individualism. This fits well with regarding independence as an in-group phenomenon. Dennis labels the second form of independence *antipartyism,* in which independence results from a negative view of parties. Antipartyism fits well with regarding independence as an out-group phenomenon—independents viewing both parties as out-groups. Dennis's third form of independence is *partisan neutrality,* in which independence results from neutrality between the parties, and his fourth form is *partisan variability,* a view of oneself as switching between the parties. These last two aspects of independence seem to fit less well with social identity theory, though they can be interpreted in terms of attitude theory more generally.

A fair question is whether all of this is just a case of putting an old theory into new jargon. Is all of this any different from the reference-group theory of the 1950s? The first answer must be that reference-group theory is no longer a topic in social psychology; the field has moved beyond that concern, and it is appropriate to modernize our theoretical basis accordingly. The second answer is that the theories discussed here separate out the different elements better than reference-group theory did. The distinction between the in-group and out-groups is fundamental to modern social psychology's treatment of group relations. Too much of the work on party identification has examined identification with the in-group without taking into account views toward the out-group.[8] Thus, there is a greater richness to the modern social psychology view of groups that should affect our understanding of party identification and also of political independence. Minimally, group-relations theory supplies us with a set of hypotheses that should be tested to see if we have more than new jargon for old theories.

The Attitudinal Basis of Party Identification

While the Michigan researchers used reference-group theory as the basis of their concept of party identification, their approach more generally was attitudinal. This was the basis of calling their approach social psychological. As Kinder has stated, "Their approach was regarded as psychological primarily in that it vested explanatory power in the concept of attitude" (1998, 779). This makes it important to embed the party-identification concept in the modern understanding of attitudes. The current treatment of attitudes will be examined next, looking in turn at the nature of attitudes and their consequences.[9]

The Nature of Partisan Attitudes

In recognizing that it is appropriate to look at the attitudes underlying voting behavior, it is essential to examine the nature of attitudes. There are three important topics to consider regarding the nature of attitudes: the definition of an attitude, its structure, and the meaning of attitude strength. Each of these topics will be examined here, with a special focus on party identification as an attitude.

The Definition of an Attitude

The most basic question to consider is what an attitude is. There are different usages of the term in the social psychology literature, and the meaning given to it has evolved over the years. The definition given in the 1998 edition of the *Handbook of Social Psychology* is that an attitude is a "psychological tendency that is expressed by evaluating a particular entity with some degree of favor or disfavor." According to this definition, an attitude is an internal state, not directly observable but inferred from observables. It "is expressed by evaluative responses of some degree of favorability or unfavorability" (Eagly and Chaiken 1998, 269). This is very different from definitions that are based on understanding the underlying mental processes, such as Fazio's (1989) definition of attitudes in terms of association in memory between an attitude object and an evaluation.[10]

Three aspects of attitudes.   Theorists over the years have also differed as to the primary basis of attitudes. Some theorists emphasize the cognitive aspect— the thoughts and beliefs about the attitude object that underlie attitudes. Others focus on the affective elements—people's feelings and emotions about the attitude object. Still other theorists focus on the behavioral side of attitudes, including both actions and intentions to act. Some would reserve the term *attitude* for just one or two of these channels. However, the current usage is that attitudes can be formed through any of these channels and that no particular channel is privileged. At the same time, attitudes do not necessarily have all three of these aspects. While the distinction among these three aspects is common, factor analysis does not always distinguish them as separate dimensions (Eagly and Chaiken 1998, 271).

A distinction is also made between attitudes and evaluations. In current usage, *affect* refers to emotions and feelings, while *evaluation* refers to states not rooted in affect. "Attitudes, understood as general evaluations of attitude objects, can stem from purely cognitive or behavioral responding and thus may have no affective aspect at all" (Eagly and Chaiken 1998, 272). Evaluation is more an intervening state between stimuli and the responses they elicit.

The tripartite approach to attitudes in terms of cognitions, affect, and behavior leads to the question of what the bases of partisan feelings are. To what extent are they cognitive? To what extent are they based on emotions? There obviously can be links between the cognitive and the affective, but social psychologists often distinguish between these different aspects of attitudes, and it is appropriate to explore the basis of party identification from this perspective. Gant and Luttbeg (1987) examine the cognitive basis of party identification. The first attempt to measure the relative importance of the cognitive and affective components of party identification is a study by Greene (1998) that used semantic-differential scales developed by Crites, Fabrigar, and Petty (1994). Greene found a preponderance of cognitive partisanship, though affective partisanship was more stable.

Introspective explanations of party identification.   A related question is how citizens explain their party identification. Do they explain it in cognitive, affective, or behavioral terms? Care must be exercised in answering this question, as respondents are not necessarily able to explain their attitudes. The work of Nisbett and Wilson (1977) particularly argues that people cannot accurately give their reasons for their actions, let alone explain their attitudes. In the current context, what we may obtain from such a study would be how people believe they are supposed to explain their party identification rather than the true explanation. Still, it is interesting to examine some introspective explanations.

The 1980 National Election Study included a question series designed to determine what respondents meant in answering the party-identification questions. Once respondents stated their party identification, they were asked a closed-ended question requiring them to choose an explanation of what they meant by that identification. Different questions were asked of strong identifiers, weak identifiers, independent leaners, and pure independents. The response categories were based on the answers that were given most often in an open-ended question asked in a previous research and development pilot study. Because the questions were asked at the end of the party-identification question series, respondents might be explaining more their second answers (strength of partisanship or direction of leaning) rather than their overall position on the seven-point party-identification scale.

The results have been summarized by Kessel (1984, 528). Majorities of strong partisans agreed with three statements: the behavioral statement that they "almost always support the Democratic (Republican) candidates" (65 percent), "ever since I can remember, I've always been a Democrat (Republican)" (63 percent), and that they were "enthusiastic about what the Democratic (Republican) party stands for" (60 percent). The only statement agreed to by a majority of weak partisans was that they would "vote for the person, not the party" (66 percent). None of the statements were agreed to by a majority of the independent partisans. A majority of pure independents agreed to two statements: "I decide on the person, not the party" (70 percent) and "I decide on the issues, not the party label" (56 percent). Many individual respondents agreed with each of the six to eleven statements offered, while no statement was agreed to by as many three-quarters of the respondents in a category.

It is difficult to divide these statements into the cognitive, affective, and behavioral categories. Always supporting their party's candidate seems to be a behavioral statement. Always having been a Democrat is a report of the past, but it virtually begs the question, as all it does is transform the issue as to why the person has always been a Democrat. Being enthusiastic about what the party stands for has both affective ("enthusiastic") and cognitive ("what the party stands for") aspects. Voting for the person or the issue and not the party is ostensibly a behavioral response, though it is more a response that sounds socially correct. All in all, this is a very blunt measure of the relevant importance of cognitive, affective, and behavioral aspects of partisanship. Indeed, if it is useful at all, it mainly is useful in demonstrating how difficult it would be to differentiate among these three aspects of attitudes on the basis of self-reports.

An alternative definition.   While the preceding is an accurate rendition of the major approach to defining attitudes in the social psychology literature, other definitions are relevant to work on party identification. In particular Bem's (1972) self-perception theory of attitude formation is that people infer attitudes that are consistent with their prior behavior. According to this theory, party identification would be based on the person's partisan behavior rather than being the unmoved mover as in most theorizing about party identification. Yet Bem's theory fits well with revisionist treatments of party identification that view it as at least partially dependent on a person's voting behavior (Jackson 1975). It also fits with Shively's (1980) finding that independents who indicate the party to which they lean are announcing their vote intentions (cf. Keith et al. 1992, 92–95).

The Structure of Attitudes

The next question of importance is how attitudes are structured. There are two aspects to this question, the internal composition of attitudes and the relationships to other attitudes. Political scientists are more familiar with the interattitudinal structure, as typified by Converse's (1964) work on belief systems, but intraattitudinal structure is more relevant to a reconsideration of party identification.

Polarity. The first concern about the internal structure of an attitude is whether it is bipolar. Attitude theorists do not assume that people encode, store, and retrieve information according to a bipolar evaluative dimension. People might conceptualize their attitudes on some issues as bipolar from the position they favor to the opposite position (Judd and Kulik 1980), as on abortion, or they could have unipolar attitudes dealing only with knowledge congruent with their own positions (Pratkanis 1989), as in areas such as music. "On many social and political issues people who strongly agree with statements at one end of a conventional attitudinal continuum may be indifferent rather than truly opposed to statements at the other end" (Eagly and Chaiken 1998, 274). Kerlinger (1984) has provided evidence of this in the political ideology field.

The obvious implication for party identification is that attitudes toward the two parties need not be bipolar. People might instead have unipolar attitudes toward one party, or they might have unipolar attitudes toward independence. Assuming bipolar party identification is an assumption that requires testing (Weisberg 1980).

Ambivalence. A related concern is attitude ambivalence. Kaplan (1972) showed that some people at the middle of bipolar attitude scales are ambivalent, with both positive and negative beliefs or feelings, rather than merely neutral or indifferent, as measured by using separate unipolar scales of positive and negative traits of the attitude objects. Cacioppo and Berntson (1994) have suggested that separating positive and negative attitudinal responses to attitude objects would be useful since they could produce separate effects, with negative reactions producing stronger effects that would not be captured by a straight additive model. However, Eagly and Chaiken find that work on ambivalence is "sparse" (1998, 281).

The concern with ambivalence supports the idea of separately measuring positive and negative reactions to parties. The National Election Studies surveys already do this in their open-ended party likes and dislikes questions ("What do you like about the Republican Party? Dislike? . . ."). In fact, Holbrook et al. (2001) found that estimating separate coefficients for candidate likes and dislikes proved to be a better predictor of vote choice than Kelley and Mirer's (1974) "simple act of voting," which uses net likes/dislikes. These indications of candidate ambivalence using open-ended measures would suggest that similar ambivalence may be found using open-ended party measures. Additionally, the NES candidate feeling questions ("Has candidate X ever made you feel angry? Proud? . . .") could be adapted to elicit positive and negative feelings toward the parties. Greene (2000) used separate positive and negative semantic scales to assess positive and negative aspects of party attitudes. One would expect that ambivalence would be related to political independence (Dennis 1988) as well as to behaviors such as split-ticket voting.

Relationship to beliefs. A basic concern dealing with the internal structure of attitudes is whether they can be predicted from beliefs. The expectancy-value model (Fishbein 1967) posits that attitudes are a function of beliefs. In this model, beliefs are treated as the sum of the expected values of the attributes ascribed to an attitude object, where the expectancy is the subjective probability that the attitude object has the attribute and the value component is the subjective evaluation of the attribute. That is, Attitude = Σ expectancy $\times$ value. Fishbein's (1967) model is

$$A_o = \sum_{i=1}^{n} b_i \times e_i,$$

where A_o is the attitude toward the object o, b_i is the strength of the belief i about o (the subjective probability that o has attribute i), e_i is the evaluation of attribute i, and n is the number of attributes. Applications of this model generally find high correlations between attitudes and expectancy values.[11]

Complexity. Another concern involves the complexity of beliefs—the number of dimensions of the attribute space. Integrative complexity involves the extent to which the dimensions are linked to one another logically or causally. Tetlock's (1989) value-pluralism model is that people who are integratively complex on an issue endorse values that have conflicting evaluative implications. Unfortunately, we know little about the structure of the mass public's beliefs about political parties.

Coherence. A final concern relating to intraattitudinal structure involves the coherence of attitudes—the consistency of beliefs with the affective and behavioral aspects of attitudes. For example, low consistency of the evaluative and cognitive aspects is interpreted as lack of coherence rather than as nonattitudes (Converse 1970). Abelson et al. (1982) show that evaluations of politicians are more consistent with affective reactions than with cognitive. Bem's (1972) self-perception theory is that people infer their attitudes from the evaluation implied by their behavior. Burden and Greene (2000) find evidence that some persons may infer their party identification from the act of party registration.

Since people may prefer consistency, as suggested in the work on cognitive dissonance, people whose behavior is opposite to their attitudes are likely to change their attitudes to fit their behavior. Indeed, people are likely to reconstruct their past behavior to fit with their current attitudes (Ross 1989). Eagly and Chaiken conclude from this that "the primary basis for an attitude may lie in the type of response—cognitive, affective, or behavioral—that produces the smallest evaluative discrepancy with the overall attitude" (1998, 279). Greene's (1999a) use of affective and cognitive discrepancies demonstrated that there is considerable variation in the coherence of partisan attitudes, though more explicit attention to the coherence of attitudes toward parties is warranted.

Interattitudinal structure.   As suggested earlier, interattitudinal structure has received considerable attention in political science because of the nonattitude controversy. In addition to looking for horizontal structure (attitudes at the same logical level being intercorrelated), it is important to look for hierarchical structures. A broad ideology could underlie a series of attitudes. Alternatively, Sears and Kinder (1985) argue that political attitudes are often grounded in attachments to groups and symbols plus moral preferences and values.

The relationships between party identification and other attitudes merit more attention. It is usually assumed that party identification affects a variety of attitudes regarding more specific issues, but how it relates to ideology and especially to values could use further examination.

The Strength of Attitudes

It has long been recognized that attitude strength is an important component of attitudes. However, the most recent review of this field concludes that "no one understanding of attitude strength dominates contemporary research" (Eagly and Chaiken 1998, 287). Indeed Krosnick and Petty describe attitude strength as "more of a vague metaphor than a formally defined social scientific construct" (1995, 2). The most comprehensive treatment of this topic in the last few years is Petty and Krosnick's 1995 *Attitude Strength,* which includes a thoughtful introduction by Philip Converse.

Characteristics of strong attitudes.   The standard position in attitude theory is that it is essential to differentiate the extremity of one's position from the strength of one's attitude. That remains the standard view, as in Fazio's (1995) argument that the location of the attitude object on a scale of favorability defines the attitude, not its strength. Extremity does not measure strength— extremity is simply distance from the neutral value of the scale. From this perspective, strength of party identification is more than just distance from political independence.

The standard party-identification scale gets around this problem in a clever way, by measuring strength of identification with a separate survey question rather than having people position themselves directly on a seven-point party-identification scale. However, social psychologists would not necessarily view self-reports of attitude strength as a valid measure. Indeed, Bassili (1996) labels such self-reports of attitude strength as "meta-attitudinal" in that people are unlikely to store attitude strength in memory. Bassili would view "operative" measures that are linked to the judgment processes as more valid, measures such as latency in response that assess the process of attitude activation.[12]

While there is disagreement within the social psychology field as to how to measure attitude strength, there is considerable agreement about its consequence: strong attitudes are durable and have impact (Krosnick and Petty 1995, 3). Stronger attitudes are more likely to be stable, to be resistant to change, to affect information processing and judgments, and to lead to behavior consistent with the attitude. What is intriguing is that several different measures of attitude strength have this set of relationships with attitude durability and impact.

Attitudes that have a dense set of associations regarding intraattitude structure should be strong in the sense that they will be more likely to stabilize over time, with resistance to isolated pieces of new information (Eagly and Chaiken 1995). Similarly, interattitude structure is an important part of attitude strength in terms of how related the attitude is to other attitudes. The more embedded the attitude is in a structure of related attitudes, the more difficult attitude change will be (McGuire 1981), particularly when we are dealing with a higher-level attitude in a hierarchical structure. Much of the treatment of this topic involves values and value centrality, as in Ostrom and Brock's (1968) work arguing that attitudes are strong when they are linked to important values.

Fazio (1995) has shown that attitudes high in accessibility are more likely to be stable, to be resistant to change, and to lead to behavior consistent with the attitude. Indeed, some attitudes can be retrieved from memory so quickly as to be automatic (Fazio et al. 1986). Accessibility may function as an indicator of the strength conferred by intraattitudinal or interattitudinal structure or may be a consequence of strength defined in these terms.

Krosnick's (1988) concept of attitude importance is the "subjective sense of the concern, caring, and significance" that the person attaches to an attitude, as indicated by self-reports (Boninger, Krosnick, and Berent 1995, 62). Attitude importance is related to indicators of strength, such as stability and resistance to change, but it could just be an indicator of structural strength (Eagly and Chaiken 1998, 290).

Dimensions of attitude strength.   A large number of strength-related aspects of attitudes have been proclaimed over the years. For example, Scott (1968) listed ten properties: extremity, intensity, ambivalence, salience, affective salience, cognitive complexity, overtness, embeddedness, flexibility, and consciousness. Raden (1985) added accessibility, evaluative-cognitive consistency, certainty, direct behavioral experience, importance, latitudes of acceptance and rejection, and vested interest to this list.

With so many different aspects of attitude strength, the next question is whether attitude strength is unidimensional. Eagly and Chaiken (1998, 290) interpret correlational studies of measures of attitude strength as showing that strength is multidimensional. Studies showing this start with Raden (1985), in which correlations among strength measures were found to be modest, followed by factor analyses that produced multiple factors (Krosnick et al. 1993).

Eagly and Chaiken's (1998, 291) reading of these studies is that there may be a more cognitive dimension and a more affective dimension of attitude strength. They support this contention with studies by Abelson (1988), in which separate emotional commitment and cognitive elaboration factors were obtained, and Pomerantz, Chaiken, and Tordesillas (1995), in which separate embeddedness and commitment factors were found.[13] Eagly and Chaiken suggest that embeddedness is cognitive, whereas the affective is related to commitment. However, other work suggests more dimensions, such as the finding of Boninger, Krosnick, and Berent (1995) that the importance of attitudes toward social issues depends on the extent to which these attitudes involve value expression, social identity, or self-interest, which may be other dimensions of attitude strength.

Krosnick and Petty (1995) settle on four strength-related dimensions of attitudes. The first dimension involves aspects of attitudes themselves—that is, extremity of the attitude and valence (positive versus negative). The second involves aspects of attitude structure, including accessibility of the attitude, links to knowledge about the attitude object, and ambivalence (conflict between positive and negative evaluations of the object). Two aspects of consistency are also part of this second dimension: evaluative-cognitive consistency (consistency of the attitude with beliefs about the object's attributes) and evaluative-affective consistency (consistency of the attitude with emotions associated with the object). Their third dimension involves subjective beliefs about people's own attitudes, such as how much people connect the attitude objects to their desires (personal relevance), how much people feel involved with the attitude object (personal involvement), and how much people feel the attitude object affects their tangible outcomes (vested interests). Two other important aspects of this third dimension are attitude importance (the psychological significance people attach to an attitude) and attitude certainty (the extent to which people are confident of their attitude). The fourth dimension involves cognitive processes, such as the amount of thinking one does about the attitude object (elaboration).

There is also an issue of what constitutes strength versus what are its antecedents or consequences. Thus, Krosnick and Petty (1995) suggest that attitude stability should be a consequence of strength rather than an indicator of it. Of course, the next question is whether different dimensions of strength have different consequences. Pomerantz, Chaiken, and Tordesillas (1995) show that their affective and cognitive strength factors influenced variables differentially, but more testing is required.

Measures of attitude strength.   Wegener et al. (1995) have provided several possible measures of these different aspects of attitude strength. Accessibility of an attitude—the ease to which the attitude comes to mind—can be measured by a response latency (the length of time between presenting the object to a person and the person's response) or by asking people how often they think or talk about the attitude object. Ambivalence—the extent to which the person has both positive and negative views of the object—can be measured by combining the number of positive and negative reactions, such as the proportion of responses that conflict with the person's dominant reaction. Certainty—the confidence with which the person holds the attitude—can be measured by asking people how certain they are of their responses. Elaboration—the extent to which the person has thought about information relevant to the object—can be measured by counting the number of thoughts the person gives about the attitude object or by asking people how much effort they put into evaluating it. Extremity—departure from neutrality—is usually measured in terms of deviation from the middle of an attitude scale. Importance—the person's perception of the importance of the attitude—can be measured by self-report of how important it is to the respondent personally, how deeply the person cares about it, and how concerned the person is about it. Knowledge—the information in memory regarding the object—can be measured by asking people to list what they know about the attitude object, by quizzing people about factual knowledge, or by asking people how much knowledge they feel they have about the object. Personal relevance—whether people believe the attitude object has consequence for their lives—can be measured by asking how likely it is to affect the respondent personally.

This listing suggests several new ways that strength of party identification might be measured, separately from partisan direction and separately from political independence (see especially Weisberg 1980). The discipline must decide which of these aspects of partisan strength is most relevant to our theories. Importance would be one obvious possibility, but it might also be useful to measure multiple aspects.

Wegener et al. (1995) also indicate some measures of structural consistency—whether the attitude is evaluated consistently with other attitudes. This can be measured by comparing within or across attitudes. Intraattitudinal consistency can be measured by comparing affective and evaluative reactions toward the object or by comparing cognitive and evaluative reactions toward the object. The latter has been done by following Fishbein's (1967) expectancy-value assessments, discussed earlier, or by comparing responses on cognitive and evaluative semantic-differential scales (Crites, Fabrigar, and Petty 1994). Interattitudinal consistency can be measured by comparing attitudes on related attitude objects, though such comparisons must be corrected for measurement error and differences in response variation. There have been studies of interattitudinal consistency involving party identification, but intraattitudinal consistency has received less focus. In particular, evaluative reactions to the parties have not been compared to either affective or cognitive reactions.

Finally, Wegener et al. (1995) point out that measuring the effects of one dimension of attitude strength requires controlling for confounding effects of the other dimensions of attitude strength, if indeed attitude strength is multidimensional. This argument implies that our estimates of the effects of strength of party identification are biased if we have not controlled for alternative dimensions of partisan strength.

Strength of party identification.   Another complication involved in the standard measurement of strength of party identification is that it combines answers to two quite different questions. People who answer the first question that they are Republicans or Democrats are asked if that identification is strong or not very strong, while people who answer that they are independents are next asked if they are closer to the Republican or the Democratic Party. The standard four-point measure of strength of identification (strong identifier, weak identifier, independent leaner, and pure independent) combines answers to these different questions. As a result, it is not surprising that "intransitivities" have been found in the relationship between strength of identification and various dependent variables (Petrocik 1974).[14]

Much of the difficulty with intransitivities for the party-identification scale results from its use of a "branching" format (Valentine and Van Wingen 1980) that does not guarantee unidimensionality (Weisberg 1980). One alternative measurement strategy would be to have respondents place themselves directly on a scale ranging from strong Republican to strong Democrat. Krosnick and Berent (1993) have reported on experiments using such a seven-point party-identification scale. They found that measure to have lower reliability than the conventional party-identification scale, though Green and Schickler's (1993) analysis of a similar seven-point self-placement scale in a 1973 National Opinion Research Center (NORC) survey found the opposite.

This lengthy review of the literature on attitude strength has several implications for the study of party identification. First, attitude strength is usually viewed as separate from attitude extremity, contrary to the customary measurement for party identification. Second, self-reports of attitude strength are not necessarily considered the most valid of measurements. Third, the consequences of attitude strength are fairly similar regardless of how it is measured, so any measurement of strength of party identification would be likely to show that stronger identification leads to attitudes that are more durable and have greater impact. Fourth, there are likely to be separate dimensions to strength of party identification, whether following the Krosnick and Petty distinctions or relying on Eagly and Chaiken's emphasis on affective versus cognitive aspects, and these separate dimensions may eventually be found to have separate effects. Fifth, combining strength of partisanship for partisans and leaning for independents leads to a less pure measure of attitude strength, which could explain the intransitivities that have been identified in the research literature.

The Consequences of Partisan Attitudes

In addition to reviewing the nature of attitudes, it is important to consider their consequences. In particular, this section will examine the effects of attitudes, their functions, and their roles as predictors of behavior.

Effects of Attitudes

One reason that attitudes are important is because of their psychological effects. In particular, attitudes exert "selectivity effects" on information processing. The dominant view is that attitudes bias this information processing in favor of information that fits with the person's attitude. This is a "congeniality effect," because people are presumed to favor information that is congenial to their attitudes (Eagly and Chaiken 1998, 292). Social psychologists have focused on three interrelated selectivity effects. Attitudes can lead to selectivity in terms of exposure and attention to information, selectivity in terms of perception and judgment, and/or selectivity in terms of memory.

Selectivity effects on memory are accepted only under particular circumstances. Selective effects on memory are considered to be minimal except when the person had to actively defend an attitude against counterarguments and when the attitude is bipolar (Pratkanis 1989). According to this view, information supportive of party identification would be remembered more by people who have had to defend their party choice. Selectivity effects on exposure and attention to information are considered to be even less likely. Early work by Festinger (1957) emphasized selectivity in terms of people favoring information that agrees with their attitudes, but Freedman and Sears (1965) concluded that there was little evidence for attitudinal selectivity in terms of exposure or attention to information. Selectivity effects are most accepted today in the area of effects on perception and judgment; Eagly and Chaiken conclude that selective evaluation is "pervasive" (1998, 294), though they view this result as an unsurprising example of balance-theory ideas.

Zaller (1992) combines selectivity effects on exposure and judgment to create a curvilinear model of political persuasion. He argues that persons with moderate levels of political knowledge and interest will be most susceptible to political attitude change. These individuals will have the exposure to new political information necessary for attitude change but not be so politically sophisticated as to successfully counterargue attitude-incongruent information. Consequently, those persons with medium exposure should be the most likely to undergo attitude change. These findings might suggest that those persons with moderately strong partisan orientations may be the most amenable to attitude change.

The early party-identification literature certainly claimed that selectivity effects existed for party identification. At that time, it was not seen as necessary to distinguish carefully among selectivity effects on memory, on exposure and attention, or on perception and judgment. There have been fewer claims for selectivity effects for party identification in the memory area, which is fortunate given the limited evidence for such effects in the more general social psychology literature. Many claims about selectivity effects for party identification focus on exposure and attention—that people pay more attention to information that favors their party and sometimes ignore information that is against their party. It is challenging to see the *Handbook of Social Psychology* (Eagly and Chaiken 1998, 294) discount that type of selectivity effect. However, it is reassuring that the *Handbook* judges selectivity effects on perception and judgment to be pervasive, as this supports the usual view of party identification affecting views on issues and candidates. Overall, more careful experimentation is called for about what selectivity effects hold and do not hold for party identification. A metanalysis of current research might suffice, but it would be useful to distinguish these different possible selectivity effects more carefully to see how potent party identification really is in this regard.

The Functions of Attitudes

What are the functions of attitudes more broadly? More specifically, what functions does party identification have as an attitude, in addition to the selectivity effects that were just reviewed? The social psychology literature identifies two main functions of attitudes: object appraisal and utilitarian. Katz (1960) first developed this distinction. Object appraisal emphasizes the knowledge function of attitudes—their role in organizing and simplifying people's experiences. The utilitarian, or instrumental, function is to maximize rewards and minimize punishments, either in terms of narrow self-interest (such as financial) or more abstract benefits (affirmation of values and self-concept). For example, symbolic politics (Kinder and Sears 1981) emphasizes the extent to which people internalize social values (symbolic beliefs) such as fairness and equity.

Other functions of attitudes that have been claimed are value expression, social adjustment, and ego defense, but these are best seen as more specific functions of some attitudes for some individuals under some circumstances. Value expression (Katz 1960) is when holding attitudes is rewarding because it satisfies needs to affirm self-concepts. This fits closely with the idea of an atti-tude hierarchy, with the self-concept leading to the overarching attitude. The social adjustive function (M. Smith, Bruner, and White 1956) emphasizes that attitudes mediate a person's relations with others. The ego-defensive function (Katz 1960) suggests that attitudes help defend the self from threatening events. Similarly, according to social identity theory (Tajfel 1981), attitudes toward out-groups and the stereotypes underlying those attitudes allow in-group members to differentiate themselves from out-group members and to justify their treatment of out-groups.

These functions of attitudes need not be seen as fixed. The functions may depend on the tasks that people face, in line with Zajonc's (1960) concept of cognitive tuning. Functions of attitudes can be assessed through self-reports, but they may also have more latent functions. Furthermore, it is important to recognize that attitudes may serve multiple functions for the same individual as well as different functions for different individuals.

The functions of party identification have not been analyzed explicitly from the perspective described in this section, but some linkages seem clear. The original view of party identification could be read as emphasizing mainly the object-appraisal function: partisanship as helping to organize our experiences in the political world. The rational choice perspective emphasizes more the instrumental aspect, choosing a party to maximize self-interest and modifying one's identification based on how the performance of the parties has affected the individual. What would be particularly interesting would be if researchers could determine whether party identification fulfills different functions for dif-ferent citizens.

There have been attempts to link party identification with other parts of the social psychology literature. For example, work on information processing leads to insights on the development of party identification (C. Smith 1993). Also, there have prominent applications of schema theory to partisan schemas (Hamill, Lodge, and Blake 1985; Richardson 1991; Rahn 1993). These uses of social psychology theory to explicate party identification differ from the attitu-dinal approach used here as regards the functions served by the psychological mechanisms. In particular, attitude theory emphasizes the object-appraisal and/or utilitarian functions served by the attitude, whereas schema theory emphasizes the use of party identification as an information shortcut.

Attitudes as Predictors of Behavior

Finally, attitudes are considered important, in large part, to the extent to which they are predictors of relevant behavior. Thus, one reason that party identification is considered such an important variable in the voting behavior field is that it is routinely found to be the best single predictor of voting in the United States.

In dealing with the issue of prediction of behavior, caution is necessary as to the exact process being implied. Do we mean to say that the attitude causes the behavior or just that it is correlated with the behavior? And, if it is just correlated with the behavior, it is possible that the causal order is reversed—that the behavior causes the attitude (Bem 1972).

The direction of causality involved in the relationship between party identification and the vote has been the subject of much work. The early Michigan studies clearly treated party identification as the causal factor. Its exogenous status is so clear in the early literature that it has been described as the "unmoved mover." Research in other countries, however, soon challenged that status. In particular, Thomassen's (1976) analysis of a panel study in the Netherlands showed that respondents were more likely to change their partisanship while maintaining their vote between elections than to change their vote while maintaining their partisanship, the opposite of the pattern that prevails in the United States. Studies such as Jackson (1975) and Franklin and Jackson (1983) in the United States also began to treat party identification as endogenous to the causal system.

Targets versus behaviors. An important distinction in the social psychology literature is between attitudes toward targets and attitudes toward behaviors. In the voting-behavior field, for example, an attitude toward a candidate would be considered an attitude toward a target. By contrast, an attitude toward a behavior would be an attitude toward the act of voting, as when some people are favorably disposed to the act of voting whereas others view it as a waste of their time. Both types of attitudes are considered important, but attitudes toward behavior are found to be "particularly effective in predicting behavior" (Eagly and Chaiken 1998, 296). That is, attitudes toward voting should be incorporated in models predicting voting behavior as well as attitudes toward the candidates.

The interesting part of this argument is that it calls attention to the question of what the behavior really is in the field of voting. We treat the vote as voting for one party or the other, but there are other ways to interpret the behavior. One alternative would be to bring multiple offices on the same ballot more into consideration by viewing the behavior in terms of the person's pattern of voting across offices.

Another interesting possibility is that the relevant behavior might be voting for or against the incumbent's party. We could call this the model of reelection and succession. This possibility fits with recent work on the "succession effect" when George Bush gained support in 1988 as the designated heir apparent of the popular Ronald Reagan (Mattei and Weisberg 1994). It also fits with the emphasis on reelection as an integral part of the election cycle (Weisberg and Box-Steffensmeier 1999). If there are two common themes to election campaigns, they are the proincumbent "don't change horses in midstream" and the anti-incumbent "throw the rascals out" themes. These themes support the view that voting is essentially a matter of support of or opposition to the incumbent's party rather than a partisan act. This interpretation of voting obviously also fits very well with Fiorina's (1981) emphasis on "retrospective voting" as well as the emphasis on performance evaluations in W. Miller and Shanks's *The New American Voter* (1996).

Correlations versus causal models. Much of the social psychology work on predicting behavior from attitudes involves correlations between the two, but some caution is required in evaluating these correlations. Fishbein and Ajzen (1974) show that a multiple-act behavior criterion yields better attitude-behavior correlations than an unreliable single-act behavior criterion. That may indeed support using multiple offices on the same ballot as the behavior to predict from partisan attitudes. Furthermore, the attitude-behavior correlation depends on how compatible the behavioral criterion is with the attitude (Ajzen and Fishbein 1977) and whether the intraattitudinal structure activated by the measurement of the attitude is the same as the structure activated when the person decides to act (Millar and Tesser 1986). As a result, high correlations are not as important as understanding the underlying psychological processes, which suggests using causal models rather than simple attitude-behavior correlations.

Social psychologists have developed several causal models detailing how attitudes impact on behavior. Expectancy-value theories have been particularly important. They are typified by Ajzen and Fishbein's (1980) theory of reasoned action (fig. 3.1), in which the intention to engage in a behavior is the proximal cause of the behavior, which is in turn caused by attitude toward the behavior. This theory sees the anticipated consequences of behavior as either utilitarian (rewards and punishments) or normative based on perceptions of others' approval or disapproval of one's behavior. This theory has stimulated other efforts. For example, self-identity consequences (affirmations and repudiations of the self-concept) can be taken into account as well as utilitarian and normative ones. Also, some behaviors can become habitual, automatic without requiring a conscious decision to act.[15]

Eagly and Chaiken (1993) have presented a composite attitude-behavior causal model (fig. 3.2). Habit, attitude toward the target, utilitarian outcomes, normative outcomes, and self-identity outcomes are seen as affecting the attitude toward the behavior. The attitude toward behavior affects the intention to act, as do the normative and self-identity consequences. Finally, the actual behavior is seen as being caused by the intention to act along with the attitude toward the behavior, plus the influence of habit, which can presumably short-circuit the other steps.

This progression from looking at correlations to developing causal models

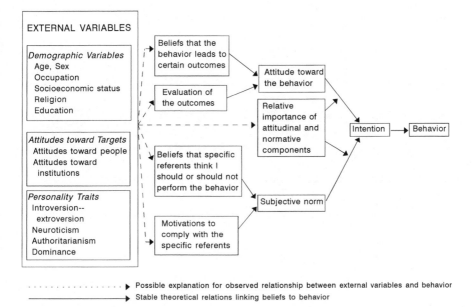

Fig. 3.1.   Representation of the theory of reasoned action. "External variables" refers to all variables not considered by the theory. (Adapted from Eagly and Chaiken 1998, 298; Ajzen and Fishbein 1980, 84.)

has been evident in the party identification literature. The early literature focused on correlating party identification with the vote and comparing that correlation with similar correlations between issue attitudes or candidate orientations with the vote. Because of the need to control simultaneously for multiple causes, the literature soon moved to causal models of the vote. However, the most sophisticated of these causal models reached somewhat different conclusions (e.g., Markus and Converse 1979 versus Page and Jones 1979), which has led to less focus on causal models of the vote decision (cf. W. Miller and Shanks 1996). It might be possible to resurrect this approach by applying some of the causal model paradigms that are currently advocated in social psychology (see especially Rahn et al. 1990). So far there have been no direct applications of either the Ajzen and Fishbein theory of reasoned action or the Eagly and Chaiken composite attitude-behavior model. Minimally, though, the correlation between party identification and vote is high enough that most researchers accept the importance of party identification to understanding the vote decision.

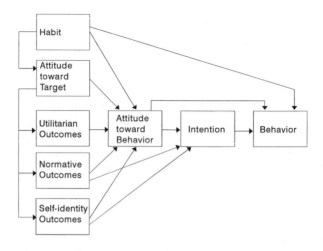

Fig. 3.2.　Representation of a composite attitude-behavior model. (Adapted from Eagly and Chaiken 1998, 298.)

Party Identification and Electoral Democracy

Before concluding, it is important to turn more explicitly to the role of party identification with respect to electoral democracy. Party identification is a basic foundation of electoral democracy in that it is one of the most important bases of individual vote choice. Extreme partisanship is sometimes seen as a danger of democracy, making it hard to achieve the compromises that are necessary to govern effectively. However, partisanship is also seen to provide a basis of stability for the political system. Converse made the most eloquent statement of this argument in his article "Of Time and Partisan Stability" (1969). As he wrote, "we conceive such aggregate levels of loyalty to existing parties in a democratic system as an important ingredient of democratic stability, and perhaps, for the mass level, *the* most important ingredient, although any such claim must remain speculative" (142). In particular, when people identify with a party for a long period of time and vote for that party, it is difficult to generate support for new extremist parties and demagogic leaders that would threaten the democracy.

If partisanship promotes political stability, then the question becomes what leads to partisan attachments. Converse's early analysis relied on arguments based on learning theory and political socialization. Whether people develop partisan ties was seen as a function of whether their parents had such ties. People whose parents had partisan ties are much more likely to have partisan ties themselves. Thus, in their best known finding, Converse and Dupeux (1962) estimate that in both the United States and France 80 percent of the people who knew their father's party have a partisan self-location themselves, compared to only half of the respondents who do not know their father's party. As to the strength component, Converse (1969) showed that length of membership in a party is the critical determinant of partisan strength of partisan attachment. Learning occurs along with socialization into politics, and both of these factors strengthen partisan attachments over time until the party system becomes frozen in place (Lipset and Rokkan 1967).

To speak of party identification as a foundation for stability in a party system also leads to an obvious corollary: weak partisan ties lead to more volatile politics. Converse and Dupeux (1962) noted that phenomenon in their discussion of French politics, where they suggest that the widespread absence of party loyalties in France at the time was linked to the development of flash party movements there as well as political turbulence more generally.

How, then, does the theoretical basis of party identification affect our understanding of the role of partisanship in undergirding electoral democracy? While the argument just given is perfectly reasonable, an alternative argument is also possible. First, the minimal-group paradigm suggests that partisan ties are easier to create than the socialization approach implies. Having one's parents identify with a party would not be the only reason for a child to develop an identification with that party, according to the minimal-group paradigm. Such identification with a party should form quite easily, in response to much milder stimuli. For example, hearing that one's racial or religious group tends to identify with a party should be sufficient to produce a partisan tie, as should realizing that most of one's coworkers identify with a party.

In addition, evidence has accumulated that party identification does not have the stability that was assumed in the early Michigan work. While the topic is still debated extensively (e.g., Green, Palmquist, and Schickler 1998), there is evidence of frequent systematic change in party identification at both the individual and the aggregate levels (MacKuen, Erikson, and Stimson 1990), though no one would view partisanship as highly volatile. Also, there is indication of weak and unstable partisanship in some other stable democracies, such as the Netherlands (Thomassen 1976). This changeability of party identification, though, challenges the claim that party identification leads to political stability for a nation. Indeed, Converse and Pierce (1986) have speculated that in some countries, people identify more with left-right ideology than with political parties, and that identification may be what produces political stability, though their results for France do not fully support that possibility.

There is indeed an alternative explanation of party system stability and change. Rational choice theorists would instead emphasize the role of electoral rules in shaping incentives for politicians. Electoral rules can affect party system stability in three ways. First, electoral rules shape the ability of parties to compete, such as by making it difficult for new parties to compete. Second, changes in electoral rules can change incentives for politicians in ways that lead to instability in the party system. Thus, changing from a single-member winner-take-all electoral system to a multimember district system with proportional representation can be expected to lead to weakening of existing parties since politicians can be elected without joining large umbrella parties. In addition, some electoral rules give politicians incentives that lead to unstable party systems. For example, electoral system reforms enacted in Japan in 1994 entitle parties to government subsidies based on their number of Diet seats, which produces an incentive for legislators who are not renominated by their party to coalesce as a new party. These legislators then can run with the benefit of those subsidies in the next election under the label of the new party, so the electoral reform has led to the formation of new parties.

Thus, a rational choice argument could explain the longevity of the party system in the United States in terms of electoral rules that do not give politicians incentives for creating new parties. New parties would form only if the incentives were changed. Important evidence on this point is provided by the change in incentives in the campaign finance reforms of the 1970s that provided funding for a party at a presidential election on the basis of its vote in the previous election. This law had minimal effect until the 1990s, when H. Ross Perot's impressive 1992 showing guaranteed substantial funding for the Reform Party in 1996 and Perot's weaker showing in 1996 still guaranteed several million dollars of funding for that party in 2000. The provision of federal funding had made the Reform Party the most important instance of a national third party that has continued across a series of elections since the birth of the Republican Party.

The preceding discussion shows that electoral rules affect the stability of a party system without having to explain such stability by the strength and stability of partisan attachments. Electoral rules can, of course, affect not only the number of parties but also divided government, interelection vote swings, the incumbency advantage, and general support for party system. Thus, electoral rules can affect electoral democracy very generally.

These several points together lead to a potential reinterpretation of the role of party identification in electoral democracy. Electoral rules would be seen as more crucial in leading to stability of the system, while partisan ties would be regarded as both easier to create and more changeable. A stable party system need not depend centrally on partisanship, though party identification can remain one of the main determinants of the vote at the individual level.

At the same time, questioning the effect of party identification as a stabilizing influence on electoral politics should not be seen as minimizing its role in promoting electoral democracy. For example, party attachments perform an important mobilizing function, drawing people into the political process. Partisans have a higher rate of voting in elections and participation in nonvoting political activities than do people without partisan ties. This mobilizing function is in its own way important for the maintenance of electoral democracy.

It is important to emphasize that the argument in this section is only a potential reinterpretation of the role of party identification in electoral democracy. However, it is an important argument regarding the basis of electoral democracy, and it leads to a vital new research agenda: disentangling the effects of party identification, ideological identification, and electoral rules in promoting democratic stability. Each of these factors may be important, so we need to devise research that tests the role of party identification in leading to the stability of political systems with these other factors fully controlled.

Conclusions

Party identification was developed in the 1950s based on reference-group theory and the more general understanding of attitude theory of that era. The field of social psychology has evolved considerably since then, but the concept and measure of party identification have survived fairly well intact. Party identification might be interpreted somewhat differently today, and social psychologists might give some additional measurement advice, but the basic concept remains intact. Yet we can learn from contemporary social psychology just as the authors of *The American Voter* learned from the social psychology of the 1950s.

The reference-group theory that undergirded the original development of the party-identification concept is passé in social psychology today. It has been replaced by a lively interest in group relations, with particular emphasis on Tajfel's social identity theory. In-group attachments are now seen as being created under conditions that are much more minimal than reference-group theory assumed. Attitudes toward out-groups are seen as separate from attitudes toward the in-group. Sources of group conflict have been investigated, with particular emphasis on the effects of categorization by itself. The development of partisan identity fits well under this new rubric (Green, Palmquist, and Schickler 2002; Greene 2002). But there should be greater focus on attitudes toward the party with which the person does not identify as well as on attitudes toward independence.

The evolution of the attitude theory field also permits a richer understanding of party identification than was possible in the 1950s. It is necessary to pull apart its cognitive, affective, and behavioral components to assess their relative importance as well as their joint contributions. Whether partisan attitudes are unipolar or bipolar should also be assessed, along with the extent and consequences of ambivalence toward the parties. The complexity of attitudes toward parties should be examined along with their coherence. Furthermore, the relationship of party identification to other attitudes, especially ideology and other underlying values, should be probed in more detail.

Partisan strength should be seen as a more complex topic than it was originally considered. The value of self-reports must be critically examined, and strength should be viewed as separate from partisan extremity. It is reassuring that social psychologists find that strong attitudes are durable and have high impact, fairly regardless of how attitude strength is measured. Still, it would be useful to determine whether different dimensions of partisan strength can be located that might have different relationships to dependent behavior, such as cognitive versus affective strength. And measures of partisan strength should not be confounded with attitudes toward political independence.

The consequences of party identification can also use further examination in light of current attitude theory. The scope of selectivity effects on information processing should be studied to separate the effects on memory, exposure and attention to information, and perception and judgment. The functions of party identification for individuals can be examined in terms of the social-psychological distinctions between object appraisal and utilitarian, with attention to whether party identification serves different functions for different individuals. Also, the relationship of party identification to voting can be reexamined, testing the theoretical payoff of different definitions of the relevant behavior as well as applying the causal models of the attitude-behavior linkage that are used now in social psychology.

Finally, it is appropriate to turn back to one of the questions raised at the beginning of this chapter, whether different social psychological theories might be appropriate for dealing with partisan direction, strength, and independence. Partisan direction can be explored as part of the general field of group relations, especially using social identity theory. Our understanding of strength of partisanship should be reexamined from the perspective of attitude theory more generally. Political independence remains more complicated to assess in social psychological terms, but minimally it is necessary to differentiate it better from strength of partisanship.

Half a century ago, a University of Michigan scholar wrote,

> Independents may be many or few; they may be increasing or not; areal patterns may or may not exist; independents may be of many undetermined types; they may be intelligent or fickle; and the effects of independent voting on the political system may be beneficent or dangerous. The state of our knowledge about independent voting is obviously not precise, well documented, or unanimous. (Eldersveld 1952, 435)

The uncertainty about the nature and extent of independence remains as true today as when Samuel Eldersveld raised those concerns. Independents can be seen as an in-group that people react positively to (see Greene 2000), as part of a rejection of both parties as out-groups, as choosing a neutral position on a bipolar partisan scale, or as a group that shares a behavior. We have been willing to lump these different types of independents (Dennis 1988) into one category on the basis of their self-identifications instead of insisting on using different labels for different types of independents. The consequence is diminished theoretical clarity about the nature of independence.

Party identification is the linchpin of our modern understanding of electoral democracy, and it is likely to retain that crucial theoretical position even if we need more research on the relative importance of partisanship and electoral rules in promoting democratic stability. However, we should move to a more contemporary understanding of the concept in terms of social identity theory and modern attitude theory. This reexamination is most likely to affect our understanding of strength of partisanship and of political independence. And it would not help if we just returned to the original party identification question: "If a presidential election were being held today, do you think you would vote for the Democratic, Republican, or for some other party?" Fortunately, the Michigan researchers of the 1950s properly recognized the necessity of embedding their work on electoral democracy in the best social psychology of the time, and that should be their enduring legacy.

NOTES

1. The National Opinion Research Center (NORC) 1944 election study pioneered in using a question measuring partisan direction but did not measure strength of partisanship. It asked, "Do you consider yourself a Democrat or Republican or something else?" with people saying that they "vote for the man" being coded as independents. This question was analyzed only in an unpublished dissertation by Sheldon Korchin (1946). The NORC 1947 and 1948 election studies asked "Do you consider yourself a Democrat, or a Republican, or do you favor some other party?" By contrast, the 1940 and 1948 studies by Columbia University's Bureau of Applied Social Research asked only about vote intention. In an oral history interview, Warren Miller told Heinz Eulau that he helped Sam Eldersveld design a 1951 survey of Ann Arbor that "was the first time that party identification was ever asked, at least by the Michigan group" (1991, 237).

2. For a recent discussion of the measurement properties of the standard party-identification question and other partisanship scales, see Weisberg 1999.

3. See Lau 1989 for one of the very few recent studies using the reference-group concept.

4. We are indebted to the faculty and students of the political psychology program at Ohio State University for many conversations over the years that have helped shape this chapter by increasing our recognition of the contributions of political psychology perspectives to our understanding of politics. Particularly influential have been discussions with Jon Krosnick, Marilynn Brewer, Tom Nelson, Margaret Hermann, David Harding, John Bruce, Charles Smith, and Zoe Oxley.

5. This review of the social psychology literature on group processes owes much to two recent reviews of that literature, Devine 1995; Brewer and Brown 1998.

6. Even if one of these characteristics is viewed as forming the basis of a group, that does not mean that the group has political relevance. The achievement of political relevance for the group should be considered a separate step, as when people's ethnic backgrounds are seen as having less political relevance than their race, gender, and religion. Group political consciousness can be even a more demanding process (Gurin, Miller, and Gurin 1980; A. Miller et al. 1981). As Kinder has written, "Identification is important, but it is but a pale shade of group consciousness. . . . Group consciousness requires membership, attachment (or identification), and, with some variation: discontent with the group's current wealth, power, or status; blame for the group's difficulties placed outside the group itself, in patterns of social discrimination or institutional bias, so that inequalities are seen as unjust; and [group consciousness requires a] commitment to collective political strategies" (1998, 805).

7. The phrase *political identity* seems to have first been used in the context of social identity theory in the title of an article by Kelly (1989).

8. A few interesting studies develop typologies of partisanship based on separate reactions to the two parties. For example, Crewe (1966) distinguished four types of partisans in Britain: (1) the "polarized," who strongly favor their party and strongly dislike the other party; (2) the "loyal," who strongly favor their party but do not strongly dislike the other party; (3) the "negative," who strongly dislike the other party but do not strongly favor their own party; and (4) the "apathetic," who have strong feelings toward neither party. It is possible to operationalize this type of classification in several ways, including through the respondent's thermometer ratings of the two parties.

9. This review of the social psychology literature on attitudes is based on the treatment of the topic by Eagly and Chaiken 1998.

10. As a result of not basing the definition of attitudes on the underlying mental processes, it is possible that attitudes that are measured are just "evaluative responding" (Eagly and Chaiken 1998, 270). That is, the attitude may be created during the task of responding to an attitude question rather than being preexisting.

11. Fishbein originally measured the beliefs with rating scales, but that approach did not rule out the possibility that the beliefs were determined by the attitude on the occasion of being measured. Other studies have used free response methods, in which people are asked to list their beliefs, but correlations with attitudes of expectancy-value products are still positive, though not as high (Eagly, Mladinic, and Otto 1994).

12. For an application of this approach to party identification in Canada, see Bassili 1995.

13. In the Abelson study, emotional commitment included "I can't imagine ever changing my mind" and "My beliefs about X express the real me," whereas cognitive elaboration included "It's easy to explain my views" and "Several other issues could come up in a conversation about it." In the Pomerantz study, embeddedness included self-reports of the centrality of the attitude to people's self-concepts and the extent to which their attitudes represented their values, whereas commitment included self-reports of certainty and the likelihood of changing opinions.

14. Keith et al. 1992 strongly argue that independent leaners should in fact be combined with weak partisans, with only pure independents treated as independents,

though Dennis 1992 shows that leaners are more like pure independents than like partisans in terms of attitudes toward independence and views of party differences.

15. By contrast, Fazio (1995) emphasized attitude accessibility (as part of attitude strength) as explaining when attitudes toward targets and behaviors will correspond. At the extreme, automatic activation of attitudes (Fazio et al. 1986) leads to the possibility of behaviors resulting without following the expectancy-value argument.

REFERENCES

Abelson, Robert P. 1988. Conviction. *American Psychologist* 43:267–75.

Abelson, Robert P., Donald R. Kinder, Mark D. Peters, and Susan T. Fiske. 1982. Affective and Semantic Components in Political Person Perception. *Journal of Personality and Social Psychology* 42:619–30.

Abrams, Dominic. 1994. Political Distinctiveness: An Identity Optimizing Approach. *European Journal of Social Psychology* 24:357–65.

Achen, Christopher H. 1989. Prospective Voting and the Theory of Party Identification. Paper presented at the annual meeting of the American Political Science Association, Atlanta.

———. 1992. Social Psychology, Demographic Variables, and Linear Regression: Breaking the Iron Triangle in Voting Research. *Political Behavior* 14:195–211.

Ajzen, I., and Morris Fishbein. 1977. Attitude-Behavior Relations: A Theoretical Analysis and Review of Empirical Research. *Psychological Bulletin* 84:888–918.

———. 1980. *Understanding Attitudes and Predicting Social Behavior.* Englewood Cliffs, N.J.: Prentice-Hall.

Bassili, John N. 1995. On the Psychological Reality of Party Identification: Evidence from the Accessibility of Voting Intentions and of Partisan Feelings. *Political Behavior* 17: 339–58.

———. 1996. Meta-Judgmental versus Operative Indexes of Psychological Attributes: The Case of Measures of Attitude Strength. *Journal of Personality and Social Psychology* 71:637–53.

Belknap, George, and Angus Campbell. 1952. Political Party Identification and Attitudes toward Foreign Policy. *Public Opinion Quarterly* 15:601–23.

Bem, Daryl J. 1972. Self-Perception Theory. In L. Berkowitz, ed., *Advances in Experimental Social Psychology,* vol. 6. New York: Academic Press.

Berelson, Bernard R., Paul F. Lazarsfeld, and William N. McPhee. 1954. *Voting.* Chicago: University of Chicago Press.

Boninger, David S., Jon A. Krosnick, and Matthew Berent. 1995. Origins of Attitude Importance: Self-Interest, Social Identification, and Value Relevance. *Journal of Personality and Social Psychology* 68:61–80.

Brewer, Marilynn B. 1979. In-Group Bias in the Minimal Intergroup Situation: A Cognitive-Motivational Analysis. *Psychological Bulletin* 86:307–24.

———. 1991. The Social Self: On Being the Same and Different at the Same Time. *Personality and Social Psychology Bulletin* 17:475–82.

Brewer, Marilynn B., and Rupert J. Brown. 1998. Intergroup Relations. In Daniel T. Gilbert, Susan T. Fiske, and Gardner Lindzey, eds. *Handbook of Social Psychology,* 4th. ed., vol. 2. Boston: McGraw-Hill.

Burden, Barry C., and Steven Greene. 2000. Party Attachments and State Election Laws. *Political Research Quarterly* 53:63–76.

Butler, David, and Donald E. Stokes. 1969. *Political Change in Britain*. New York: St. Martin's.

Cacioppo, John T., and Gary G. Berntson. 1994. Relationship between Attitudes and Evaluative Space: A Critical Review, with Emphasis on the Separability of Positive and Negative Substrates. *Psychological Bulletin* 115:401–23.

Campbell, Angus, Philip E. Converse, Warren E. Miller, and Donald E. Stokes. 1960. *The American Voter*. New York: Wiley.

Campbell, Angus, Gerald Gurin, and Warren E. Miller. 1954. *The Voter Decides*. Evanston, Ill.: Row, Peterson.

Campbell, Donald T. 1958. Common Fate, Similarity, and Other Indices of the Status of Aggregates of Persons as Social Entities. *Behavioural Science* 3:14–25.

———. 1965. Ethnocentric and Other Altruistic Motives. In D. Levine, ed., *Nebraska Symposium on Motivation*. Lincoln: University of Nebraska Press.

Converse, Philip E. 1964. The Nature of Belief Systems in Mass Publics. In David E. Apter, ed., *Ideology and Discontent*. New York: Free Press.

———. 1966. The Concept of the Normal Vote. In Angus Campbell, Philip E. Converse, Warren E. Miller, and Donald E. Stokes, *Elections and the Political Order*. New York: Wiley.

———. 1969. Of Time and Partisan Stability. *Comparative Political Studies* 2:139–71.

———. 1970. Attitudes and Non-Attitudes: Continuation of a Dialogue. In Edward R. Tufte, ed., *The Quantitative Analysis of Social Problems*. Reading, Mass.: Addison-Wesley.

———. 1976. *The Dynamics of Party Support*. Beverly Hills, Calif.: Sage.

Converse, Philip E., and Georges Dupeux. 1962. Politicization of the Electorate in France and the United States. *Public Opinion Quarterly* 26:1–23.

Converse, Philip E., and Gregory B. Markus. 1979. *Plus ça change . . .* The New CPS Election Study Panel. *American Political Science Review* 73:2–49.

Converse, Philip E., and Roy Pierce. 1985. Measuring Partisanship. *Political Methodology* 11:143–66.

———. 1986. *Political Representation in France*. Cambridge: Harvard University Press.

Crewe, Ivor. 1966. Party Identification Theory and Political Change in Britain. In Ian Budge, Ivor Crewe, and Dennis Farlie, eds., *Party Identification and Beyond*. London: Wiley.

Crites, Stephen, Leandre Fabrigar, and Richard E. Petty. 1994. Measuring the Affective and Cognitive Properties of Attitudes: Conceptual and Methodological Issues. *Personality and Social Psychology Bulletin* 20:619–34.

Dennis, Jack. 1988. Political Independence in America, Part II: Towards a Theory. *British Journal of Political Science* 18:197–219.

———. 1992. Political Independence in America, Part III: In Search of Closet Partisans. *Political Behavior* 14:261–96.

Devine, Patricia G. 1995. Prejudice and Out-Group Perception. In Abraham Tesser, ed., *Advanced Social Psychology*. New York: McGraw-Hill.

Eagly, Alice H., and Shelly Chaiken. 1993. *The Psychology of Attitudes*. Fort Worth, Tex.: Harcourt, Brace, Jovanovich.

———. 1995. Attitude Strength, Attitude Structure, and Resistance to Change. In

Richard E. Petty and Jon A. Krosnick, eds., *Attitude Strength: Antecedents and Consequences*. Mahwah, N.J.: Erlbaum.

———. 1998. Attitude Structure and Function. In Daniel T. Gilbert, Susan T. Fiske, and Gardner Lindzey, eds. *Handbook of Social Psychology,* 4th ed., vol. 1. Boston: McGraw-Hill.

Eagly, Alice H., A. Mladinic, and S. Otto. 1994. Cognitive and Affective Bases of Attitudes toward Social Groups and Social Policies. *Journal of Experimental Social Psychology* 30:113–37.

Eldersveld, Samuel. 1952. The Independent Vote: Measurement, Characteristics, and Implications for Party Strategy. *American Political Science Review* 46:732–53.

Fazio, Russell H. 1989. On the Power and Functionality of Attitudes. In A. R. Pratkanis, S. J. Breckler, and Anthony G. Greenwald, eds. *Attitude Structure and Function.* Hillsdale, N.J.: Erlbaum.

———. 1995. Attitudes as Object-Evaluation Associations: Determinants, Consequences, and Correlates of Attitude Accessibility. In Richard E. Petty and Jon A. Krosnick, eds., *Attitude Strength: Antecedents and Consequences*. Mahwah, N.J.: Erlbaum.

Fazio, Russell H., D. M. Sanbonmatsu, M. C. Powell, and F. R. Kardes. 1986. On the Automatic Activation of Attitudes. *Journal of Personality and Social Psychology* 44:723–35.

Festinger, Leon. 1950. Informal Social Communication. *Psychological Review* 57:271–82.

———. 1957. *A Theory of Cognitive Dissonance.* Evanston, Ill.: Row, Peterson.

Fiorina, Morris P. 1977. An Outline for a Model of Party Choice. *American Journal of Political Science* 21:601–26.

———. 1981. *Retrospective Voting in American National Elections.* New Haven: Yale University Press.

Fishbein, Morris. 1967. A Behavior Theory Approach to the Relations between Beliefs about an Object and the Attitude toward the Object. In Morris Fishbein, ed., *Readings in Attitude Theory and Measurement.* New York: Wiley.

Fishbein, Morris, and I. Ajzen. 1974. Attitudes toward Objects as Predictors of Single and Multiple Behavioral Criteria. *Psychological Review* 81:59–74.

Franklin, Charles, and John E. Jackson. 1983. The Dynamics of Party Identification. *American Political Science Review* 77:957–73.

Freedman, J. L., and David O. Sears. 1965. Selective Exposure. In L. Berkowitz, ed., *Advances in Experimental Social Psychology*, vol. 2. New York: Academic Press.

Gant, Michael, and Norman Luttbeg. 1987. The Cognitive Utility of Partisanship. *Western Political Quarterly* 40:499–517.

Gilbert, Daniel T., Susan T. Fiske, and Gardner Lindzey, eds. 1998. *The Handbook of Social Psychology.* 4th ed. Boston: McGraw-Hill.

Green, Donald Philip, and Jack Citrin. 1994. Measurement Error and the Structure of Attitudes: Are Positive and Negative Judgments Opposite? *American Journal of Political Science* 38:256–81.

Green, Donald Philip, Bradley Palmquist, and Eric Schickler. 1998. Macropartisanship: A Replication and Critique. *American Political Science Review* 92:883–99.

———. 2002. *Partisan Hearts and Minds: Political Parties and the Social Identities of Voters.* New Haven: Yale University Press.

Green, Donald Philip, and Eric Schickler. 1993. Multiple-Measure Assessment of Party Identification. *Public Opinion Quarterly* 57:503–35.

Greene, Steven. 1998. Affective and Cognitive Components of Partisanship. Paper presented at the annual meeting of the Midwest Political Science Association, Chicago.

———. 1999a. Exploring the Structure of Party Identification: The Cognitive, Affective, and Social Identity Components of Partisanship. Ph.D. diss., Ohio State University.

———. 1999b. Understanding Party Identification: A Social Identity Approach. *Political Psychology* 20:393–403.

———. 2000. The Psychological Sources of Partisan-Leaning Independence. *American Politics Quarterly* 28:511–37.

———. 2002. The Social-Psychological Measurement of Partisanships. *Political Behavior* 24:171–97.

Gurin, Patricia, Arthur H. Miller, and Gerald Gurin. 1980. Stratum Identification and Consciousness. *Social Psychology Quarterly* 43:30–47.

Hamill, Ruth C., Milton Lodge, and Frederick Blake. 1985. The Breadth, Depth, and Utility of Class, Partisan, and Ideological Schema. *American Journal of Political Science* 29:850–70.

Hogg, Michael, and Dominic Abrams. 1988. *Social Identifications*. London: Routledge.

Holbrook, Allyson, Jon Krosnick, Penny S. Visser, Wendi L. Gardner, and John T. Cacioppo. 2001. Attitudes toward Presidential Candidates and Political Parties. *American Journal of Political Science* 45:930–50.

Hyman, Herbert H. 1942. The Psychology of Status. *Archives of Psychology*, no. 269.

Hyman, Herbert H., and Eleanor Singer, eds. 1968. *Readings in Reference Group Theory and Research*. New York: Free Press.

Insko, Chester A., and John Schopler. 1987. Categorization, Competition, and Collectivity. In C. Hendrick, ed., *Group Processes: Review of Personality and Social Psychology*, 8:213–51. Beverly Hills, Calif.: Sage.

Jackson, John E. 1975. Issues, Party Choice, and Presidential Votes. *American Journal of Political Science* 19:161–85.

Judd, Charles M., and J. A. Kulik. 1980. Schematic Effects of Social Attitudes on Information Processing and Recall. *Journal of Personality and Social Psychology* 38:469–78.

Judd, Charles M., and B. Park. 1988. Out-Group Homogeneity: Judgments of Variability at the Individual and Group Levels. *Journal of Personality and Social Psychology* 54:778–88.

Kaplan, K. J. 1972. On the Ambivalence-Indifference Problem in Attitude Theory and Measurement: A Suggested Modification of the Semantic Differential Technique. *Psychological Bulletin* 77:361–72.

Katz, Daniel. 1960. The Functional Approach to the Study of Attitudes. *Public Opinion Quarterly* 24:163–204.

Keith, Bruce, David Magleby, Candice Nelson, Elizabeth Orr, Mark Westlye, and Raymond Wolfinger. 1992. *The Myth of the Independent Voter*. Berkeley: University of California Press.

Kelley, Stanley, Jr., and Thad W. Mirer. 1974. The Simple Act of Voting. *American Political Science Review* 68:572–91.

Kelly, Caroline. 1988. Intergroup Differentiation in a Political Context. *British Journal of Social Psychology* 27:319–32.

———. 1989. Political Identity and Perceived Intragroup Homogeneity. *British Journal of Social Psychology* 28:239–50.

————. 1990. Social Identity and Intergroup Perceptions in Minority-majority Contexts. *Human Relations* 43:583–99.
Kerlinger, F. N. 1984. *Liberalism and Conservatism: The Nature and Structure of Social Attitudes.* Hillsdale, N.J.: Erlbaum.
Kessel, John H. 1984. *Presidential Parties.* Homewood, Ill.: Dorsey.
Kinder, Donald R. 1998. Opinion and Action in the Realm of Politics. In Daniel T. Gilbert, Susan T. Fiske, and Gardner Lindzey, eds., *Handbook of Social Psychology,* 4th ed., vol. 2. Boston: McGraw-Hill.
Kinder, Donald R., and David O. Sears. 1981. Prejudice and Politics: Symbolic Racism versus Racial Threats to the Good Life. *Journal of Personality and Social Psychology* 40:414–31.
Korchin, Sheldon. 1946. Psychological Variables in the Behavior of Voters. Ph.D. diss., Harvard University.
Krosnick, Jon A. 1988. Attitude Importance and Attitude Change. *Journal of Experimental Social Psychology* 24:240–55.
Krosnick, Jon A., and Matthew K. Berent. 1993. Comparisons of Party Identification and Policy Preferences: The Impact of Survey Question Format. *American Journal of Political Science* 37:941–64.
Krosnick, Jon A., D. S. Boninger, Y. C. Chuang, Matthew K. Berent, and C. G. Carnot. 1993. Attitude Strength: One Construct or Many Related Constructs? *Journal of Personality and Social Psychology* 65:1132–51.
Krosnick, Jon A., and Richard E. Petty. 1995. Attitude Strength: An Overview. In Richard E. Petty and Jon A. Krosnick, eds., *Attitude Strength: Antecedents and Consequences.* Mahwah, N.J.: Erlbaum.
Lau, Richard R. 1989. Individual and Contextual Influences on Group Identification. *Social Psychology Quarterly* 52:220–31.
Lazarsfeld, Paul F., Bernard Berelson, and Hazel Gaudet. 1949. *The People's Choice.* New York: Columbia University Press.
Lipset, Seymour M., and Stein Rokkan. 1967. *Cleavage Structures, Party Systems, and Voter Alignments.* New York: Free Press.
MacKuen, Michael B., Robert S. Erikson, and James A. Stimson. 1990. Macropartisanship. *American Political Science Review* 89:1125–42.
Markus, Gregory B., and Philip E. Converse. 1979. A Dynamic Simultaneous Equation Model of Electoral Choice. *American Political Science Review* 73:1055–70.
Mattei, Franco, and Herbert F. Weisberg. 1994. Presidential Succession Effects in Voting. *British Journal of Political Science* 24:269–90.
McGuire, William J. 1981. The Probabilogical Model of Cognitive Structure and Attitude Change. In Richard E. Petty, Thomas M. Ostrom, and Timothy C. Brock, eds., *Cognitive Responses in Persuasion.* Hillsdale, N.J.: Erlbaum.
Merton, Robert K. 1957. *Social Theory and Social Structure.* Rev. ed. Glencoe, Ill.: Free Press.
Millar, M. G., and Abraham Tesser. 1986. Effects of Affective and Cognitive Focus on the Attitude-Behavior Relation. *Journal of Experimental Social Psychology* 32:561–79.
Miller, Arthur H., Patricia Gurin, Gerald Gurin, and Oksana Malanchuk. 1981. Group Consciousness and Political Participation. *American Journal of Political Science* 25:494–511.

Miller, Arthur H., and Christopher Wlezien. 1993. The Social Group Dynamics of Partisan Evaluations. *Electoral Studies* 12:5–22.

Miller, Warren E. 1991. Interview by Heinz Eulau. In Michael A. Baer, Malcolm E. Jewell, and Lee Sigelman, eds., *Political Science in America: Oral Histories of a Discipline.* Lexington: University Press of Kentucky.

Miller, Warren E., and J. Merrill Shanks. 1996. *The New American Voter.* Cambridge: Harvard University Press.

Mullen, B., Rupert Brown, and C. Smith. 1992. Ingroup Bias as a Function of Salience, Relevance, and Status: An Integration. *European Journal of Social Psychology* 22:103–22.

Nisbett, R. E., and Timothy D. Wilson. 1977. Telling More Than We Can Know: Verbal Reports on Mental Processes. *Psychological Review* 84:231–59.

Ostrom, Thomas M., and Timothy C. Brock. 1968. A Cognitive Model of Attitudinal Involvement. In Robert P. Abelson, Elliot Aronson, William J. McGuire, Theodore M. Newcomb, Milton J. Rosenberg, and P. H. Tannenbaum, eds., *Theories of Cognitive Consistency: A Sourcebook.* Chicago: Rand McNally.

Page, Benjamin I., and Calvin C. Jones. 1979. Reciprocal Effects of Policy Preferences, Party Loyalties and the Vote. *American Political Science Review* 73:1071–89.

Perdue, C. W., J. F. Dovidio, M. B. Gurtman, and R. B. Tyler. 1990. "Us" and "Them": Social Categorization and the Process of Intergroup Bias. *Journal of Personality and Social Psychology* 59:475–86.

Petrocik, John R. 1974. An Analysis of the Intransitivities in the Index of Party Identification. *Political Methodology* 1:31–47.

Petty, Richard E., and Jon A. Krosnick. 1995. *Attitude Strength: Antecedents and Consequences.* Mahwah, N.J.: Erlbaum.

Pomerantz, E. M., Shelly Chaiken, and R. Tordesillas. 1995. Attitude Strength and Resistance Processes. *Journal of Personality and Social Psychology* 69:408–19.

Popkin, Samuel L. 1991. *The Reasoning Voter.* Chicago: University of Chicago Press.

Pratkanis, A. R. 1989. The Cognitive Representation of Attitudes. In A. R. Pratkanis, S. J. Breckler, and Anthony G. Greenwald, eds., *Attitude Structure and Function.* Hillsdale, N.J.: Erlbaum.

Quattrone, G. A. 1986. On the Perception of a Group's Variability. In S. Worchel and W. G. Austin, eds., *Psychology of Intergroup Relations,* 2d ed. Chicago: Nelson-Hall.

Rabbie, J. M., and M. Horwitz. 1988. Categories versus Groups as Explanatory Concepts in Intergroup Relations. *European Journal of Social Psychology* 18:117–23.

Rabbie, J. M., J. C. Schot, and L. Visser. 1989. Social Identity Theory: A Conceptual and Empirical Critique from the Perspective of a Behavioural Interaction Model. *European Journal of Political Psychology* 19:171–202.

Raden, D. 1985. Strength-Related Attitude Dimensions. *Social Psychology Quarterly* 48:312–30.

Rahn, Wendy. 1993. The Role of Partisan Stereotypes in Information Processing about Political Candidates. *American Journal of Political Science* 37:472–96.

Rahn, Wendy, John Aldrich, Eugene Borgida, and John Sullivan. 1990. A Social-Cognitive Model of Candidate Appraisal. In John Ferejohn and James Kuklinski, eds., *Information and Democratic Processes.* Urbana: University of Illinois Press.

Richardson, Bradley. 1991. European Party Loyalties Revisited. *American Political Science Review* 85:751–76.

Ross, M. 1989. Relation of Implicit Theories to the Construction of Personal Histories. *Psychological Review* 96:341–57.

Sachdev, L., and R. Y. Bourhis. 1987. Status Differentials and Intergroup Behaviour. *European Journal of Social Psychology* 17:277–93.

Scott, W. A. 1968. Attitude Measurement. In Gardner Lindzey and Elliot Aronson, eds., *Handbook of Social Psychology*, 2d ed. Reading, Mass.: Addison-Wesley.

Sears, David O., and Donald R. Kinder. 1985. Whites' Opposition to Busing: On Conceptualizing and Operationalizing Group Conflict. *Journal of Personality and Social Psychology* 48:1141–47.

Sherif, Muzafer, O. J. Harvey, B. Jack White, William R. Hood, and Carolyn W. Sherif. 1954. *Experimental Study of Positive and Negative Intergroup Attitudes between Experimentally Produced Groups: Robbers Cave Experiment*. Norman: University of Oklahoma, Institute of Group Relations.

Shively, W. Phillips. 1980. The Nature of Party Identification: A Review of Recent Developments. In John C. Pierce and John L. Sullivan, eds., *The Electorate Reconsidered*. Beverly Hills, Calif.: Sage.

Smith, Charles E. 1993. An Information-Processing Theory of Party Identification. Ph.D. diss., Ohio State University.

Smith, M. Brewster, J. S. Bruner, and R. W. White. 1956. *Opinions and Personality*. New York: Wiley.

Sumner, W. 1906. *Folkways*. New York: Ginn.

Tajfel, Henri. 1970. Experiments in Intergroup Discrimination. *Scientific American* 223(2): 96–102.

———. 1978. Social Categorization, Social Identity, and Social Comparisons. In Henri Tajfel, ed., *Differentiation between Social Groups*. London: Academic Press.

———. 1981. *Human Groups and Social Categories*. Cambridge: Cambridge University Press.

———. 1982. Social Psychology of Intergroup Attitudes. *Annual Review of Psychology* 33:1–39.

Tajfel, Henri, C. Flament, M. G. Billig, and R. F. Bundy. 1971. Social Categorization: An Intergroup Phenomenon. *European Journal of Social Psychology* 1:149–77.

Tajfel, Henri, and John C. Turner. 1986. The Social Identity Theory of Intergroup Behaviour. In S. Worchel and W. G. Austin, eds., *Psychology of Intergroup Relations*. Chicago: Nelson.

Tetlock, Philip E. 1989. Structure and Function in Political Belief Systems. In A. R. Pratkanis, S. J. Breckler, and Anthony G. Greenwald, eds., *Attitude Structure and Function*. Hillsdale, N.J.: Erlbaum.

Thomassen, Jacques. 1976. Party Identification as a Cross-National Concept: Its Meaning in the Netherlands. In Ian Budge, Ivor Crewe, and Dennis Farlie, eds., *Party Identification and Beyond*. New York: Wiley.

Turner, John C., Michael A. Hogg, Penelope J. Oakes, S. Reicher, and M. Wetherell. 1987. *Rediscovering the Social Group: A Self-Categorization Theory*. Oxford: Basil Blackwell.

Valentine, David C., and John R. Van Wingen. 1980. Partisanship, Independence, and the Partisan Identification Question. *American Politics Quarterly* 8:168–86.

Wegener, Duane T., John Downing, Jon A. Krosnick, and Richard E. Petty. 1995. Measures and Manipulations of Strength-Related Properties of Attitudes: Current Practice and Future Directions. In Richard E. Petty and Jon A. Krosnick, eds., *Attitude Strength: Antecedents and Consequences*. Mahwah, N.J.: Erlbaum.

Weisberg, Herbert F. 1980. A Multidimensional Conceptualization of Party Identifica-
tion. *Political Behavior* 2:33–60.
———. 1999. Political Partisanship. In John P. Robinson, Phillip R. Shaver, and
Lawrence S. Wrightsman, eds., *Measures of Political Attitudes*, rev. ed. San Diego:
Academic Press.
Weisberg, Herbert F., and Janet M. Box-Steffensmeier. 1999. Reelection: The 1996 U.S.
Election. In Herbert F. Weisberg and Janet M. Box-Steffensmeier, eds., *Reelection
1996: How Americans Voted*. Chatham, N.J.: Chatham House.
Weisberg, Herbert F., and Edward B. Hasecke. 1999. What Is Partisan Strength? A Social
Identity Theory Approach. Paper presented at the annual meeting of the American
Political Science Association, Washington, D.C.
Zajonc, Robert B. 1960. The Process of Cognitive Tuning in Communication. *Journal of
Abnormal and Social Psychology* 61:159–67.
Zaller, John. 1992. *The Nature and Origins of Mass Opinion*. Cambridge: Cambridge
University Press.

4
Process Matters:
Cognitive Models of
Candidate Evaluation

Marco R. Steenbergen and Milton Lodge

Of Philip Converse's many contributions to political behavior, two stand out in our minds. First, Converse was a key player in the development of a psychological perspective on public opinion and voting behavior. Second, he has raised some of the most fundamental normative questions in political behavior.

Even today, the normative questions that Converse raised remain relevant and continue to guide a great deal of research in political science. But the social psychology that we see today differs greatly from the social psychology that informed Converse's work. Social psychology has undergone enormous change, and among the most dramatic developments has been the rise of the social cognitive paradigm, which has resulted in a voluminous literature on political cognition. The objective of this chapter is to provide a summary of the literature on political cognition, keeping an eye on the normative concerns that Converse raised in his work.

We intend this chapter to be a review of the state of the art in political cognition. Much of the research in this field has occurred on the topic of candidate evaluation. Consequently, this will be our focus in this chapter, although we shall take an occasional detour into other domains. The chapter is organized as follows. First, we motivate the cognitive approach to political behavior. Next, we outline the structural model of the mind that forms the cornerstone of political cognition. In the following section, we provide a detailed discussion of key findings—and some unresolved issues—concerning different stages of information processing. Next, we discuss competing theories of how information processing affects candidate evaluation. We conclude by discussing the normative implications of the findings in political cognition to date.

Motivating Political Cognition

The cognitive approach to political behavior is of relatively recent origin, dating back to the early 1980s.[1] It was motivated in large part by the belief that existing explanations of political behavior were lacking in an important way. Specifically, these explanations did not describe how the human mind forms decisions, even though decision making is central to political behavior.

For example, voting behavior has a five-decade research history. This research has suggested a series of factors that affect the way in which voters evaluate candidates and determine their vote, including issue positions (see, e.g., Davis, Hinich, and Ordeshook 1970; Rabinowitz and Macdonald 1989), partisanship (see, e.g., Campbell et al. 1960), social context (see, e.g., Berelson, Lazarsfeld, and McPhee 1954; Beck et al. 2002), evaluations of the economy (see, e.g., Fiorina 1981; MacKuen, Erikson, and Stimson 1992), character assessments of candidates (see, e.g., Kinder 1986; Just et al. 1996), and ideology (see, e.g., Downs 1957; Hinich and Munger 1997). What has been missing from this literature, however, is a theory of how the human mind processes these factors—how it takes in information about these factors, combines it, and translates it into a judgment or choice.

The goal of political cognition is to fill these gaps in our knowledge. Electoral research has only scratched the surface of voter decision making. This may be sufficient to obtain adequate predictions of electoral outcomes, but it is not sufficient to understand those outcomes. Ultimately, electoral choices can only be grasped when we have good insights about the mental processes that lead to those choices.

Understanding these mental processes is also important from a normative perspective. Political theorists have sometimes posited an image of the citizen as a political animal who absorbs lots of political information, reasons carefully about political issues, and makes informed choices. A great deal of empirical evidence, however, calls into question both citizens' knowledge about politics and their motivation (Delli Carpini and Keeter 1996). One could use this evidence to support the assumption of certain elite theorists that most citizens are not capable of sound political judgment and that important decisions are therefore best left to a political elite (Schumpeter 1976). But this conclusion does not necessarily follow from the empirical evidence. If we understood better how citizens make decisions in the light of limited knowledge and motivation, as the cognitive approach tries to do, we may find that citizens are quite capable of sound judgment despite these limitations. Indeed, we shall see that a number of studies suggest this to be the case.

The task at hand, then, is to get inside voters' minds: we need to open the black box that transforms campaign stimuli into overt choices on election day. This means that we need to take account of the information-processing mechanisms that underlie voting behavior (Lodge, Stroh, and Wahlke 1990) because cognitive psychology has demonstrated powerfully that the connection between information and behavior lies in the mechanisms by which information is processed (see the reviews by Lachman, Lachman, and Butterfield 1979; Gardner 1985; Eysenck and Keane 1995). Thus, process is the ultimate focus of the cognitive approach to political behavior.

To political cognition, voting models that are not also information-processing models are at best incomplete and at worst misleading. Further progress in electoral research can be made only when our studies concentrate on developing psychologically realistic models of information processing during campaigns (and at other times). This premise forms the backdrop for the remainder of this chapter.

The Structural Model of the Mind

To understand information-processing theory, we need to understand the model of the mind that underlies it. Most cognitive models in political science posit a two-component architecture of the mind (see Lachman, Lachman, and Butterfield 1979; Gardner 1985; Sanford 1987; Eysenck and Keane 1995; Ottati and Wyer 1990; Lodge and Stroh 1993; Wyer and Ottati 1993; Lodge 1995). The first of these components is long-term memory (LTM), which stores our everyday knowledge about the world. The second component is working memory (WM), also known as short-term memory, which consists of the small part of LTM to which a person is consciously attending at a particular moment. The structural features of both components and the interplay between them determine in large part how information is processed.

Working Memory

In crude terms, working memory can be compared to random access memory (RAM) on a microcomputer.[2] Like RAM, WM serves two functions: (1) it is a temporary holding place for information that has been attended to; and (2) it is the place where operations on information are performed. Also similar to RAM, WM is rather limited, especially in comparison to LTM.

The limitations of WM are threefold. First, WM can hold only a limited amount of information. The magic number that is often given is 7 ± 2 bits or chunks of information (G. Miller 1956). Bits refer to discrete pieces of information, such as the digits of a telephone number. By combining these pieces into a package—a process called chunking—larger sets of information may be retained in WM. However, even in this case, the overall amount of information in WM remains small.

A second limitation of WM is that attention is serial. Once WM fills up, new information can enter only when an old piece of information is lost. This loss can be permanent (the information is forgotten) or temporary (the information is moved to LTM). Because of this serial nature of attention, the number of considerations in WM is likely to be small at any point in time. For example, it is unlikely that decision makers can attend to all aspects of a decision-making task at a particular point in time (Payne 1982).

Finally, the fixation rate in WM is slow. By this we mean that it takes a long time to transfer information from WM to LTM—perhaps eight to ten seconds to assemble information and store it as a new chunk (Simon 1978). This attribute, in combination with the serial processing attribute, implies that much information in WM is probably lost permanently, as it never makes it into LTM.

All of these limitations make WM the bottleneck of information processing. That is, most limitations in human information processing can be attributed to WM. In particular, the loss of information, breakdowns in operations performed on information, and incomplete processing of information can often be attributed to the structural features of WM.

This analysis of WM has important ramifications for the possibility for rational choice. Economic theory has handed us a decision-making model that postulates substantive rationality: decision makers make decisions according to a calculus that maximizes expected utility (Simon 1985). This model has guided much of electoral research, in particular spatial models of the vote (see Downs 1957; Davis, Hinich, and Ordeshook 1970; Hinich and Munger 1997).

From what we know about WM, however, it is questionable that people can live up to the decision calculus of rational choice. Optimization requires a complex set of operations, and it is not clear that WM can handle this. Instead, decision makers may only be able to satisfice—make a decision that is "good enough" (Simon 1959).[3] In doing so, decision makers look for procedures that can lead to reasonable, if not optimal, choices. Decision making, then, is procedurally rational but not substantively rational. Or, to put it in another way, decision making is characterized by bounded rationality (Simon 1985).[4]

Long-Term Memory

To understand LTM, we can invoke another computer analogy: LTM is similar to storage on a microcomputer—it is the place where information is kept. Information is moved back between LTM and WM just like it is moved between storage and RAM on a computer. And just as storage is organized in directories or folders, LTM is organized as well (see Judd and Krosnick 1989; McGraw and Steenbergen 1995; Rahn 1995).

There has been extensive debate about the nature of the organization of

LTM. Here we shall discuss the so-called associative network model, which has been widely accepted in the literature (J. Anderson 1983). Later we shall point to some alternative models as well.

Associative Network Model

The associative network model stipulates that LTM is organized in terms of a series of associations, involving concepts. These concepts are represented as nodes. These are connected to each other in a network of associations and by a simple mechanism, spreading activation, for transferring information from LTM to WM and back (Collins and Quillian 1969; Collins and Loftus 1975; J. Anderson 1983). Figure 4.1 illustrates these ideas through an associative network fragment from a hypothetical voter. This fragment contains four concepts—Clinton, Democrats, gun control, and scandal—that are represented as nodes by way of ellipses. Associations between the nodes—the links—are depicted through lines. Thus, there are associations between Clinton and Democrats, Clinton and gun control, Clinton and scandal, and Democrats and gun control.

In our associative network Clinton is the main node, the hub from which other nodes extend. This reflects our belief that in the context of elections (at least in the United States), associative networks tend to be candidate centered. This is consistent with social-psychological research on person perception (Sedikides and Ostrom 1988).[5]

In the associative network model, links represent beliefs. We can capture these links through statements of the form "I believe that NODE is/is not (favors/does not favor; involves/does not involve) OTHER NODE." As this semantic representation illustrates, nodes can be either positively linked (X is Y) or negatively linked (X is not Y). Figure 4.1 captures this through a series of positive and negative signs. Thus, our voter believes that Clinton is a Democrat, that Clinton favors gun control, and that Democrats favor gun control. However, our voter does not believe that Clinton is involved in a scandal.

Beliefs vary in their degree of certainty or confidence,[6] a feature represented in associative network models by the notion of belief strength, here denoted by the size of the plus and minus signs. Thus, the strongest belief of our voter is that Clinton is a Democrat, followed by the beliefs that Clinton favors gun control and that Democrats favor gun control. The weakest belief of the voter is that Clinton is not involved in scandals (i.e., the voter believes there is a good possibility that Clinton is involved).

Belief strength has implications for spreading activation. Spreading activation theory stipulates that nodes can be activated—that is, brought into WM—in two different ways. First, a node can be activated directly by referring to a concept. For example, the Clinton node may be activated when a news story

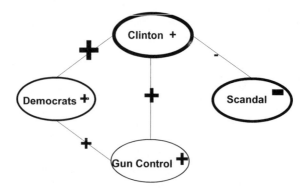

Fig. 4.1.   Illustration of an associative network model

contains the word *Clinton* in its headline. Second, a node can be activated because activation energy has spread from another node (Collins and Quillian 1969; Collins and Loftus 1975; J. Anderson 1983).

The more strongly two nodes are associated (i.e., the greater belief strength is), the greater the probability that activation of the first node will spread to the other node, thereupon increasing the probability that the belief will make its way into WM. In the case of our voter, a newspaper headline about Clinton will directly activate the Clinton node, which will spread a trickle of activation to the scandal node, more activation to the gun control node, and most activation to the Democrats node. Thus, our associative network fragment implies that the belief about Clinton's partisanship will spring to mind most quickly and effortlessly, as this is the voter's strongest belief. Barsalou (1992) shows that the activation threshold is almost instantaneous (on the order of 100–200 milliseconds).

Some nodes are more accessible than others—some are even "chronically accessible" (see Lau 1989; Iyengar 1990)—because they are more frequently thought about in the course of everyday information processing or have been thought about more recently. In our associative network architecture, we represent this residual impact of past activation as node strength, depicted here by the thickness of the ellipses that represent concepts. Node strength represents the accessibility of a node in LTM—that is, the ease with which a stored attribute can be retrieved from LTM. For our voter, Clinton has the greatest node strength, followed by scandal, Democrats, and gun control. The large node strengths of Clinton and scandals could result from the frequent discussion of these concepts in the media, from recent thought about these concepts, or from both.

Node strengths vary over time through a simple process. Node strengths increase as activation becomes more frequent and recent and weaken as activation becomes less frequent and more distant (J. Anderson 1983). Indeed, when nodes have not been activated for a long time, they lose all of their strength and may no longer be accessible. This is tantamount to saying that information has been forgotten from LTM.

At the time of this writing, the concepts *Clinton* and *scandal* were in the news often, so that both were activated frequently (and recently), leaving a large pocket of residual activation energy. Only a few years ago, Clinton's involvement with scandal received much less attention. At that time, the Brady Bill and gun control received greater priority in the media. Therefore, it is likely that the node strength for scandal would have been much weaker and that for gun control much stronger.

Most associative network models end with this discussion of the concepts of nodes, links, belief strengths, and node strengths. In our minds, however, one more concept is necessary to do justice to the way voters represent information about candidates and issues. That concept is affect. On the whole, cognitive models tend to be remarkably silent about the role of affect in memory representations. This poses no problem when the memory representation concerns concepts toward which a person feels neutral (cold cognition). Politics is qualitatively different. Citizens evaluate the concepts that enter their associative networks, such as candidates, groups, and issues. Indeed, citizens often feel very strong affect toward these objects, and this affect gives direction to their political behavior (Schwartz and Clore 1988; Abelson and Prentice 1989; Devine 1989; Pratkanis 1989; Kunda 1990, 1999; Damasio 1994; Fazio 1995; Schwartz 1998). Politics, then, is about "hot cognition"—cognition (beliefs) intertwined with affect (Abelson 1963; Zajonc 1980; Abelson and Prentice 1989).[7]

To integrate affect into the cognitive architecture, we posit that all nodes in memory are affectively charged (Sears, Huddy, and Schaffer 1986; Fazio 1995), some positively, others negatively, and some strongly, others weakly (see Lodge and Taber 2000). The affective tag is tied directly and inseparably to the concept node[8] and is represented in figure 4.1 with plus and minus signs at the nodes. Negative signs indicate negative affect, while positive signs indicate positive affect. The size of these signs represents the strength of the affect that is felt. In our example, affect toward Clinton is weakly positive, affect toward Democrats is moderately positive, affect toward gun control is strongly positive, and affect toward scandal is strongly negative.

The complete associative network, then, postulates that information is stored in LTM in the form of affective nodes of various strengths. Connections between those nodes represent beliefs of various strengths. By activating nodes, either directly or through spreading activation, stored information is transferred into WM. There it is operated on—perhaps updated with new information—before it is stored back into LTM.

Alternative Models of LTM

The associative network model is widely accepted, but several alternatives exist. One of these alternatives is connectionism, which shares many similarities with the associative network model. Connectionists view knowledge as a neural network of connections among nodes. Mental processes involve the activation of these connections, which occurs through a turnament (Fodor 1979). A political application of connectionist ideas can be found in Lupia and McCubbins (1998).

Second, we call attention to the bin model developed by Wyer and Srull (1986). This model postulates that information is organized in bins, each of which has a header denoting its contents. This header may carry an affective tag and forms the basis of memory searches. Within the bin, information is stored in layers, with newer information units deposited on top of older ones. The bin model has not found much application in political cognition (but see Ottati and Wyer 1990; Wyer and Ottati 1993), probably because associative network models provide a more parsimonious memory structure that appears to explain empirical patterns just as well or better than the bin model.

The best-known alternative is the schema concept, which was popular with psychologists and political scientists through the 1980s.[9] Schemata are broadly defined as organizational structures in memory (for a review, see Fiske and Taylor 1991), but beyond this broad definition there is little consensus (see Kuklinski, Luskin, and Bolland 1991). For example, the term *schema* has been used to refer to memory structures broadly or to specific structures pertaining to narratives or pictures (see Hastie 1981; Taylor and Crocker 1981). Because associative network models are defined much more precisely, they promise to provide a more attractive framework for electoral research.

Another memory structure is that of stories (Schank and Abelson 1995). The idea here is that information is packaged in narratives, rather than nodes and links. That is, people construct stories to interpret events and experiences, and these stories are stored into LTM as a single package. This idea has found some application in political science (see Cappella and Jamieson 1997), but its utility still has to be demonstrated in the context of electoral decision making. We are not convinced that the story concept cannot be broken down into nodes and links, with some nodes being episodic in nature. Neither are we convinced that larger, more comprehensive knowledge structures could not be treated more promisingly within McGuire and McGuire's (1991) thought-systems approach.

Stages of Informational Processing

Information processing is a dynamic process. To understand the cognitive approach, we need to understand something about the dynamics of information processing. It is common to conceive of four stages in information processing: (1) exposure and attention; (2) encoding; (3) evaluation; and (4) storage (see Ottati and Wyer 1990; Lodge and Stroh 1993; Wyer and Ottati 1993; Lodge 1995). We shall discuss each in turn.

Exposure and Attention

For information to play any role in political behavior, citizens need to be exposed and attend to it. That is, the information needs to make its way into WM. Thus, the first stage of information processing concerns exposure and attention, which drive the acquisition of information.[10]

Experimental Evidence Concerning Exposure and Attention

Because of the limitations of WM, citizens can attend only to a small subset of the information that is available at any given point in time. A lack of motivation can further curtail the amount of information that is attended to. Thus, the evidence suggests that citizens at best attend to a small portion of the available political information—exposure and attention are selective (Frey 1986; Iyengar 1990).

The best evidence concerning exposure and attention on political matters comes from experiments using information boards.[11] These boards show information about decision attributes (for example, issues) listed by decision alternatives (for example, candidates). The information is covered up, and participants in these experiments decide which information to uncover and consult (Herstein 1981). Sometimes a price is attached to uncovering the information, simulating information costs. At other times, the information search through the board is subject to time constraints, simulating the limited time span of events such as campaigns. For example, information may scroll by on a computer screen, giving experimental subjects only limited time to access this information (Lau and Redlawsk 1997).

Information board experiments have demonstrated that people typically access only a small portion of the information available to them (Herstein 1981, 1985; Lau 1995; Lau and Redlawsk 1997). For example, Herstein (1981) found that his experimental subjects often compared candidates on just a few attributes before making a vote choice (see also Lau 1995; Lau and Redlawsk 1997).

These findings have important implications for rational choice theory. While the finding of limited information acquisition is consistent with some versions of this theory (Lupia and McCubbins 1998), it poses a problem for versions that assume compensatory decision rules. With compensatory decision rules (such as the expected utility model) negative attributes of alternatives can be compensated by positive attributes (see, e.g., Fischer and Johnson 1986). But

such trade-offs are possible only when citizens collect information about multiple attributes for each alternative. The evidence suggests that most citizens do
not operate this way.

Determinants of Exposure and Attention

If attention is limited, as the evidence shows, then the next question becomes
what determines what people attend to. Although a wide range of determinants
of exposure and attention has been studied (for reviews see Wheeless and Cook
1985; Fiske and Taylor 1991), we will focus on those determinants that are politically the most relevant. In our view, there are three such determinants: attitude importance, the mass media, and motivated reasoning.

Attitude Importance.   People attend to what is important to them. For
example, a great deal of social-psychological evidence suggests that people
attend to others who are relevant to their situation (e.g., Erber and Fiske 1984).
Thus, political candidates who are perceived to be long shots may have a
difficult time capturing voters' attention simply because they are less likely to
affect voters' lives. In terms of issues, too, there is evidence that attention is a
function of importance. Converse (1964) suggested that different parts of the
American public attended to and were concerned about different issues. He
called these subsets of citizens "issue publics." Krosnick (1990) operationalized
the concept of issue publics in terms of personal attitude importance. He found
that the mass public is divided into different subgroups of people who differ in
the attitudes that are important to them. Moreover, important attitudes are
attended to in forming candidate evaluations (see also Krosnick 1988).

The Mass Media.   The role of the mass media in determining attention is
well established in research. As early as 1963, Cohen (1963) raised the possibility that the media may have a much greater impact on what issues the mass
public thinks about then on the opinions that people hold about those issues.
McCombs and Shaw (1972) developed this suggestion into a theory about
agenda setting that holds that the attention that people give to issues mirrors
the amount of attention that the media give to those issues. This effect was
demonstrated in survey data by Funkhouser (1973), who found that the attention paid by the national press to issues was reflected in the mass public's
assessment of the most important issues of the day. Iyengar and Kinder (1987)
analyzed the agenda-setting effect in a more rigorous experimental setting in
which they controlled how much emphasis different issues received. They also
found profound agenda-setting effects. However, at the same time, certain
issues were so important to the mass public that it was impossible to manipulate the amount of importance placed on them. One could say that these issues
were chronically important: citizens attended to them regardless of the amount
of media emphasis.

Motivated Reasoning.   Earlier we argued that political cognition is hot cognition: citizens often are emotionally invested in their opinions. This implies that citizens are motivated to hold on to their opinions (Kunda 1990, 1999; Lodge and Taber 2000; Taber and Lodge 2000). The implications this has for information acquisition have long preoccupied scholars.

The theory of motivated reasoning claims that people are goal-oriented information processors. Simplifying things considerably, motivations (goals) fall into two categories. First, information processing may be dominated by accuracy goals, which motivate an individual to reach a correct or otherwise optimal conclusion. Obtaining the truth is the ultimate goal in this "intuitive scientist" mode (Fiske and Taylor 1991; Baumeister and Newman 1994). Second, voters may pursue directional goals that motivate them to justify a specific, preselected conclusion (Kruglanski and Webster 1996). Thus, "partisanship" characterizes this mode of reasoning. In reality, people pursue both goals, but the relative weight of each may differ across situations and individuals. The partisan mode of information processing is likely to dominate when voters have a strong commitment to an opinion. Intuitive science is much more likely to take over when the personal consequences of an opinion, when acted on, are severe (Lodge and Taber 2000; Taber and Lodge 2000).

If citizens act in partisan mode, as we expect to be the case in politics quite frequently, they have every reason to expose themselves and attend to information selectively. Several studies suggest such a selective acquisition of information. For example, Lazarsfeld, Berelson, and Gaudet (1948) discussed how the impact of the 1944 presidential campaign was limited because voters selected information to reinforce their prior opinions (see also Barlett et al. 1974). Granberg (1971) found evidence that opponents of desegregation paid less attention to the media coverage of the assassination of Martin Luther King Jr. In a similar vein, Sweeney and Gruber (1984) discovered that supporters of Richard Nixon showed less interest in and paid less attention to coverage of the Watergate hearings in 1973, resulting in less knowledge about those hearings. Most recently, Taber and Lodge (2000) demonstrated a confirmation bias. In an experimental investigation concerning two political issues, affirmative action and gun control, they found that participants showed a tendency to seek out information from sources that would be likely to confirm the participants' prior opinion.

The theory of motivated reasoning, however, suggests that we should not always observe selective exposure and attention. Citizens are to some extent driven by accuracy goals, and such goals predict an even-handed search for information rather than a directional search.[12] Thus, information acquisition is driven in part by citizens' information-processing goals. While we are beginning to learn more about those goals (Kunda 1990, 1999; Lodge and Taber 2000; Taber and Lodge 2000), there is considerable room for further research in this area.[13]

Consequences of Exposure and Attention

The importance of exposure and attention lies in the gatekeeping role that they play. During the exposure/attention stage of information processing, the massive amount of political information that exists at any point in time is filtered out. Some information makes it into WM and can be processed further, but the majority of the information never makes it into WM and hence does not play a role in decision making. As one might imagine, the political consequences of this filtering effect can be enormous.

Interpretation and Encoding

Information is not by itself meaningful. Meaning derives from linking the information to existing knowledge, which has meaning to the decision maker. This linking process starts almost immediately on encountering information and guides attention. However, it comes into full force once information is in WM. At that point, an internal representation of the information is formed through a process called encoding. This process consists of two subprocesses, comprehension and elaborative reasoning.[14]

Comprehension

Comprehension means that semantic meaning can be given to the information. For example, to understand a news story about a political candidate, one needs first to understand the words. Such understanding comes from linguistic knowledge structures in LTM. These structures are generally applicable, as opposed to being specific to a particular object (e.g., the candidate in the news story). Comprehension is essential to information processing; if citizens attend to political information but fail to comprehend it, no impact of the information on political behavior can be expected (Hovland, Janis, and Kelley 1953; Zaller 1992).

Elaborative Reasoning

Elaborative reasoning also involves the use of old information in LTM, but this information is specific to the object of the information. For example, on reading a story about Clinton, our hypothetical voter depicted in figure 4.1 would download nodes from her associative network for Clinton. The information in the story would then be linked to this existing information. Which nodes will make it into WM at the encoding stage depends on the nature of spreading activation, a topic we discussed earlier. The important point is that new information is integrated with old information to form a new knowledge structure.

The Role of Recognition

The encoding process can be very fast and automatic (Bargh 1997) or very slow and deliberative. Which of these processes unfolds depends a lot on the familiarity of the information object. The more familiar the object is, the better developed the knowledge structure for that object is, and the easier it is to encode new information about the object.

We can illustrate the importance of recognition by considering a primary election that involves a relatively large field of candidates. Most voters can recognize some of these candidates, but few can recognize all of them. For example, in the 1996 Republican primaries, Dole, Gramm, and Buchanan were relatively well known candidates, while Keyes was hardly recognized at all (except perhaps by voters from the Religious Right). Here, recognition means that the candidate and his or her features map onto an existing knowledge structure for that candidate, however sparse that structure may be. If such a knowledge structure exists, one or more nodes in it are activated and become available in WM for the encoding of new information. Recognition is an automatic, unconscious process that occurs very fast, usually in a split second (Neely 1977). It is usually unambiguous: mapping occurs onto only one knowledge structure. Thus, in the context of the 1996 elections, most voters would recognize the name Dole as a presidential candidate, not as a brand of bananas. And on recognition, they would use prior knowledge about Dole to make sense of incoming information about him.

When recognition fails, as was the case for most voters with Keyes in 1996, two alternative routes of encoding are possible (aside from discarding the information). First, a voter may try to map a candidate's features onto another knowledge structure that is available in LTM. For example, the voter may have recognized Keyes's partisan label. This would have caused the categorization of Keyes as an instance (exemplar) of the label *Republican*. Alternatively, the voter may choose to build a memory representation for the candidate from scratch (see Fiske and Pavelchak 1986; Fiske and Ruscher 1989; Fiske and Neuberg 1990; Lodge and Stroh 1993).[15]

The first scenario is referred to as labeling or as stereotyping (Lodge and Stroh 1993). Instead of developing a personalized memory structure for an object (e.g., candidate), the object is seen as an example of a broader category (e.g., Republican). Features of this category become associated with the candidate, even if the candidate does not possess these features. For example, the category *Republican* may be linked (stereotypically) to the category *white*. Consequently, the voter might infer from the categorization of Keyes as a Republican that this candidate is white. While this inference is obviously incorrect, there is evidence that labeling is an automatic process and that it requires cognitive effort to correct stereotypes (Devine 1989; Blair and Banaji 1996).[16]

Categorization may be adequate for disinterested citizens, but it is probably not for those who take campaigns seriously or those who are driven by accuracy goals. These citizens are motivated to build a memory structure for the previously unknown object (i.e., candidate), a process that is sometimes referred to as personalization (Lodge and Stroh 1993) or individuation (Fiske and Neuberg 1988). Developing this memory structure is effortful: it requires piecemeal information processing, whereby the citizen builds a candidate knowledge structure attribute by attribute. Voters generally make this effort only if categorization fails and if they are highly motivated (Fiske and Pavelchak 1986; Fiske and Neuberg 1988; Fiske and Ruscher 1989; Lodge and Stroh 1993).

Consequences of Encoding

Encoding is arguably the most important stage of information processing. There are two reasons for this. First, the gatekeeping process, which begins with exposure and attention, continues in the encoding stage. Information that cannot be comprehended or recognized may well be discarded. Second, and more important, during encoding, information inputs are transformed. Elaborative reasoning implies that information is actively processed and manipulated. Information is linked to prior knowledge and is absorbed into a new knowledge structure. Aspects of the information inputs that do not fit into this structure may be discarded. Remaining knowledge gaps may be filled through inferences. Thus, the end product of elaborative reasoning may look little like the information inputs at the beginning of this process. Moreover, interindividual differences in encoding imply that the same set of information inputs can lead to very different knowledge structures for different people. Ultimately, these knowledge structures, rather than the original information inputs, influence decision making. For this reason, understanding encoding is of great importance to understanding candidate evaluation and public opinion.

Evaluation

The third stage of information processing is evaluation. In many ways, this is the most controversial stage; it may also be the least well-understood stage. Leaving aside for now the controversy, to which we shall return later in the chapter, let us sketch briefly what is known about evaluation.

To understand evaluation, we need to know the answers to three questions. First, how do citizens evaluate the attributes of evaluation targets (e.g., candidates)? Second, how do they integrate these attribute evaluations into an overall evaluation of the target? Finally, is this overall evaluation made in terms of a trade-off between likes and dislikes, or is it made on separate dimensions for likes and dislikes? For example, imagine a voter who receives the following headline: "Despite Booming Economy, Scandal Jeopardizes Clinton." How should the voter use this headline to form (or update) an evaluation of Clinton? She could transfer the affect associated with "booming economy" and "scandal" to Clinton. But this raises further questions: (1) What determines the affect toward these attributes? (2) How should these attributes be integrated into an overall evaluation of Clinton? (3) Does the voter make a trade-off between her likes and dislikes of Clinton, or does she use both of these evaluative dimensions separately?

Evaluating Attributes

Very little is known about the way in which people evaluate attributes, but recent work by Brendl and Higgins (1996) holds a great deal of promise. These authors propose four valence mechanisms, all of which have clear political relevance. First, valence can be informed by goal supportiveness. Attributes that promote a voter's goals are positively valued, whereas attributes that are inconsistent with those goals are negatively valued. Goal supportiveness is the valence mechanism that rational choice theorists propose, although they cast it in utilitarian terms (Downs 1957; Hinich and Munger 1997). In the preceding example, it is plausible that goal supportiveness would drive the valence placed on the state of the economy.

Second, referential status can inform valence: does an attribute put a person in the domain of losses or in the domain of gains relative to some reference point? Attributes that result in gains are positively valued, while attributes that result in losses are negatively valued. This valence criterion plays a central role in prospect theory, which further predicts that negative valences carry more weight than positive valences (Kahneman and Tversky 1979, Tversky and Kahneman 1992). Referential status, too, gives a plausible explanation for the evaluation of the state of the economy.

A third criterion for valence involves a conditioning process similar to that proposed by behaviorism. A neutral attribute is paired with a stimulus of strong valence and gradually absorbs the valence of that stimulus. The negative valence that most people accord to scandal may well derive from such a process.

Finally, people may determine the valence of an attribute by considering society's reaction to certain outcomes. For example, by monitoring the collective disdain for scandals, a citizen would infer that scandals are bad. She would accept as her own the reactions of others.

As far as we know, these valence criteria have not yet been systematically researched in the political domain, especially not in electoral research.[17] Most political scientists are satisfied with recording how a person values certain attributes. Where those evaluations come from is deemed less interesting from a political point of view. However, we believe that knowing where attribute

evaluations come from is of great political importance because such evaluations can be manipulated by politicians, for example through framing (see
Kinder and Sanders 1990).

Information Integration

Once the attributes of alternatives have valences, they need to be integrated
into an overall evaluation. In the domain of candidate evaluations, political scientists have modeled this process of information integration mostly in terms of
a weighted additive model. This model expresses the evaluations of alternatives
as a weighted sum of their attribute valences:

$$E = \sum_j w_j v_j .$$

Here E is the overall evaluation of an alternative (i.e., candidate); w_j is the
weight (e.g., importance) of an attribute, j, of the alternative; and v_j is the
valence of this attribute. The weighted additive model can be found, for example, in spatial theories of voting behavior (Davis, Hinich, and Ordeshook 1970).

From a normative perspective, the weighted additive model is attractive
because it captures optimal decision making: in theory, no other decision rule
performs better (Payne, Bettman, and Johnson 1988). Nonetheless, the model
has been subject to severe criticisms. Not only is it very demanding of citizens
(exceeding WM constraints), it also ignores important phenomena like infor-
mation-order effects (J. Anderson 1983; N. Anderson 1981). Alternative models,
such as Norman Anderson's (1991) information-integration theory, are better
equipped to deal with information sequence.

To date, few tests in political science compare the weighted additive model
with plausible alternatives. An exception is Taber and Steenbergen's (1995)
analysis of the predictive power of various information-integration rules. The
authors collected evaluations and importance ratings for a wide range of issues
in a pretest. A subset of these issues was presented as candidate attributes in an
experiment that manipulated information load and was conducted on the participants from the pretest. At the end of the experiment, the participants were
asked to evaluate the candidates and choose between them. Taber and Steenbergen contrasted these evaluations and choices with ones that were derived
from different simulated information-integration rules. These rules included
both noncompensatory models (such as models in which voters consider only
the candidate attribute that is most important to them) as well as complex
sequential rules.

Taber and Steenbergen found few differences between the rules' ability to
predict the participants' candidate evaluations and choices. In fact, simpler

decision rules typically performed very well, suggesting that citizens can make good choices without the elaborate decision calculus of the weighted additive rule (for a similar point see Lau and Redlawsk 1997). However, further research is needed to disentangle the precise conditions under which different information-integration rules display convergent and divergent behavior.

One or Two Dimensions of Evaluation?

Most political science models assume that voters evaluate candidates on a single like-dislike dimension. Of necessity this implies that voters make trade-offs in candidate evaluation: an increase in the likes for a political candidate means that there is a corresponding decrease in the dislikes. As a voter moves toward one pole of the evaluative continuum, she necessarily moves away from the other pole.

Recent research in social psychology, however, calls this conventional wisdom into question. This research argues that evaluations are made in a bidimensional space that is formed by positivity and negativity dimensions. The positivity dimension indicates likes for an attitude object, while the negativity dimension captures dislikes toward this object (see Cacioppo and Berntson 1994; Cacioppo, Gardner, and Berntson 1997). These dimensions are not perfectly correlated, as traditional theories of candidate evaluation assume. On the contrary, these dimensions may be perfectly orthogonal.

An important implication of this theory is that voters can be ambivalent about their candidate evaluation (Cacioppo and Berntson 1994; Thompson, Zanna, and Griffin 1995; Priester and Petty 1996; Tesser and Martin 1996; Cacioppo, Gardner, and Berntson 1997; Lavine 2001; Lavine et al. 1998). That is, a candidate may simultaneously score high on the positivity dimension and high on the negativity dimension. For example, when reading the headline described earlier in this section, our hypothetical voter may increase her likes for Clinton because of the booming economy but at the same time increase her dislikes for the president because of the mention of scandals.

Meffert, Guge, and Lodge (2000) found considerable evidence for ambivalence in candidate evaluation. For example, in 1996 48.9 percent of the ANES respondents were found to be indifferent toward Clinton in that they listed both likes and dislikes for the president as well as positive and negative emotional reactions. Considering all presidential elections since 1980, ambivalence ranged between a low of 29.2 percent (Mondale in 1984) and a high of 56.9 percent (Bush in 1992).

Ambivalence in candidate evaluation has important consequences. Meffert, Guge, and Lodge found that ambivalent ANES respondents gave less extreme feeling thermometer ratings for candidates and were more wavering in their approval of the president. At the same time, ambivalent respondents were more accurate in their placement of candidates on the issues, even after controlling for political knowledge. Other studies have found that ambivalence is associated with a delay in the formation of a vote intention, with a weaker correlation between vote intention and vote choice, and with a reduced predictability of candidate evaluation from candidate traits and issues (Lavine 2001). In addition, work by Alvarez and Brehm (1995) shows that ambivalence may lead to greater variability in the survey response.[18]

In our view, the idea that candidate evaluations are bidimensional is intriguing and deserves further exploration. Important questions remain. To what extent does the finding of ambivalence depend on the way in which ambivalence is measured? Under what circumstances can ambivalence be increased or decreased? What are the psychological characteristics of ambivalent and nonambivalent people? The answer to these questions will help us better understand the nature of candidate evaluation.

Storage and Retrieval

The final stages in the information-processing sequence are storage and retrieval. At the storage stage, encoded information and any evaluations that have been made are transferred from WM into LTM. This process is subject to the slow fixation rate of WM, so not all encoded information will make it into LTM. At the retrieval stage, the reverse process takes place: information is transferred from LTM to WM, perhaps as part of the encoding process.

We have described the most important characteristics of storage in our discussion of LTM. We should say a little more about retrieval, however. One of the most important questions about the retrieval stage in social and political cognition has been whether memory is selective. Specifically, is it easier for people to remember information that is consistent with expectations or evaluations? A series of studies in social psychology suggests that this is the case (Higgins and Bargh 1987; Stangor and McMillan 1992; Olson, Roese, and Zanna 1996). However, memory for consistent information is improved only when certain conditions are in place. First, it occurs only when an impression of a target has been formed (or else, the whole idea of consistency becomes questionable). Second, it occurs mostly when accuracy goals take second place to partisan goals (Higgins and Bargh 1987; Stangor and McMillan 1992). We suspect that both of these conditions are satisfied quite often in the electoral arena.

Selective memory has important political implications. Klayman and Ha (1987) found that increased memorability of consistent information causes people to exaggerate the extent to which their beliefs and opinions are supported by information. This may lead to a false sense of confidence and a corresponding reduction of ambivalence, both of which may cause more extreme and polarized attitudes.

Influences on Information Processing

There are important individual and contextual differences in the nature of information processing. Four factors have a particularly strong influence on political cognition: (1) motivation, (2) importance, (3) political sophistication, and (4) information-presentation effects. We shall briefly comment on current insights about each.

Information processing can be quite effortful. Motivated decision makers are likely to make this effort, but unmotivated decision makers are likely to look for shortcuts (Petty and Cacioppo 1986; Ottati 1990; Popkin 1994). In elections, a first shortcut would be to make a quick judgment of the relevance of a candidate to the voter. If the candidate is deemed irrelevant, then the voter can stop further information processing (Fiske and Ruscher 1989). If the candidate is relevant, then further processing will take place. This processing may be subject to further shortcuts. For example, when recognition of a candidate fails, unmotivated voters may opt for labeling instead of personalization, because the latter is much more effortful (Lodge and Stroh 1993). These voters may also come to rely more on inference than on information acquisition. That is, when confronted with new information, uninterested voters may forgo careful processing of the information and infer the information contents instead (Hamill, Lodge, and Blake 1985; Conover and Feldman 1986; Popkin 1994). Alternatively, these voters may rely on opinion leaders to obtain the gist of information rather than processing the information themselves (Lazarsfeld, Berelson, and Gaudet 1948; Popkin 1994; Zaller 1992; Lupia and McCubbins 1998).

Motivation often means that a citizen deems the issues at hand as important. A large body of research by Krosnick and others reveals that importance has strong effects on information processing. Judd and Krosnick (1989) reasoned that importance is reflected in node strengths and that stronger nodes tend to also be evaluatively more consistent. Berent and Krosnick (1995) show that LTM is better organized when information is considered personally important then when it is considered unimportant. Perhaps as a consequence of this, Berent (1990) found that recall and recognition of information relevant to important attitudes was better than that for unimportant attitudes. There also is evidence that recall was more accurate for information related to important attitudes. Finally, the priming literature suggests that candidate evaluations tend to be influenced most by those considerations that are most important, perhaps as a consequence of media emphasis (Iyengar and Kinder 1987; J. Miller and Krosnick 2000).

Aside from motivation, political sophistication—often measured as information (Zaller 1992)—is an important determinant of information processing. Work by Fiske, Kinder, and Larter (1981) and Judd and Krosnick (1989) shows that sophisticates recognize many more political objects than do nonsophisticates and have more elaborate memory structures. McGraw and Steenbergen (1995) find evidence that information is organized differently in LTM for sophisticates and nonsophisticates. In an experiment in which information about a candidate's personal attributes and issue stances were offered, all participants showed a greater proclivity for memory organization by personal attributes. However, sophisticates showed a significantly greater proclivity to do so than did nonsophisticates, who showed a greater tendency toward evaluative memory organization, with likes being grouped together and dislikes being grouped together. These results about involvement and expertise can be understood in terms of depth of processing (Craik and Lockhart 1972), with motivated and sophisticated voters processing information more deeply than their less motivated and less sophisticated brethren. The consequence is more elaborated memory structures that produce better recall and recognition.[19]

Depth of processing is not the only influence on information processing, however. The information environment also influences the nature of information processing. Rahn (1995) has done important work to show these effects. In several experiments, she manipulated how candidate information was presented. In some experimental conditions, subjects were exposed to all information about a candidate before moving on to the next candidate. In other conditions, subjects received information about multiple candidates for a single attribute. Rahn observed that memory organization was more person focused in the first condition and more attribute focused in the second condition. This finding contrasts with our earlier assumption that campaign information is structured around candidate nodes. However, a limitation of Rahn's work—as well as our own (McGraw and Steenbergen 1995)—is that she only investigated memory organization in terms of a single organizing dimension. We cannot eliminate the possibility that memory is organized multidimensionally, perhaps in terms of attributes within candidates (see Buschke 1977).

In sum, while the basics of information processing are probably universal, there is considerable variation in how these basics play out. A lot of progress has been made in terms of understanding individual differences in information processing. Much less is known about contextual differences, although Rahn's works serve as a promising starting point.

Conclusion

Our discussion so far has uncovered the information-processing framework that underlies political cognition. We have tried to give an evenhanded treatment of this framework, but we have also pointed to our own theoretical beliefs. By now it should be obvious that there have been heated debates about the nature of information processing despite general consensus about the terms of the information-processing framework. These debates have been particularly vehement in electoral research. It is time, then, to consider in more detail how political scientists have used information processing to analyze electoral choice.

Modeling Candidate Evaluation

Information processing is an important element of several theories about candidate evaluation. We can divide these theories into three groups: (1) memory-based models, (2) the on-line model, and (3) hybrid models. These groups are distinctive in terms of their assumptions about the evaluation and storage stages of information processing. The resulting views of the way in which voters make candidate evaluations are very different.

Memory-Based Models

Memory-based models of candidate evaluation stipulate that citizens base their candidate evaluations on the facts, figures, and attributes they can recall from LTM. These considerations are then integrated into an evaluation of the candidate. This integration process is held in abeyance until an evaluation is called for (e.g., on election day).

The classical statement of a memory-based model is Kelley and Mirer's (1974) article about the simple act of voting. Their model holds that voters recall their likes and dislikes for each of the candidates. The likes are weighted equally and added, as are the dislikes. The dislike count is then subtracted from the like count to form a net likability score—the overall evaluation of the candidate. Finally, a vote is cast for the candidate with the highest net likability score. If there is a tie, voters use partisanship to inform their vote choice (see also Kelley 1983).

While Kelley and Mirer may have presented the purest statement of the memory-based model, other theories are based on a similar logic. For example, empirical tests of spatial models of the vote choice often rely on recall (e.g., Westholm 1997). The question is what assumptions do we have to make about information processing to believe these theories?

Information-Processing Mechanism

The memory-based model implies that evaluation can be delayed. In particular, the evaluation of candidates does not take place automatically, immediately on encoding. Rather, if we accept the idea of candidate-centered memory representations—an assumption with which some memory-based theories would take issue—the candidate is stored as a node without affect. This node is associated with other nodes representing attributes that have been associated with the candidate. These nodes carry valence or at least their valence can be easily

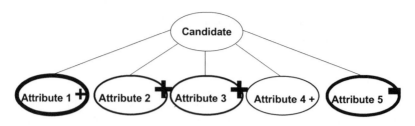

Fig. 4.2.   Memory organization under memory-based processing

inferred. A schematic presentation of the structure of LTM can be found in figure 4.2.[20]

In this figure, the affect-free candidate node has several attribute nodes associated with it. The links indicate that these attribute nodes have relevance to the candidate. The nodes in figure 4.2 vary in strength. Typically, we expect the candidate node to be relatively weak, as citizens may not do most of their information processing in terms of the candidate.

Notice that we sketch a situation in which the attribute nodes have affect associated with them, much as Kelley and Mirer (1974) suggested. However, it is sufficient to assume that affect for the attribute nodes can be easily inferred. Thus, under memory-based processing assumptions, the entire memory structure for the candidate may initially be without affect.

Candidate evaluation takes place by recalling the attribute nodes from LTM. Voters then infer affect from these nodes. That is, on recognition of the candidate's name, associations are downloaded into WM when an evaluation or choice is called for. These nodes, a mixture of positive and negative considerations, are only now integrated into a summary evaluation following one or another information-integration rule. We do not expect the downloaded nodes to capture everything a voter knows about the candidate. The limitations of WM usually preclude this. So does the typically low level of voter motivation, which promotes top-of-the head responses. Thus, the downloaded nodes are best viewed as a possibly biased sample of considerations (Zaller 1992; Zaller and Feldman 1992).

Which attribute nodes make it into working memory depends on several factors. First, some nodes may have been activated in the recent past, making it more likely for them to be reactivated. The same holds true for frequently accessed nodes. However, it is also possible that certain nodes are activated because of immediately salient stimulus cues. For example, a survey question can be framed to tap certain nodes. Or the person who asks the question can cause certain nodes to fire (interviewer race and gender effects). The impact of these cues on evaluation is discussed by Zaller and Feldman (1992) and Feldman (1995).

The memory model that we have presented is consistent with the model presented by Zaller (1992; Zaller and Feldman 1992). Zaller speaks of opinions as distributions of considerations or, in our words, bundles of attribute nodes that carry different affective tags over which a distribution can be defined. Sampling from this distribution allows the voter to construct and report an opinion. The sampling could be performed at random but is more likely to be biased in favor of frequently or recently accessed nodes or of nodes that have been triggered by cues. The impact of new information in memory-based models depends on the number of considerations the voter brings to mind. The greater the number of considerations, the less weight new information will carry in shaping opinions. This means that sophisticates will generally display the least sensitivity to new information and consequently the greatest stability in their responses. Nonsophisticates will be considerably more sensitive to new information, but only if they are capable of processing that information (Zaller 1992; Zaller and Feldman 1992).

In sum, the memory-based model suggests that voters store candidate attributes, which they integrate into candidate evaluations after recall. Recall can be selective and influenced by cues. Moreover, new information may be combined with old information at the time of evaluation. This new information is then likely to be stored along with old information in LTM.

Evidence Concerning Memory-Based Models

What is the evidence in support of memory-based processing? One way to answer this question is to look at the predictive power of memory-based models. By this standard, these models perform very well. For example, Kelley and Mirer (1974) report accuracies of the vote prediction between 86.5 and 90.7 percent. This is quite typical of similar results reported for other memory-based models (see Kelley 1983).

There are problems with assessing the predictive power of memory-based models, however. First, high predictive power is typically achieved only with survey data. Experiments, in which the researcher controls what subjects know and learn about the target person, usually show that the model fares poorly (see Lodge, McGraw, and Stroh 1989). Second, and more troubling, the direction of causality in memory-based models is unclear given the lack of control over the judge's prior knowledge. These models postulate that evaluation follows recall. However, when tested with survey data, it is not at all clear whether evaluation truly follows or precedes recall.

Several studies have studied the direction of causality between recall and evaluation. One argument is that memory is in large part reconstructed: after voters evaluate a candidate, they will reconstruct a rationalization when called on to justify their judgment, for example in a survey question that asks about the likes and dislikes for a candidate (Lodge and Stroh 1993).[21] If this argument is true, the causal arrow should flow from candidate evaluation to recall, not the other way around, as memory-based models suggest. Indeed, using survey data from a panel in Ohio, Rahn, Krosnick, and Breuning (1994) found that voters often report reasons for their vote choice that are rationalizations rather than the true reasons behind their behavior. Lodge, Steenbergen, and Brau (1995) found similar results in an experimental investigation of candidate evaluation. They observed some residual impact of recall on candidate evaluation, but this effect was relatively small and did not produce the kind of predictive power for memory-based processing that is usually reported.

These results call into question how well memory-based models really predict. But perhaps questions about predictive power are misguided. Maybe we should ask about the explanatory power of memory-based models: how plausible is their account of political information processing, and how well can they accommodate empirical patterns?

To start with the second question, memory-based models are quite successful in accounting for many empirical patterns that we observe in surveys. Question wording and question order effects are easily accommodated in these models, as are interviewer effects and response instability. These can all be seen as influences on the sampling process of considerations, and they can be built into a model of the survey response (Zaller and Feldman 1992; Feldman 1995).

The first question, however, renders memory-based models problematic. How plausible is it that voters delay candidate evaluation when they know all along in an election that they will soon have to evaluate the candidate? How plausible is it to assume that the affect associated with attribute nodes does not flow to the candidate node at some point before election day? How likely is it that voters will engage in memory-based processing, which is often viewed as more effortful (Kitayama and Burnstein 1989), when we know that they typically have low levels of motivation? Is it realistic to assume that people construct opinions over and over again by sampling from a distribution of considerations? Why would not they use a previous evaluation instead? In our mind, memory-based models do not provide a satisfactory answer to these questions. The question is, then, what alternative models exist.

The On-Line Model

The on-line model—also known as the impression-driven model—finds its roots in the person-perception literature in social cognition. In that literature, researchers have often observed that the correlation between recalled attributes of a person and the evaluation of that person is low. This suggests that memory-based information processing may not drive impression formation.

Instead, information often affects impressions directly, without mediation by recall or recognition (Hastie and Park 1986; M. Brewer 1988).[22]

Information can have a direct effect on impressions only if its valence is assessed immediately, at the time of encoding or very shortly thereafter. Decision makers cull the affect of information as they encounter it and use it to form or update an impression of the target person. Thus, the target (node) has an affective tag attached to it—the so-called on-line tally—that is updated immediately as new information becomes available (Lodge and Taber 2000). One can think of this on-line tally as an implicit attitude (see Betsch et al. 2001).

The on-line model has found application in the domain of voting behavior through our own work (Lodge, McGraw, and Stroh 1989; Lodge, Steenbergen, and Brau 1995). The premise of this work is that forming impressions about candidates is not fundamentally different from forming impressions about other social targets. Thus, people can use the same processing mechanisms for the evaluation of political candidates that they would use for the evaluation of people, be they friends, job candidates, potential spouses. An unresolved issue is whether the same mechanism applies to groups, places, things, and issues (Zaller 1992).

Information-Processing Mechanism

The critical assumption of the on-line model is that voters typically do not and usually cannot delay evaluation. The moment they have completed encoding of candidate-relevant information, they immediately derive the affective implications of the information and use it to infer an evaluation of the candidate. This evaluation is stored as part of the candidate node and is inseparable from the candidate. Thus, evaluation precedes storage in the on-line model.

The information inputs that were encoded are stored as part of the memory representation of the candidate. This information is captured in attribute nodes, similar to what we have described for memory-based models. However, the linkage of the attribute nodes to the candidate node is subject to a different set of dynamics in the on-line model. Since evaluation is immediate in on-line processing, cognitive consistency becomes an important consideration. Imagine that the voter holds a mixture of positive and negative attribute nodes. Under memory-based processing, this poses no consistency problems, because evaluation of the candidate is delayed. Under on-line processing, however, either the positives or the negatives will conflict with the candidate evaluation. For example, when the overall impression is positive, then the negative attribute nodes are inconsistent with that impression. The result is cognitive dissonance.

The on-line model that we developed assumes a dynamic process of dissonance reduction that is not relevant in the context of memory-based information processing. Several mechanisms are at work in this process. First, consistent attribute nodes may be more closely connected to the candidate node than are inconsistent attribute nodes, making it easier to recall the consistent nodes than the inconsistent nodes, especially under time constraints on recall (Kitayama and Burnstein 1989). This is in keeping with the finding of selective memory effects discussed earlier. Consequently, we propose that attitude-consistent attribute nodes are more strongly connected to the candidate node than are inconsistent attribute nodes. Second, voters may relieve inconsistencies between the valences of the attribute nodes and the candidate nodes by adding rationalizations to the associative network for the candidate. We shall return to this topic shortly.

The top panel of figure 4.3 shows an example of the memory representation for a candidate after on-line impression formation. The favored status of consistent information is reflected in the strength of the links. The candidate node now has affect and is among the strongest nodes in the associative network. This is because the candidate takes a central place in the voter's mind, a target that is continuously recalled when new information becomes available for processing.

Once established, the on-line tally becomes an important determinant of subsequent information processing. We call the mechanism by which this occurs the "how do I feel?" heuristic (Schwartz and Clore 1988). This heuristic captures the on-line tally from memory without having to access the considerations that originally entered into the evaluation. Consequently, the voter is continuously informed about how much she likes the candidate. This heuristic is both a virtue and a vice (Clore and Isbell 2001). On the one hand, reliance on the on-line tally allows one to avoid the more cognitively taxing task of constructing a judgment from whatever evidence is available in memory (Kitayama and Burnstein 1989). On the other hand, the same mechanisms that bring the on-line tally to mind and thereby promise reasonable, experience-based evaluations are very likely to bias the processing of new information, since voters know how much they like or dislike the political object at the moment they are evaluating the new evidence and also know whether a piece of tally-relevant information is pro or con.

Because the on-line tally drives so much of information processing, memory representation will undergo considerable change over time. There are three types of change. First, when new information becomes available, it has the potential to change the affective tag associated with the candidate, especially when the information supports the on-line tally. In addition, this information is likely to be stored in the associative network for the candidate.

Second, new information is processed by recalling the candidate node but not necessarily by recalling any of the attribute nodes representing old information. This means that many of these attribute nodes will not be accessed frequently. Over time, then, their strength will fade, and they ultimately may

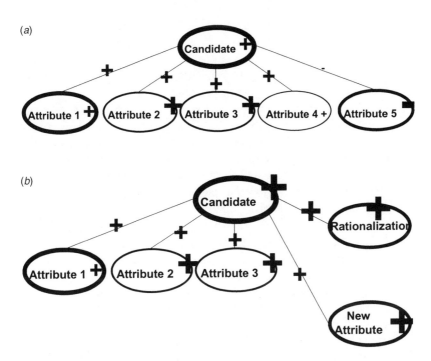

Fig. 4.3. Memory organization under on-line processing: (*a*) memory structure at *t*, (*b*) memory structure at *t* + 1.

become detached from the candidate node. In this case, they can no longer be recalled as part of the memory structure for the candidate (Lodge, Steenbergen, and Brau 1995). This is the likely fate of many attribute nodes, so we believe that the number of attribute nodes under on-line processing is relatively small. The first nodes to disappear are those with low initial strength and those that are only loosely connected to the candidate node.

Finally, it is possible that voters construct rationalizations for their impressions of candidates. These rationalizations are supporting reasons for liking or disliking a candidate drawn from LTM, but not the actual reasons that initially influenced candidate evaluation. They may be stored in LTM along with the information on which the impressions are based (Lodge and Stroh 1993). Rationalization provides further protection against cognitive dissonance and is very common (Lodge, Steenbergen, and Brau 1995; Rahn, Krosnick, and Breuning 1994). Because rationalizations require a lot of elaborative reasoning, their connection to the candidate node is likely to be particularly strong.

The bottom panel of figure 4.3 illustrates these changes to the associative network. One attribute node (attribute 5) has disappeared, probably because of its inconsistency with the on-line tally. New consistent information has been added to the network, and the positive affect of this node is one reason why the on-line tally of the candidate has become stronger. The figure also shows the addition of a rationalization that is strongly associated with the candidate node. This rationalization, too, may have bolstered the on-line tally.

In sum, the on-line model postulates that voters evaluate candidates on the fly, as voters are exposed to information. They store their impressions of candidates in an on-line tally attached directly to a candidate node. Along with that node, some of the information may be stored in the form of attribute nodes. However, these nodes are usually not accessed often—especially when they are inconsistent nodes—so that they may decay quite rapidly. In their place may come rationalizations, which are particularly likely to emerge when voters have the expectation that they may have to defend their impression at some time in the future (Lodge and Stroh 1993).

Evidence Concerning the On-Line Model

The on-line model has found considerable support in experimental research. The on-line tally proves to be a better summary of a voter's past evaluative experiences than are preferences based on the recollection of pros and cons that come to mind on the spur of the moment (Lodge, McGraw, and Stroh 1989; Sanbonmatsu and Fazio 1990; Lodge, Steenbergen, and Brau 1995) or, worse yet, evaluations based on the reasons people give when they are asked explicitly why they like or dislike some person, place, or thing (Wilson and Hodges 1992). In an experimental setting, then, on-line processing appears to provide a good account of the formation of impressions of candidates (but see Redlawsk 2001).

The specific predictions of the on-line model are also supported handsomely by the experiments. Our own experimental evidence reveals a great deal of rationalization. It also shows that the nodes for old information decay very quickly, the half-life for recall being less than one week (Lodge, Steenbergen, and Brau 1995).[23]

Conversely, the experiments suffer from limitations. One shortcoming is that they are rarely concerned with the type of election that engages Americans. In most cases, the experiments have focused on one or two candidates about whom voters received limited information in a single shot. As our critics have been quick to point out, this may be a good model of elections someplace in the world, but one may wonder legitimately whether the experiments can be generalized to the information-rich context of U.S. presidential or congressional elections, where, for example, voters are inundated with redundant information over the course of weeks rather than a single forty-five-minute or so session.

In defense of the experimental evidence, we argue that the on-line model has found support in other analyses (see Graber 1984). We think there is room for improvement in the experiments, but we believe they have uncovered real empirical patterns, as evidenced by the fact that we have replicated our basic findings in several other studies. On a more general note, experimentation is probably the only way in which the on-line model can be tested. Because it is important to separate rationalizations from other nodes in memory, it becomes essential to use hypothetical candidates about whom experimental subjects do not know anything prior to the experiment. Only in this case can we be sure that memory-based explanations are tested fairly instead of receiving the benefit of rationalization.

Hybrid Models

As the review so far suggests, the differences between memory-based and on-line models of candidate evaluations are vast. Nonetheless, several scholars have made attempts at joining the on-line model with aspects of memory-based processing. This work presents an interesting synthesis of different processing modes that warrants further investigation.

Saris's Modified On-Line Model

One shortcoming of the on-line model is that it cannot easily accommodate response effects in surveys. When a voter is asked whether she likes or dislikes a candidate, the on-line model predicts that the voter retrieves the on-line tally from LTM and translates this into a survey response. While there is room for unsystematic measurement error in this translation process, it is harder to explain why the voter would be influenced by such systematic factors as the interviewer, question wording, or question order. Nonetheless, we know that these factors are influential in surveys.

To accommodate response effects, Saris (1997) has proposed a modified version of the on-line model. In this model, a person's evaluation of the candidate is based not solely on the on-line tally, as we have assumed so far. Instead, this evaluation is the product of the on-line tally plus any immediate cues provided by the survey. These cues are stored in WM and may influence candidate evaluation in the near future. Some cues may even make it into LTM, so that Saris's model has a memory-based component. However, the effect of the cues is usually short-lived, and the tally is the only truly stable element in a voter's mind.

This modification of the on-line model is intriguing, but so far it has not been tested empirically. Such a test may be hard to obtain, because the resulting response model contains many parameters and is therefore not easily identified. However, we believe that further exploration of this model is worthwhile.

Inference-Memory-Based Models

Hastie and Pennington (1989) have proposed an inference-memory-based model that is situated somewhere between pure on-line and pure memory-based information processing. In this model, decision makers make inferences about a target person from information to which they are exposed. These inferences are made on line and stored in LTM. However, evaluation of the target person is memory based. That is, the person is not evaluated until a judgment is called for. At that time, the decision maker downloads the on-line inferences into WM and integrates them to form an evaluation.

Just et al. (1996) present evidence that inference-memory-based models may be relevant for understanding political campaigns. Using focus groups, these authors found that voters had few difficulties with producing descriptions of candidates during the 1992 presidential elections. Many of these descriptions pertained to trait inferences, which were significant predictors of candidate evaluation. It looks, then, as if voters made trait inferences on line and retrieved the on-line tallies from memory. However, the fact that recall of these inferences predicts candidate evaluation suggests the presence of memory-based processing as well.

This account of candidate evaluation is again intriguing and deserves further exploration. We believe, however, that the evidence to date is inconclusive. Just et al. relied on very small samples from which it may be difficult to generalize. What is more problematic, however, is that these authors have no way of disentangling rationalizations from considerations that entered candidate evaluation. Who is to say that the inference that "Clinton is competent" is not a convenient rationalization of a favorable evaluation of this candidate? Without a mechanism for answering this question, we find it difficult to take these authors' findings at face value.

Determinants of Information-Processing Mode

There has been a tendency, for which we carry some responsibility, to pit memory-based models against the on-line model in a zero-sum context. Some scholars have called this a false dichotomy (Hastie and Pennington 1989; Just et al. 1996; Redlawsk 2001), and we agree. People are not just memory-based processors or on-line processors. Rather, people engage in one type of information processing under some circumstances and in another under different circumstances.

Several conditions have been shown to affect the mode of information processing that occurs. The most fundamental of these conditions is decision task. If the objective is to form an impression, people are much more likely to engage in on-line processing than when the objective is to learn the information for recall (Hastie and Park 1986; Sanbonmatsu and Fazio 1990). We have always maintained that the impression-formation goal is of paramount importance during campaigns. Others have called this into question. For example, Just et al. (1996) claim that voters sometimes encounter information haphazardly, in which case the information may not be used to update an on-line tally. There may be some truth to this proposition, although we think that impression-formation goals ultimately take over, especially at the end of a campaign, when election day approaches quickly.

Another factor that affects whether voters engage in memory-based or on-line information processing is political sophistication. Although on-line processing provides an economic way of absorbing political information, it requires an ability on the part of voters to cull affect immediately after the information has been encoded. Political sophisticates may be much more able to engage in this process than are nonsophisticates. Thus, on-line processing may be more common among sophisticates, with memory-based processing more common among nonsophisticates. Indeed, an experimental investigation by McGraw, Lodge, and Stroh (1990) finds some evidence for exactly this pattern (see also McGraw and Pinney 1990).

Political sophistication also interacts with the presentation format of candidate information. Rahn, Aldrich, and Borgida (1994) manipulated two information-presentation formats. In one format, experimental subjects were exposed to information about all of the attributes of a candidate before moving to the next candidate. In another format, information about a particular attribute was displayed for all of the candidates before moving onto another attribute. On-line processing was much more prevalent in the first condition than in the second. Nonsophisticates, in particular, appeared to rely heavily on memory-based processing when candidate information was presented within attributes. This suggests that debates may not provide a suitable platform for on-line processing, whereas campaign advertisements may.[24] Other evidence concerning the role of presentation format comes from Redklawsk's (2001) study using dynamic information boards. This study showed a mix of on-line and memory-based effects, suggesting that a dynamic information flow may trigger both kinds of processing simultaneously.

These studies show that there is considerable variation in the mode of information processing, variation that is driven both by individual and contextual factors. Given this variation, it is incorrect to state the dichotomy between memory-based and on-line processing too strongly. Indeed, we think that both processes occur, perhaps even within the same voter.

Building Bridges: A Modified Memory-Based Model

Is it possible to build a bridge between memory-based and on-line information processing? We think it is, but it requires us to modify an important assumption of memory-based models—namely, that candidate nodes are always affect-free. If this assumption is relaxed, it is possible to think of candidate evaluation as a natural progression from a memory-based process to an on-line process.

In our minds, the least plausible assumption of memory-based models is that candidate nodes remain affect-free throughout the campaign. This assumption suggests that voters explicitly evaluate the candidate only once, on election day. In reality, we think voters evaluate candidates multiple times—for example, when discussing an election with others or when responding very strongly to information received. What happens over the course of these repeated evaluations is that the candidate node becomes affectively laden. At the beginning of an election, voters may only gather facts about the candidate, especially when the candidate is unfamiliar and voters engage in personalization. These facts are stored as affectively laden attribute nodes that are associated with a candidate node. Perhaps the candidate node itself remains affect-free until voters feel comfortable that they have gathered sufficient evidence to form a candidate evaluation. At this point, affect from the attribute nodes is transferred to the candidate node; an on-line tally is established. It is implausible that this tally disappears from LTM immediately after a judgment has been made. Indeed, the evidence suggests that the on-line tally is remarkably resistant to memory decay (Lodge, Steenbergen, and Brau 1995). How quickly the on-line tally is established is not clear, but research by Park (1986) suggests that impression formation occurs rather rapidly in social settings, and we suspect that politics is not much different. Indeed, there is evidence that the formation of the on-line tally is automatic: the encoding of value-charged stimuli is sufficient to initiate this process (Betsch et al. 2001).

With an on-line tally established, cognitive consistency mechanisms come into play. Thus, attribute nodes that are consistent with the tally become more strongly associated with the candidate node, whereas inconsistent attribute nodes become more weakly associated. At first this process is weak, because the voter may not be terribly confident about her judgment of the candidate. Over time, however, the process is likely to become more important.

As long as the voter is not perfectly convinced about her evaluation of the candidate, she may continue to rely primarily on memory-based processing. However, the affect-laden candidate node is now also downloaded in WM each and every time information is encoded—the "how do I feel?" heuristic. It is likely that this node colors the way new information is encoded, leading to multiple, serious biases in judgment (Edwards and Smith 1996; Lodge, Taber, and Galonsky 1999; Lodge and Taber 2000; Taber and Lodge 2000). In particular, information may be selectively encoded to bolster the on-line tally. When this happens, the voter may become ever more confident in her judgment of the candidate.

At some point, the voter may have enough confidence in the on-line tally that she will rely primarily on on-line processing. There is no longer reason to be cautious and delay the evaluation of the candidate. Rather, the on-line tally is updated instantaneously. This means that attribute nodes become of secondary importance. They will be accessed relatively infrequently, and many of them will consequently decay. The end result is a memory structure that mimics that of figure 4.3.

We have no empirical evidence to support these propositions. However, they appear to provide a plausible account of political information processing under different conditions. It is worthwhile to investigate this model further, because it may provide important information about the candidate-evaluation process.

Conclusion

The distinction between memory-based and on-line models of candidate evaluation has colored much of the discussion about voting behavior in the 1990s. Memory-based models have long been part of the received wisdom about voting behavior. The on-line model was pitted against these models to reveal their limitations and to point out a plausible alternative for candidate evaluation. While the debate between advocates of both types of models has by no means ended, we are well on our way to understanding when each model applies. Now, at the end of a decade of controversy, it is becoming quite clear that people are not memory-based processors all of the time, but neither do they form impressions uniquely on line. More research obviously needs to be done on these models of candidate evaluation and on the hybrid models. But a decade of research has brought great improvements to our understanding of the cognitive psychology of candidate evaluation, as this section has demonstrated.

Normative Implications

Our review of the state of political cognition would be incomplete without a consideration of the normative implications of research findings. A recurring theme in the literature has been the extent to which citizens make sound political judgments despite their limited motivation and despite the constraints on WM. On balance, we believe that the cognitive literature on candidate evaluation gives reason for guarded optimism about democratic citizenship.

The task that democratic citizens face is quite complex. Just focusing on elections, citizens are bombarded in a relatively short time span with lots of information about candidate attributes, including numerous political issues. Competing candidates provide very different pictures of the state of the political world and very different remedies for social and economic problems. Talking heads, experts, and pundits add to this information flow by giving their own interpretations of the issues and the campaign. During the primary season, citizens are asked to evaluate what may be as many as ten candidates who all vie for the party's nomination. And this picture even ignores the added complexity of multiple races, proposition ballots, and referenda.

In this pandemonium, citizens show a remarkable capacity of making sound judgments. Although it often appears from surveys that citizens cannot recall much about political candidates, our own research has demonstrated that they do attend to candidate information and use it to form candidate impressions (Lodge, Steenbergen, and Brau 1995). Although citizens rely extensively on shortcuts in information processing, the evidence suggests that they usually draw reasonable inferences about candidates (Popkin 1994; but see Kuklinski and Hurley 1994). Although few citizens rely on the weighted additive rule for information integration, which is the normative ideal, it appears that they usually make good judgments and decisions anyway (Taber and Steenbergen 1995; Lau and Redlawsk 1997).

All of this is good news. Imperfect as citizens are, these imperfections do not have to intrude on sound political judgment. At least in the electoral context, it appears that the state of democratic citizenship is considerably less bleak than earlier empirical studies showed, including those of Converse (1964).

It would be incorrect, though, to assume that all is well with the quality of citizens' decision making. Both memory-based and on-line models of candidate evaluation call attention to attributes of decision making that are less desirable. One of the greatest normative concerns raised by memory-based models is the malleability of opinion. If citizens do not have real attitudes but hold only bundles of considerations from which they sample, and if this sampling is affected by external cues, then the question is to what extent autonomous public opinion exists. If politicians and other powers can manipulate the frames of questions and thereby elicit very different responses from citizens, then public opinion may be little more than a distillate of elite opinion (see Entman 1989).

The on-line model raises similarly troublesome questions. If citizens hold true attitudes in the form of an on-line tally, then their susceptibility to manipulation by political elites is considerably less. But the on-line model suggests that the pendulum may have swung too far in the other direction—citizens may not be susceptible to persuasion by reasonable arguments and evidence presented by elites. If the on-line tally colors the way citizens respond to new information and if citizens act as partisan information processors, as implied by the notion of hot cognition, then they may become dogmatic in their political beliefs and in their evaluations of political candidates. This could spell trouble for high-quality democratic citizenship.

The findings that people forget information and rationalize their evaluations are also problematic. Political theorists increasingly stress the importance of discussion and deliberation for democracy (e.g., Fishkin 1995). These acts require that citizens can make arguments to defend their opinions. If citizens have forgotten the reasons for their opinions or if they can present only self-serving rationalizations, then real political communication between citizens becomes difficult. If, in addition, partisan motivations dominate, then citizens may be unable to listen to contrary viewpoints, ending any hope for deliberative democracy (see Just et al. 1996).

These prospects are troublesome for democratic citizenship. But here, too, there is reason for hope. For example, while a considerable literature has demonstrated framing effects (e.g., Kinder and Sanders 1990; Zaller 1992), there is evidence that citizens can resist elite frames (see P. Brewer 1999). And while a partisan mode of reasoning has the potential to blind citizens to new information, people do respond to information that overwhelmingly contradicts their prior attitude. As Kunda states, "we are not at liberty to conclude whatever we want to conclude simply because we want to" (1999, 224). People need to be able to justify their beliefs and attitudes, and, in the absence of supporting evidence, it is unlikely that people will hold onto beliefs and attitudes, as doing so would be delusional.

Conclusion

We started this chapter by noting the important role that Converse has played in developing a psychological approach to politics. In this chapter, we have tried to present an overview of two decades of psychological research that did not exist at the time that Converse was writing. This research provides a cognitive perspective on political behavior.

The cognitive perspective differs markedly from the perspective we find in Converse's work. While it shares with Converse an emphasis on beliefs and attitudes, it derives them from an information-processing framework that depicts citizens as active processors of political information. Partisanship plays a role in this framework, but other factors are relevant as well, including issues.

Nonetheless, it is hard to escape the similarities between the cognitive approach and the work that Converse pursued. In many respects, the cognitive approach was developed to address the same normative questions that Converse asked. Some cognitive theories, like memory-based models, have come to answers that are consistent with Converse's conclusions. Other theories, like our on-line theory, have resulted in answers that are inconsistent with Converse's claim. But the fact that we are still trying to address Converse's puzzles is a tribute to the wisdom of his insights and the quality of his scholarship. In this sense, political cognition is nothing but the next step on a road that Converse traveled before us. This chapter has tried to provide readers with a map of this road and a sense of future direction.

NOTES

Inquiries about this paper should be directed to Professor Marco Steenbergen, Department of Political Science, University of North Carolina at Chapel Hill, Chapel Hill NC 27599–3265, e-mail: msteenbe@email.unc.edu. This manuscript was supported in part through an NSF grant (SES-9310351).

1. It is difficult to determine exactly when political cognition originated. We believe it first was firmly established in the early 1980s, with the publication of important works by Fiske and Kinder (1981), Herstein (1981), and Graber (1984). However, preludes to political cognition can be found much earlier, in Lippmann's (1922) writings about public opinion, McPhee's (1963) work on voting behavior, and Axelrod's (1973) work on schemata.

2. In general, there are dangers in using a computer metaphor of the mind (see Bruner 1990). For pedagogical purposes, however, such a metaphor is often useful, and this is why we pursue it here.

3. Lupia and McCubbins (1998) have recently argued that citizens are typically not fully informed as a result of limitations on information processing. However, within this limited information set, citizens still seek optimal decision making. This model of low information rationality presents an interesting challenge to Simon's notion of satisficing. We shall return to this model when we discuss models of information integration.

4. Scholars sometimes conflate bounded rationality with the notion that citizens are cognitive misers (see Stroh 1995), but we would like to separate these concepts. Bounded rationality refers to structural limitations of the human mind that prevent people from optimizing behavior under all but the simplest circumstances. Cognitive miserliness arises from a motivational state: citizens shun effortful information processing because the decision task holds little interest for them.

5. For an alternative view of the structure of associative networks in the context of elections, see Rahn 1995.

6. This point is well known in social psychology (see, e.g., Fishbein 1963). In political science it has received much less attention (but see Alvarez 1997).

7. A more general discussion of the role of affect in politics can be found in Marcus, Neuman, and MacKuen 2000.

8. Judd and Krosnick (1989) have proposed a slightly different model that states that affective tags are associated with candidates with varying strengths.

9. In electoral behavior, examples of applications of schema theory include Conover and Feldman 1984, 1986; Hamill, Lodge, and Blake 1985; and Lau 1986.

10. Important differences exist between exposure and attention, but as Wheeless and Cook (1985) note, it is often very difficult to empirically distinguish between these processes. For this reason, we treat these processes together. For a discussion of their differences, see Wheeless and Cook 1985.

11. Surveys that ask respondents to recall political facts are a complementary source of information about attention. To the extent that respondents fail to recall facts, one

could argue that they also failed to pay attention to those facts. Indeed, recall measures typically show that citizens can recall only a small amount of information (see, e.g., Delli Carpini and Keeter 1996). However, recall measures are impure measures of attention because the process of forgetting may make it impossible for respondents to recall information even if they attended to it (Lodge, Steenbergen, and Brau 1995; for a defense of recall-based measures of exposure, see Price and Zaller 1993).

12. The differences in processing goals may be one more explanation for the mixed empirical record concerning selective exposure and attention (see Freedman and Sears 1965; Sears and Freedman 1967; Wheeless and Cook 1985; Frey 1986).

13. Affect does not always hamper exposure or attention. Marcus, Neuman, and MacKuen (2000) have demonstrated that anxiety generates learning (see also Marcus and MacKuen 1993). This finding contradicts the findings reported by Taber and Lodge (2000). The key to this difference may lie in the nature of the affect that is involved— aversion may prompt a "partisan" mode, while anxiety may cause citizens to be more open-minded and focused on accuracy goals (see MacKuen et al. 2001).

14. Fiske and Taylor (1991) include attention as a third component of the encoding process. While attention and encoding are obviously closely related, we follow Ottati and Wyer (1990; Wyer and Ottati 1993) and keep separate these two stages of information processing.

15. This distinction is consistent with certain dual-process models in psychology, which posit a distinction between automatic processing and deliberative processing (see, e.g., Chaiken and Trope 1999).

16. The inferences from categories are not always problematic. For example, Popkin (1994) has argued convincingly that partisan labels are a convenient and reasonable shortcut for citizens to learn about the political world. However, Kuklinski and Hurley (1994) have demonstrated that shortcuts do not always produce sound inferences.

17. The growing popularity of prospect theory in international relations has made the referential criterion an important focus of research in that field (see, e.g., McDermott 1998).

18. A logical question is whether ambivalence carries over in the area of political issues. Steenbergen and Brewer (2000) looked into this question for four issues: affirmative action, gay rights, welfare, and abortion. Surprisingly, the authors found very little evidence of ambivalence, although it should be noted that they employed different ambivalence measures than did Meffert, Guge, and Lodge (2000) and Lavine (2001).

19. A study by McGraw and Pinney (1990) suggests that it is important to consider different concepts of political sophistication. This study distinguished between general and domain-specific sophistication and found that their impacts on memory were distinct.

20. This representation builds on work by Kitayama and Burnstein (1989) but deviates from it in important ways. First, Kitayama and Burnstein argue that the gist, which would be the candidate node in our model, contains affect. Second, attribute nodes that are consistent with the gist are more easily remembered. We think these assumptions violate the spirit of memory-based processing.

21. For a contradictory view, see Wilson and Hodges 1992.

22. While most of the evidence for the on-line model is based on correlations between recall and evaluation, Hertel and Bless (2000) discuss the use of response latencies to discriminate between on-line and memory-based cognition.

23. Cappella and Jamieson (1997) have called this result into question, arguing that our recall task was so difficult that even our highly educated sample had problems with it. We find this ironic. Reading a mock campaign brochure, our subjects learned the candidates' positions on seven issues plus a handful of background characteristics that included partisanship. If this is deemed an excessively difficult decision task, we hold little hope for American democracy. In any case, we would expect recall in the normal campaign environment to be even lower than ours—not better—because more information is typically available to voters.

24. Rahn, Aldrich, and Borgida (1994) did not control for rationalization effects, so that some of the evidence for high correlations between judgments and recall may be overstated.

REFERENCES

Abelson, Robert P. 1963. Computer Simulation of "Hot" Cognition. In *Computer Simulation of Personality: Frontier of Psychological Theory,* ed. Silvan S. Tomkins and Samuel Messick. New York: Wiley.

Abelson, Robert P., and Deborah A. Prentice. 1989. Beliefs as Possessions: A Functional Perspective. In *Attitude Structure and Function,* ed. Anthony R. Pratkanis, Steven J. Breckler, and Anthony G. Greenwald. Hillsdale, N.J.: Erlbaum.

Alvarez, R. Michael. 1997. *Information and Elections.* Ann Arbor: University of Michigan Press.

Alvarez, R. Michael, and John Brehm. 1995. American Ambivalence toward Abortion Policy: Development of a Heteroskedastic Probit Model of Competing Values. *American Journal of Political Science* 39:1055–82.

Anderson, John R. 1983. *The Architecture of Cognition.* Hillsdale, N.J.: Erlbaum.

Anderson, Norman H. 1981. *Foundations of Information Integration Theory.* New York: Academic Press.

Axelrod, Robert. 1973. Schema Theory: An Information Processing Model of Perception and Cognition. *American Political Science Review* 67:1248–66.

Bargh, John A. 1997. The Automaticity of Everyday Life. In *The Automaticity of Everyday Life: Advances in Social Cognition,* ed. Robert S. Wyer, vol. 10. Mahwah, N.J.: Erlbaum.

Barlett, Dorothy L., Pamela B. Drew, Eleanor G. Fahle, and William A. Watts. 1974. Selective Exposure to a Presidential Campaign Appeal. *Public Opinion Quarterly* 38:264–70.

Barsalou, Lawrence W. 1992. *Cognitive Psychology: An Overview for Cognitive Scientists.* Hillsdale, N.J.: Erlbaum.

Baumeister, Roy F., and Leonard S. Newman. 1994. Self-Regulation of Cognitive Inference and Decision Processes. *Personality and Social Psychology Bulletin* 20:3–19.

Beck, Paul A., Russell J. Dalton, Steven Greene, and Robert Huckfeldt. 2002. The Social Calculus of Voting: Interpersonal, Media, and Organizational Influences on Presidential Choices. *American Political Science Review* 96:57–73.

Berelson, Bernard R., Paul F. Lazarsfeld, and William N. McPhee. 1964. *Voting: A Study of Opinion Formation in a Presidential Campaign.* Chicago: University of Chicago Press.

Berent, Matthew K. 1990. Attitude Importance and the Recall of Attitude Relevant Information. Master's thesis, Ohio State University.

Berent, Matthew K., and Jon A. Krosnick. 1995. The Relation between Political Attitude Importance and Knowledge Structure. In *Political Judgment: Structure and Process*, ed. Milton Lodge and Kathleen M. McGraw. Ann Arbor: University of Michigan Press.

Betsch, Tilmann, Henning Plessner, Christiane Schwieren, and Robert Gütig. 2001. I Like It but I Don't Know Why: A Value-Account Approach to Implicit Attitude Formation. *Personality and Social Psychology Bulletin* 27:242–53.

Blair, Irene V., and Mahzarin R. Banaji. 1996. Automatic and Controlled Processes in Stereotype Priming. *Journal of Personality and Social Psychology* 70:1142–63.

Boynton, G. Robert, and Milton Lodge. 1994. Voter's Image of Candidates. In *Presidential Campaigns and American Self Images*, ed. Arthur H. Miller and Bruce E. Gronbeck. Boulder, Colo.: Westview.

Brendl, C. Miguel, and E. Tory Higgins. 1996. Principles of Judging Valence: What Makes Events Positive or Negative? *Advances in Experimental Social Psychology* 28:95–160.

Brewer, Marilynn B. 1988. A Dual Process Model of Impression Formation. In *Advances in Social Cognition*, vol. 1: *A Dual Process Model of Impression Formation*, ed. Thomas K. Srull and Robert S. Wyer. Hillsdale, N.J.: Erlbaum.

Brewer, Paul R. 1999. Values, Public Debate, and Policy Opinions. Ph.D. diss., University of North Carolina at Chapel Hill.

Bruner, Jerome. 1990. *Acts of Meaning*. Cambridge: Harvard University Press.

Buschke, Herman. 1977. Two-Dimensional Recall: Immediate Identification of Clusters in Episodic and Semantic Memory. *Journal of Verbal Learning and Verbal Behavior* 16:201–15.

Cacioppo, John T., and Gary G. Berntson. 1994. Relationship between Attitudes and Evaluative Space: A Critical Review, with Emphasis on the Separability of Positive and Negative Substrates. *Psychological Bulletin* 115:401–23.

Cacioppo, John T., Wendi L. Gardner, and Gary G. Berntson. 1997. Beyond Bipolar Conceptualizations and Measures: The Case of Attitudes and Evaluative Space. *Personality and Social Psychology Review* 1:3–25.

Campbell, Angus, Philip E. Converse, Warren E. Miller, and Donald E. Stokes. 1960. *The American Voter*. Chicago: University of Chicago Press.

Cappella, Joseph N., and Kathleen Hall Jamieson. 1997. *The Spiral of Cynicism: The Press and the Public Good*. New York: Oxford University Press.

Chaiken, Shelly, and Yaacov Trope. 1999. *Dual-Process Theories in Social Psychology*. New York: Guilford.

Clore, Gerald L., and Linda M. Isbell. 2001. Emotion as Virtue and Vice. In *Citizens and Politics: Perspectives from Political Psychology*, ed. James H. Kuklinski. New York: Cambridge University Press.

Cohen, Bernard C. 1963. *The Press and Foreign Policy*. Princeton: Princeton University Press.

Collins, Allan M., and Elizabeth F. Loftus. 1975. A Spreading-Activation Theory of Semantic Processing. *Psychological Review* 82:407–28.

Collins, Allan M., and M. Ross Quillian. 1969. Retrieval Time from Semantic Memory. *Journal of Verbal Learning and Verbal Behavior* 8:240–47.

Conover, Pamela J., and Stanley Feldman. 1984. How People Organize the Political World: A Schematic Model. *American Journal of Political Science* 28:95–126.

———. 1986. The Role of Inference in the Perception of Political Candidates. In *Political Cognition*, ed. Richard R. Lau and David O. Sears. Hillsdale, N.J.: Erlbaum.

Converse, Philip E. 1964. The Nature of Belief Systems in Mass Publics. In *Ideology and Discontent*, ed. David E. Apter. London: Collier-Macmillan.

Craik, Fergus I., and Robert S. Lockhart. 1972. Levels of Processing: A Framework for Memory Research. *Journal of Verbal Learning and Verbal Behavior* 11:671–84.

Damasio, Antonio R. 1994. *Descartes' Error: Emotion, Reason, and the Human Brain.* New York: Putnam.

Davis, Otto A., Melvin J. Hinich, and Peter C. Ordeshook. 1970. An Expository Development of a Mathematical Model of the Electoral Process. *American Political Science Review* 64:426–48.

Delli Carpini, Michael X., and Scott Keeter. 1996. *What Americans Know about Politics and Why It Matters.* New Haven: Yale University Press.

Devine, Patricia G. 1989. Stereotypes and Prejudice: Their Automatic and Controlled Components. *Journal of Personality and Social Psychology* 56:5–18.

Downs, Anthony. 1957. *An Economic Theory of Democracy.* New York: Addison, Wesley, and Longman.

Edwards, Kari, and Edward E. Smith. 1996. A Disconfirmation Bias in the Evaluation of Arguments. *Journal of Personality and Social Psychology* 71:5–24.

Entman, Robert M. 1989. *Democracy without Citizens: Media and the Decay of American Politics.* New York: Oxford University Press.

Erber, Ralph, and Susan T. Fiske. 1984. Outcome Dependency and Attention to Inconsistent Information. *Journal of Personality and Social Psychology* 47:709–26.

Eysenck, Michael W., and Mark T. Keane. 1995. *Cognitive Psychology.* Mahwah, N.J.: Erlbaum.

Fazio, Russell H. 1995. Attitudes as Object-Evaluation Associations: Determinants, Consequences, and Correlates of Attitude Accessibility. In *Attitude Strength: Antecedents and Consequences*, ed. Richard E. Petty and Jon A. Krosnick. Mahwah, N.J.: Erlbaum.

Feldman, Stanley. 1995. Answering Survey Questions: The Measurement and Meaning of Public Opinion. In *Political Judgment: Structure and Process*, ed. Milton Lodge and Kathleen M. McGraw. Ann Arbor: University of Michigan Press.

Fiorina, Morris P. 1981. *Retrospective Voting in American National Elections.* New Haven: Yale University Press.

Fischer, Gregory, and Eric J. Johnson. 1986. Behavioral Decision Theory and Political Decision Making. In *Political Cognition*, ed. Richard R. Lau and David O. Sears. Hillsdale, N.J.: Erlbaum

Fishbein, Martin. 1963. An Investigation of the Relationships between Beliefs about an Object and the Attitude toward that Object. *Human Relations* 16:233–39.

Fishkin, James S. 1995. *The Voice of the People: Public Opinion and Democracy.* New Haven: Yale University Press.

Fiske, Susan T., and Donald R. Kinder. 1981. Involvement, Expertise, and Schema Use: Evidence from Political Cognition. In *Personality, Cognition, and Social Interaction*, ed. Nancy Cantor and John F. Kihlstrom. Hillsdale, N.J.: Erlbaum.

Fiske, Susan T., Donald R. Kinder, and W. Michael Larter. 1981. The Novice and the

Expert: Knowledge-Based Strategies in Political Cognition. *Journal of Experimental Social Psychology* 19:381–400.

Fiske, Susan T., and Steven Neuberg. 1990. A Continuum Model of Impression Formation from Category-Based to Individuating Responses: Influences of Information and Motivation on Attention and Interpretation. *Advances in Experimental Social Psychology* 23:1–75.

Fiske, Susan T., and Mark A. Pavelchak. 1986. Category-Based Versus Piecemeal-Based Affective Responses: Developments in Schema-Triggered Affect. In *Handbook of Motivation and Cognition: Foundations of Social Behavior,* ed. Richard M. Sorrentino and E. Tory Higgins. New York: Guilford.

Fiske, Susan T., and Janet B. Ruscher. 1989. On-Line Processes in Category-Based and Individuating Impressions: Some Basic Principles and Methodological Reflections. In *On-Line Cognition in Person Perception,* ed. John N. Bassili. Hillsdale, N.J.:Erlbaum.

Fiske, Susan T., and Shelley E. Taylor. 1991. *Social Cognition.* New York: McGraw-Hill.

Fodor, Jerry A. 1979. *The Language of Thought.* Cambridge: Harvard University Press.

Freedman, Jonathan L., and David O. Sears. 1965. Warning, Distraction, and Resistance to Influence. *Journal of Personality and Social Psychology* 1:262–66.

Frey, Dieter. 1986. "Recent Research on Selective Exposure to Information." *Advances in Experimental Social Psychology* 19:41–80.

Funkhouser, G. Ray. 1973. The Issues of the Sixties: An Exploratory Study in the Dynamics of Public Opinion. *Public Opinion Quarterly* 37:62–75.

Gardner, Howard. 1985. *The Mind's New Science: A History of the Cognitive Revolution.* New York: Basic Books.

Graber, Doris A. 1984. *Processing the News: How People Tame the Information Tide.* New York: Longman.

Granberg, Daniel. 1971. Selectivity in Exposure and the Effect of Attitudes on Judgments of the Mass Media Coverage of the King Assassination. *Journal of Social Psychology* 85:147–48.

Hamill, Ruth, Milton G. Lodge, and Frederick Blake. 1985. The Breadth, Depth, and Utility of Class, Partisan, and Ideological Schemata. *American Journal of Political Science* 29:850–70.

Hastie, Reid. 1981. Schematic Principles in Human Memory. In *Social Cognition: The Ontario Symposium,* ed. E. Tory Higgins, Charles Herman, and Mark P. Zanna, vol. 1. Hillsdale, N.J.: Erlbaum.

———. 1986. A Primer of Information-Processing Theory for Political Scientists. In *Political Cognition,* ed. Richard R. Lau and David O. Sears. Hillsdale, N.J.: Erlbaum.

Hastie, Reid, and Bernadette Park. 1986. The Relationship between Memory and Judgment Depends on Whether the Judgment Task Is Memory-Based or On-Line. *Psychological Review* 93:258–68.

Hastie, Reid, and Nancy Pennington. 1989. Notes on the Distinction between Memory-Based versus On-Line Judgments. In *On-Line Cognition in Person Perception,* ed. John N. Bassili. Hillsdale, N.J.: Erlbaum.

Herstein, John A. 1981. Keeping the Voter's Limits in Mind: A Cognitive Process Analysis of Decision Making in Voting. *Journal of Personality and Social Psychology* 40:843–61.

———. 1985. Voter Thought Processes and Voting Theory. In *Mass Media and Political*

Thoughts: An Information-Processing Approach, ed. Sidney Kraus and Richard M. Perloff. Beverly Hills, Calif.: Sage.

Hertel, Guido, and Herbert Bless. 2000. "On-Line" und erinnerungsgestützte Urteilsbildung: Auslösefaktoren und empirische Unterscheidungsmöglicheiten ("On-Line" and Memory-Based Judgment: Triggering Conditions and Empirical Methods of Differentiation). *Psychologische Rundschau* 51:19–28.

Higgins, E. Tory, and John A. Bargh. 1987. Social Cognition and Social Perception. *Annual Review of Psychology* 38:369–425.

Hinich, Melvin J., and Michael C. Munger. 1997. *Analytical Politics.* New York: Cambridge University Press.

Hovland, Carl I., Irving L. Janis, and Harold H. Kelley. 1953. *Communication and Persuasion: Psychological Studies of Opinion Change.* New Haven: Yale University Press.

Huckfeldt, Robert, and John Sprague. 1988. Choice, Social Structure, and Political Information: The Information Coercion of Minorities. *American Journal of Political Science* 32:467–82.

Iyengar, Shanto. 1990. Shortcuts to Political Knowledge: The Role of Selective Attention and Accessibility. In *Information and Democratic Processes,* ed. John A. Ferejohn and James H. Kuklinski. Urbana: University of Illinois Press.

Iyengar, Shanto, and Donald R. Kinder. 1987. *News That Matters: Television and American Opinion.* Chicago: University of Chicago Press.

Judd, Charles M., and Jon A. Krosnick. 1989. The Structural Bases of Consistency among Political Attitudes: Effects of Political Expertise and Attitude Importance. In *Attitude Structure and Function,* ed. Anthony R. Pratkanis, Steven J. Breckler, and Anthony G. Greenwald. Hillsdale, N.J.: Erlbaum.

Just, Marion R., Ann N. Crigler, Dean E. Alger, Timothy E. Cook, Montague Kern, and Darrell M. West. 1996. *Crosstalk: Citizens, Candidates, and the Media in a Presidential Campaign.* Chicago: University of Chicago Press.

Kahneman, Daniel, and Amos Tversky. 1979. Prospect Theory: An Analysis of Decision under Risk. *Econometrica* 47:263–92.

Kelley, Stanley. 1983. *Interpreting Elections.* Princeton: Princeton University Press.

Kelley, Stanley, and Thad W. Mirer. 1974. The Simple Act of Voting. *American Political Science Review* 68:572–91.

Kinder, Donald R. 1986. Presidential Character Revisited. In *Political Cognition,* ed. Richard R. Lau and David O. Sears. Hillsdale, N.J.: Erlbaum.

Kinder, Donald R., and Lynn M. Sanders. 1990. Mimicking Political Debate with Survey Questions: The Case of White Opinion on Affirmative Action for Blacks. *Social Cognition* 8:73–103.

Kitayama, Shinobu, and Eugene Burnstein. 1989. The Relation between Opinion and Memory: Distinguishing between Associative Density and Structural Centrality. In *On-Line Cognition in Person Perception,* ed. John N. Bassili. Hillsdale, N.J.: Erlbaum.

Klayman, Joshua, and Young-Won Ha. 1987. Confirmation, Disconfirmation, and Information in Hypothesis Testing. *Psychological Review* 94:211–28.

Krosnick, Jon A. 1988. The Role of Attitude Importance in Social Evaluation: A Study of Policy Preferences, Presidential Candidate Evaluations, and Voting Behavior. *Journal of Personality and Social Psychology* 55:196–210.

———. 1990. Government Policy and Citizen Passion: A Study of Issue Publics in Contemporary America. *Political Behavior* 12:59–92.

Kruglanski, Arie W., and Donna M. Webster. 1996. Motivated Closing of the Mind: "Seizing" and "Freezing." *Psychological Review* 103:263–83.

Kuklinski, James H., and Norman L. Hurley. 1994. On Hearing and Interpreting Political Messages: A Cautionary Tale of Citizen Cue-Taking. *Journal of Politics* 56:729–51.

Kuklinski, James H., Robert C. Luskin, and John Bolland. 1991. Where Is the Schema? Going Beyond the "S" Word in Political Psychology. *American Political Science Review* 85:1341–56.

Kunda, Ziva. 1990. The Case for Motivated Reasoning. *Psychological Bulletin* 108:480–98.

———. 1999. *Social Cognition: Making Sense of People.* Cambridge: MIT Press.

Lachman, Roy, Janet L. Lachman, and Earl C. Butterfield. 1979. *Cognitive Psychology and Information Processing: An Introduction.* Hillsdale, N.J.: Erlbaum.

Lau, Richard R. 1986. Political Schemata, Candidate Evaluations, and Voting Behavior. In *Political Cognition,* ed. Richard R. Lau and David O. Sears. Hillsdale, N.J.: Erlbaum.

———. 1989. Construct Accessibility and Electoral Choice. *Political Behavior* 11:5–32.

———. 1995. Information Search during an Election Campaign: Introducing a Process-Tracing Methodology for Political Scientists. In *Political Judgment: Structure and Process,* ed. Milton Lodge and Kathleen M. McGraw. Ann Arbor: University of Michigan Press.

Lau, Richard R., and David P. Redlawsk. 1997. Voting Correctly. *American Political Science Review* 91:585–98.

Lavine, Howard. 2001. The Electoral Consequences of Ambivalence toward Presidential Candidates. *American Journal of Political Science* 45:915–29.

Lavine, Howard, Cynthia J. Thomsen, Mark P. Zanna, and Eugene Borgida. 1998. On the Primacy of Affect in the Determination of Attitudes and Behavior: The Moderating Role of Affective-Cognitive Ambivalence. *Journal of Experimental Social Psychology* 34:398–421.

Lazarsfeld, Paul F., Bernard Berelson, and Hazel Gaudet. 1948. *The People's Choice: How the Voter Makes up His Mind in a Presidential Campaign.* New York: Columbia University Press.

Lippmann, Walter. 1922. *Public Opinion.* New York: Harcourt, Brace.

Lodge, Milton. 1995. Toward a Procedural Model of Candidate Evaluation. In *Political Judgment: Structure and Process,* ed. Milton Lodge and Kathleen M. McGraw. Ann Arbor: University of Michigan Press.

Lodge, Milton, Kathleen M. McGraw, and Patrick Stroh. 1989. An Impression-Driven Model of Candidate Evaluation. *American Political Science Review* 85:399–419.

Lodge, Milton, and Marco Steenbergen, with Shawn Brau. 1995. The Responsive Voter: Campaign Information and the Dynamics of Candidate Evaluation. *American Political Science Review* 89:309–26.

Lodge, Milton, and Patrick Stroh. 1993. Inside the Mental Voting Booth: An Impression-Driven Process Model of Candidate Evaluation. In *Explorations in Political Psychology,* ed. Shanto Iyengar and William J. McGuire. Durham: Duke University Press.

Lodge, Milton, Patrick Stroh, and John Wahlke. 1990. Black-Box Models of Candidate Evaluation. *Political Behavior* 12:5–18.

Lodge, Milton, and Charles Taber. 2000. Three Steps toward a Theory of Motivated

Political Reasoning. In *Elements of Reason: Cognition, Choice, and the Bounds of Rationality,* ed. Arthur Lupia, Matthew D. McCubbins, and Samuel L. Popkin. New York: Cambridge University Press.

Lodge, Milton, Charles Taber, and Aron Chase Galonsky. 1999. An Exploration of the Mechanisms of Motivated Reasoning. Paper presented at the annual meeting of the Midwest Political Science Association, Chicago.

Lupia, Arthur, and Matthew D. McCubbins. 1998. *The Democratic Dilemma: Can Citizens Learn What They Need to Know?* New York: Cambridge University Press.

MacKuen, Michael B., Robert S. Erikson, and James A. Stimson. 1992. Peasants or Bankers? The American Electorate and the U.S. Economy. *American Political Science Review* 86:597–611.

MacKuen, Michael, George E. Marcus, W. Russell Neuman, Luke Keele, and Jennifer Wolak. 2001. Emotions, Information, and Political Cooperation. Paper presented at the annual meeting of the American Political Science Association, San Francisco.

Marcus, George E., and Michael B. MacKuen. 1993. Anxiety, Enthusiasm, and the Vote: The Emotional Underpinnings of Learning and Involvement during Presidential Campaigns. *American Political Science Review* 87:688–701.

Marcus, George E., W. Russell Neuman, and Michael MacKuen. 2000. *Affective Intelligence and Political Judgment.* Chicago: University of Chicago Press.

McCombs, Maxwell E., and Donald Shaw. 1972. The Agenda-Setting Function of the Mass Media. *Public Opinion Quarterly* 36:176–87.

McDermott, Rose. 1998. *Risk-Taking in International Politics: Prospect Theory in American Foreign Policy.* Ann Arbor: University of Michigan Press.

McGraw, Kathleen M., Milton Lodge, and Patrick Stroh. 1990. On-Line Processing in Candidate Evaluation: The Effects of Issue Order, Issue Importance, and Sophistication. *Political Behavior* 12:41–58.

McGraw, Kathleen M., and Neil Pinney. 1990. The Effects of General and Domain Specific Expertise on Political Memory and Judgment. *Social Cognition* 8:9–30.

McGraw, Kathleen M., and Marco Steenbergen. 1995. Pictures in the Head: Memory Representations of Political Candidates. In *Political Judgment: Structure and Process,* ed. Milton Lodge and Kathleen M. McGraw. Ann Arbor: University of Michigan Press.

McGuire, William J., and Claire V. McGuire. 1991. The Content, Structure, and Operation of Thought Systems. In *The Content, Structure, and Operation of Thought Systems,* ed. Robert S. Wyer and Thomas K. Srull. Hillsdale, N.J.: Erlbaum.

McPhee, William N. 1963. *Formal Theories of Mass Behavior.* New York: Free Press of Glencoe.

Meffert, Michael F., Michael Guge, and Milton Lodge. 2000. Good, Bad, and Ambivalent: The Consequences of Multidimensional Political Attitudes. In *The Issue of Belief: Essays in the Intersection of Non-Attitudes and Attitude Change,* ed. Willem E. Saris and Paul Sniderman. Amsterdam: Amsterdam School of Communications Research.

Miller, George A. 1956. The Magical Number Seven, Plus or Minus Two: Some Limits on Our Capacity for Processing Information. *Psychological Review* 63:81–97.

Miller, Joanne M., and Jon A. Krosnick. 2000. News Media Impact on the Ingredients of Presidential Evaluations: Politically Knowledgeable Citizens Are Guided by a Trusted Source. *American Journal of Political Science* 44:301–15.

Neely, James. 1977. Semantic Priming and Retrieval from Lexical Memory: Roles of Inhibitionless Spreading Activation and Limited Capacity Attention. *Journal of Experimental Psychology: General* 106:226–54.

Olson, James M., Neal J. Roese, and Mark P. Zanna. 1996. Expectancies. In *Social Psychology: Handbook of Basic Principles*, ed. E. Tory Higgins and Arie W. Kruglanski. New York: Guilford.

Ottati, Victor C. 1990. Determinants of Political Judgments: The Joint Influence of Normative and Heuristic Rules of Inference. *Political Behavior* 12:159–79.

Ottati, Victor C., and Robert S. Wyer. 1990. The Cognitive Mediators of Political Choice: Toward a Comprehensive Model of Political Information Processing. In *Information and Democratic Processes*, ed. John A. Ferejohn and James H. Kuklinski. Urbana: University of Illinois Press.

Park, Bernadette. 1986. A Method for Studying the Development of Impressions of Real People. *Journal of Personality and Social Psychology* 51:907–17.

Payne, John W. 1982. Contingent Decision Behavior. *Psychological Bulletin* 92:382–402.

Payne, John W., James R. Bettman, and Eric J. Johnson. 1988. Adaptive Strategy Selection in Decision Making. *Journal of Experimental Psychology: Learning, Memory, and Cognition* 14:534–52.

Petty, Richard E., and John T. Cacioppo. 1986. *Communication and Persuasion: Central and Peripheral Routes to Attitude Change*. New York: Springer.

Popkin, Samuel L. 1994. *The Reasoning Voter: Communication and Persuasion in Presidential Campaigns*. Chicago: University of Chicago Press.

Pratkanis, Anthony R. 1989. The Cognitive Representation of Attitudes. In *Attitude Structure and Function*, ed. Anthony R. Pratkanis, Steven J. Breckler, and Anthony G. Greenwald. Hillsdale, N.J.: Erlbaum.

Price, Vincent, and John Zaller. 1993. Who Gets the News? Alterative Measures of News Reception and Their Implications for Research. *Public Opinion Quarterly* 57:133–64.

Priester, Joseph R., and Richard E. Petty. 1996. The Gradual Threshold Model of Ambivalence: Relating the Positive and Negative Bases of Attitudes to Subjective Ambivalence. *Journal of Personality and Social Psychology* 71:431–49.

Pryor, John B., and Thomas M. Ostrom. 1981. The Cognitive Organization of Social Information: A Converging-Operations Approach. *Journal of Personality and Social Psychology* 41:628–41.

Rabinowitz, George, and Stuart Elaine Macdonald. 1989. A Directional Theory of Issue Voting. *American Political Science Review* 83:93–121.

Rahn, Wendy M. 1995. Candidate Evaluation in Complex Information Environments: Cognitive Organization and Comparison Process. In *Political Judgment: Structure and Process*, ed. Milton Lodge and Kathleen M. McGraw. Ann Arbor: University of Michigan Press.

Rahn, Wendy M., John H. Aldrich, and Eugene Borgida. 1994. Individual and Contextual Variations in Political Candidate Appraisal. *American Political Science Review* 88:193–99.

Rahn, Wendy M., Jon A. Krosnick, and Marijke Breuning. 1994. Rationalization and Derivation Processes in Survey Studies of Political Candidate Evaluation. *American Journal of Political Science* 38:582–600.

Redlawsk, David P. 2001. You Must Remember This: A Test of the On-Line Model of Voting. *Journal of Politics* 63:29–58.

Sanbonmatsu, David M., and Russell H. Fazio. 1990. The Role of Attitudes in Memory-Based Decision Making. *Journal of Personality and Social Psychology* 59:614–22.

Sanford, Anthony J. 1987. *The Mind of Man: Models of Human Understanding.* New Haven: Yale University Press.

Saris, Willem E. 1997. Multi-Trait Multi-Method Models of Public Opinion. Paper presented at the conference "No Opinion, Instability, and Change in Public Opinion Research," Amsterdam.

Schank, Roger C., and Robert P. Abelson. 1995. Knowledge and Memory: The Real Story. In *Knowledge and Memory: The Real Story,* ed. Robert S. Wyer. Hillsdale, N.J.: Erlbaum.

Schumpeter, Joseph A. 1976. *Capitalism, Socialism, and Democracy.* New York: Harper-Collins.

Schwartz, Norbert. 1998. Warmer and More Social: Recent Developments in Cognitive Social Psychology. *Annual Review of Sociology* 24:239–64.

Schwartz, Norbert, and Gerald L. Clore. 1988. How Do I Feel about It? Informative Functions of Affective States. In *Affect, Cognition, and Social Behavior: New Evidence and Integrative Attempts,* ed. Klaus Fiedler and Joseph Forgas. Toronto: C. J. Hogrefe.

Sears, David O., and Jonathan L. Freedman. 1967. Selective Exposure to Information: A Critical Review. *Public Opinion Quarterly* 31:194–213.

Sears, David O., Leonie Huddy, and Lynitta G. Schaffer. 1986. A Schematic Variant of Symbolic Politics Theory, as Applied to Racial and Gender Equality. In *Political Cognition,* ed. Richard R. Lau and David O. Sears. Hillsdale, N.J.: Erlbaum.

Sedikides, Constantine, and Thomas M. Ostrom. 1988. Are Person Categories Used When Organizing Information about Unfamiliar Sets of Persons? *Social Cognition* 6:252–67.

Simon, Herbert A. 1955. A Behavioral Model of Rational Choice. *Quarterly Journal of Economics* 69:99–118.

———. 1959. Theories of Decision-Making in Economics and Behavioral Science. *American Economic Review* 49:253–83.

———. 1978. Rationality as a Process and Product of Thought. *American Economic Review: Proceedings* 68:1–16.

———. 1985. Human Nature in Politics: The Dialogue of Psychology with Political Science. *American Political Science Review* 79:293–304.

Stangor, Charles, and David McMillan. 1992. Memory for Expectancy-Congruent and Expectancy-Incongruent Information: A Review of the Social and Social Developmental Literatures. *Psychological Bulletin* 111:42–61.

Steenbergen, Marco R., and Paul R. Brewer. 2000. The Not-So Ambivalent Public: Policy Attitudes in the Political Culture of Ambivalence. In *The Issue of Belief: Essays in the Intersection of Non-Attitudes and Attitude Change,* ed. Willem E. Saris and Paul Sniderman. Amsterdam: Amsterdam School of Communications Research.

Stroh, Patrick. 1995. Voters as Pragmatic Cognitive Misers: The Accuracy-Effort Trade-Off in the Candidate Evaluation Process. In *Political Judgment: Structure and Process,* ed. Milton Lodge and Kathleen M. McGraw. Ann Arbor: University of Michigan Press.

Sweeney, Paul D., and Kathy L. Gruber. 1984. Selective Exposure: Voter Information

Preferences and the Watergate Affair. *Journal of Personality and Social Psychology* 46:1208–21.

Taber, Charles, and Milton Lodge. 2000. Motivated Skepticism in the Evaluation of Political Beliefs. Paper presented at the annual meeting of the American Political Science Association, Washington, D.C.

Taber, Charles, and Marco R. Steenbergen. 1995. Computational Experiments in Electoral Behavior. In *Political Judgment: Structure and Process,* ed. Milton Lodge and Kathleen M. McGraw. Ann Arbor: University of Michigan Press.

Taylor, Shelley E., and Jennifer Crocker. 1981. Schematic Bases of Social Information Processing. In *Social Cognition: The Ontario Symposium,* ed. E. Tory Higgins, Charles Herman, and Mark P. Zanna, vol. 1. Hillsdale, N.J.: Erlbaum.

Tesser, Abraham, and Leonard Martin. 1996. The Psychology of Evaluation. In *Social Psychology: Handbook of Basic Principles,* ed. E. Tory Higgins and Arie W. Kruglanski. New York: Guilford.

Thompson, Megan M., Mark P. Zanna, and Dale W. Griffin. 1995. Let's Not Be Indifferent about (Attitudinal) Ambivalence. In *Attitude Strength: Antecedents and Consequences,* ed. Richard E. Petty and Jon A. Krosnick. Hillsdale, N.J.: Erlbaum.

Tversky, Amos, and Daniel Kahneman. 1974. Judgment under Uncertainty: Heuristics and Biases. *Science* 185:1124–31.

———. 1992. Advances in Prospect Theory: Cumulative Representation of Uncertainty. *Journal of Risk and Uncertainty* 5:297–323.

Westholm, Anders. 1997. Distance versus Direction: The Illusory Defeat of the Proximity Theory of Electoral Choice. *American Political Science Review* 91:865–83.

Wheeless, Lawrence R., and John A. Cook. 1985. Information Exposure, Attention, and Reception. In *Information and Behavior,* ed. Brent D. Ruben, vol. 1. New Brunswick, N.J.: Transaction.

Wilson, Timothy D., and Sara D. Hodges. 1992. Attitudes as Temporary Constructions. In *The Construction of Social Judgments,* ed. Leonard L. Martin and Abraham Tesser. Hillsdale, N.J.: Erlbaum.

Wyer, Robert S., and Victor C. Ottati. 1993. Political Information Processing. In *Explorations in Political Psychology,* ed. Shanto Iyengar and William J. McGuire. Durham: Duke University Press.

Wyer, Robert S., and Thomas K. Srull. 1986. Human Cognition in Its Social Context. *Psychological Review* 93:322–59.

Zajonc, Robert. 1980. Feeling and Thinking: Preferences Need No Inferences. *American Psychologist* 39:151–75.

Zaller, John. 1992. *The Nature and Origins of Mass Opinion.* New York: Cambridge University Press.

Zaller, John, and Stanley Feldman. 1992. A Simple Theory of the Survey Response: Answering Questions versus Revealing Preferences. *American Journal of Political Science* 36:579–616.

5

Policy Issues and
Electoral Democracy

Stuart Elaine Macdonald, George Rabinowitz,
and Holly Brasher

Politics deals with the allocation of values—whose ideas and interests will be supported by government decisions, and whose ideas and interests will be opposed or ignored. For example, should there be universal health insurance? How much income should be taken in taxes, and whose income? How much attention should be given to preserving and protecting the environment? These are all questions of whose values the government will favor and whose it won't. Democracy gives common people a voice in this allocation process by letting the general populace determine who controls government. Elections are the mechanism through which the mass public can exert influence over the policies under which they live.

Yet, one of the early insights of modern social science was that people tend to be poorly informed about most policy issues. Indeed, not only are citizens often ignorant of what is being debated in government, they also show considerable instability in their own preferences (A. Campbell et al. 1960; Converse 1964, 1970; Converse and Markus 1979; Zaller and Feldman 1992). While this might suggest that issues are irrelevant to elections, that is not the case. Current evidence supports the view that issues make a substantial contribution to voting decisions. Illustrative is Miller and Shanks's (1996) analysis of the 1992 election, which shows that issues are as important in explaining the vote as party identification, the single variable most closely associated with voting behavior in the United States.

Thus, we have some obvious questions to consider. How is it that people are generally uninformed about issues, but issues are still important to electoral outcomes? What, if any, consequences does the chronically low information level have for the way in which citizens are likely to process issue information? What are the consequences of individual issue processing for how parties and candidates compete for votes and for how the mass public influences policy-making?

In this chapter, we compare and contrast two models of candidate evaluation based on issues. We then observe how issues operated to influence feelings toward the candidates in the 1996 U.S. presidential election. We conclude by considering the general role of issues in elections and the nature of mass control of public policy. We selected the 1996 election because it provides an unusually good venue for investigating the impact of issues, as the National Election Study (NES) included a large battery of policy questions in that year. The NES is the leading academic survey of the U.S. public for the purpose of understanding voting behavior.

How People Understand Political Issues: An Example

We begin by considering an issue question asked of a sample of U.S. citizens during the 1996 presidential campaign. The NES regularly includes a set of seven-point issue questions, of which the following is illustrative:

> Some people think we need much tougher government regulations on business in order to protect the environment. (Suppose these people are at one end of a scale, at point 1.) Others think that current regulations to protect the environment are already too much of a burden on business. (Suppose these people are at the other end of the scale, at point number 7.) And, of course, some other people have opinions somewhere in between at points 2, 3, 4, 5 or 6.
>
> Where would you place YOURSELF on this scale, or haven't you thought much about this?

The respondent is shown a card displaying the issue scale with the seven points marked and the cue "Tougher regulations on business needed to protect the environment" at point 1 and the cue "Regulations to protect environment already too much of a burden on business" at point 7. The format of the card is illustrated in figure 5.1.

Now we'd like to turn the tables a bit and ask you, the reader, to respond to the survey question. What point would you select—1, 2, 3, 4, 5, 6, or 7? After you've made your choice, reflect for a moment on how you reached your decision. Did you think of a specific mix of environmental concern and desire for low regulation? Or did you think of which side you agreed with more?

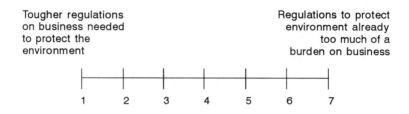

Fig. 5.1.   Illustration of NES issue question format

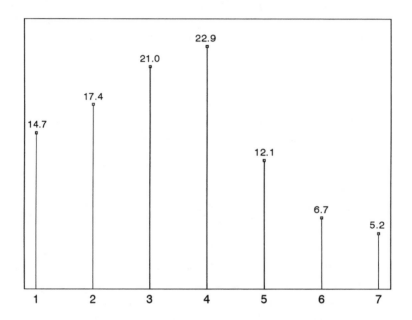

Fig. 5.2.   Distribution of respondents on environmental regulation question

Two Models of Issue Voting

To understand the link between issues and either public policy or electoral competition, it is necessary to have a systematic model that relates the issue position of individuals to their evaluation of candidates and parties. To give this assertion some meaning, it is useful to begin by examining the actual distribution of opinion on the environmental regulation question. In 1996 the sample of respondents was distributed as shown in figure 5.2. The greatest density of voters is at positions 3 and 4 on the scale, with 4 the modal category.

Given this distribution of opinion, what is the optimal position for a candidate to take? Before reaching any conclusions, it might be helpful to see where

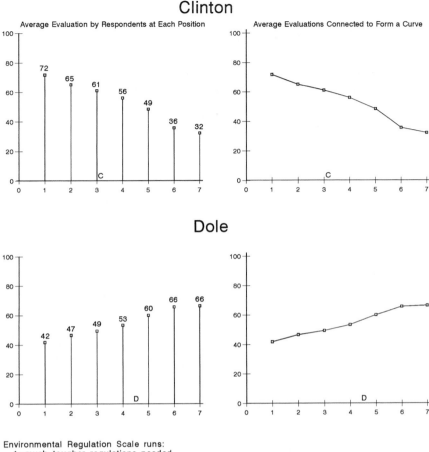

Fig. 5.3.   Evaluation as a function of position on environmental regulation scale

the candidates were located and how voters at each location evaluated them. The NES survey asked respondents where they would place each of the candidates on the issue scale. The average perception of Clinton's position was 3.18 and of Dole's position was 4.62.[1] Based on the environmental issue, which group of voters do you think will give Clinton the highest evaluation? Which group will give Dole the highest rating? Will the candidates be liked best by the voters closest to them?

Figure 5.3 shows the average evaluation of the candidates by voters at each of the locations on the environmental regulation scale. Clinton was perceived to stand at 3.18 on the scale, and voters at position 3 gave him an average evaluation of 61 degrees on the feeling thermometer. But notice that voters at position 2 and especially position 1 gave him higher ratings on average. The ratings decline from 1 through 7.

Now what about Bob Dole? The Republican candidate was located at 4.62, in between positions 4 and 5 on the scale. His average evaluation from voters at those locations were 53 and 60 degrees, respectively. But those were not the voters who liked him best—his highest evaluations came from voters at positions 6 and 7.

Do these results surprise you? We suspect they do, if the model you had in mind was the traditional proximity model in which voters evaluate candidates based on distance. If proximity were the key to evaluation, then voters nearest the candidate's position would give the highest ratings. But that does not occur.

If voters don't evaluate candidates based on proximity, how do voters evaluate candidates? Let us develop a somewhat different line of reasoning and begin by recalling the words of the authors of *The American Voter:* "In the electorate as a whole, the level of attention to politics is so low that what the public is exposed to must be highly visible—even stark—if it is to have an impact on opinion" (A. Campbell et al. 1960, 60). With this in mind, we begin with a strong presumption: when an issue is debated in the public arena, it becomes a contest of two competing sides. The many alternative policies that legislators might actively consider are not part of the issue debate the public sees. The essence of any issue debate in the mass domain is which of two sides one favors.

Thus, for an issue to have an impact on a voter's evaluation of a candidate, two conditions must be met. First, the voter must prefer one side or the other of the issue debate—otherwise, there is no basis for evaluating the candidate on the issue. Second, the candidate must provide strong enough cues in favor of one side or the other to cross the voter's "threshold of awareness."

Now consider two voters evaluating a moderately pro-environment candidate, located at 2.9 on the environmental scale. One voter is at position 1 and the other at position 3. If we divide the scale into two sides, both individuals are on the left—the pro-environment side. What distinguishes the voter at 1 is neither the side she favors nor any particular policy position; it is her certainty or intensity compared to the voter at position 3. In placing herself at position 1, the respondent is showing enthusiastic agreement with the left cue, while the voter at 3 is more ambivalent. Thus, an extreme—or distal—location on the issue scale signifies a strong desire for policy in the stated direction rather than a desire for an extreme policy option.

Given that the candidate is on the pro-environment side, which of these voters is likely to rate him more favorably on the basis of the environment—the one who is more intense about the issue or the one who is less intense? The more intense voter is more sensitive to environmental cues and reacts more strongly to the candidate's pro-environment stance; therefore, she would be expected to evaluate him more highly. Recall that this is what we saw in the evaluation curves in figure 5.3: the more intense voters liked Clinton more, even though he was closer to position 3. And the more intense voters on the pro-business side liked Dole more.

Now suppose a candidate were to give even stronger cues in favor of the environment. How would that affect his evaluations? The answer is that stronger cues would stimulate even stronger support from those who were pro-environment and stronger opposition from those who were pro-business. There is, however, a potential complication. If a candidate is effectively labeled an extremist, he or she will suffer because of that label. Thus, a candidate's cues must be strong enough to stimulate support but not so strong as to lead the media to stigmatize the candidate as irresponsible.

In general, in this framework evaluation is an interplay of voter and candidate intensity. Voters at distal positions on the scale react more strongly to candidates than do voters at more central positions. Candidates who give strong cues are evaluated more dramatically than those who give weaker cues. Candidates who fail to cross the threshold of awareness on an issue—either unintentionally or by design—make the issue irrelevant to their evaluation. Candidates labeled extremist are penalized.

In figure 5.4, panel A, four hypothetical candidates are evaluated by voters. The candidates are located at four different positions on the issue scale: center (*C*), moderate right (*MR*), right (*R*), and far right (*FR*). For each candidate, a curve is drawn to show how voters at each location on the issue scale would evaluate the candidate. The higher the curve, the more favorably voters at that position rate the candidate.

Consider first the curve for the center candidate. The curve is entirely flat, showing that the candidate receives the same evaluation from voters everywhere on the scale. The center reflects an absence of issue stimulation, so everyone has a neutral reaction to the candidate. Even voters who place themselves in the center do not feel favorably toward the center candidate, who is rated no differently by them than by voters on the left or right.

For the three candidates on the right side of the scale, evaluations are always highest from voters on the far right and decrease monotonically. Observe that the slope of the evaluation curve varies according to the candidate's location. The more intense a candidate is on an issue, the more the candidate's evaluation depends on the issue.

One additional feature of the figure is striking. The curves for the center, moderate right, and right candidates all intersect at the fifty-degree mark in the

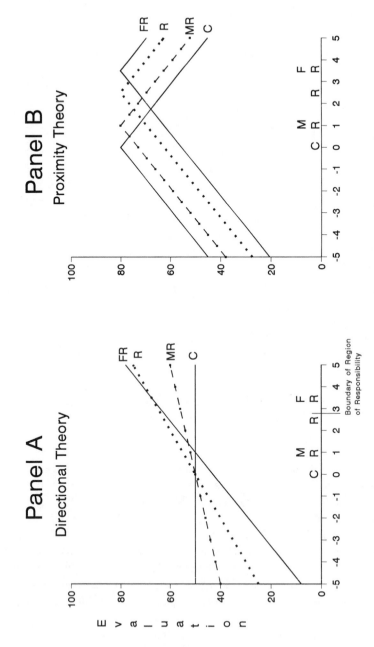

Fig. 5.4. Illustrative sketches comparing the two theories. (C denotes a candidate at the center, MR at the moderate right, R at the right, and FR at the far right.)

center of the scale, but the far right candidate receives distinctly lower evaluations from center voters and even from many voters on the right. Only the most intense voters on the right give the far right candidate higher evaluations than the other right candidates.

The evaluation of the far right candidate illustrates the principle that generating very high intensity comes at a price. A candidate who takes very intense stands is apt to be labeled an extremist, perhaps because he or she is perceived to lack the pragmatic flexibility that many voters see as essential to handling the ebb and flow of political events (see, e.g., Lipset and Rokkan 1967). In the United States, some major-party presidential candidates—Goldwater and McGovern most recently—have suffered from the extremist label, as did Ralph Nader in the 2000 election. Figure 5.4A includes a line identified as the boundary of the region of responsibility; this denotes the point beyond which a candidate is labeled an extremist.

Candidate issue intensity works something like a dimmer switch on a powerful light. When the switch is turned down, the issue disappears and becomes invisible. As the switch is turned up, the issue becomes increasingly visible and thus available for use in evaluating the candidate. If the light becomes too bright, however, it becomes a source of discomfort and distraction.

The model depicted in panel A of figure 5.4 is the directional model of candidate evaluation. It is useful to contrast this with the proximity model, displayed in panel B. In the proximity model, voters like best candidates who share their own issue position. Each evaluation curve peaks at the exact location of the candidate and declines monotonically with distance.

The two theoretical models can be nicely compared by focusing on their core questions. In the proximity model, the voter asks of a candidate, "How close is your position to mine?" In the directional model, the voter asks, "Are you on my side of the issues?" and "Can I trust you to be responsible?" From the voter's standpoint, the directional questions are inherently simpler. It takes a good deal of political knowledge to know what policy options are actively under consideration and which option specifically one would prefer. As Converse (1964) showed years ago, very few voters can meet exacting standards of policy information. In contrast, knowing whether a candidate is on one's side or not is a relatively simple task and can be made even simpler if the candidate sends out clear signals.

Candidate Strategies

The directional and proximity models suggest that different strategies should guide candidate behavior. Let us briefly consider what those strategies are. For simplicity, we restrict our attention to competitions involving only two candidates in a single dimension.

In the unidimensional case where only one issue or a single ideological dimension determines choice, the proximity model gives an unequivocal answer to the best strategy. That strategy is to adopt the position of the median voter (Downs 1957). This is illustrated in figure 5.5A, which shows a distribution of eleven voters labeled V1 to V11. Any candidate adopting the position of V6 will necessarily win the election, because that candidate will capture V6 and five other voters, no matter where the opposing candidate locates. If the opponent adopts a position to the right of V6, the candidate will capture the five voters to the left of V6; if the opponent adopts a position to the left of V6, the candidate will win the five voters to the right of V6.

The optimal strategy in directional theory in the unidimensional case is

Panel A.   Proximity Model

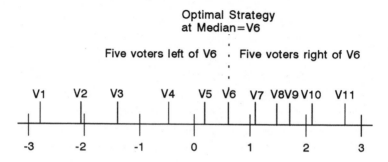

Panel B.   Directional Model

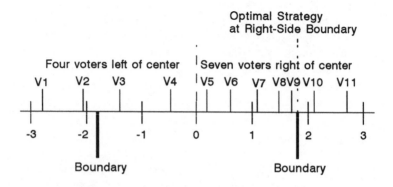

Fig. 5.5.   Optimal position in unidimensional competition. (*A*) Proximity model: Optimal position at median; (*B*) Directional model: Optimal position at boundary

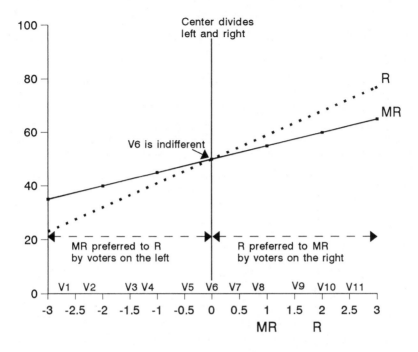

Fig. 5.6.   **Lack of optimum when median voter is at center**

somewhat less clear-cut but will generally constitute a less centrist strategy than under the proximity model. Given the voter distribution in figure 5.5 and the boundary points marked on the figure in panel B, the optimal candidate position is exactly at the right-side boundary. Let us see why that is the case.

In figure 5.5 there are more voters on the right than on the left, so winning the voters on the right will guarantee victory. If one candidate locates on the right and the opposing candidate locates on the left, then any position on the right will win. But if the opposing candidate also locates on the right, then the candidate who most effectively attracts the right-side voters will win. In directional theory, the key to turning on voters is to take strong stands. Thus, the winning candidate will be the one who is most clearly on the right without being an extremist. That is the candidate at the boundary of the region of responsibility.[2]

In the figure, a candidate at the boundary is guaranteed the support of voters V5 through V11, compared to any candidate left of the boundary point. In general, the boundary point on the side of the issue that has the plurality of voters is the dominant position in directional theory.

The less clear-cut nature of the optimum in directional theory derives from two considerations: (1) the exact location of the boundary of the region of responsibility is unknown, and (2) there is no optimum if an equal number of voters are on each side of the center position. The second point is illustrated in figure 5.6, which displays a new distribution of eleven voters with V6 now exactly in the middle of the continuum. Evaluation curves are shown for a candidate on the moderate right and the right. Both candidates are within the region of responsibility.

In this case, the two candidates will divide the vote equally, with the voters on the right supporting the right candidate and the voters on the left supporting the moderate right candidate. More generally, for any pair of candidates within the region, the candidate further to the right will win the voters on the right, the candidate further to the left will win the voters on the left, and V6 at the center will be indifferent between the various choices. The election will be a draw.

Which Model Is Right?

Models at the level of abstraction of directional and proximity theory are never perfectly right or wrong—they serve as abstract representations of processes that are far more complex than any simple model can possibly capture. Nevertheless, one model is almost surely more correct than the other, and the question of which one is better is of real consequence. The view that candidates should match the policy position of the median voter follows directly from the proximity model and goes to the heart of how we understand the mass public to influence the policy debate. In contrast, under the directional model, candidates define issues with an eye toward contesting the election on issues on which they are advantaged. Both the politics and public policy implications are different depending on which of the two models provides a more accurate perspective on politics. And without a model to guide our understanding, all we have is descriptive information about voter location—we have no ability to translate that information into a meaningful interpretation of politics.

So which model is better? We began our discussion with the illustrative issue of government regulation to protect the environment (see fig. 5.3). On that issue, it is clear that the evaluation pattern closely fits the predictions of directional theory and fails to conform to the expectations of proximity theory. Evaluations for Clinton are highest among those on the far left side of the issue and decline consistently as voters take positions to the right; evaluations for Dole peak at the far right and decline as voters move leftward. Voters close to Clinton's position like him less well than voters who are more distal on his side; similarly, more distal voters on the other side like Dole best.

Of course, the environment is just one issue, and elections usually involve many issues. So it is necessary to embed the theories in a richer and more complex issue environment and to see how they compare empirically when they are put to a systematic test. This requires translating the verbal descriptions of the theories into mathematical formulations.

Mathematical Descriptions of the Theories

The Proximity Model

Proximity or distance is such a natural idea that most people give it very little thought. But distance can have a couple of different meanings. The most common way to think of distance is as Euclidean distance. The Euclidean distance between a voter and a candidate can be expressed using the following formula:

$$\text{Distance}_{CV} = [\Sigma_k \text{Importance}_k \, (\text{Issue Position}_{Ck} - \text{Issue Position}_{Vk})^2]^{1/2}$$

where
   Importance_k represents the importance of issue k in the election,
   $\text{Issue Position}_{Ck}$ represents the position of candidate C on issue k,
   $\text{Issue Position}_{Vk}$ represents the position of voter V on issue k.

Euclidean distance is a good representation of distance as we commonly visualize it when we look at two points or as we experience it when we go between places without obstacles between them. The formula itself follows directly from the Pythagorean theorem that in right triangles the length of the hypotenuse is the square root of the sum of the squares of the two sides.

The formula we present includes one addition to the standard distance formula, the introduction of the importance of issue k. If one issue is very important and other issues are less important, then the degree to which a voter separates from a candidate on the important issue is more significant than on the less important issues. In geometric terms the space is stretched when an issue is important, making differences on that issue more consequential for judgments.

Euclidean distance is not the only kind of distance. If you are in a city and want to go between two locations that are not on the same block—a restaurant and a movie theater, for example—it is usually impossible to walk or drive in a straight line. Instead, it is necessary to follow the block contour of the city. If your trip involves going three blocks in a north-south direction and four blocks in an east-west direction, you must travel a total of seven blocks. The same trip in Euclidean space would allow you to move in a straight line, and the distance would be five blocks.[3]

The city-block distance formula is somewhat simpler than the Euclidean formula. It is

$$\text{Distance}_{CV} = [\Sigma_k \text{Importance}_k |\text{Issue Position}_{Ck} - \text{Issue Position}_{Vk}|]$$

where the symbols | | indicate the absolute value. In a city-block metric, it is strictly the difference between the voter and candidate on each of the issues that is added up to determine the distance.

In most empirical situations, it makes little difference which type of distance is considered, as they tend to yield similar results. In the analysis we do, we use city-block distance because it is easier to analyze in a multivariate model.

The Directional Model

The directional model relies on the directional compatibility between the voter and the candidate and their intensities. This is nicely summarized by simply multiplying the position of the candidate by the position of the voter, provided the issue scale has been appropriately centered. To center the scale, subtract the center position on the original scale (position 4) from the issue position of the voter and the candidate. Using the same notation as before,

$$\text{Centered Issue Position}_{Vk} = (\text{Issue Position}_{Vk} - \text{Center Position}_k)$$

The centered position has a sign and a magnitude. It is positive if the voter is to the right of the center position and negative if the voter is to the left. The further to the left the person is, the larger the negative value will be; and the further to the right, the larger the positive value. Thus, on the 7-point environmental scale with 4 being the center position, a voter at position 1 will have a value of -3 on the centered scale. Instead of going from 1 to 7, the values on the centered scale go from -3 to $+3$.

Once the scales are centered, the computation of the product of the voter and candidate positions is the building block of directional theory. The sum of these products over all the issues is called the scalar product. We can write the scalar product as follows:

$$\text{SP}_{CV} = \Sigma_k \text{Importance}_k \times \text{Centered Issue Position}_{Ck} \times \text{Centered Issue Position}_{Vk}$$

When the candidate and the voter are on the same side, the product of their issue positions will be positive, and when they are on opposite sides, the product will be negative. The more intense either the voter or the candidate is, the larger the product will be. Being more intense leads to higher positives from those who agree with the candidate and higher negatives from those who disagree. A voter at the exact center has a zero value on the centered scale; therefore, the product will be zero regardless of whether the candidate is left, right, or center. The same holds true for a candidate exactly in the center: the product will be zero, no matter where the voter is located. Thus, candidates who convey a strong message generate dramatic evaluations, while center candidates are neither loved nor hated.

Intensity has another effect as well: as we discussed earlier, the electorate will penalize a candidate who is effectively labeled an extremist. Therefore, candidates walk a fine line between the need to stimulate support and the need to appear responsible. This constraint is incorporated in directional theory by including a penalty that applies to candidates located outside the boundary of the region of responsibility. The evaluation of a candidate under the directional model is

$$\text{DIR}_{CV} = \Sigma_k \, \text{Importance}_k \times \text{Centered Issue Position}_{Ck} \\ \times \text{Centered Issue Position}_{Vk} - \text{Penalty}_{CV}$$

where $\text{Penalty}_{CV} = 0$ whenever $\Sigma_k \, (\text{Centered Issue Position}_{Ck})^2 \leq r^2$, where r is the radius of the region of responsibility.

In U.S. presidential elections since 1972, every major party candidate has been within the region of responsibility, so the directional penalty has not been a factor. The penalty concept is more critical, however, in multiparty competitions where gaining a fixed number of votes can lead to parliamentary seats. Parties can more readily succeed with an extremist label when they must only win the support of a limited number of voters.

Testing the Theories in the 1996 Presidential Election

The 1996 U.S. presidential election followed a congressional election in which the Republican Party had taken control of the House of Representatives for the first time since 1952, ending forty years of Democratic domination of that chamber. The elections of 1996 presented the Republican Party with its first realistic opportunity since the Great Depression to gain complete control of the U.S. national government. Its only obstacle was William Jefferson Clinton. While Clinton had been widely discounted as a potential repeat winner after the 1994 Republican sweep, he was very much alive and kicking by 1996. With a good economy and generally favorable reviews from the public, he was a formidable incumbent who represented a test likely to try any challenger.

The challenger's hat went to Bob Dole. A longtime contender for the Republican nomination, Dole finally achieved his goal in 1996. His credentials as Senate majority leader were impeccable, and he was well liked by the Republican leadership and Republicans in the electorate. Based on the early polls, the most serious threat to his nomination was Colin Powell, the African American general who had led U.S. troops in the Gulf War. Powell, however, chose not to put his name in contention. The two most interesting challenges to Dole's nomination came from Steve Forbes, a wealthy magazine publisher who favored a flat tax, and Pat Buchanan, who favored traditional social values and less open borders—both in terms of economic protectionism and in terms of fewer immigrant families. Buchanan never rose very high in national polls rating the candidates, perhaps because he was the only serious nomination contender to draw an extremist label. Forbes's flat tax had some early resonance with voters, but once the economic consequences of the flat tax became better known (particularly in New Hampshire), voters appeared to cool to the idea and to Forbes.[4]

The Empirical Test

To test the two theories, data must be collected on where the voters and the candidates are located on the key issues of the day. The 1996 NES asked eleven issue questions that included both respondent and candidate placements.

Nine of the questions were asked in exactly the same seven-point format used in the illustrative environmental regulation question. These questions dealt with

1. Government services versus reduced government spending
2. Increased versus decreased defense spending
3. Government versus private health insurance
4. Government versus private responsibility for providing jobs and living standards
5. Government help for blacks versus blacks helping themselves
6. Reduced crime through attacking social problems versus catching, convicting, and punishing criminals
7. Environmental protection versus jobs
8. Environmental protection versus regulation of business (the sample question)
9. Equal roles for women and men versus a woman's place is in the home

A tenth question focused on abortion and provided the respondent with four specific alternatives:

1 = by law, abortion should never be permitted

2 = the law should permit abortion only in case of rape, incest, or when the woman's life is in danger

3 = the law should permit abortion for reasons other than rape, incest, or danger to a woman's life, but only after the need for the abortion has been clearly established

4 = by law, a woman should always be able to obtain an abortion as a matter of personal choice

The eleventh question asked respondents to place themselves and the candidates on a seven-point ideology scale. Here the choices were 1 = extremely liberal, 2 = liberal, 3 = slightly liberal, 4 = moderate/middle of the road, 5 = slightly conservative, 6 = conservative, and 7 = extremely conservative.

To test the theories, we compare their ability to predict the evaluation of Clinton and Dole. Evaluation is measured in the NES by feeling thermometer ratings of the candidates on a zero- to one hundred degree scale.[5] First we analyze evaluation taking only issues into account, then we add the possibility that candidates themselves might have a unique nonissue effect on evaluation, and then we add a set of background characteristics to see how that influences the impact of issues. Individuals are located where they placed themselves on the issue scales, and each candidate is located at his median perceived position. We estimate the models using ordinary least squares regression.[6]

The results are summarized in table 5.1. The values displayed in the table are unstandardized regression coefficients, appropriate for comparing the impact of the issues within a given model. They are not useful for comparing across the theories because the variables are measured in different units.[7]

The directional model provides a better accounting of how people evaluate candidates based on issues. This can be seen by comparing the adjusted R-squared values at the bottom of the table. These values reflect the percent of variation in candidate affect that the models successfully predict. The first set of columns (Model I) reports the results of the simple issue analysis. Notice that the directional model of issues accounts for about 35 percent of the variance, compared to 29 percent for the proximity model. The second set of columns (Model II) incorporates the idea that other aspects of the candidates quite independent of issues can influence their evaluation. While the basic results remain the same, we see a tendency for people to evaluate Clinton somewhat better than would be expected on the basis of issues alone. The positive values in the Clinton dummy row show how much more favorably the typical voter rates Clinton than Dole after taking issue effects into account. The final set of columns (Model III) controls for a variety of social characteristics. Some of the issue effects weaken when the demographic variables are included, but the overall pattern is maintained.

The results in table 5.1 show the dominance of the directional model over the proximity model. They also demonstrate that the issues have decidedly dif-

TABLE 5.1. Effect of Issues on the Evaluation of Clinton and Dole in the 1996 Presidential Election Based on a Pooled OLS Regression

	Model I Issues Only		Model II Issues + Clinton Dummy		Model III Issues + Clinton Dummy + Demography	
	Proximity Model	Directional Model	Proximity Model	Directional Model	Proximity Model	Directional Model
Liberal-conservative	-8.05*	3.50*	-8.25*	3.62*	-7.71*	3.66*
Government services	-3.58*	3.82*	-3.81*	3.89*	-2.92*	3.34*
Defense spending	0.63	0.69	0.92	0.51	0.45	0.69
Environment versus jobs	0.31	0.60	0.61	0.37	-0.12	1.18
Environmental regulation	-1.02	2.57*	-0.69	2.38*	-0.61	1.63*
Health insurance	-2.93*	1.57*	-3.02*	1.55*	-2.64*	1.36*
Jobs and living standards	-0.84	0.86	-1.25	0.98*	-0.66	0.81
Abortion	-1.79*	0.72*	-1.67*	0.66*	-1.62*	0.73*
Aid blacks	-0.59	-0.34	-1.14	-0.10	-1.24	-0.24
Approach to crime	0.10	-0.34	0.11	-0.34	-0.27	-0.23
Women's role	-0.75	0.72*	0.16	0.59*	-0.24	0.60*
Intercept	85.47*	51.58*	81.94*	50.46*	75.26*	45.41*
Clinton dummy			5.98*	2.94	4.61	1.69
Demography					—[a]	—[a]
Adjusted R^2	0.290	0.352	0.298	0.353	0.351	0.386
N of cases	1,815	1,815	1,815	1,815	1,815	1,815

Note: Coefficients are unstandardized regression coefficients from a pooled OLS regression.

[a] Eighteen demographic effects were estimated separately for each candidate, for a total of thirty six demographic effects. All of the demographic variables were dummy variables that took on a value of 1 for those included in the category and a value of 0 for those excluded. The dummy variables were (1) black, (2) south, (3) female, (4) married, (5) Hispanic, (6) union household, (7) public sector worker, (8) self-employed, (9) Protestant, (10) Catholic, (11) Jew, (12) those who believe "the Bible is the actual word of God and is to be taken literally, word for word," (13) age low, (14) age high, (15) education low, (16) education high, (17) income low, and (18) income high. Using a .01 level of significance, the demographic effects that were significant in the proximity model were black/Clinton (coefficient = 24.90), Hispanic/Clinton (8.53), Jew/Clinton (19.98), education low/Clinton (9.99) and public sector/Dole (5.68). In the directional model, effects were significant for black/Clinton (coefficient = 18.33), Hispanic/Clinton (6.96), education low/Clinton (10.09), and public sector/Dole (6.74). The adjusted R-squared for a model including only the demographic variables and the Clinton dummy was 0.150.

*Significant at the .01 level.

ferent effects. We turn now to consider these effects and their political meaning.

The Role of Issues

Our discussion focuses on the results of the directional model, as it more accurately reflects the role of issues in evaluating candidates. Six issues show a consistently significant impact across the three statistical analyses: liberal-conservative position, attitude toward government services, abortion, environmental regulation, health insurance, and women's role. A seventh issue, jobs and living standards, has a borderline effect that registers significance in just one of the three specifications. No issue is significant in the proximity analysis that fails to show significance in the directional analysis. Notably, the environmental issue has a sizable effect in the directional model but is not significant in any of the proximity analyses.

We rely on the issue analysis including the Clinton dummy (Model II) because it incorporates the most critical control—that of overall candidate impact—while maintaining a direct focus on the issues. We are not arguing this is the most preferred analysis, but it has the advantage of being the least arbitrary in terms of its specification.[8] Let us now make some political sense of the results.

As we saw earlier, three factors determine the effect of an issue on the evaluation of a candidate:

(1) the importance of the issue,
(2) the position of the candidate,
(3) the position of the voter.

The estimated directional coefficient for environmental regulation in table 5.1 is 2.38. That value reflects the importance of the issue but in itself does not reveal much about the issue's impact. To know its influence on a candidate's evaluation, we must know where the candidate stands on the issue, and to know its influence on the differential evaluation of the two candidates, we need to know the difference in the candidates' positions.

In the case of the environmental issue, we know that Clinton's median perceived position in 1996 placed him at −.82 left of center. We can calculate the expected impact on Clinton's evaluation of a shift in a voter's position one unit further to the right on the environmental regulation scale as follows:

$$\text{Effect} = \text{importance} \times \text{Clinton position} \times \text{change in voter position}$$
$$= 2.38 \quad \times (.82) \quad \times 1$$

$$\text{Effect} = -1.95$$

Clinton's evaluation would be expected to decline 1.95 degrees on the feeling thermometer for each unit shift to the right on the environmental scale. The effect is determined as a product of the importance of the issue as assessed in the regression (2.38) and the directional intensity of the candidate (−.82). The minus sign means that evaluation will decline as voters are located further to the right. Intensity controls the expected amount of change. If Clinton had been more intensely pro-environment, the estimated impact would have been greater. If he had been more centrist, the estimated impact would have been less. Since our goal is to assess the impact of a one-unit shift to the right in the voter's position, the change in voter position is fixed at +1. While a value of +1 does not affect the multiplication, we display the value to reinforce the fact that voter position is itself a critical component of the effect.

In 1996 Dole's perceived position on the environmental scale was .62 units to the right of center. A similar set of calculations for the Republican candidate shows:

Predicted Change in Dole's Evaluation = 2.38 × (.62) × 1 = 1.48

Dole's evaluation would be expected to increase by 1.48 thermometer evaluation units for each unit shift to the right on the scale. Dole's more centrist position (.62) induces a slightly weaker predicted effect than Clinton's does. And, of course, because Dole is on the right, his evaluation is predicted to increase as a voter moves to the right, whereas Clinton's is predicted to decrease.

What is most critical to the outcome of the election is the net effect of the issue on the difference in evaluation of the two candidates. The net effect on candidate difference is determined by how far apart the candidates are on the issue. The fact that Clinton was at −.82 and Dole at .62 means that they were 1.44 units apart. Therefore the predicted change is calculated as follows:

Predicted Change in (Dole − Clinton) Difference = 2.38 × (1.44) × 1 = 3.43

This value (within rounding error) can also be obtained by taking the difference between the previous calculations: 1.48 − (−1.95) = 3.43.

Table 5.2 summarizes the impact of each of the six significant issues and shows the impact of a one-unit, four-unit, and six-unit change. The six-unit effect is the maximum potential impact of an issue, comparing those on the far left with those on the far right. The four-unit effect provides a more modest—and more realistic—assessment of the effect by showing the difference between those with a clear left and a clear right position on the issue.

Looking at the table, we see two reversals in the impact of issues once the location of the candidates is taken into consideration. The issue with the

TABLE 5.2. Estimated Potential Impact of Six Issues on the Evaluation of Clinton and Dole in 1996

	Regression Coefficient	Clinton Location	Dole Location	Location Difference	1-Unit Effect[a]	4-Unit Effect	6-Unit Effect
Liberal-conservative	3.62	-1.06	+1.56	2.62	9.49	37.9	56.9
Government services	3.89	-1.04	+0.94	1.97	7.68	30.7	46.1
Environmental regulation	2.38	-0.82	+0.62	1.44	3.44	13.8	20.6
Health insurance	1.55	-1.40	+1.19	2.59	4.02	16.1	24.1
Abortion[b]	0.66	-2.26	+0.81	3.07	2.01	8.0	12.1
Women's role	0.59	-2.13	-0.59	1.54	0.90	3.6	5.4

Note: Candidate locations are based on the interpolated median of the placements given by respondents. Government services and abortion were reverse coded.

[a]The 1-unit effect is determined by multiplying the regression coefficient by the location difference. Because of rounding, the 4- and 6-unit effects are sometimes not exact multiples of the 1-unit effect.

[b]The abortion values were rescaled to match the 7-point format of the other issues by multiplying the original value by 2 and subtracting 1.

strongest potential effect is liberal-conservative, because Clinton and Dole diverged more clearly on the ideological spectrum than on government services. Similarly, the issue of health insurance overtakes environmental regulation because of the candidates' more distinctive stands on medical care. Some of the issue effects are quite substantial.

For understanding the effect of an issue on an election, however, a critical piece of the story is still missing. What ultimately determines an issue's impact is both its potential potency as shown in table 5.2 and where the voters are located. If voters are equally divided on both sides of an issue, the issue can be quite powerful in determining evaluations, but in the end the advantage that accrues to a candidate from voters on one side of the issue will be offset by losses from voters on the other side. Only when a disproportionate number of voters is on one side or the other of an issue will the issue help or hurt a candidate's electoral performance.

The issues in the 1996 election had quite different voter distributions, as shown in figure 5.7 and table 5.3. For the two most important issues in terms of their potential impact on evaluation—liberal-conservative and government services—the weight of the distribution was on the right, favoring Dole. For the government services issue, however, the balance favoring the Republican side was modest, and for both issues, the center category was the mode, where according to directional theory there is little anticipated impact. With that said, however, the advantage accruing to the Republican candidate on the basis of attitudes toward the liberal-conservative spectrum was impressive. If the election had been contested solely on this issue, the Republicans would have had a very marked advantage. Thus, it is hardly surprising that in the debates and in his ads, Dole worked to associate himself closely with the conservative label and to associate Clinton with the liberal label. This issue works extremely well for the Republican Party.

The issue of environmental regulation clearly favored the Democratic Party. While its predicted effect as measured by the regression coefficient was less than half that of the previous issues, its net impact was actually greater than government services and only slightly less than liberal-conservative. The fact that so many voters took the pro-environment side gave the issue its potency. When compared to either liberal-conservative or government services, the environment is a relatively one-sided issue.

The health insurance issue is intriguing. Here the advantage that accrued to either party was minimal because the distribution was relatively evenly balanced: among those taking the most intense positions, the number on the far left narrowly exceeded the number on the far right, while in the other two categories the edge reversed but remained small. Given that voters at the endpoints are more influenced by an issue than those near the center, health insurance represented the closest thing to a perfect standoff between the parties. According to

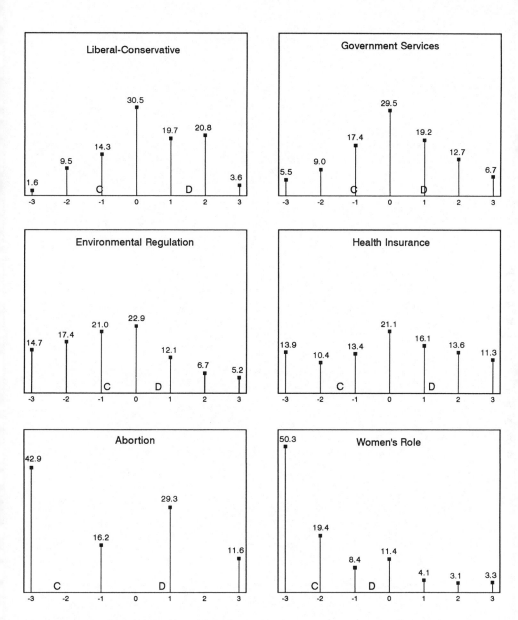

Fig. 5.7. Distribution of respondents on six issues in the 1996 presidential election. (C indicates Clinton's position on each issue, D indicates Dole's position.)

TABLE 5.3.   Candidate Advantage on Six Issues by Intensity Level of Respondents

Advantage by Intensity Level[a]

Liberal-Conservative
Advantage Dole: 18.7% more respondents on the right. All intensity levels favor the right.

Low	Medium	High
5.4 R	11.3 R	2.0 R

Government Services
Advantage Dole: 6.7% more respondents on the right. All intensity levels favor the right.

Low	Medium	High
1.8 R	3.7 R	1.2 R

Environmental Regulations
Advantage Clinton: 29.1% more respondents on the left. All intensity levels favor the left.

Low	Medium	High
8.9 L	10.7 L	9.5 L

Health Insurance
Advantage Unclear: 3.3% more respondents on the right. The strongest intensity level favors the left.

Low	Medium	High
2.7 R	3.2 R	2.6 L

Abortion
Advantage Clinton: 18.2% more respondents on the left. The strongest intensity level favors the left.

Low	High
13.1 R	31.3 L

Women's Role
Advantage Clinton: 67.6% more respondents on the left. All intensity levels favor the left.

Low	Medium	High
4.3 L	16.3 L	47.0 L

[a]This is the difference between the percentage of respondents on the right and the percentage of respondents on the left at each level of intensity. Respondents at −1 and +1 have a low level of intensity, −2 and +2 a medium level, and −3 and +3 a high level. If the percentage of respondents on the left side of the issue is larger, the percentage difference is followed by an L; if the percentage on the right is larger, the difference is followed by an R.

directional theory, this is an issue on which neither party would have an incentive to converge. And apparently there was no convergence, as both candidates took stands outside the middle range of −1 to +1 on the issue scale.

On abortion, the intense voters fell disproportionately on the Democratic side, with a Clinton edge of more than 30 percent among those taking the strongest stand for or against abortion. Among the more moderate, the edge was in Dole's favor, with 13 percent more opposed to general abortion rights. The net effect was clearly pro-Clinton, as both the greater preponderance of voters and the greater preponderance of intense voters favored allowing abortions. The overall impact of the issue was limited, however, by the relatively small regression coefficient.

The issue of women's role was the most one-sided of the six issues. There is very strong support in the electorate for the view that women should have an equal role with men. Consistent with this, women's role was the only issue on which both candidates were located on the same side. The relative closeness of the candidates and the small regression coefficient both worked to limit the issue's net impact, although it was clearly in Clinton's favor.

It is natural to ask, Who would have won based strictly on these six issues? To answer this question, we make a prediction for each voter based on the voter's issue position, the importance of the issue, and the position of the candidates. This entails calculating the product for each issue and then adding up the set of products to obtain a predicted evaluation for Clinton and then repeating the process for Dole. If the predicted evaluation is higher for Clinton, we predict a Clinton vote by the individual; if it is higher for Dole, we predict a Dole vote. The net prediction is a 52.9 to 47.1 percent victory for Clinton.[9] The advantages that accrued to Clinton on the basis of the environment, abortion, and women's role were more than enough to offset his liabilities on the liberal-conservative and government services issues. The health insurance issue served to inflame passions on both sides but with no serious detriment to either candidate.

Real Politics

In the real world of politics, policy issues are one of the elements that presidential candidates can use to draw support from voters. What issues do they discuss? And how do they discuss them? If candidates were entirely free to take any position imaginable, the logic of directional politics would be for candidates to get on the correct (i.e., plurality) side of every issue and then to emphasize those issues where they had a clear advantage over their opponent. In directional theory, a candidate is neither advantaged nor disadvantaged by being in the center. The center is a place where candidates who are well liked based on personality or past accomplishments can rest and keep issues out of a campaign. If, however, the contest is lively and no candidate has laurels on which to rest, the center is not the right place to be.

In the press—and perhaps even in the minds of practicing political scientists—there is often confusion between a centrist strategy and a plurality strategy. A centrist strategy is one in which the candidate tries to locate at the position of the median voter on each issue; in a plurality strategy, the candidate tries to be on the plurality side of each issue. Plurality-seeking politicians are not centrists—they want to be clearly associated with the plurality side of the issue, not in the center. They might appropriately be called opportunistic because they do not conform to a preexisting ideological orthodoxy, but that is different from taking a determinedly center position on each issue. With his mix of health care, environment, balanced budget, and welfare reform, Clinton was not attempting to reproduce the policy positions of the median voter; he was attempting to draw the support of the plurality of the electorate by taking the popular side of as many issues as possible.

Another national-level candidate whose behavior conformed to the logic of directional politics was John McCain. McCain mounted a surprisingly credible challenge to George W. Bush in the 2000 Republican primary contest and was the plurality winner of the open primary ballot in California. What distinguished McCain's candidacy were his strong issue positions, many of which ran counter to the usual ideology of his party. McCain first emerged in the national spotlight when he advocated tough controls on tobacco products; then in the 2000 election he argued forcefully for campaign finance reform. In each case, McCain advanced a position on the plurality side of the issue and was the single politician most closely identified with that side of the debate. McCain was not a centrist on either issue, yet those were the issues that gained him national prominence.

In general, four guidelines seem appropriate for candidates to follow in their campaigns.

(1) Candidates should stress issues on which they have a natural advantage—that is, where a greater number of voters are on their side of the issue than the side of their opponent (see Petrocik 1996).

(2) The issues should be credible to debate. Simply raising an issue that the media will consider illegitimate or the public will think is insignificant will not generate much support. In other words, issues differ in their potential for activating support (see, e.g., Rabinowitz, Prothro, and Jacoby 1982).

(3) Candidates should be sensitive to the possibility of issue reframing by a determined opponent. If a candidate defines an issue but the opponent can redefine it in terms of a different dichotomy on which the candidate is on the wrong side, then the strategy can backfire (see Riker 1990; Macdonald and Rabinowitz 1993).

(4) Candidates should be careful to be seen as responsible. Taking a stand or set of stands that can be readily labeled as extremist will threaten the overall credibility of a candidate, even if the stand itself is popular.

It is beyond the scope of this essay to chronicle candidate strategies in the United States over the past several decades. Nevertheless, it is striking that Republican candidates at least since Reagan have been fairly determinedly directional, while only Clinton of recent Democrats has followed a similar directional strategy. The Republican Party's Contract with America, formulated in the context of the 1994 congressional elections, conformed well to the directional stratagem in delineating ten issue positions, each of which had strong plurality support. Bush's selection of tax reduction as his paramount issue in the 2000 campaign also fit the mold.

Public Policy and Directional Voting

From a public policy perspective, presidential candidates present directions and, if elected, try to effect policy that conforms to their directional promises (Ginsberg 1976; Budge and Farlie 1983). Elections do not provide a fixed policy prescription but rather a loose guide to where the country should be going. In this regard, every election is a consideration of which of two directions the country favors. The United States presents such formidable obstacles to policy enactment via its separation of powers that even if specific policies were presented and debated, they would be unlikely to be enacted. It is important to realize, however, that the degree to which any mass public can digest the specifics (and often even the generalities) of public policy debate is quite limited.

Directional politics serves two functions. It encourages parties and candidates to seek issues on which they can build advantage, and it encourages candidates to simplify issues so that they can be digested at least by the more aware citizens. Directional politics thus provides a strong entrepreneurial incentive for elites to be responsive to mass concerns.

Elections, however, are unlikely to fit well within the classic context of the mass public exerting direct influence on public policy. Policy-making beyond the lowest level is simply not in the mass domain. And the very process of dichotomizing and simplifying issues will necessarily encourage a politics in which symbolism often dominates substance.

While we have focused exclusively on issues in this essay, much of winning and losing elections hinges on how well a party performs in office (Kramer 1971; Fiorina 1981; J. Campbell 1992; Lewis-Beck and Rice 1992; Gelman and King 1993). This is an important fact to bear in mind, for it places a limit on symbolic manipulation and gives parties a clear incentive to formulate policies that work. Combining the politics of reward and punishment based on performance with a directional politics based on issues produces a dual mechanism encouraging policy that is sensitive to mass preferences. If the mechanism is less than one of direct mass control, that can hardly be seen as a disappointment.

NOTES

1. The average perception is the interpolated median of the placements given for each candidate.

2. Figure 5.4A showed that the candidate at the right-side boundary has a higher evaluation curve for voters on that side than do any of the other candidates within the region. We assume that the penalty for extremism is sufficiently large that a candidate located beyond the boundary is guaranteed to lose to a candidate at the boundary.

3. The square root of $(3^2 + 4^2 = 25) = 5$.

4. There has been a good deal of scholarly work on the 1996 election; see, for example, Abramson, Aldrich, and Rohde 1999, Alvarez and Nagler 1998, Pomper 1997, and Weisberg and Box-Steffensmeier 1999.

5. The wording of the feeling thermometer question is as follows: "I'd like to get

your feelings toward some of our political leaders and other people who are in the news these days. I'll read the name of a person and I'd like you to rate that person using something we call the feeling thermometer. Ratings between fifty degrees and one hundred degrees mean that you feel favorable and warm toward the person. Ratings between zero degrees and fifty degrees mean that you don't feel favorable toward the person and that you don't care too much for that person. You would rate the person at the fifty-degree mark if you don't feel particularly warm or cold toward the person. If we come to a person whose name you don't recognize, you don't need to rate that person. Just tell me and we'll move on to the next one."

6. The evaluations of Clinton and Dole are pooled and analyzed in the same model.

7. In each theory, the explanatory variables involve voter and candidate issue positions, but in the proximity model they are city-block distances, which are in linear units, while in the directional model they are scalar products, which are in squared units.

8. Scholars might differ in terms of what they feel are appropriate demographic controls.

9. The prediction includes only people who reported that they voted and is based exclusively on the issues. Incorporating the Clinton dummy would lead to a larger predicted victory for Clinton.

REFERENCES

Abramson, Paul R., John H. Aldrich, and David W. Rohde. 1999. *Change and Continuity in the 1996 and 1998 Elections.* Washington, D.C.: CQ Press.

Alvarez, R. Michael, and Jonathan Nagler. 1998. Economics, Entitlements, and Social Issues: Voter Choice in the 1996 Presidential Election. *American Journal of Political Science* 42:1349–63.

Budge, Ian, and Dennis J. Farlie. 1983. *Explaining and Predicting Elections.* Winchester, Mass.: Allen and Unwin.

Campbell, Angus, Philip E. Converse, Warren E. Miller, and Donald E. Stokes. 1960. *The American Voter.* New York: Wiley.

Campbell, James E. 1992. Forecasting the Presidential Vote in the States. *American Journal of Political Science* 36:386–407.

Converse, Philip E. 1964. The Nature of Belief Systems in Mass Publics. In David E. Apter, ed., *Ideology and Discontent.* Glencoe, Ill.: Free Press.

———. 1970. Attitudes and Non-Attitudes: Continuation of a Dialogue. In Edward R. Tufte, ed., *The Quantitative Analysis of Social Problems.* Reading, Mass.: Addison-Wesley.

Converse, Philip E., and Gregory B. Markus. 1979. *Plus ça change . . .* The New CPS Election Study Panel. *American Political Science Review* 73:32–49.

Davis, Otto, Melvin J. Hinich, and Peter Ordeshook. 1970. An Expository Development of a Mathematical Model of the Electoral Process. *American Political Science Review* 64:426–48.

Downs, Anthony. 1957. *An Economic Theory of Democracy.* New York: Harper and Row.

Enelow, James M., and Melvin J. Hinich. 1984. *The Spatial Theory of Voting: An Introduction.* New York: Cambridge University Press.

Fiorina, Morris. 1981. *Retrospective Voting in American National Elections.* New Haven: Yale University Press.

Gelman, Andrew, and Gary King. 1993. Why Are American Presidential Election Campaign Polls So Variable When Votes Are So Predictable? *British Journal of Political Science* 23: 409–20.

Ginsberg, Benjamin. 1976. Elections and Public Policy. *American Political Science Review* 70:41–49.

Kramer, Gerald H. 1971. Short-Term Fluctuations in U.S. Voting Behavior, 1896–1964. *American Political Science Review* 65: 131–43.

Lewis-Beck, Michael S., and Tom W. Rice. 1992. *Forecasting Elections.* Washington, D.C.: CQ Press.

Lipset, Seymour M., and Stein Rokkan. 1967. Cleavage Structures, Party Systems, and Voter Alignments: An Introduction. In Seymour M. Lipset and Stein Rokkan, eds., *Party Systems and Voter Alignments.* New York: Free Press.

Macdonald, Stuart Elaine, and George Rabinowitz. 1993. Direction and Uncertainty in a Model of Issue Voting. *Journal of Theoretical Politics* 5:61–87.

Macdonald, Stuart Elaine, George Rabinowitz, and Ola Listhaug. 1995. Political Sophistication and Models of Issue Voting. *British Journal of Political Science* 25:453–83.

Miller, Warren E., and J. Merrill Shanks. 1996. *The New American Voter.* Cambridge: Harvard University Press.

Petrocik, John R. 1996. Issue Ownership in Presidential Elections, with a 1980 Case Study. *American Journal of Political Science* 40:825–50.

Pomper, Gerald M., ed. 1997. *The Election of 1996: Reports and Interpretations.* New York: Chatham House.

Rabinowitz, George, and Stuart Elaine Macdonald. 1989. A Directional Theory of Issue Voting. *American Political Science Review* 83:93–121.

Rabinowitz, George, James W. Prothro, and William Jacoby. 1982. Salience as a Factor in the Impact of Issues on Candidate Evaluation. *Journal of Politics* 44:41–63.

Riker, William. 1990. Heresthetic and Rhetoric in the Spatial Model. In James M. Enelow and Melvin J. Hinich, eds., *Advances in the Spatial Theory of Voting.* Cambridge: Cambridge University Press.

Rosenstone, Steven J. 1983. *Forecasting Presidential Elections.* New Haven: Yale University Press.

Weisberg, Herbert F., and Janet M. Box-Steffensmeier, eds. 1999. *Reelection 1996: How Americans Voted.* New York: Chatham House.

Zaller, John R., and Stanley Feldman. 1992. A Simple Theory of the Survey Response: Answering Questions versus Revealing Preferences. *American Journal of Political Science* 36:579–616.

6

Elections and the Dynamics
of Ideological Representation

Michael B. MacKuen, Robert S. Erikson,
James A. Stimson, and Kathleen Knight

The nature of democratic government depends in large part on citizens' and politicians' ability to communicate with each other about their preferences and actions. In the contemporary United States, as in many other industrialized nations, the shorthand language of "ideology" facilitates such communication. Here by *ideology*, we mean the notions of liberalism and conservatism or left and right that are used in everyday political discourse. While it is clear that *liberalism* and *conservatism* may have different meanings and surely confound multiple dimensions (Converse 1975), it is also clear that the general terms are used by newspaper reporters, editorialists, lobbyists, politicians, party activists, and informed citizens. These are central terms in the lingua franca of Washingtonians and those who seek to influence them.

In this chapter we explore the extent to which politicians and citizens use ideology effectively to connect with each other in the electoral arena. We shall examine the ways that some citizens rather than others use ideology to inform their voting decisions. We shall see that the "ideologically literate" have characteristically different political preferences than others and that they have a heavy, though not dominant, impact on electoral outcomes. In addition, we shall see that electoral candidates appreciate the ideological character of the informed voters and position themselves accordingly. These connections, as one might expect, vary by the level of political office—running from the presidency to the House of Representatives—but ideology plays an important role throughout.

In the end, we see that ideological representation works fairly well. Electorates elect candidates with political views that are consistent with the electorates' preferences. Politicians react strategically, working hard to anticipate the electorates' demands before election time. It is when politicians are surprised that the power of ideological representation becomes most obvious—incumbents get thrown out of office. Finally, we see that equilibrium between people's ideological preferences and their party loyalties seems to be driven by elite debate and politicians' strategic choices. In the contemporary United States, this equilibrium seems to have settled down so that the politics of party and the politics of ideology appear indistinguishable.

Theory

Our starting point is the spatial modeling theory associated with Anthony Downs and his classic *An Economic Theory of Democracy* (1957). Downs elaborated on the familiar idea in which candidates (and parties) gain votes by appealing to moderate voters in the political center. Downs's specific model made two crucial assumptions about the motivations of voters and parties/candidates. Downs assumed that voters select candidates based solely on ideological proximity. He assumed that candidates are motivated solely by winning. The theoretical result from these assumptions for a two-candidate race is that candidates have a (Nash) equilibrium outcome, where each has an incentive to stay, once it is reached. This outcome is the "median voter outcome," or the ideological preference of the median voter at the 50th percentile of ideological liberalism/conservatism. This is the equilibrium result because if either candidate strays from the median voter outcome, the opponent wins the election.

In the abstract, the Downs model is simple and logical. But it is too simple to be an accurate description of electoral politics. Voters do not make choices purely on ideological grounds, and candidates do not position themselves exactly at the median voter's preference point.

First, we must take into account that voters are motivated only partially by the goal of selecting the most ideologically agreeable candidate. Decades of voting studies have shown the importance of other variables in the voters' calculus, especially partisan dispositions and candidate evaluations. And of course, some voters care only about specific single issues rather than about the overall ideological landscape. In fact, many voters totally ignore the ideological debate, develop minimal order to their own political views, understand little about ideological language, and miss the news that Democrats are more liberal and Republicans more conservative than their partisan opponents. Thus, it will prove crucial that we distinguish between that part of the public that is paying minimal attention and that which is not (as is clearly suggested by Converse 1964).

Second, parties and candidates are motivated only partially by the goal of winning elections. Political activists and candidates are themselves driven by ideology and seek electoral victory to achieve their own ideological agendas.

And even the most cynical value-free politician must take into account the ideological preferences of the party's activists and financial backers. The fact that voters are not very ideological encourages parties and candidates to seek ideological satisfaction at the expense of pandering to the median voter's more moderate preference. And of course, in the United States, the Democrats and Republicans are typically aligned to the ideological left and right of the median voter position, thus presenting the electorate with an ideological basis for electoral choice.

Yet in all this, the connection between the public's preferences and electoral outcomes is highly uncertain. Candidates operate in a political battlefield where the ideological location of the median voter is only approximately known. Even with the modern instrument of survey research, the electorate's collective preferences are never known in any exact way. An election will have a victor, but because voters select on ideological grounds plus other motivations, how much the outcome represents an ideological judgment by the electorate cannot be known for sure. We might think that the next election would decide this matter. But since the next election, like all others, will be decided by a combination of ideological and nonideological considerations, the policy verdict will be debatable all over again.

Fortunately for democratic theory, even when many voters are motivated by considerations other than ideology, the pressures for ideological representation need not break down. Imagine the following two types of voters: most vote randomly, as if throwing darts at the ballot; a significant minority, however, votes based on ideological preference, as prescribed here. Alternatively, imagine individual voters to be a mix of the two—voting partially on ideology but with individual quirks so that vote decisions appear to contain a purely random component as well. If voting is partly a function of systematic ideological voting and partly random, the "errors" due to the random component will cancel out in what has been called the miracle of aggregation (Converse 1990). The result will be ideological representation: the systematic component of the vote due to ideological voting is the dominant signal from the electorate; anticipating this, candidates are responsive ideologically in terms of the choices they offer.

Accepted uncritically, this argument can make it seem that ideological representation is automatic, even if many voters are largely ignorant or capricious. But we cannot automatically expect this happy result. The reason is that the nonideological portion of the vote will in large part also be systematic. Among other nonideological criteria, voters select on the basis of party identification and on evaluations of candidate competence.[1]

In any given election, we would not expect the ideologically favored candidate to win with certainty. But the ideological bias of any one election may itself be the transient result of unique circumstances. If so, the pattern of bias will itself be random, favoring neither liberals nor conservatives, Democrats nor Republicans. The long-run expectation would be that on average, election outcomes would converge to their equilibrium outcome—reflecting voters' preferences.

Complicating matters, ideological preferences can change. Suppose, for example, that nonideological voters were to awaken ideologically, perhaps responding to their currently dormant political interests. The ideological distribution would then change, and the location of an ideological equilibrium point on the left-right continuum would change accordingly.

This discussion can be made less abstract. We can reframe it in terms of two possible scenarios—one conservative and one liberal—regarding the location of an ideological equilibrium.

The conservative version goes as follows: For the past quarter century, surveys have shown that the electorate is conservative in ideological identification. Yet Democrats (liberals) tend to have the upper hand electorally, especially below the office of president. This combination of circumstances would seem to represent an ideological imbalance whereby voters are subject to forces that push them to vote for the candidate more liberal than their ideological tastes. One likely culprit would be party identification, with voters resisting their conservative impulse as a result of the pull of their vestigial Democratic party identifications. Increase political awareness, so the conservative's argument goes, and the hold of inherited party identification would lessen. With newly enlightened conservatives voting their views, the ideological balance would be restored, with more people voting Republican.

Our contrasting liberal's scenario goes as follows. It is true that more people call themselves conservatives than liberals. But election results favor conservatives more than they should because people do not always recognize their liberal interests. Many people call themselves conservatives unknowingly; many others do not even hold an ideological identification but are drawn from among the disadvantaged and therefore "should" be liberals. Increase political awareness, so the liberal's argument goes, and the uninformed will see their liberal interests and vote accordingly, creating a more natural ideological balance.

All this matters, of course, only if ideology plays an important role in connecting politicians and citizens. We shall see that it does.

Measurement Issues

The goal of this chapter is simple. We seek to estimate the degree to which the ideological preferences of the electorate influence election outcomes. We also seek to estimate the correspondence between the electorate's ideological preferences and the policy positions of the politicians they elect. At the outset, we must acknowledge the challenge that measurement issues pose.

When we demonstrate a statistical association between aggregate opinion and policy or behavior, the variables are measured in incomparable measurement units. Public preferences are measured from survey responses, aggregated. Policies are measured by actions. Sometimes these actions can be readily quantified, as with indexes of roll call ideology. Causal inferences can be made from correlating constituency ideology with roll call ideology (e.g., Erikson and Wright 2001). But from correlation evidence alone, one cannot say for sure how closely roll calls match the electorate's preferences.

Lacking instruments of common calibration, we face difficulty placing candidate and party positions in relationship to the distribution of ideological positions among the electorate. Consider the Downs model, where parties are motivated toward the center because of electoral considerations. Conversely, parties are pushed toward their ideological extremes by their own tastes and those of their ideological followers, fiscal backers, and their primary electorates. Empirically, where do voters see the parties relative to their own collective preferences? Are parties viewed as near the center or out by the two peripheries, relative to the electorate's ideological distribution?

Ideally, our knowledge of representation would say something about contemporary politics. Lacking a common calibration of the variables, however, claims about the degree of electoral representation at any particular moment are severely circumscribed. For example, is it plausible that the ideological verdict of an election necessarily represents the ideological tastes of the electorate? With election results representing an uncertain mix of ideological and nonideological considerations, the degree to which electoral choice represents an ideological mandate is itself uncertain.

In principle there is one way to estimate whether candidates and elected leaders are too liberal, too conservative, or just right for the voters. The solution is to ask the voters. If, for example, voters persistently see the leaders they elect as more conservative (liberal) than the voters are, then there must be some conservative (liberal) bias embedded in the voters' vote equation that pushes their vote decisions in the conservative (liberal) direction. If it turns out that voters tend to elect candidates with whom they disagree ideologically, we could then probe further to ascertain why this is so.

NES Ideological Data, 1972–96

This chapter addresses these questions using as its database individual-level National Election Study (NES) data from 1972 to 1996. The NES self-placement scale offers respondents seven choices ranging from 1 (extremely liberal) to 7 (extremely conservative), with midpoint 4 labeled moderate/middle of the road. As with similar measures of ideological identification, responses to the NES ideological question tend in the conservative direction. Because the NES

attempts to filter out responses from those without actual ideological preferences ("or haven't you thought much about it?"), a sizable minority in NES
surveys, between 20 and 30 percent, do not classify themselves on the liberal-
conservative scale.

In all thirteen elections between 1972 and 1996, NES respondents have also
been asked to place the two major parties on the ideological scale. In all presidential elections starting with 1972, respondents have been asked to place both
major-party presidential candidates. In all midterm elections starting with 1978
(as well as 1980 and 1996), respondents have been asked to place both major-
party House candidates. Also, in the three separate NES Senate Election Studies of 1988, 1990, and 1992, voters were asked to evaluate their two sitting senators and (if there was a Senate election) all major party senatorial candidates.

Preliminaries: Ideological and Nonideological Voters

One obvious obstacle to a study of ideological voting is that many voters in fact
do not have meaningful ideological preferences. Many fail to locate themselves
on the ideological continuum, and of those who do, many reveal little understanding of ideological terms. Here we consider a minimum requirement of
ideological literacy: recognition that the Democratic party is to the left of the
Republican party and, where candidate evaluation is relevant, that the Democratic candidate is to the left of the Republican opponent. Many voters fail
these tests, as table 6.1 shows.[2]

**TABLE 6.1. Perceptions of Ideological Distinction between the Parties, 1972–96
(in percentages)**

	See Democrats Left of Republicans		See Democrats Left of Republicans and Democratic Presidential Candidate Left of Republican Presidential Candidate	
	All Respondents	Voters Only	All Respondents	Voters Only
1972	38	54	35	49
1974	42	51		
1976	46	56	41	50
1978	43	53		
1980	41	51	35	44
1982	45	55		
1984	47	56	43	53
1986	47	58		
1988	46	58	41	53
1990	43	54		
1992	52	61	49	57
1994	56	67		
1996	61	69	57	65

Identifying the ideologically aware voters, those who possess a minimal amount of ideological literacy, will prove helpful for this chapter. We shall term these people *ideologically literate, ideologically aware,* and even *ideologicals* to indicate that they are familiar with the language of ideology as it is practiced in U.S. politics and can fit their own preferences and the parties into this frame-work. These are not necessarily *ideologues* in the Converse 1964 meaning of the term—they may or may not conceptualize of politics in ideological terms. As with any language, some people may be familiar with the terminology without actually thinking in the language. We may compare our "literacy" standard with the now-classic *levels of conceptualization* (hand coded from the original inter-view protocols by others [see Hagner and Pierce 1982, Knight 1985] for the years 1972–88). We see that almost all ideologues are in fact ideologically literate but not all ideologically literate are ideologues. While about 20 percent of the public are ideologues in the sense that they talk about politics in ideological terms, an additional 30 percent are literate in the sense that they are aware of the political meaning of ideology even if they do not use the language spontaneously.

Although not so clearly ideological as the ideologues, the literate do make sense of the ideological debate. For example, we examine the relationship between expressed ideological preferences and preferences for increased gov-ernment spending on services to see if ideology carries a meaningful translation into a straightforward liberal-conservative policy issue. We expect to see that liberals prefer more government services while conservatives prefer lower taxes. Using data from the years 1984–88, when all relevant measures are at hand, we see that pure ideologues' ideological and policy preferences are closely interlinked ($r = .54$) and that nonideologue literates' preferences are modestly correlated ($r = .32$). In contrast, ideology and policy are unrelated ($r = .01$) for the ideological illiterates.

In the main, we shall focus on the ideological choices of the ideological lit-erates, those who correctly place the parties on the ideological scale. It is for the literates that ideology carries real meaning. Later, we shall compare the prefer-ences and behavior of the ideologically literate to those of the ideologically illit-erate to see how the total electorate reflects this mixture of ideological and non-ideological components.

First, we consider the long-term trend in ideological literacy. Table 6.1 shows that the proportion of people who pass the bar increases over time: in 1972 only 38 percent could say that Republicans were more conservative than Democrats, while by 1996 fully 61 percent could do so. Among those who vote—of those more politically engaged—the levels of ideological literacy have risen from the low 50s in the 1970s to almost 70 percent in 1996. Whatever one makes of the overall level here, we see signs of the public's beginning to acquire the ideological lingo.

When we add the proviso that people get not only the parties but also the presidential candidates right, we see that the levels of literacy stay about the same (they drop, but only modestly, about 3–4 percentage points). Thus, we have some confidence in our measure, and we have the ability to go farther.

Concentrating on the ideological choices of the ideologically literate provides a handle for placing voters relative to candidates or parties. If all relevant ratings place the Republican candidate to the right of the Democrat, we can create a seven-point scale of respondent placement relative to the candidates. For any voter, this scale goes as follows:

-3 Left of both candidates

-2 Same as Democratic candidate

-1 In between, closer to Democrat

 0 Equidistant

 1 In between, closer to Republican candidate

 2 Same as Republican candidate

 3 Right of both candidates

Similar scales can be made for voters relative to the two parties. We call these relative proximity scores.

These simple measures provide the tools with which to assess ideological representation in the electoral system. We can mark those voters who feel that both parties are too far to the center (liberals and conservatives being –3 and 3), those who feel that one party is "just right" (–2 and 2), and those in between the parties who have either a mild ideological preference or who are indifferent (–1, 1, and 0).[3] Aggregating, we can now understand whether the parties and candidates are typically at the center of the public's ideological distribution, to the extremes, or somewhere in between. And we can tell whether the candidates are typically displaced to the right or the left. And especially important for representation, we can tell when election winners come from the center, from the right, or from the left.

Ideological Representation in Presidential Elections

Following a presidential election, the interpretation of the outcome will often be given an ideological connotation, with observers claiming that the winner won more votes (at least in part) because of ideology. But does the U.S. electorate vote for president on an ideological basis? This was once a highly debatable question, with the literature following the lead of the classic voting study *The American Voter* (Campbell et al. 1960). *The American Voter* emphasized the public's lack of ideological awareness at the time of the book's writing in the quiescent 1950s. The subsequent literature was cautious in attributing causality, even when ideology and vote decisions were found to correlate with one another. (For a review, see Niemi and Weisberg 1993.) Since the time of *The American Voter*, ideological awareness has increased. Scholars now recognize the electoral significance of the sometimes-small band of voters who do vote ideologically (Stimson 1975; Nie, Verba, and Petrocik 1976; Knight 1985; Jacoby 1991). Not all voters may be ideological, but those who do observe presidential politics from an ideological perspective do vote ideologically. And their collective behavior carries electoral consequences.

In this section, we offer our evaluation of ideological voting in presidential elections. To what extent do the electorate's ideological evaluations of the candidates account for presidential election outcomes? A slightly different question is: To what extent do presidential election outcomes reflect the ideological preferences of the electorate? Our investigation involves the intersection of the micro and macro levels of analysis. We begin with microlevel analysis, pooling responses from seven NES presidential election surveys (1972–96). From the coefficients of this microlevel analysis and the macrolevel distributions of voter attributes, we infer the contribution of ideological evaluations to electoral change.

A useful starting point is to array the distribution of ideological voters relative to their individual perceptions of the two candidates' ideological positions (see fig. 6.1). These are the relative proximity scores described earlier. The columns at the left and the right of the distributions represent voters at the ideological wings, those who see *both* candidates as too far to the right or to the left, respectively. The middle three columns are voters who see themselves flanked by the Democrats on the left and the Republicans on the right. The remainder see one of the parties as just right.

An appreciable proportion of ideological voters see themselves outside the range of the two candidates—either to the right or left of both the Democrat and the Republican. The frequency with which voters see themselves outside the range of the candidates varies in predictable fashion. Voters see themselves as relatively extreme in elections where the candidates are generally perceived as centrists (e.g., Carter versus Ford in 1976). Where one candidate is viewed as quite extreme (McGovern in 1972, Reagan in 1980, 1984), relatively few see themselves as more extreme themselves. This pattern makes sense and corroborates the measurement technique. But it does more.

One important feature of a party system is the relative placement of the party positions in the ideological space. Downs's theory, taken in its simple form, predicts that the parties and candidates will take centrist positions and thus that most people will see both parties as to the left or right of their own

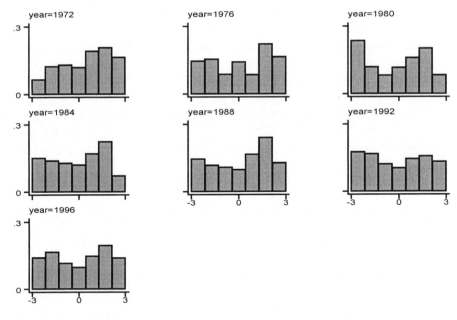

Fig. 6.1.   Voter conservatism relative to presidential candidates

positions. (That is, all conservatives will see both parties—who lie at the center—as too liberal, and all liberals will see both parties as too conservative.) Other theories suggest that the parties and candidates will stand well to the left or right of the distribution. (That is to say, all voters but the most extreme wings will see the parties as flanking their own voters' preferences.) This distinction is important because in the first Downsian case the parties will chase the center but fail to provide voters ideological alternatives from which to choose. Representation will be implicit—driven by elite perceptions rather than by voter actions. In the second case, the parties present quite distinct alternatives that reflect the parties' rather than the voters' preferences, and the choices over policy are made explicitly by the voters.

These relative proximity data can inform our understanding about these different party and candidate strategies. In terms of figure 6.1, the Downs "centrist" prediction is that almost all voters will place themselves in columns 1 and 7, at the end points of the "relative proximity" distributions. The "parties as ideological purists" view predicts that almost all voters will be in the three middle columns, flanked by the relatively extreme party positions.

Here we see strong evidence that neither view is solely correct and that the situation changes from year to year. At least as far as ideology is concerned, the parties' candidates frequently alter their relative positions, sometimes more centrist and sometimes more ideologically purist, and the electorate recognizes those alterations. Importantly for understanding the party system, the candidates' positions are most often somewhere between a centrist and a purist strategy. Aggregating over the years, about 28 percent of the voters see the candidate pairs as centrists, and another 38 percent see the candidate pairs as purists. Thus, we see that the parties try to balance between the centrist and purist strategies and that their balancing act noticeably shifts the weights from one campaign to the next.

In terms of relative ideological advantage, Republican candidates have had a slight edge (the overall mean is 0.10). The Republicans' strongest ideological advantages were in 1972 and 1988, and one could easily argue that their victories depended on these advantages. They lost in 1976 despite this advantage as a result of Watergate and other factors. In the remaining elections, including both Reagan wins, the net ideological advantages were smaller and did not determine the final outcome.

Shifts in mean ideological perceptions of candidates correspond loosely at best with election results. One might be tempted to conclude that ideology does not matter much in presidential elections. But that would be premature. Statistically, three issues are at stake. First, how much does ideological proximity affect individual votes? Second, are changes in relative ideological proximity (the data we have just observed) sufficient to generate much net macrolevel change in the vote? And, third, to what extent do other forces determining elections swamp ideologically driven change?

Questions such as these have a long history, going back at least to *The American Voter* (Campbell et al. 1960). Beginning with Stokes (1966), a number of studies have estimated the "variance components" of electoral change from the early NES presidential series (see also Popkin et al. 1976; Kagay and Caldeira 1980).

The findings of these studies examined open-ended likes-dislikes responses and ignored any overt measurement of ideological evaluation. Here we will examine ideology, party identification, and other unobserved sources of election-to-election differences, which are referenced by year dummy variables in the pooled NES data set.

Microlevel Analysis

First we assess whether ideology matters for voters. As a first cut, we examine the simple bivariate relationship between ideological proximity and the vote, for the ideologically literate part of the electorate. Figure 6.2 plots relative conservatism (on the horizontal axis) against the percentage voting Republican (on the vertical axis) for 1972–96. It is immediately apparent that those with a

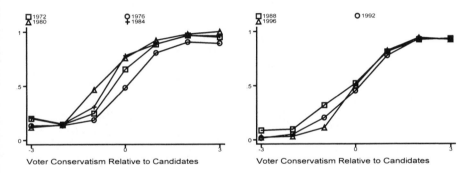

Fig. 6.2.   Relative conservatism and Republican presidential vote (ideologically literate)

clear ideological preference (scored –3 and –2 for liberals and 2 and 3 for conservatives) vote overwhelmingly for the appropriate presidential candidate. Liberals vote for the Democrat and Conservatives vote for the Republican, with loyalty rates in the 90 percent range. If anything, the clarity of this relationship has increased over the decades, with ideology being almost synonymous with the vote during the post-Reagan era.

We get stronger and more systematic statistical evidence when we model vote choice as a function of ideological proximity for all nine presidential elections between 1972 and 1996. Here we combine the NES samples to produce a large pool of late-twentieth-century voters, using election-specific intercepts to pick up systematic nonideological factors associated with each campaign.[4] The first column of table 6.2 shows the results, with a statistically robust coefficient (0.61) connecting ideology with vote. The pseudo-R^2 of .45 indicates that ideology accounts for almost half the variance in voting. At least among the ideologically aware, it is clear that voting and ideological preferences are closely connected.

We gain further confidence in this inference when we introduce party identification. Using the familiar NES seven-point measure, we scale the variable from –3 (Strong Democrat) to +3 (Strong Republican) with the "pure" Independent position as the neutral point. Thus, partisanship is directly comparable to ideological proximity in these estimates. When we observe the impact of ideology while modeling the impact of partisanship, we exert a statistical control for the ideology-partisanship connection. In fact, we can see that ideology's impact persists even after the control for partisanship.

To underscore the point, column 2 shows that the relative impact of ideology on the vote (0.42) is nearly identical to that of partisanship (0.45). As components of the vote choice, ideology stands about equal with partisanship. (To be sure, there are more "strong partisans" than "ideologically committed," so the comparison is rough rather than exact.) The electoral relevance of ideology thus seems well established for the ideologically aware part of the electorate.

Next we reintroduce the remainder of the electorate—the nonideological respondents, those who evince no awareness of ideological meanings. We do this in part to compare ideological and nonideological voters in terms of their responsiveness to party identification and year effects. We also observe the additive coefficient for being a nonideological voter. The question is whether nonideological voters tend to vote differently from ideological voters, taking into account the year and their specific party identification and (for ideological voters) relative ideological position.

Column 3 of table 6.2 now includes all voters (nonideological voters are scored as neutral or 0 on candidate proximity). The coefficients change little,

TABLE 6.2.   Presidential Vote by Ideological Proximity and Other Variables, 1972–96

	Ideologically Aware		All Voters
Relative Ideological Proximity	0.61**	0.42**	0.42**
	(43.79)	(25.09)	(26.02)
Party Identification		0.45**	0.44**
		(28.01)	(44.41)
Not Ideologically Aware, dummy variable			−0.11**
			(−2.97)
Year effects			
1972	0.32**	0.63**	0.70**
	(5.58)	(9.78)	(15.29)
1976	0.01	0.15	0.15**
	(0.22)	(2.21)	(3.07)
1980	0.60**	0.72**	0.57**
	(6.82)	(7.05)	(9.57)
1984	0.50**	0.61**	0.54**
	(8.49)	(8.50)	(10.91)
1988	0.13	0.11	0.16**
	(2.08)	(1.40)	(3.12)
1992	−0.11	−0.16	−0.07
	(−1.81)	(−2.16)	(−1.42)
1996	−0.08	−0.17	−0.28**
	(−1.27)	(−2.18)	(−4.74)
Pseudo-R^2	0.45	0.60	0.46
N	(4,708)	(4,702)	(8,717)

Source: Data from National Election Studies.
Note: Each column represents a probit model. Z-values in parentheses. Pseudo-R^2 is the Zavoina-McKelvay pseudo-R^2 for probit equations.
**Significant at .01.

indicating that the impact of partisanship and election-specific short-term forces are about equal for both ideological and nonideological voters. Interestingly, the estimated constant for the ideologically unaware is mildly negative and marginally significant: nonideological voters typically lean a bit to the Democrats. As we shall see, this phenomenon is both interesting and important.

A telling question at this point is whether the equations for ideological and nonideological voters are the same, apart from ideology and the coefficient for the nonideological dummy variable. To see, we generated equations with interaction terms for year effects times "nonideological voter" and for party identification times "nonideological voter." Neither the party identification interaction nor the set of year interactions was significant; nor was the combination. Since these negative significance tests resulted in an analysis with more than eight thousand cases, we can be statistically confident that we have not omitted any serious interactions. The substantive conclusion is that ideological and nonideological voters are no different from each other in terms of their vote's responsiveness to party identification or short-term forces represented by year effects. What separates the two groups is their ability and willingness to use ideology as a meaningful voting criterion.[5]

Macrolevel Analysis

We have divided presidential voters into those who are ideological and those who are not. When we compare the collective vote decisions of the two groups, we find that the ideologically aware voters are far more Republican in their choice—by 15 percentage points or more. Several factors account for the Republican tilt among the ideologically aware. First, the ideologically aware generally (but not always) tilt Republican in their relative candidate placement. Second, as we shall explore, they disproportionately identify with the Republican party. Third, residual year effects favor the Republicans. Even when partisanship and ideology are set to neutral (i.e., independents in terms of partisanship, moderates ideologically), ideologically aware voters are more likely to vote Republican.

Does ideology matter for election outcomes? While we now know that ideology carries weight for a substantial portion of the electorate, this does not necessarily imply that ideology drives elections. In the pure Downsian model of party competition, the two candidates converge on the median voter position and essentially neutralize ideology as an electoral determinant. This is true when (by assumption) all voters choose candidates entirely on ideological grounds. Thus, even when voters are ideological and candidates pay consuming attention to the voters' preferences, the impact of ideology on outcomes will be zero. Of course, to the extent to which the candidates fail to converge (and we have instances of this), then we shall see that ideology does matter when it comes to determining the winners of election campaigns.

A revealing exercise is to decompose the aggregate vote into three components: the portions resulting from ideological proximity, party identification (macropartisanship), and residual short-term forces captured by the year effects dummy variables. This is a bit tricky, because the microlevel (dichotomous) vote is not a linear function of the probit coefficients in table 6.2. Fortunately, however, in the range of actual outcomes, the macrolevel vote of the NES samples does approximate very closely an exact linear function of the three components. Using a conversion formula,[6] the sample vote can be broken down into its three additive components: net ideological proximity, net party identification (macropartisanship), and residual short-term forces, or year effects.

Figure 6.3 shows the results. On average, the Democratic edge in macropartisanship is worth about two percentage points, while the Republican edge in ideological proximity has been worth about one point. This net ideological advantage has ranged from +3 in the Republicans' favor in 1972 to –1 in the Democratic direction in 1992. Most of the action in terms of year-to-year variation in the vote has been due to factors other than ideological proximity or changes in macropartisanship. Simply put, elections result mainly from short-term variation in candidate attractiveness.

This empirical pattern suggests that the competing presidential campaign teams are generally pretty good about balancing a need to satisfy their ideological supporters with a need to appeal to the broader ideologically aware and more centrist public. The largest net effect, 3 points for the 1972 McGovern campaign that was seen as markedly leftist for its day, makes sense but also cautions about the limited magnitude of the purely ideological impact.[7] Ideology matters when one candidate fails to manage well the supporters-versus-centrists trade-off, but ideology can be decisive only in close elections.

In terms of ideological representation, ideologically aware voters generally see presidential election winners as more conservative than themselves:

	See Self to Left of Winner	See Self to Right of Winner
1972: Nixon	63%	16%
1976: Carter	15%	70%
1980: Reagan	71%	8%
1984: Reagan	70%	22%
1988: Bush	63%	13%

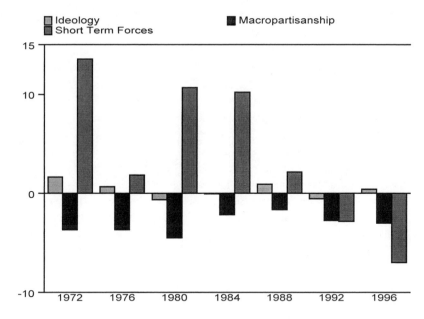

Fig. 6.3.   Impact of components on election outcome

1992: Clinton	18%	66%
1996: Clinton	14%	69%

This pattern obviously is a function of the run of Republican presidential successes, for which voter ideology is only partially responsible.

Ideology and U.S. Senate Elections

Although less visible than presidential contests, Senate elections are typically hotly contested and draw considerable interest. In the popular press, victorious Senate candidacies are often attributed to being in ideological tune with the state, just as rare incumbent losses are attributed to ideological discrepancies. Empirical studies of Senate contests show that ideology plays a major role, with state electorates voting ideologically and sitting senators responding with ideological responsiveness in terms of Senate roll call voting (Wright and Berkman 1986; Erikson 1990; Erikson, Wright, and McIver 1993, chap. 8)

In this section, we utilize the NES 1988–90–92 Senate studies to evaluate ideology in the context of U.S. Senate elections. In each of these years, the NES interviewed a sample of approximately eighty respondents from each state.

State size was kept approximately equal for efficient analysis of separate state Senate elections. In the analysis below, the data are not weighted. In this way, we generalize to fifty state electorates rather than the U.S. population. The patterns are similar, however, if the data are weighted.

Given the staggered six-year Senate terms and two senators from every state, roughly two-thirds of all voters face a Senate contest every election year. Of these senatorial voters, we counted ideologically aware voters the same way as for presidential elections. Assuming each contest's Democratic candidate is to the left of the Republican opponent, we counted ideologically aware Senate voters as those who saw the Democratic candidate to the left of the Republican and the Democratic party to the left of the Republicans. Thirty-nine percent of Senate voters passed this test. Senate voters were almost equally divided left and right relative to the candidates, with a very slight tilt to the left, or closer to the Democrat.[8]

Microlevel Analysis

As with presidential elections, we pooled our samples to estimate the impact of ideology on voter choice. Table 6.3 shows two probit equations predicting the vote from ideological proximity, party identification, incumbency, and year effects. Column 1 represents ideological voters only. The equation of column 2 represents all voters and includes interaction terms involving ideological awareness.

The results from both specifications indicate that ideological proximity clearly matters in Senate elections but does so somewhat less than for president. The year effects are trivial in size, suggesting the virtual absence of national short-term forces in at least these three years of Senate elections. Based on the interaction terms, party identification has a stronger effect among ideologically aware voters, while incumbency matters more to the less aware.

Macrolevel Analysis

Are the ideological verdicts of Senate elections ideologically balanced, as perceived collectively by ideological Senate voters? Table 6.4 presents the data. Of the 1,740 ideologically aware voters, 33 percent saw themselves as to the left of the Senate winner, and 49 percent saw themselves to the right. This imbalance occurred even though ideological voters generally voted for the more ideologically proximate candidate and even though ideological voters on average were equally proximate to the Democratic and Republican candidates. As a group, ideological voters voted for only slightly more Republicans than Democrats. Their collective ideological imbalance, where more see themselves to the right than the left of the victor, results from the partisan asymmetry of ideological

TABLE 6.3. Senate Vote by Ideological Proximity and Other Variables, for All Voters, 1988–92

	Ideologically Aware	All Voters
Relative Ideological Proximity	0.28**	0.28**
	(11.06)	(11.08)
Party Identification	0.35**	0.35**
	(14.77)	(14.76)
Incumbency ($D = -1$, $R = 1$)	0.46**	0.46**
	(9.35)	(9.36)
Not Ideologically Aware, dummy variable		−0.06
		(−1.14)
Year effects		
1998	−0.01	
	(−0.12)	
1990	0.05	
	(0.64)	
1992	−0.01	
	(−0.10)	
Party ID* Not Ideologically Aware		−0.11**
		(−3.88)
Incumbency* Not Ideologically Aware		0.20**
Pseudo-R^2	0.59	0.52
N	(1,477)	(3,770)

Source: Data from NES Senate Studies.
Note: Each column represents a probit model. Z-values in parentheses. Pseudo-R^2 is the Zavoina-McKelvay pseudo-R^2 for probit equations.
*significant at .05; **significant at .01.

TABLE 6.4. Perceptions of Ideological Distance from Elected Senator (in percentages)

	1988	1990	1992
Left of elected senator	38	34	38
Same as elected senator	19	21	17
Right of elected senator	43	45	45
	100	100	100
N	(458)	(477)	(561)

Note: Based on responses of voters who rated Democratic candidate to the left of the Republican and the Democratic party to the left of the Republican party.

218   ELECTORAL DEMOCRACY

and nonideological voters. It is the by-product of Democratic voting by non-ideological voters, as we shall see.

One aspect of senatorial representation is whether the positions of the Democratic and Republican candidates are responsive to state opinion—or in our case, state-level ideological preference. We have an easy test, using state-level measures of mean ideology from CBS News/*New York Times* polls (Erikson, Wright, and McIver 1993). The test is to regress ideological proximity on state ideology. A positive coefficient would mean that conservative states see themselves as more conservative than the perceived midpoint between the two candidates. A negative coefficient would mean the opposite. In fact, the regression coefficient is nonsignificant, indicating that senatorial candidates get it just right:[9]

$$Relative\ Proximity = -0.18 + 0.01\ State\ Conservatism$$
$$(R - D) \qquad (-1.71)\ (1.74)$$

$(N = 1,740;$ Adjusted $R^2 = 0.00;$ SEE $= 3.04)$

The clear implication is that Democratic candidates are to the left of voters by about the same amount in each state and Republicans are to the right by about the same amount in each state, no matter how liberal or conservative the state.

We can also ascertain the responsiveness of winner ideology relative to state opinion. We have seen that winners on average are seen to be slightly more liberal than ideological voters see themselves. Does this gap vary with state ideology? The answer is yes:

$$Relative\ Proximity\ to\ Winner = 0.35 - \ 0.17\ State\ Conservatism$$
$$(7.57)\ (-5.88)$$

$(N = 1,740;$ Adjusted $R^2 = 0.02;$ SEE $= 0.89)$

This result means that the more conservative the state, the more the state electorate sees itself to the *left* of the winning Senate candidate. (That is to say, conservative states produce winners even more conservative than one would expect.) This is hyperrepresentation, where the effect of opinion on (perceived) winner behavior has a "coefficient" of greater than 1.00.

Partisan voting is responsible. With perceived ideological distance between each party's candidate and the voter invariant with state preference (as discussed previously), party voting should be orthogonal to state preferences. In fact, however, liberal states tend to vote more Democratic than average. Thus, liberal states tend to elect Democrats who are more liberal than the state electorate and conservative states tend to elect Republicans who are more conservative than the state electorate.

Ideology and U.S. House Elections

Even in the down-ballot elections for the U.S. House of Representatives, ideology matters. In the popular lore, the Democrats who lost their House seats in the 1994 Republican landslide lost because they were too liberal. In the earlier Democratic landslides of 1964 and 1974, Republicans more conservative than their districts were clearly the most vulnerable (Wright 1978). In general, when holding constant constituency opinion, moderate House candidates get the most votes. And anticipating electoral sanctions, House members from the most marginal districts are the most moderate (Erikson 1971; Erikson and Wright 2001).

Candidates are far less ideologically visible in House elections than even candidates for the U.S. Senate. In the seven NES studies that have questioned respondents about the ideological positions of congressional candidates, 37 percent of congressional voters rated their incumbent candidates; 14 percent their challenger; in between these numbers, 26 percent were able to rate open-seat candidates. When we set the challenge to be how many were able to rate both the Democratic and Republican candidate (and the two parties), the number bottoms out at 18 percent. Thus, roughly one in five congressional voters both places the two parties correctly and evaluates the two congressional candidates ideologically.

Microlevel Analysis

Using the same format as for Senate elections, table 6.5 presents two probit equations predicting the congressional vote. The results are similar to those for Senate voting. The coefficients are smaller for ideological proximity than for party identification. As for Senate voting, party identification effects are intensified for ideologically aware voters, while incumbency effects are intensified for nonaware voters. But in all this, ideology clearly matters a great deal.

The year coefficients are generally negligible, which means that voters scoring neutral on the usual indicators—zero on proximity, party identification (independent), and incumbency (open seat)—were equally disposed to vote Democratic or Republican in those years. The one exception was the strongly positive 1994 coefficient, indicating an unusual Republican tilt. For congressional voters (as for presidential but not senatorial voters), the dummy variable for not ideologically aware shows a significant negative coefficient. Everything

else being equal (including party identification), nonideological voters are predisposed to vote Democratic.

Macrolevel Analysis

Next, let us examine the ideological satisfaction obtained by ideological voters
in congressional elections. Specifically, do voters with an ideological perception of their representative tilt toward seeing their representative as too liberal
or too conservative, or is there an even balance? Table 6.6 presents the relevant
data for 1978–96. The table shows how ideological voters (who see parties' and

TABLE 6.5. Vote for House of Representatives by Ideological Proximity and Other Variables, for All Voters, Selected Years (Probit)

	Ideologically Aware	All Voters
Relative Ideological Proximity	0.27**	0.27**
	(8.89)	(9.00)
Party Identification	0.41**	0.41**
	(13.07)	(13.01)
Incumbency $(D = -1; R = 1)$	0.43**	0.43**
	(6.64)	(6.80)
Not Ideologically Aware, dummy variable		−0.18
		(−1.41)
Party ID* Not Ideologically Aware		−0.05
		(−1.65)
Incumbency* Not Ideologically Aware		0.47**
		(6.99)
Year effects		
1978	0.09	0.03
	(0.58)	(0.37)
1980	0.10	0.21**
	(0.66)	(2.86)
1982	0.13	0.02
	(0.82)	(0.25)
1986	−0.08	−0.05
	(−0.59)	(−0.74)
1990	−0.05	−0.01
	(−0.26)	(−0.07)
1994	0.31**	0.26**
	(2.69)	(3.67)
1996	0.04	0.09
	(0.29)	(1.28)
Pseudo-R^2	0.55	0.46
N	(1,105)	(6,324)

Source: Data from National Election Studies.
Note: Z-values in parentheses. Pseudo-R^2 is the Zavoina-McKelvay probit pseudo-R^2.
*significant at .05; **significant at .01.

candidates' relative positions correctly) rate the winners of local elections. With a slight imbalance, ideologically literate voters more often see their elected representatives as too liberal rather than too conservative.

Why do ideological voters receive what from their perspective is an excessively liberal House of Representatives? As for the Senate, the reason why ideological congressional voters get a more liberal representation than they collectively desire is that nonideological voters also drive elections, and they are somewhat more Democratic.

Just as for Senate elections, for House elections we can ask whether (perceived) ideological positions of the party candidates vary as a function of constituency opinion. For House districts, we have no direct measure of constituency ideology. In its place, we use the 1988 Republican (Bush) presidential vote as a surrogate measure of constituency ideology to predict relative candidate proximity. The results are as for the Senate: constituency ideology (Bush vote) is not significantly related to relative proximity:[10]

$$\textit{Relative Proximity to Candidate Pair} = -0.26 + 0.01 \ \textit{District Percent Bush 1988}$$
$$(-0.68) \ (1.77)$$

$$(N = 846; \text{Adjusted } R^2 = 0.00; \text{SEE} = 2.18)$$

The conservatism of the constituency does not predict relative respondent closeness to the Republican or Democratic House candidate between 1982 and 1990. Liberal or conservative, the district candidates are seen as equally close to ideological voters. In this way, candidate positions respond to constituency opinion. Democrats are always to the left and Republicans to the right by about the same amount regardless of constituency ideology.

But just as for Senate elections, in House elections voters are more likely to see themselves to the left of the winner if the voters are in a conservative district:

TABLE 6.6.   Ideology Relative to Perceptions of Elected House Member (in percentages)

Respondent Is	1978	1980	1982	1986	1990	1994	1996
Left of representative	37	35	34	44	39	32	41
Same as representative	23	25	25	25	18	27	23
Right of representative	41	40	41	31	43	41	36
	100	100	100	100	100	100	100
N	(175)	(146)	(166)	(203)	(144)	(333)	(190)

Note: Based on response of voters who rated Democratic candidate to the left of the Republican and the Democratic party to the left of the Republican party.

Relative Proximity to Winner = 0.93 − 0.02 *District Percent Bush 1988*
$$(6.32) \ (-6.25)$$

$(N = 846; \text{ Adjusted } R^2 = 0.04; \text{ SEE} = 0.85)$

Again, we have hyperrepresentation, and again the likely culprit is party voting. As liberal districts vote Democratic, they elect representatives more liberal than themselves. As conservative districts vote Republican, they elect representatives more conservative than themselves.

But this is not a simple as it sounds. To the extent that liberal and conservative districts choose candidates on the basis of ideology, there is no reason to expect that they will choose Democratic or Republican candidates. After all, we have just seen that the candidates get their competitive ideological posturing just about right, with ideological voters dispersed about equally around the relatively liberal and conservative candidates. The prediction is that the outcome will reflect the ideological voters' preferences, not that it will exaggerate their preferences. This poses a puzzle, the solution of which requires a bit of a detour.

Ideological Representation and the Preferences of Ideological and Nonideological Voters

To understand ideological representation, we must ultimately understand the motivations of nonideological voters, the illiterate voters we have largely ignored. In this section, to maintain continuity over presidential and nonpresidential election years, we define nonideological voters by the standard of whether they show the most minimal of ideological understanding—correct placement of the Democratic party to the left of the Republicans. That is to say, we score as ideologically aware those who get the parties straight and ignore their views about the candidates.

The surprising aspect of the nonideologicals' survey responses is the set of responses they give to the ideological question. If anything, their verbalized ideological preferences are more conservative than those of the ideologically alert. That is, the greatest preference for the conservative label is among voters whose ideological preferences are irrelevant because they do not know party positions. This result occurs even though such voters gravitate toward the midpoint of 4 on the continuum. It can be most readily seen from the relative directions of respondents who choose the liberal or conservative side, ignoring degree of preference and excluding respondents' choosing the moderate ideological midpoint. In general, the stronger the evidence that the respondent lacks understanding of partisan ideological differences, the more likely that a reported ideological preference will be for the conservative label. Figure 6.4 graphs this trend over time—net conservative/liberal preferences by the ideo-

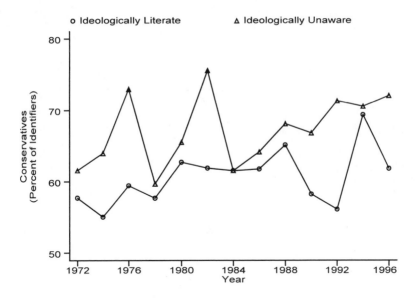

Fig. 6.4. Conservatism and ideological literacy

logically literate and the ideologically unaware. Overall, 60 percent of the ideologically literate call themselves conservative, while 66 percent of illiterates choose that label.

This distaste for the liberal label among the ignorant is probably a result of social learning. But since these individuals do not associate the ideological terms properly with party labels, their excess "conservatism" has little impact other than to distort polls of ideological preference. And for their sakes, happily so. While the ideologically literate clearly get their ideological attachments right with respect to their preferences for governmental policy, it seems that the ideologically illiterate do not. In fact, the relationship between their policy views and their nominal ideological identifications is essentially zero.[11]

The other aspect of the difference between ideological and nonideological voters is one we have already noted: the nonideologicals vote Democratic. The same difference can be observed when considering party identification. As figure 6.5 shows, the ideologically unaware are decidedly Democratic in party preference, while the ideological literates are trending in the Republican direction.

These Democratic leanings make common sense. On average, the nonideologicals have lower education and lower incomes and probably should prefer Democratic social welfare policies. We check this by assessing their preferences on a survey question (repeated biennially since 1982) on whether the govern-

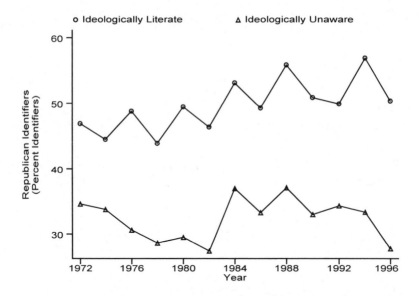

Fig. 6.5.   Partisanship and ideological literacy

ment should increase spending on social services or should cut taxes. As ordinary understanding suggests, we see that the ideological literates and illerates have very different preferences: the literates favor tax cuts, while the illiterates prefer social spending.[12] Notwithstanding their nominal "conservatism," the nonideologicals' Democratic preferences make good sense. And the apparent tension between the conservative-leaning ideological and Democratic-leaning nonideological voters merely reflects the fundamental socioeconomic divisions in U.S. politics.

But the question remains, why do liberal districts produce winners more liberal than their electorates and conservative districts produce winners more conservative than their electorates? A ready answer lies in the preferences of the nonideological voters. In a simple world, we might expect that genuinely conservative areas—for example, rural regions or rich suburbs—would produce ideological voters who properly choose the conservative side and nonideologicals who (in proxy fashion) choose a relatively Republican partisanship. Urban districts would generate liberals and Democrats.

Our best evidence indicates that this picture largely holds for smallish geographical regions—say, congressional districts. Here we create twenty-five-year pooled aggregates of the NES-sampled congressional districts to obtain estimates of a geographical region's ideology, policy preferences, and partisanship. While we cannot treat these aggregates as precise samples of any given congressional district, we shall treat them as rough approximations.[13] We can examine the within-area relationships between the ideological and partisan inclinations of the ideologically aware and unaware.

The simple answer is that the within-district correspondence between the views of ideological and nonideological voters runs through partisanship rather than ideology. The district-level correlation between the ideological stances of the two types of voters is −0.04. This makes sense because the individual-level ideological views of the unaware seem not to be tied to more specific political views that might be rooted in common experience. (Given their ideological ignorance, there is no reason for the ideologically unaware to adopt ideological preferences similar to their more aware neighbors.) Conversely, the correlation between the ideologically awares' ideology and the ideologically unawares' partisanship is 0.30.[14] To the extent to which the ideologically unaware half of the electorate affects candidate policies, it communicates its preferences through partisan rather than ideological signals. Districts get hyperrepresentation because they generate nonideological votes that are not independent of but instead reinforce their ideological neighbors' choices.

Toward an Equilibrium?

So far, we have treated ideological representation as a cross-sectional phenomenon rather than examined its dynamic properties. Indeed, for much of the period of analysis, there is little dynamic to observe. In part this is because comparative survey analysis is a poor way to identify true macrolevel trends.

Yet we know certain trends are in the background, most notably a persistent increase in Republican identification over the period. Except for 1994, there is no clear movement of ideological direction over the period. But the data do suggest a rise in ideological awareness, especially in the 1990s. Since ideological voters vote more Republican, could we infer that increased ideological awareness is the cause of Republican renewal?

First, we know that ideology and partisanship are connected to one another. Liberals will find their views better expressed by Democrats, and conservatives find representation in Republicans. When political debate is framed as liberal versus conservative, when political conflict pits liberals against conservatives, when political analysts constantly describe trends toward liberalism or conservatism, we should expect that voters should come around to the idea that their political preferences and partisan loyalties are tied together.[15] And when partisanship and ideology reinforce one another, we are much more likely to obtain a politics colored by the ideological divide.

We also know that politics has taken on an increasingly ideological tone. In elite political debate, participants have lined up in predictable ways: it has become difficult to find intellectuals or commentators who are either liberal

Republicans or conservative Democrats. And ideologues have seized the high ground within each organized political party to paint their standards in ideological hues. Importantly, the parties' politicians have become increasingly polarized in their congressional voting. Figure 6.6 shows the ideological polarization—the difference in liberal voting for Democrats and Republicans—averaged for both houses of Congress since 1968.[16] By the late 1970s and early 1980s, polarization reached a level not previously seen in postwar America. And that bar was raised again in the 1990s. It would be hard for politically conscious citizens to miss these unmistakable cues.

In fact, the correspondence between citizen ideology and partisanship has been on the rise over the past quarter century. Figure 6.7 shows how ideologues have come to translate ideology into partisanship by plotting the regression of partisanship on ideology by year over time. (The plotted points are regression coefficients—a high score means that partisanship accords with ideology.) The top two panels produce the patterns for the South and North separately, while the bottom panel gives the national trend. It is clear that this relationship has grown substantially over time. In 1972, many voters were quite likely to hold partisan loyalties distinct from their ideology, especially in the South, with its Dixiecrat legacy of conservatism and allegiance to the Democrats. However, the South very quickly lost its distinctiveness, so by the late 1970s, both regions evinced higher and similar levels of consistency. This trend has continued, so that by the 1990s there exists a one-to-one correspondence between ideology and partisanship. Decades of increasingly explicit ideological debate have brought citizens to sort themselves into largely unified partisan and ideological camps.

We get a more formal sense of this dynamic relationship when we regress the citizen-level ideology-partisanship correspondence (figure 6.7) on congressional polarization (from figure 6.6). The evidence comes from a quarter century's political change (1972–96).[17]

$$Ideology\text{-}Partisan\ Correspondence_t = 0.39 + 0.91\ Congressional\ Polarization_{t-1}$$
$$(5.22)\ \ (6.32)$$

$(N = 12;\ Adjusted\ R^2 = 0.78;\ SEE = 0.047)$

This relationship between politicians and their publics is an instance of an "issue evolution" system (Carmines and Stimson 1989). Perhaps the most famous single case is that of civil rights and the political fortunes of the Democratic and Republican parties. The combination of elite politics and a set of historical accidents turned the GOP away from and the Democrats toward civil rights in the early 1960s. The public reacted. First political activists and then the mass public sent signals to politicians, either of support or opposition, and the

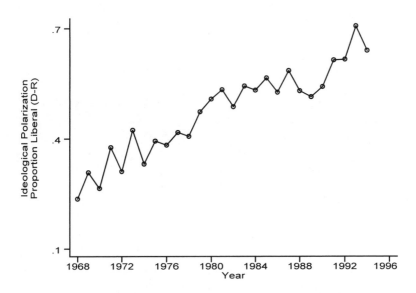

Fig. 6.6. Ideological polarization of congressional parties

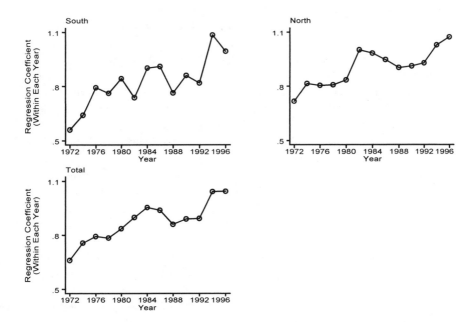

Fig. 6.7. Correspondence of ideology and partisanship (by region and then total United States)

politicians then responded in kind. After a decade or so, the civil rights issue, which had previously been unattached to either political party, began to dominate the partisan division. This "realignment" or "issue evolution" is often seen as the key to understanding the demise of the New Deal coalition and the rise of the modern southern-based Republican party.

We now see the outlines of a similar positive feedback dynamic operating on ideology as an "evolving issue." Starting from the civil rights issue evolution and the Watergate setback, Republicans have enthusiastically embraced the conservative banner and attracted an ever more energetic band of activists. Democrats have sometimes awkwardly accepted the liberal flag. By the 1990s, political commentators came to refer to party politics as a culture war, with both sides self-righteously proclaiming their ideological dicta.

As politics have become increasing ideological and as ideological voters tend toward the Republicans, does this mean that the Republican party can expect to continue a long-term resurgence? We obtain crucial evidence by examining the election year–to–election year equations predicting party identification from relative party placement among the ideologically aware. That is to say, we study the ideological and the nonideological components that underlie partisanship over time. In particular, the intercepts of these equations take on special significance because they represent the net nonideological influences on party identification. A positive intercept would indicate, for example, that respondents seeing themselves equidistant ideologically between the parties nevertheless lean in the Republican direction in terms of identification. The fact is that these intercepts once tilted Democratic, a matter of some electoral consequence.[18]

Figure 6.8 shows these estimates of nonideological influences on party identification over time. In the 1970s, reflecting the Democratic party's general advantage in the post–New Deal era, these nonideological influences favored the Democrats, so that people averaged a fraction of a point more Democratic than they "should" have based solely on perceived ideological distance. Since about 1984, however, the intercepts have converged toward zero, suggesting a new equilibration with this former Democratic advantage now neutralized. An ideologically neutral voter is now about equally likely to be a Republican or a Democrat.

This pattern helps to account for the precipitous decline in Democratic identification, beginning in about 1984. This evolution may have now stopped, however, with the party identifications of ideologically aware voters now aligned more exactly with their ideological perceptions. Republicans were correct to argue that partisanship had lagged behind the conservative direction of ideological preferences. However, the correction appears to have now been in place for about a decade.

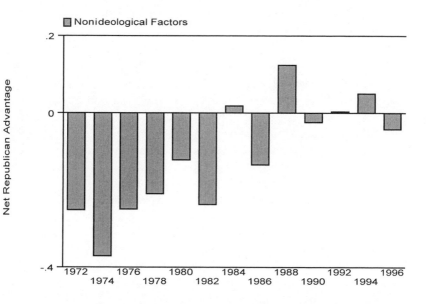

Fig. 6.8.   Net impact of nonideological factors on macropartisanship

The Dynamics of Ideological Representation

Representation, of course, is a dynamic phenomenon as well as a cross-sectional one. In other work (Stimson, MacKuen, and Erikson 1995; Erikson, MacKuen, and Stimson 2002), we have argued that politicians pay attention to the public's changing preferences for policy direction and react by producing the appropriate policy shifts. One key feature in this understanding is the fact that politicians rationally anticipate the electorate's preferences and try to provide the proper signals to their constituencies before election time. When incumbents are successful at anticipation and at political action, they will be difficult to unseat. Such a mechanism provides incentives for effective dynamic representation.

Crucially, it is surprises—unexpected developments—that provide the spur to partisan change. Of course, for any particular campaign in a particular constituency, such surprises include a variety of factors including personal issues such as scandals, campaign issues of the sort associated with the dance of modern mudslinging, and specific policy questions that get framed in ways that incumbents find difficult to handle. For national policy-making, however, such idiosyncratic factors play only a modest part—they are likely to be randomly scattered over time and ideological persuasion. It is the more systematic exceptions that prove more interesting.

Consider the possibility of movement on the ideological spectrum. Could 1994 provide such an example? When the Clinton administration took office in 1993, it faced a backlog of "liberal" legislation that had been stalled by twelve years of Republican control of the presidency. Having won office, the new Democratic administration naturally supposed that the public supported its agenda. The Democrats successfully pushed their program in 1993, receiving at first muted and later strident protests from the conservative opposition. And, by the election of 1994, the Democratic party lost control over the House for the first time in half a century.

Could Democratic incumbents have been systematically surprised by the public's reaction? Our evidence suggests that there was a genuine change in the public's policy and ideological evaluation of the parties and their congresspersons. First, to get a sense of the dramatic change, look at the sea change in public opinion about governmental action, Policy Mood, shown in figure 6.9. Policy Mood may be thought of as the proportion of the public that takes a conservative position on questions about governmental policy.[19] Within one election cycle we see an almost ten-point shift in people's reactions to policy questions—this is about half the entire range of Mood over the past fifty years. The largest movement was in 1993, but it continued apace in 1994 as well. Could this sudden surge in conservative evaluations have surprised House incumbents and produced the Republican Revolution of 1994?

Ideology, of course, is not equivalent to Policy Mood, which implicitly incorporates a thermostatic component. Ideology reflects an overall stance, while Policy Mood reflects a comparison of that preference with perceptions of what is currently going on. Thus, rather than simply looking at people's self-identifications, we also need to examine their assessments of the parties' candidates. We find that people—the ideologically literate—moved in a conservative direction (see fig. 6.4). Simultaneously their perceptions of the candidates also changed, and they saw the Republicans as more conservative and Democrats as more liberal. This combination proved a deadly surprise to Democratic incumbents. Politicians typically try to position themselves around the ideological center, but occasionally they make mistakes. We get a sense of the Democratic error by looking at a graph of relative ideology in figure 6.10. Here we see the ideologically literates' conservatism relative to each year's candidate posturing.

Again, this relative conservatism indicates whether voters felt to the left or to the right of a competitive center—when both candidates get the ideological battle about right, the score should be zero. In our years, to be sure, the Republicans have enjoyed a modest advantage in ideology. This was larger during the Watergate era simply because Democratic House candidates had a nonideolog-

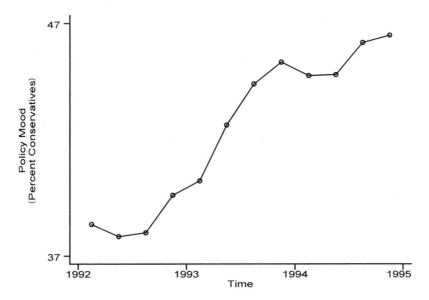

Fig. 6.9.   Dynamics of policy mood and the 1994 election

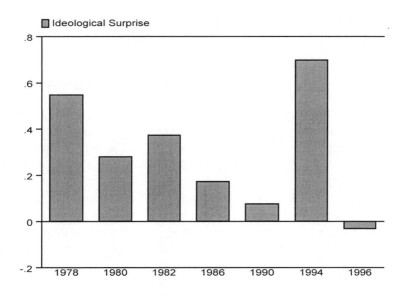

Fig. 6.10.   Ideological surprises to House candidates

ical surplus to trade off against policy.[20] By the late 1980s that surplus vanished and the Democrats had adjusted to eliminate their ideological disadvantage. But note the sharp surprise associated with 1994. The sudden step rightward by the ideologues coupled with a quick shift in their assessments of candidates' positions shocked the standard Democratic strategies (to the tune of about 5 percent of the vote) and led to a turnover in Congress.

Politicians—successful politicians—learn. We see that while the public remained conservative in its policy and ideological views through 1996, the candidates' readjusted their policy positions to produce a competitive set of House campaigns, with neither party enjoying a net advantage. This action and reaction of politicians and citizens is characteristic of a system of dynamic representation. Accordingly, when we search for explanations of movement in election outcomes and policy-making, we should consider ideological movement by voters and candidates as central suspects.

Conclusions

This essay has explored ideological representation in contemporary electoral politics. In presidential elections, we have seen the presence of considerable ideological voting at the micro level. However, ideology appears swamped by other forces in terms of determining macrolevel change in presidential outcomes.

In congressional elections—Senate and House—where ideological attention and information are at far lower levels at the micro level, macrolevel ideological representation appears to be strong. A unit change of constituency ideological preferences appears to produce on average a unit change—or even more—to congressional representation. At the same time, congressional voters generally elect representatives slightly more liberal than the districts' ideologues because of the voting influence of Democratic nonideological voters.

Party identification plays an important role in ideological representation. When partisanship and ideology reinforce one another, at the micro level or the macro level, ideology carries surprising weight in electoral outcomes. As recently as the early 1970s, party and ideology were separate sorts of things. However, since that time, the increasing polarization of elite debate and politicians' behavior has led to a public aligned along virtually identical partisan and ideological grounds. The politics of parties and the politics of ideology have become nearly the same.

In all, the evidence supports the idea that contemporary politics in the United States can be described in ideological terms. While nonideological factors are powerfully at work, it surely seems that voters are connected to policymakers though the language of political ideology. Politicians adjust their policy stances to accommodate voters, and voters throw their support behind politicians who play the ideological political game. And these ideological politics penetrate well into the mass public—our measure of ideological literates now includes two-thirds of Americans. Furthermore, the extension of ideological capacity seems to have increased in several bursts in the past two decades.

The dynamics of the past quarter century, however, give pause. The description of ideological politics that applies to the 1980s and 1990s applies less well to the early 1970s. And side evidence suggests that the politics of the late 1950s and 1960s were even less ideological. Instead, the pattern of political elites deciding to pursue ideological politics—and thus reshaping mass politics—closely resembles the pattern of issue evolution. On reflection, there appears nothing permanent about the selection of liberal-conservative symbolism over which to contest political power—that particular choice is surely subject to future historical accidents and political strategies.

NOTES

1. The arguments resemble those involving ecological inference and aggregate data analysis. Ecological correlations tend to be high, but they can also go haywire to the point of showing the wrong sign. Similarly, systematic nonideological influences can distort ideological representation.

Suppose that in a particular election, perhaps because of candidate attractiveness on nonideological grounds, voters favor the conservative candidate more than that candidate deserves based on ideological proximity alone. The outcome would then depend on two factors: the relative ideological proximity of the candidates to the median voter and the exact degree of asymmetrical attraction to the conservative candidate. Given our limited description of this contest, the more liberal candidate might win, but only by passing a high ideological threshold. The less popular liberal would need to be closer to more than half the voters to win. We might choose to describe this hypothetical election as ideologically biased in the sense that one candidate will earn more votes than he or she would win based solely on ideology.

2. As assurance that candidates and parties rarely are perceived as projections of respondent positions, relatively few of those scored as ideologically illiterate rate parties or candidates opposite of the correct left-right direction. Among presidential voters scored as ideologically illiterate, only 11 percent scored either the Democratic party or the Democratic presidential candidate to the right of the Republican counterpart. An additional 20 percent, while avoiding this mistake, did get scored as ideologically illiterate by rating the parties and/or candidates at an ideological tie.

3. Happily, this measure avoids the problematic assumption that citizens calibrate the seven-point "ideological" scale with identical metrics.

4. It is possible, of course, that the relative impact (the coefficient) of ideology might vary in accord with each distinct election campaign. In these analyses, the election-specific differences are not statistically important, a fact that allows our simple pooled statistical work.

5. An important literature (Converse 1962; Zaller 1992) has argued that the less informed are available for political persuasion because of their lack of stored information. The lack of significant interactions involving ideological knowledge and partisanship or year effects helps to illustrate how this works. Nonideological voters show more change over time in their votes. And in a given year, nonideological partisans are more up for grabs than their ideological counterparts. The reason is not that they care more about the short-term forces represented by year effects. It is that they lack the ideological position that normally bolsters a partisan choice. Ideological voters show less movement because their ideological orientations and party identifications reinforce one another.

6. Precisely, sample percent republican = 21.2 × Z, Adj. R^2 = 0.99; where $Z = b_I(I_y)$ + $b_P(P_y)$ + b_y and b_I and b_P represent the probit coefficients for ideological proximity and party identification, respectively; (I_y) and (P_y) represent the mean values of ideological proximity and party identification in year y, respectively; and b_y represents the dummy variable coefficient for year y (where the coefficients are from table 6.2, column 3).

7. We suspect that these net ideology estimates may be incomplete as they stem from a narrow macrolevel extrapolation from microlevel findings. Variation from one election to the next in terms of ideological proximity or macropartisanship might bring about hidden contextual effects beyond their observable additive effects. Consider, for example, the 1972 election that supposedly represented the rejection of Democratic candidate McGovern's "extreme" platform. It is plausible that McGovern's net loss from his liberalism greatly exceeded the observable three points, as aversion to the platform reverberated down from elites to masses, with specific objections translating into vague complaints about competence. More generally, when knowledgeable voters perceive a candidate as too conservative or too liberal and start turning away in larger numbers than usual, they may have only a marginal impact on the outcome. However, their systematic movement might well provide powerful cues for less attentive voters to the effect that it is time to vote differently than normal.

8. As with presidential voters, ideologically aware Senate voters voted slightly more Republican than their nonideological counterparts (52 percent to 45 percent). Again, the ideologically aware tend modestly toward Republican partisanship.

9. State-level ideology is calibrated here as percent liberal minus percent conservative. In each equation, the t-statistics appear in parentheses under the coefficients.

10. The Bush-Dukakis campaign was intentionally framed (by Bush strategists) in ideological terms. It provides a clear case of ideological distribution of districts during a year in which nonideological issues may have been less important than usual. The t-statistics appear in parentheses under the coefficients.

11. Recall that, ideology means something in terms of ordinary policy preferences. For the ideologically literate, we see a very substantial correlation (0.43) between ideology and views on government spending on social programs. For the unaware, the correlation is essentially zero (0.00). In fact, the unaware do better using partisanship rather than ideology as a cue for policy voting. (The correlation between partisanship and policy preference is 0.38.)

12. Among those who are "government-spending literate," the overall mean for 1982–96 is almost exactly 4.0, the scale midpoint. Ideologues take a (relatively conservative) position of 3.79, while nonideologues weigh in at 4.55.

13. These "district" aggregates are best thought of as tests of relationships between ideologues and nonideologues within geographic areas. The "district" samples were not typically meant to represent the congressional districts but instead more generic area samples. To be sure, the congressional district boundaries will have changed during our time frame, though largely at the margins. Of course, there are occasional instances of major changes. To the extent to which we treat these samples as representative of specific districts, those changes are problematic. But when we treat them as simple geographic concentrations, we worry less.

In the analysis that follows, we aggregate by nominal (state) congressional district and take means over ideology and partisanship for both ideologues and nonideologues. We discard the aggregates of fewer than thirty respondents and then do a weighted least squares analysis (using the square root of the within-district sample) to correct for theoretical sampling error.

14. The first relationship is statistically indistinguishable from zero (with a p value of 0.58), while the second is highly significant ($p = 0.0000$). The correlation between the ideologues' and nonideologues' partisanship is higher, of course, at 0.52.

15. One might reasonably expect that the predominance of ideological symbols as a major form of communication would generate correspondence between preference and partisanship. For ideologically aware citizens, anomalies between their policy views and their party allegiances must cry out for resolution. To the extent to which politics has become nationalized, the old excuses of being a "southern" Democrat have gone away. While there remain numbers of liberal Republicans and conservative Democrats, it is increasingly hard for them to find friends and allies with whom to share public life.

16. This measure is simply the proportion of Democrats who vote on the liberal side of an issue minus the proportion of Republicans voting liberal on that issue. Were both parties equally divided—not polarized—the score would be zero. Were all Democrats liberal and all Republicans conservative—absolutely polarized—the score would be 1.00.

17. Here we use lagged congressional polarization (from the previous year) to keep the causal direction straight. A parallel analysis, additionally controlling for previous ideology-partisan correspondence to take out the long-term trend, yields the following:

$$Ideology\text{-}Partisan = 0.38 + 0.66 \ Congressional + 0.17 \ I - P \ Correspondence_{t-2}$$
$$Correspondence_t \qquad\qquad Polarization_{t-1}$$
$$(2.86) \ (3.08) \qquad\qquad\qquad (0.48)$$

where the lagged term is statistically insignificant. The reverse feedback exists, of course, but is considerably weaker and statistically insignificant. Given the small number of years, it is difficult to be sure about null relationships. The t-statistics are given in parentheses below each coefficient.

18. It is clear that the aggregate distribution of macropartisanship responds to the performance of the parties in office, including their management of both economics and political drama (see MacKuen, Erikson, and Stimson 1989).

19. Policy mood is a sophisticated "splicing together" of different series of survey questions on a wide range of policy matters. The postwar history of policy mood can be well summarized by a single dimension—what we normally think of as liberal versus conservative reactions. Policy mood contains an implicit thermostatic component in

the sense that questions usually ask whether the government is doing too much or should do more. For a detailed explanation, see Stimson 1999. Here we reverse policy mood to point in the conservative direction to parallel our other graphics.

20. That is, the typical candidate (a Democrat from a fairly safe district) could count on some "unfair advantage" because of partisanship in the district and probably an additional personal constituency. This would allow the representative to take policy positions to the left of the district's center to maintain support among financial and ideological backers, to accommodate the pursuit of political power in Washington, or to formulate what the representative thought were good public policies.

REFERENCES

Campbell, Angus, Philip E. Converse, Warren E. Miller, and Donald E. Stokes. 1960. *The American Voter.* New York: Wiley.

Carmines, Edward B., and James A. Stimson. 1989. *Issue Evolution: Race and the Transformation of American Politics.* Princeton: Princeton University Press.

Converse, Philip E. 1962. Information Flow and the Stability of Partisan Attitudes. *Public Opinion Quarterly* 26:578–99.

———. 1964. The Nature of Belief Systems in Mass Publics. In David Apter, ed., *Ideology and Discontent.* New York: Free Press of Glencoe.

———. 1975. Public Opinion and Voting Behavior. In Fred Greenstein and Nelson Polsby, eds., *Handbook of Political Science,* vol. 4. Reading, Mass.: Addison-Wesley.

———. 1990. Popular Representation and the Distribution of Information. In John A. Ferejohn and James H. Kuklinski, eds., *Information and Democratic Processes.* Urbana: University of Illinois Press.

Downs, Anthony. 1957. *An Economic Theory of Democracy.* New York: Harper and Row.

Erikson, Robert S. 1971. The Electoral Impact of Congressional Roll Call Voting. *American Political Science Review* 65:1018–32.

———. 1990. Reputations, Representation, and Roll Calls in U.S. Senate Elections. *Legislative Studies Quarterly* 15:623–42.

Erikson, Robert S., Michael MacKuen, and James A. Stimson. 2002. *The Macro Polity.* New York: Cambridge University Press.

Erikson, Robert S., and Gerald C. Wright. 2001. Voters, Candidates, and Issues in Congressional Elections. In Lawrence C. Dodd and Bruce I. Oppenheimer, eds., *Congress Reconsidered,* 7th ed. Washington, D.C.: CQ Press.

Erikson, Robert S., Gerald C. Wright, and John P. McIver. 1993. *Statehouse Democracy: Public Opinion and Policy in the American States.* New York: Cambridge University Press.

Hagner, Paul R., and John C. Pierce. 1982. Conceptualization and Party Identification. *American Journal of Politics* 26:377–87.

Jacoby, William G. 1991. The Sources of Liberal-Conservative Thinking: Education and Conceptualization. *Political Behavior* 10:316–32.

Kagay, Michael R., and Greg A. Caldeira. 1980. A Reformed Electorate? Well, at Least a Changed Electorate. In William J. Crotty, ed., *Paths to Political Reform.* New York: Heath.

Knight, Kathleen. 1985. Ideology in the 1980 Election: Sophistication Matters. *Journal of Politics* 47:828–53.

Knight, Kathleen, and Robert S. Erikson. 1997. Ideology in the 1990s. In Barbara Norrander and Clyde Wilcox, eds., *Understanding Public Opinion*. Washington, D.C.: CQ Press.

MacKuen, Michael B., Robert S. Erikson, and James A. Stimson. 1989. Macropartisanship. *American Political Science Review* 83:1125–42.

Nie, Norman, Sidney Verba, and John R. Petrocik. 1976. *The Changing American Voter*. Cambridge: Harvard University Press.

Niemi, Richard G., and Herbert F. Weisberg. 1993. What Determines the Vote? In Richard G. Niemi and Herbert F. Weisberg, eds. *Classics of Voting Behavior*. Washington, D.C.: CQ Press.

Popkin, Samuel L., John W. Gorman, Charles Phillips, and Jeffrey A. Smith. 1976. What Have You Done for Me Lately? Toward an Investment Theory of Voting. *American Political Science Review* 70:779–805.

Stimson, James A. 1975. Belief Systems: Constraint, Complexity, and the 1972 Election. *American Journal of Political Science* 19:393–417.

———. 1999. *Public Opinion in America: Moods, Cycles, and Swings*. 2d ed. Boulder, Colo.: Westview.

Stimson, James A., Michael B. MacKuen, and Robert S. Erikson. 1995. Dynamic Representation. *American Political Science Review* 89:543–65.

Stokes, Donald E. 1966. Some Dynamic Elements of Contests for the Presidency. *American Political Science Review* 60:19–28.

Wright, Gerald C. 1978. Candidate Policy Positions and Voting in U.S. House Elections. *Legislative Studies Quarterly* 3:445–64.

Wright, Gerald C., and Michael Berkman. 1986. Candidates and Policy in U.S. Senate Elections. *American Political Science Review* 80:253–83.

Zaller, John. 1992. *The Nature and Origins of Mass Opinion*. Cambridge: Cambridge University Press.

7

The Heavenly Public:
What Would a Fully Informed
Citizenry Be Like?

Robert C. Luskin

It has been widely remarked, and mainly deplored, that most people live their lives in blissful ignorance of politics. Not everyone, to be sure. At the individual level, political awareness has "low mean" but "high variance" (Converse 1990). At the national level, the variation is clearly much smaller (and harder to document), but there does seem to be some, cross-nationally at least, if only very secularly and modestly over time.[1]

What we are talking about here is something like cognitive participation in politics: the quantity of mental representations of political stimuli stored in memory. Variously got up, this variable may have held the limelight more than any other in the modern study of mass politics. It appears as "political sophistication," "political expertise," "political information," "political knowledge," "political awareness," and "political cognitive complexity," terms differing only in effectively minor detail. *Knowledge* implies factual accuracy as well as quantity. *Sophistication, expertise,* and *complexity* imply organization as well as quantity, as may *awareness,* the vaguest of these terms. But since both accuracy and organization are highly correlated with quantity, these additional requirements do not make much practical difference.[2] I shall therefore use all these terms synonymously, and while elsewhere I have favored "sophistication," both from force of habit and because the most theoretically relevant variable is quantity *plus* (or, more precisely, *times*) organization, here I shall make nearly equal use of "information," on the grounds that it is the core variable, the common denominator, of this cluster.

The public's level of political information is no new concern. Acute observers going back at least to Lord Bryce (1904) and Walter Lippmann (1922) have noted the variable's radically skewed distribution. In the early survey era,

Berelson, Lazarsfeld, and McFee (1954) added the authority of survey data and provided a Schumpeterian (1950), elite-driven view of how real-world democracies could function in the absence of much public involvement. But the studies most responsible for shaping our view of political information and convincing us of its importance have been Campbell et al.'s *The American Voter* (1960) and Converse's long chapter, "The Nature of Belief Systems in Mass Publics" (1964). The latter in particular sketched lightly but vividly some plausible implications of low and uneven levels of political information for public opinion and electoral outcomes.

Much of this variable's popularity stems from its utility for understanding. Theoretically and empirically, it affects a variety of mass attitudes and behaviors. In the way of main effects, the better informed are more participatory, more committed to democratic norms, but (arguably) more extreme in their policy views. In the way of conditioning or interaction effects, the better informed (also arguably) attach greater weight to policy considerations and lesser weight to candidate personalities and other policy-irrelevant matters in voting. Their policy views, in turn, should be more snugly reasoned from their more fundamental values and interests, however construed (a question to which we shall return). The very well informed, like "the very rich," according to Fitzgerald, "are different."

But another large share of political information's popularity stems from its utility for evaluation. Most of us are democrats, small *d,* and care about the extent to which real-world democracies approach the democratic ideal. What constitutes the democratic ideal is of course a large question, but we need not attempt to specify it completely to know that some of the desiderata must concern the behavior of ordinary citizens and that some close familiarity with public affairs is surely one of them. Thus we partly care about political information for its implications for the gap between the real and the ideal.

All this leads to the effectively compound question I wish to explore here, what would the ideal democratic public, the "heavenly public" of the Augustinian title, be like? As stated, the question is ambiguous. It could be procedural, concerning the ways in which ideal democratic citizens relate to politics: *How much,* and *how,* do they think, know, talk, and act politically? As the "talk" and "act" in this last phrase suggest, other characteristics besides information are undoubtedly involved, and, among other things, I want to consider what some of them might be. This is the independent-variable side of the question.

The other sense of the question is substantive. Given whatever procedural characteristics we require, *what* would the ideal democratic public think and do? What policy views would its members hold and work toward? For what candidates or parties would they vote? This is the dependent-variable side of the question. What *other* characteristics would procedurally ideal citizens tend to display?

I want here to address both sides of the question, first sketching explicitly, if somewhat diffidently, the procedural ideal and then considering, also somewhat diffidently, its implications for other, posterior variables, particularly policy views and voting decisions. My driving concern is with the second endeavor, but the second makes sense only in light of the first.

Defining the Ideal

Let me begin by narrowing my scope. Democracy has been promoted in various lights. It is claimed to be good for society, most centrally as a decision-making device—as a way of determining, as defensibly as possible, what policies should be chosen and by whom. It is also claimed to be good for the individual, as a way of maximizing autonomy and self-fulfillment. The two sorts of benefits are related, of course, but analytically separable.[3] Here I shall focus on democracy as decision making. Although I do consider this its most central role, its raison d'être, in fact, I do not mean to slight its other virtues. Given constraints of time and space, I simply leave them for another day.

For similar reasons, we may forgo a fully specified definition of democracy. Suffice it to remark that it revolves around some version of majority rule, which provides a powerfully, indeed primitively, appealing means of deciding conflicts over policy choices and who should make them, as well as of reconciling the losers to current defeat.[4] Subsidiarily, it also presumes the political freedoms necessary to make majorities meaningful expressions of popular will and allow minorities the hope of becoming majorities. Prefatory adjectives like *direct, representative, liberal, strong,* or *deliberative* may of course add ingredients, but these two seem to me the core meaning.

Democracy is thus procedural. People sufficiently devoted to certain policy outcomes may attempt to smuggle them into the definition, as in the traditional Marxist refusal to regard as truly democratic any system not producing economic leveling. But these are just efforts by undemocratic ideologies to hijack an approbatory term. Democracy is quite centrally about good losing, what the minority must do under majority rule. As long as the procedures are legitimate, the minority must be prepared to live with distasteful, even abhorrent results—at least until the next election.

For citizens, too, the democratic ideal is procedural. It requires citizens who care and think about policies yet do not mind efforts by others who think differently to see other preferences prevail. It does not require citizens who prefer particular policies. The ideal public may happen to favor (or oppose) economic leveling (or any other outcome) but is not required to do so by definition.

Let me turn, then, to the ingredients of this procedural ideal. I have sorted a number of possibilities into *defining* properties, which are essential; *elective* properties, which may arguable be; and *related* properties, which are not. Most of these last are instrumental, redundant as part of the ideal but still important for their effects on it. Although I should be astonished to find the properties I discuss exhaustive, I do hope to have caught the main ones.

Defining Properties

Sophistication

The ideal public cannot be ignorant: that much seems obvious. The reason, which may be less obvious, is that the normative value of the majorities in majority rule depends critically on the level of thought and information behind the preferences being counted.

Appeals to Condorcet, à la Page and Shapiro (1992), yield little comfort. As Bartels (1996) remarks, this sort of miracle-of-aggregation argument depends critically on the assumption of random error (see also Luskin 2002a, 2002b). To see this more clearly, imagine individual i's propensity y_i^* to vote for a given candidate or party, say the Republican, in a two-party contest to be a linear combination of his or her interests, given by the vector x_i and an error term ε_i:

$$y_i^* = \gamma_0 + \gamma_1' x_i + \varepsilon_i, \tag{1}$$

where γ_1' is a correspondingly dimensioned parameter vector, and γ_0 is a scalar constant. The error could arise from the voter's mistaking his or her interests, miscalculating which candidate or party would best serve them, or both.[5]

Even under the happiest assumptions—that all the ε_i have means of zero, are uncorrelated for different individuals, have constant variance across individuals, and are independent of interests for any given individual—the results of any given election will never be exactly what they would sans error.[6] It is true that over infinitely repeated hypothetical iterations of the same election, they will average out to roughly what they would be sans error and that, in any given election, they should rarely stray all that far from it.[7] But again these properties depend on the assumptions just stated.

So now imagine, more realistically, that one or more of these assumptions is seriously wrong. One very real possibility is that variance of ε_i varies across individuals (a matter of heteroskedasticity). The errors may average out to zero across the society, and do so for everyone, but some people, from certain sectors of society, may tend to make much larger errors, while others, from other sectors of society—and thus having different interests—tend to make much smaller ones. Over infinitely repeated iterations of the same election, those groups less prone to error will vote against their interests in appreciable numbers less frequently. Since it is those in relatively privileged social locations, the natural clientele of the right, whose information and other resources should enable them to make smaller errors, this sort of heteroskedasticity could be expected to redound to the advantage of parties and candidates of the right.

A second very real possibility is that mean of ε_i is nonzero, that over infinitely repeated iterations of the same election, the average vote totals are not what they would be sans error but tend to favor one side or other. This could occur through media bias, although which side benefits and by how much are matters of debate.[8] A likelier suspect is the generally greater financial resources enjoyed by parties and candidates of the right, which would again seem to tilt the results rightward.

The third possibility, also very real, indeed anticipated in the reasoning about the partisan implications of the first two, is that ε_i is correlated with interests. The more people's interests should incline them to the left, the more they may err to the right, owing to the combination of greater financial and thus persuasive resources on the right and lesser information among those whose interests should incline them to the left. Given the standard presumption that the latter are generally a majority, the right, yet again, could be expected to benefit.

Now, this reasoning may be too simple in ways I shall presently sketch (and any inference from these past few paragraphs that my own sympathies are decidedly left of center would be mistaken), but the general lesson remains: there is every reason to expect both public opinion and vote totals to be deflected by widespread public ignorance from what they would be if everyone were well informed—and were thus subject to smaller and more equal error.

We shall come to the evidence regarding the existence and nature of such consequential ignorance anon. For the moment, it suffices to establish its plausibility and to raise the question of its implications for democracy. How satisfying, how fair, is majority rule when the majority might well change with full, or fuller, information? It may still, in the spirit of Churchill's description of democracy as the worst form of government except for all the rest, be fairer than any other principle of aggregating preferences in something like a mean-squared-error sense (averaging over infinitely repeated elections). But it is now a long way from the ideal. "Majorities, if heavily of the bamboozled or distracted, lose much of their normative value" (Luskin and Globetti 1997, 6).

This is the primary reason we should want the ideal public to be highly (and homogenously) sophisticated: a sufficiently sophisticated public would have preferences true to its interests. A necessary further premise, widely but not universally shared, is that the distributions of preferences true to interests would often be appreciably different from the real-world distributions we actually see. I shall return to this issue below.

Of course, *representative* democracy may be viewed as a strategy for mitigating mass ignorance by confining the public's decision making to the choice of representatives and delegating the actual policy-making to the representatives chosen (Fishkin and Luskin 2000). But even the choice among candidates or parties, though much less cognitively demanding than the choice among policies, entails the same possibilities for error. Thus the public's being highly sophisticated remains a key part of the democratic ideal, even in representative democracy.

Participation

In addition to any good done the individual (as claimed most famously by Mill 1859, 1861; and more recently by Pateman 1970 and Barber 1984, among others), participation is essential for the proper functioning of the democratic system. Thus consider voting, in either direct or representative democracy. Voters are always a self-selected sample, but only trivially so (i.e., the same as the population) when there are no abstentions. The more numerous the abstentions, the greater the gap between population and sample, and the greater the likely bias. In most elections, there seem to be only small differences between the voting and other preferences of voters and nonvoters (Wolfinger and Rosenstone 1980; Schaffer 1982; Gant and Lyons 1993; cf. Bennett and Resnick 1990; Verba, Schlozman, and Brady 1995), but the difference (a) might well be greater if the nonvoters, who tend to be particularly unsophisticated, had more information and (b) is appreciable in some elections as it is. At least sometimes, and probably often, the distribution of votes would therefore be different if everyone voted. Abstention thus undermines the democratic principle of equality (see Fishkin and Luskin 2000).

Respect

The democratic ideal also requires the acceptance of principled disagreement. This is a matter of attitudes and behavior toward other citizens holding opposing views. There is quite a literature on *political tolerance,* defined as one's willingness to allow minorities, even those one despises, the freedoms necessary for them to have the chance of becoming majorities (e.g., Sullivan, Piereson, and Marcus 1982; McClosky and Brill 1983; Gibson 1988, 1992; Sniderman and Fletcher 1996). But mere toleration, though necessary, is not enough. Ideal citizens *respect* those whose only known demerit is being on the other side of one or more important issues, regarding them as misguided rather than bad hearted. Behaviorally, respect facilitates *civility.*

Elective Properties

The two properties I put under this heading are sociotropism and deliberation. There is reason to doubt the necessity of requiring either, especially sociotropism, although there is also some case to be made for requiring each, especially deliberation.

Sociotropism

There is a great and highly relevant divide between those who consider there, at least sometimes, to be some common interest to be striven toward and those who believe there to be only individual interests to be aggregated in some fashion. On the second view, the great virtue of democracy is that it allows a free and fair contest among individual interests. People may cloak their interests in arguments about some fictional common interest, but that is just rhetoric. Ideal citizens pursue their interests as accurately and efficiently as they can. This is what Mansbridge (1980) calls "adversary democracy."

On the first view, the great virtue of democracy is that it provides a forum for deciding among competing conceptions of the common interest or, in a more extreme version, that it facilitates convergence on a common notion of the common interest. Here ideal citizens think not of their individual interests, however generously defined, but of the common interest. In Kinder and Kiewiet's (1979) term, they are *sociotropic*, in Wilson and Banfield's (1964) *public-regarding*, in Mill's (1859) *public-spirited*. This is what Mansbridge (1980), terms "unitary democracy."[9]

The reality of course may lie in between. There may be a common interest on some issues but not others. Or given interests may be common to varying degrees—a possibility leading to an awkward question for those whose ideal involves convergence on a common interest: How common a common interest are we talking about, and on what dimension? Is it the interest of the nation? Why not of all humanity? Or, in the other direction, is it the interest of the state, the region, or the community? Or, on nongeographic lines, the interest of a racial, ethnic, or religious group? An occupational one? There is a wide variety of possible interests greater than one's own. My own view, as may already be evident, is that there are few if any truly common interests, at least for entities of any size or heterogeneity, but I am content to leave the question open.

Does democracy benefit, then, from extreme sociotropism? That is a nice question. What if given individuals, facing given issues or electoral choices, have more than one common interest? Toward what groups should we wish them to be sociotropic? What if there is actually no common interest? Might not the aggregate satisfaction of individual interests be maximized by everyone's pursuing his or her individual interest rather than some mythical common interest? What if common and individual interests exist side by side? How much should people pursue the common interest? Entirely, not at all, or partially? With what weight, if partially? In sum, it is by no means clear that more sociotropism is categorically better.

The cognitive aspect of sociotropism may arguably be entailed in sophistication. People who learn enough should learn, among many other things, about the needs and circumstances of others very different from themselves. In the real world, when people learn more about politics, they tend to keep their learning within more or less familiar channels and so may not learn what is like to be African American, middle class, or from Alaska.[10] But high enough—ideal—sophistication would surely include some acquaintance with such other perspectives.

That by itself would not ensure sociotropic preferences, of course. Recognizing others' needs and thus presumably respecting their preferences is one thing, factoring their needs into one's own preferences something else again. For that, some motivational element, some altruistic desire to further others' interests, even to the detriment of one's own, is also necessary.

But again it is by no means clear that we should always want everyone—or anyone—to be sociotropic. There may arguably be issues where interests are mostly common, and with respect to which we should want people to be broadly sociotropic, thinking of the societal good; certainly there are issues where interests are more particular, and with respect to which we should presumably want people to be thinking of the good of much narrower circles, perhaps just themselves. What may make sense to require is therefore an appropriate—not necessarily high—degree of sociotropism, where what is appropriate will depend on the nature of the issue, and where knowing what is appropriate requires sophistication.

Deliberation

Among the hottest topics in political theory is "deliberative democracy" (e.g., Dryzek 1990; Spragens 1990; Fishkin 1991, 1997; Bessette 1994; Bohman 1996; Bohman and Rehg 1998; Elster 1998). As Young puts it, "recent years have seen an explosion of theorizing about democracy as a discussion-based form of practical reason" (1996: 486). Empirically, James Fishkin, assorted other collaborators, and I have been exploring the consequences of deliberation by means of Deliberative Polling (Fishkin 1991, 1997; Luskin and Fishkin 1998; Fishkin and Luskin 1999; Luskin, Fishkin, and Jowell 2002; Luskin et al. 1999; Luskin, Fishkin, and Plane 1999).

A parenthesis about Deliberative Polling may be in order at this juncture, since I shall refer to the project several times as the discussion unfolds. Briefly, a Deliberative Poll is a quasi-experiment bringing local, regional, or national probability samples to some single site to discuss a set of policy issues for a weekend. We have now superintended twenty of these, including eleven national ones—five in Britain, two each in the United States and Australia, and one each in Denmark and Bulgaria. The basic design is to question the participants via a more or less standard telephone or in-person interview, send them carefully balanced briefing materials outlining the chief policy proposals and the arguments for and against each, bring them to the common site for a mix of moderated discussions in randomly assigned small groups and plenary question-and-answer sessions with panels of experts and/or policymakers, and finally have them answer the same survey questions as at the beginning. Note, importantly for the quality of deliberation, that random assignment makes the groups much more heterogeneous than discussion partners tend to be in real life.

It may help in thinking about deliberation to distinguish several related processes. How would ideal citizens greet a new issue? They would absorb information, they would think about it, and they would talk it over—processes we may distinguish as *learning, rumination,* and *discussion.* Rumination is solo, and learning may frequently be, but discussion is inherently social. *Deliberation* may refer to the three activities as a group or simply to discussion. In any case, it is discussion that is the distinctive aspect of deliberation and the sense in which I shall mainly use the term here.

The question about deliberation is not whether it is an important part of the life of the ideal citizenry. Most assuredly, it is. The question is whether that must be true by definition. From our present perspective on democracy as decision making, the ideal public doubtless will engage in a great deal of serious political discussion, but only because discussion fosters (and stems from) sophistication, participation, respect, and sociotropism. The discussion is merely—if highly—instrumental. It is perhaps particularly relevant to sociotropism and respect. "Tout comprendre rend très indulgent," wrote Madame de Staël.[11] Citizens talking with one another may gain a deeper appreciation of each others' needs and constraints, which should help widen the "common" in any effort to take account of a common interest. By the same token, they may gain a deeper appreciation of the reasons for views with which they still disagree. But the role of discussion here is still instrumental rather than intrinsic.

On the other hand, this is one place where my having restricted our attention to democracy's functions for society, and specifically for decision making, may make some difference. It could be argued that, no matter how limited its necessity for democracy as decision making, discussion is an essential part of its benefits for the individual, that it enlarges the soul.

Related Properties

What I am calling related properties are a mix of consequences, causes, and assorted other correlates of the defining ones. Most are instrumental, in the sense described above. All have some plausible claim on being made part of the definition, but none, on close scrutiny, seems necessary.

Education

Education is commonly thought to promote a very wide assortment of civic virtues, including sophistication, participation, and respect, and although I do not believe that it in fact has much effect on sophistication, it does seem to affect participation and respect (Luskin 1990; Luskin and Ten Barge 1995; cf. Nie, Junn, and Stehlik-Barry 1996). At the same time, it is hard to see how it could matter to ideal citizenship except through these or similar intervening variables.

Interest

It is possible to be well informed and participatory but uninterested. People may acquire information willy-nilly, from spouses or jobs. They may get roped into working on campaigns or voting. But such cases are relatively rare. Interest is heavily bound up with both sophistication and participation (Luskin 1990; Luskin and Ten Barge 1995). It is important for democracy that citizens be interested in politics, but mainly so that they may learn about and participate in it.

Attention

It is surprisingly hard to demonstrate much effect of political media exposure on political sophistication or political interest (Luskin 1990), although there must surely be some, if the media exposure variable is carefully enough drawn (and sophistication finely enough measured). Even then, however, it is hard to see how attention matters, except through sophistication and participation.

Intelligence

The matching of preferences to interests may be facilitated by cognitive ability or intelligence as well as by sophistication. Brighter people should do better at spotting their interests and tailoring their policy preferences to them. Indeed, intelligence and information may to some degree substitute for one another. People who are sharp enough may see connections that others need more knowledge to detect; people who know enough may see connections that others would need to be sharper to detect. (See Luskin and Ten Barge 1995 for further argument on these lines.)

Intelligence is in many quarters an unwelcome variable these days, and I raise it as a possible criterion with some trepidation, even though I raise it only to reject it. But surely it would be helpful to democracy, surely it would increase the extent to which everyone acted in keeping with his or her own interests (or the common interest, if one prefers), if everyone were highly intelligent. The evidence is that intelligence affects performance on almost every task involving nontrivial mentation. The effects may not usually be more than modest, but they are pervasive (Brody 1992; Gordon 1997; Gottfredson 1997). To some extent, intelligence may be regarded as instrumental for sophistication, given the strong correlation between ability and knowledge (in no matter what domain). But it is not purely instrumental. There remains the question of how accurately people reason from given (even high) levels of information.

No, the main problem with requiring universally high intelligence is not instrumentality but impracticability. A public whose members are all highly knowledgeable is utopian enough; one whose members are all highly intelligent is qualitatively more so. At least in principle, the ignorant can learn; the mentally dull cannot be made sharp. Making everybody highly intelligent is *too* ideal.

Indeterminacies: How Ideal Is "Ideal"?

This brings us to the general question of how ideal to make the ideal, which is actually two questions. The first, as we have just seen, is of what properties to require. Some are more radically and intractably counterfactual than others. If we were talking about adult individuals' participation in basketball rather than politics, we might well make height a desideratum. But, then again, if the object were to evaluate the population's performance, we might not. Height, for given individuals in adulthood, is unalterable.[12] Like intelligence with respect to politics, it may be relevant but too intractable to be useful as part of a not-too-ideal ideal.

A similar issue concerns the quality of thought in sophistication. Is it enough that people have thought more about politics, as in variables like sophistication, expertise, or cognitive complexity, conventionally defined, or must they think "better"—more logically, more as decision theory says they should? This is a stiffer requirement than high sophistication, which entails extensive psycho-logic (in Abelson and Rosenberg's [1958] old distinction), not necessarily rigorous logic.

The other question, for the properties we do require, is of degree. I have been using phrases like "highly sophisticated," but how highly is "highly"? Equivalently, in the literature calling this variable "information," what is "full information"? Is it omniscience—what God knows? That would make high sophistication/full information easy to define but hard to operationalize. Or it could be some very high level short of omniscience, but in that case we should have to draw an arbitrary line, making high sophistication/full information easy to operationalize but hard to define.

In some degree, the same question arises for any desideratum, although it may be particularly acute for information, whose maximum seems to stretch especially far from zero. *How* tolerant and respectful should we require our ideal citizens to be? How participatory? How sociotropic? There are almost literally innumerable opportunities to participate, electorally and otherwise; groups, causes, and individuals to respect and tolerate; issues on which to consider some more common interest than one's own; and definitions of "common" (supersets of oneself). Where to locate the threshold of the ideal is hard to know.

What Would the Ideal Public Be Like? Political Sophistication and Policy and Vote Preferences

On the substantive side, too, I must begin by narrowing the question. The respects in which a public ideally sophisticated, respectful, and participatory would differ from the public we actually see are plural, perhaps many. The ideal public may be more civil and less violent. Its preferences may be more (or less) extreme. They may be more sociotropic. But constraints of time and space again force me to set these and other possible consequences aside. Specifically, and aptly for our special concern with democracy as decision making, I shall focus on the effects on policy and vote preferences.

Much ink has been spilt over the question of whether these effects are nontrivial. A Frank-Capra-ish literature has contended that despite massive ignorance, citizens manage, either individually or in the aggregate, to reach the same policy preferences they would have held and the same vote choices they would have made under full information (Popkin 1991; Page and Shapiro 1992; Lupia and McCubbins 1998). It is now pretty clear, however, both from survey-based studies simulating the effects of full information (Delli Carpini and Keeter 1996; Bartels 1996; Luskin and Globetti 1997; Althaus 1998) and quasi-experimental devices like the Deliberative Poll (Fishkin 1997; Luskin and Fishkin 1998; Fishkin and Luskin 1999; Luskin, Fishkin, and Jowell 2002; Luskin et al. 1999; Luskin, Fishkin, and Plane 1999) and the choice questionnaire (Neijens 1987; Neijens, de Ridder, and Saris 1992) that this is not so. Taking that much for granted, I shall instead concentrate here on the as-yet little addressed but vitally important question of the effects' signs and shapes.

The Nature of the Relationship

As previously argued, policy and vote preferences should depend partly on interests, values, and other more basic dispositions. Algebraically, a relatively general statement of this hypothesis might be

$$E(y_i|x_i) = g(\gamma_0 + \gamma_1' x_i), \tag{2}$$

where y_i is either a policy preference measured numerically or a binary vote choice scored $\{0,1\}$, x_i is a $K \times 1$ vector of interests or other underlying dispositions, γ_1' is a $1 \times K$ parameter vector and γ_0 a scalar constant, g is the identity function for numerical y_i and either logit or probit for binary y_i, $E(y_i|x_i)$ is the expected value of y_i conditional on x_i, and the i subscript denotes the ith observation. Note that this model can be derived from (1), and that $E(y_i|x_i)$ equals the probability that $y_i = 1$ (also conditional on x_i) in the case of binary vote choice.[13]

The relevance for present concerns lies in the expansion of (2) to allow for conditioning by information and perhaps other relevant variables. Apart from taking the steam out of the worries about the error term raised in connection with (1), this enables us to examine the question of how the reasoning and thus the preferences of the real-world and fully informed publics would differ. The question is the nature of this conditioning. One seemingly straightforward notion, at least implicit in Converse (1964), is that the relationships between the right-hand-side variables and left-hand-side preference are accentuated by sophistication. To express this, we expand the equation to

$$E(y_i|x_i,S_i) = g(\gamma_0 + \gamma'_1 x_i + \gamma'_2 x_i S_i), \tag{3}$$

where S_i is a scalar measure of political information, γ'_2 is another $1 \times K$ parameter vector, the conditioning is now on S_i as well as x_i, and everything else is the same.[14] This formulation covers the analyses in Delli Carpini and Keeter 1996; Bartels 1996; Luskin and Globetti 1997; and Althaus 1998.[15]

Interests, Values, and Other Right-Hand-Side Variables

It remains to elaborate on the right-hand-side variables. I shall continue finessing the definition of interests and values, for want of space or need for greater precision, but should explicitly note that I mean people's "interests" to be their own, although they may take account of others' interests or of a common interest (where and to the extent that one exists) as well.

Take first the case where y_i is vote choice. The equation's focus could be very close up, in which case the x_i's could include such proximate influences on vote choice as party identification, policy distances, perceptions of the candidates as people, and retrospective judgments of the parties' performance in office, as in Luskin and Globetti (1997). Or it could be more telescopic, in which case the x_i's might be interests or values. If instead y_i is a policy preference, some of these more proximate variables become irrelevant, and others, notably including party identification, incur endogeneity problems, but a reduced form in terms of interests or values still works.

But should it be interests or values? The question is not actually either-or, but the pluses and minuses are worth examining. The simpler alternative is values, which can be measured directly, if not necessarily well. One need merely ask survey respondents or experimental subjects to rate or rank the importance of various, usually instrumental needs, although the responses are often disappointing. Ratings often show little variation (just about everything is highly important to just about everyone), while rankings are often noisy (because difficult for many respondents to deal with). But these measurement issues are mainly another story.

Theoretically, the drawback to focusing on values lies in its missing some important possibility of error. Values are subjective, interests objective. It is impossible to get one's values wrong, but not everyone perceives his or her interests correctly. The translation from values to preferences involves only errors of calculation, whereas that from interests to preferences involves errors of perception as well. Issues of measurement aside, prediction from interests is thus less certain but more interesting.

The problem with interests, however, is gauging them. Who are we—how is anyone but God—to say what a given voter's interests are? The best we can do is to use as wide as possible an array of sociodemographic variables to index them. Variables like age, sex, race, and income are not interests themselves but do affect them. Hence interests become latent variables intervening between the sociodemographic array and vote choice. Delli Carpini and Keeter (1996), Bartels (1996), and Althaus (1998) all use sociodemographic arrays, on something like this reasoning.

This strategy effectively substitutes the voters' average judgment of what is in their interests for ours. To put it too simply, in view of the pervasive nonadditivities with which interests must be fraught, if being black raises a person's probability of voting Democratic, all other sociodemographic variables being equal, it must be in black people's interest to vote Democratic. The presumption is that even though individual members of a given category may get their interests wrong, the whole category membership will, on average, get them right. The assumption is neither unreasonable nor entirely safe.

One other difficulty in working with interests is the extreme nonadditivity with which sociodemographic variables can most accurately index them. In the arguments of (2) and (3), the sociodemographic characteristics combine only additively with one another (though nonadditively with sophistication). The actual relationship between interests and sociodemographic variables, however, must be highly configural. What determines one's interests is being in some particular combination of sociodemographic categories. The interests of blacks may depend on whether they are men or women; the interests of black men may depend on what region they live in; the interests of southern black men may depend whether they live in the city or in the country; and so on, ad nearly infinitum.

But modeling this more complex relationship into equations like (2) or (3) may pose collinearity or even degrees-of-freedom problems. Both Delli Carpini and Keeter and Bartels have sociodemographic variables numbering in the low twenties. Suppose for concreteness' sake that we have twenty-two of these. They, their one-way (pairwise) interactions with sophistication, and their one-way interactions with one another would account for $22 + 22 + 231 = 275$ regressors. Adding just the two-way interactions with both sophistication and one another makes for a total of $275 + 231 + 1,540 = 2,046$ regressors. Obviously, the model must be far less configural than the reality or it will not be estimable. We cannot really examine the multielement combinations of sociodemographic characteristics that actually determine interests. I do not regard this limitation as fatal, but it is a limitation.

The Role of Sophistication

Another right-hand-side variable is sophistication. Operationally, this is usually a numerical variable, a count or proportion of factual or quasi-factual items answered correctly. Sometimes the count or proportion is reduced to a dichotomy, distinguishing high- from low-information respondents. In this case, the results from estimating (3) are the same as from estimating (2) for high- and low-information respondents separately when g is the identity function and generally similar, though not quite the same, when g is logit or probit.[16]

The standard expectation is that increasing sophistication should reinforce the sociodemographic variables' main effects. If Jews, for example, tend to vote Democratic, politically sophisticated Jews should do the same, only more so. In terms of (3), this means that the corresponding coefficients in the vectors γ'_1 and γ'_2 share the same sign. This is how I too used to think the story ran.

Now, however, I am not so sure. The results so far, based on the observable range of information, are mixed. Delli Carpini and Keeter (1996), estimating a series of equations like (3) with policy opinions on the left (of the equation) and an array of sociodemographic variables on the right (of the equation), find that increasing sophistication to its maximum shifts the distributions of opinion to the left (politically). On the other hand, Bartels (1996), estimating a series of equations also like (3) but with presidential vote choices rather than policy opinions on the left, finds that in most recent presidential elections, increasing sophistication to its maximum would have shifted the distributions of votes to the right (toward the Republican). Yet again, Luskin and Globetti (1997), estimating an equation with presidential vote choice on the left and more proximate, psychological influences on vote choice, notably including perceived policy proximities and perceptions of the candidates as people, on the right, find that increasing sophistication to its maximum moves the distribution of votes to the left (toward the Democrat). Indeed, in their results, a fully sophisticated public elects Michael Dukakis in 1988, a possibility that helps underscore the importance of this whole question.

An additional source of uncertainty concerns the monotonicity of sophistication's effect. What is the impact of truly full information? It is pointless to pretend that the maximum level of information that can be measured in a survey or imparted in a Deliberative Poll is Safire- or Kinsley-like, let alone God-like. Increases up to the measured maximum may increase the magnitudes of the sociodemographic variables' coefficients, but what would the effect of further increases be? More attitude change in the same direction, or some reversal? That depends on what happens to people's understandings of their interests. Perhaps the conventional understanding by a given set of people, working-class whites, that they ought to favor policy X is based only on the direct and short-term consequences of X and its alternatives. The ignorant will of course fail to see even these, but, in some cases, at least, there may be indirect or long-term consequences that would persuade the sufficiently sophisticated to favor Y instead.

This question of monotonicity has implications for the bottom line: what happens to the overall distributions of policy and vote preferences as the public approaches the ideal? The conventional view, rehearsed briefly above and clearly visible in Converse (1964), is that people in disadvantaged social locations have interests that would be served by the policies of the left. When they gain information, therefore, they move left. This much may well be true, at least in the main, despite the diversity of results just cited, so long as only the short-term and direct effects of the policies of the left and the readily observable part of the information continuum are considered.

But then the question of monotonicity arises. What really serves the interests of most people is the stuff of political debate, and it is perfectly possible to construct plausible arguments, for example, of the "rising tide lifts all boats" variety, that most of the less advantaged would actually be better off, absolutely if not relatively, under the policies favored by parties of the right. Of course many of those on the right making such arguments may be motivated heavily by their own short-term and direct self-interest, but that does not necessarily make the arguments wrong. And if they are right, those who gain enough information might see more long-term and indirect effects and, after initially moving left, drift back to the right.

But this, too, may be too simple. The preceding discussion implicitly assumes classic redistributive issues, but social issues revolving around the treatment of relatively disfavored groups may plausibly display the opposite pattern. Here the right's positions may be the more easily grasped, and learning enough to see who benefits and who suffers may move people right, while learning still more—enough to understand others' needs or circumstances— may move them back left. Notice, by the way, that the mechanism here, not just the pattern, is different. With respect to redistributive issues, my speculation is that people who learn beyond a certain point revise their understandings of *their* interests; with respect to these social issues, it is instead that they begin to take more account of *other people's* interests. Of course, these *are* both speculations. I am not committed to either. The point is that nonmonotonicities like these are plausible and need thinking about.

The Role of Deliberation

As if this were not complication enough, there is also the possibility of conditioning by other variables associated with ideal citizenship, notably including deliberation. We may or may not define deliberation into the citizenly ideal, but it is in any case closely associated with it, as a principal means of achieving sophistication (or sociotropism, if the latter is defined into the ideal). It is indeed this association with sociotropism commands attention as a possible conditioning mechanism. As previously argued, discussing politics with others much different from oneself may not only increase one's appreciation of other people's interests but widen the framing of one's own.

Expanding (3) accordingly, we have

$$E(y_i|x_i,S_i,D_i) = g(\gamma_0 + \gamma_1'x_i + \gamma_2'x_iS_i + \gamma_3'x_iD_i), \qquad (4)$$

where D_i represents some measure of deliberation, γ_3' is a third $1 \times K$ parameter vector, and the rest is a straightforward extension of (3).

My expectations of the conditioning by deliberation are just the opposite of my expectations of the conditioning by sophistication. Deliberation with a sufficiently diverse collection of others should diminish rather than increase people's concentration on their individual interests. The coefficients in γ_3', consequently, should oppose those in γ_1' and γ_2'. The combination leaves open the question of whether the relationships between sociodemographic characteristics (or values) are stronger or weaker in a sophisticated and deliberative public than in the one we actually have.

One vehicle for addressing this question is the Deliberative Poll, whose experimental intervention increases both deliberation (qua discussion) and sophistication (via learning and rumination), although the Deliberative Polling data are currently still a blunt instrument for disentangling the one's effects from the other's. We do have measures of information but do not have very refined measures of the deliberative experience. As a matter of relatively casual impression, my colleagues and I all believe from observing the small-group discussions that deliberation makes at least some participants more sociotropic, which in turn affects their policy and electoral preferences.

The most relevant sort of analysis we have tried estimates the parameters of models of the form of (2) separately before and after deliberation. The dependent variables are policy attitudes, and we have tried both values and sociodemographic variables proxying interests (separately) on the right. If learning and rumination, producing sophistication gains, are what is driving attitude change, the coefficients should generally strengthen, without changing sign, from time 1 to time 2, and the (population) R^2 should increase. If, on the other hand, the attitude change is driven by deliberation with others different from oneself, the coefficients and the R^2 should weaken. We have seen some results of both sorts.

This question of the sign carried by other conditioning variables associated with ideal citizenship has bottom-line implications as well. To the extent that the ideal is sociotropic, that deliberation is one of the main avenues to sophistication, or that sophistication itself entails *tout-comprendre*-ing, we should expect some tempering (or even, conceivably, reversal) of whatever pattern people's maximally efficient pursuit of their interests would produce. The Deliberative Polling results to date, like those from the statistical simulations previously cited, have been mixed. The net change of preference has been sometimes leftward, sometimes rightward, depending on the issue (as any survey of the results in Luskin and Fishkin 1998; Fishkin and Luskin 1999; Luskin, Fishkin, and Jowell 2002; Luskin, Fishkin, and Plane 1999; and Luskin et al. 1999 will confirm). Overall, I should describe the variation in sign as somewhat greater than in the statistical simulations, consistent, perhaps, with the operation of a second conditioning variable.

In sum, the bottom line remains unclear, for reasons I hope I am making clear. It does seem a safe bet, however, that the differences between the earthly and heavenly publics are more varied across issues and elections, and the effects of ascending from the one to the other less uniformly favorable to the left, than many, including me, seem to have thought.

Envoi

This closing section is too modest to be called "Conclusion" or even "Discussion." Many of the questions with which the empirical literature on mass politics has been grappling, not to mention others it has so far brushed past, have profound implications for democratic theory. At the same time, democratic theory can help direct attention to the most important questions for the empirical literature on mass politics. It is an old story: the study of what might be needs to be informed by what is, and the study of what is may be oriented by what might be.

This chapter has considered the properties that might ideally be expected of democratic citizens and what the distributions of public opinion and electoral outcomes might be if the public actually approached this ideal. That the distributions of public opinion and electoral outcomes would be affected now seems clear (pace Popkin 1991; Page and Shapiro 1992; and Lupia and McCubbins

1998). Precisely how they may be affected is much less clear, although I have tried to blaze some of the likely contingencies.

I have concentrated on the handful of citizen characteristics essential to democracy as decision making, which I see as its core function, leaving aside any other functions that may serve for either society or individual citizens. I have also concentrated on just one set of implications (for public opinion and electoral outcomes) of just one element (sophistication) of the democratic ideal for ordinary citizens. Other implications of sophistication (for example, for the unidimensionality and extremity of policy views) remain to be explored, as do the implications of other elements of the citizenly ideal (participation, respect, arguably sociotropism, and arguably deliberation).

The basic questions remain. What can and should be expected of democratic citizens, and what consequences can those attributes be expected to have for both the polity and the citizens themselves? This is far from the first word on these subjects but much further from the last.

NOTES

This chapter was revised while I was a Fellow at the Center for Advanced Study in the Behavioral Sciences, and I am grateful to the William and Flora Hewlett Foundation (Grant 2000–5633); the Center General Fund; and the University Research Institute of the University of Texas, from which I had a faculty Research Assignment, for their financial support. My thinking on these subjects has been stimulated by my participation in the Deliberative Polling project and by conversations with some of the others involved, notably including James Fishkin, Roger Jowell, Norman Bradburn, and Kenneth Rasinski. I am also grateful to Bruce Ackerman, David Brady, Henry Brady, Richard Brody, Shanto Iyengar, Dennis Plane, and, above all, David Braybrooke and Jane Mansbridge for comments. The responsibility for these remarks, however, is strictly mine.

1. For a sense of the cross-national variation, see Klingemann 1979; Dimock and Popkin 1997; S. Gordon and Segura 1997; Dalton 1998. On the absence of much over-time variation, at least in the United States, see Luskin 1987; Smith 1989; Bennett 1989, 1993, 1995; Nie, Junn, and Stehlik-Barry 1996; Price 1999.

2. Yet other variables, like *attitude crystallization* and *schema development*, are just sophistication/expertise/cognitive complexity writ small, defined on just one slice of the political domain. For more on these and other samenesses and differences, see Luskin 1987, 2002a.

3. The distinction between the citizenly virtues required by democracy's decision-making function and those required by its serving as a means to self-actualization bears some rough correspondence to Nie, Junn, and Stehlik-Barry's (1996) distinction between "engagement" and "enlightenment." In their terms, this chapter concerns engagement.

4. I hasten to emphasize the phrase "some version." The question of how majorities are characteristically formed—particularly of how far they are negotiated—may be left open. So may the question of how large a majority is required. Thus I take "consen-

sus" to be a perfect (100%) majority, and "consensus" and "consociational" democracy (Lijphart 1968, 1969, 1999) to be (admittedly distinctive) species of majority rule.

5. This model is entirely consistent with—indeed, can be seen as underlying—that of (2)–(4) (whose phrasing in terms of expected values keeps the error submerged) below. See also n. 12.

6. More precisely, the assumptions are that $E(\varepsilon_i) = 0$, $E(\varepsilon^2_i) = \sigma^2_\varepsilon$, and $E(\varepsilon_i x_i) = 0$ for all i and, more innocuously, $E(\varepsilon_i \varepsilon_j) = 0$ for all $i \neq j$.

7. This unbiasedness is only approximate for vote totals because the propensity y^*_i must be translated into probabilities of voting for one candidate or other by some non-linear function like logit or probit. The small sampling variance stems from the extremely large size of the "sample," in this setup the voting electorate.

8. For a recent meta-analysis suggesting essentially zero bias in newspapers and magazines, albeit a slight liberal bias on TV, see D'Alessio and Allen 2000.

9. Barber's (1984) "strong democracy" is similar.

10. Deliberative Polling, with its random assignment to discussion groups, is another story. See below.

11. An apter quote than her better known but merely attributed "tout comprendre c'est tout pardonner."

12. There is the further similarity that the distributions of both height and intelligence can vary over time and place as a function of environmental causes (including indeed some of the same ones, like pre- and postnatal nutrition), although there is the further difference that the distribution of intelligence can be influenced by the *social* environment—by "coaching"—as well.

13. For continuous y_i like policy preferences, we simply set $y^*_i = y_i$ and $\varepsilon_i = u_i$ (submerged in the expected value). For binary vote choice, we assume the underlying propensity to be centered at 0, so that $y_i = 1$ for $y^*_i = \gamma'_0 + \gamma'_1 x_i > -\varepsilon_i$, and $y_i = 0$ for $y^*_i = \gamma_0 + \gamma'_1 x_i \leq \varepsilon_i$. Then $p(y_i = 1|x_i) = E(y_i|x_i) = g(\gamma_0 + \gamma'_1 x_i)$, as in (2), where the form of g depends on what distribution we assume for ε_i. If ε_i is logistic, g is logit; if ε_i is standard normal, g is probit. The extension to polychotomous vote choice is straightforward. See, e.g., Maddala 1983; Aldrich and Nelson 1984.

14. I have written the equation as theoretically indicated; in practice, analysts with sufficiently little faith in their theory or measurements may add a main effect term for S_i.

15. The literature on the role of uncertainty in electoral choice (e.g., Bartels 1988; Franklin 1991; Alvarez and Franklin 1994; Alvarez 1997) tells a similar story. The main right-hand-side variables are typically policy proximities, mediating in the present context between interests and preferences, and the conditioning variables are uncertainties about the candidates' locations in the policy space, explicitly made a function of information.

16. Education is often used to proxy sophistication—unwisely, except when more direct measures are unavailable. See Luskin and Ten Barge 1995; Luskin 2002b.

REFERENCES

Abelson, Robert P., and Milton J. Rosenberg. 1958. Symbolic Psycho-Logic: A Model of Attitudinal Cognition. *Behavioral Science* 3:1–13.

Aldrich, John H., and Forrest D. Nelson. 1984. *Linear Probability, Logit, and Probit Models.* Newbury Park, Calif.: Sage.

Althaus, Scott. 1998. Information Effects in Collective Preferences. *American Political Science Review* 92:545–58.

Alvarez, R. Michael. 1997. *Information and Elections.* Ann Arbor: University of Michigan Press.

Alvarez, R. Michael, and Charles H. Franklin. 1994. Uncertainty and Political Perceptions. *Journal of Politics* 56:671–89.

Barber, Benjamin R. 1984. *Strong Democracy: Participatory Politics for a New Age.* Berkeley: University of California Press.

Bartels, Larry M. 1988. *Presidential Primaries and the Dynamics of Public Choice.* Princeton: Princeton University Press.

———. 1996. Uninformed Voters: Information Effects in Presidential Elections. *American Journal of Political Science* 40:194–230.

Bennett, Stephen Earl. 1989. Trends in Americans' Political Information, 1967–1987. *American Politics Quarterly* 17:422–35.

———. 1993. Out of Sight, Out of Mind: Americans' Knowledge of Party Control of the House of Representatives, 1960–1984. *Political Research Quarterly* 46:67–81.

———. 1995. Americans' Knowledge of Ideology, 1980–1992. *American Politics Quarterly* 23:259–79.

Bennett, Stephen Earl, and David Resnick. 1990. The Implications of Nonvoting for Democracy in the United States. *American Journal of Political Science* 34:771–803.

Berelson, Bernard R., Paul F. Lazarsfeld, and William N. McFee. 1954. *Voting.* Chicago: University of Chicago Press.

Bessette, Joseph M. 1994. *The Mild Voice of Reason: Deliberative Democracy and American National Government.* Chicago: University of Chicago Press.

Bohman, James. 1996. *Public Deliberation: Pluralism, Complexity, and Democracy.* Cambridge: MIT Press.

Bohman, James, and William Rehg, eds. 1998. *Deliberative Democracy: Essays on Reason and Politics.* Cambridge: MIT Press.

Brody, Nathan. 1992. *Intelligence.* San Diego, Calif.: Academic Press.

Bryce, James. 1904. *The American Commonwealth.* 3d ed. New York: Macmillan.

Campbell, Angus, Philip E. Converse, Warren E. Miller, and Donald E. Stokes. 1960. *The American Voter.* New York: Wiley.

Converse, Philip E. 1964. The Nature of Belief Systems in Mass Publics. In David E. Apter, ed., *Ideology and Discontent.* New York: Free Press.

———. 1990. Popular Representation and the Distribution of Information. In John A. Ferejohn and James H. Kuklinski, eds., *Information and Democratic Processes.* Urbana: University of Illinois Press.

D'Alessio, David, and Mike Allen. 2000. Media Bias in Presidential Elections: A Meta-Analysis. *Journal of Communication* 50:133–56.

Dalton, Russell J. 1998. *Citizen Politics: Public Opinion and Political Parties in Advanced Western Democracies.* 2d ed. Chatham, N.J.: Chatham House.

Delli Carpini, Michael X., and Scott Keeter. 1996. *What Americans Know about Politics and Why It Matters.* New Haven: Yale University Press

Dimock. Michael A., and Samuel L. Popkin. 1997. Political Knowledge in Comparative Perspective. In Shanto Iyengar and Richard Reeves, eds., *Do the Media Govern? Politicians, Voters, and Reporters in America.* Newbury Park, Calif.: Sage.

Dryzek, John. 1990. *Discursive Democracy.* Cambridge: Cambridge University Press.

Elster, Jon, ed. 1998. *Deliberative Democracy.* Cambridge: Cambridge University Press.

Fishkin, James S. 1991. *Democracy and Deliberation: New Directions for Democratic Reform.* New Haven: Yale University Press.

———. 1997. *The Voice of the People: Public Opinion and Democracy.* Rev. ed. New Haven: Yale University Press.

Fishkin, James S., and Robert C. Luskin. 1999. Bringing Deliberation to the Democratic Dialogue. In Maxwell McCombs and Amy Reynolds, eds., *The Poll with a Human Face: The National Issues Convention Experiment in Political Communication.* Mahwah, N.J.: Erlbaum.

———. 2000. The Quest for Deliberative Democracy. In Michael Saward, ed., *Democratic Innovation: Deliberation, Association, and Representation.* New York: Routledge.

Franklin, Charles H. 1991. Eschewing Obfuscation? Campaigns and the Perception of U.S. Senate Incumbents. *American Political Science Review* 85:1193–1214.

Gant, Michael M., and William Lyons. 1993. Democratic Theory, Nonvoting, and Public Policy. *American Politics Quarterly* 21:185–204.

Gibson, James L. 1988. Political Intolerance and Political Repression during the McCarthy Red Scare. *American Political Science Review* 82:511–29.

———. 1992. Alternative Measures of Political Tolerance: Must Tolerance Be "Least Liked?" *American Journal of Political Science* 36:560–77.

Gordon, Robert A. 1997. Everyday Life as an Intelligence Test: Effects of Intelligence and Intelligence Context. *Intelligence* 24:203–320.

Gordon, Stacy B., and Gary M. Segura. 1997. Cross-National Variation in the Political Sophistication of Individuals: Capability or Choice? *Journal of Politics* 59:126–47.

Gottfredson, Linda S. 1997. Why *g* Matters: The Complexity of Everyday Life. *Intelligence* 24:79–132.

Kinder, Donald R., and R. Roderick Kiewiet. 1979. Economic Discontent and Political Behavior: The Role of Personal Grievances and Collective Economic Judgments in Congressional Voting. *American Journal of Political Science* 23:498–527.

Kinder, Donald R., and David O. Sears. 1985. Public Opinion and Political Action. In Gardner Lindzey and Elliot Aronson, eds., *Handbook of Social Psychology,* vol. 2. New York: Random House.

Klingemann, Hans-Dieter. 1979. Measuring Ideological Conceptualizations. In Samuel H. Barnes and Max Kaase, eds., *Political Action: Mass Participation in Five Western Democracies.* Beverly Hills, Calif.: Sage.

Lijphart, Arend. 1968. Typologies of Democratic Systems. *Comparative Political Studies* 1:1–44.

———. 1969. Consociational Democracy. *World Politics* 21:207–25.

———. 1999. *Patterns of Democracy: Government Forms and Performance in Thirty-Six Countries.* New Haven: Yale University Press.

Lippmann, Walter. 1922. *Public Opinion.* New York: Macmillan.

Lupia, Arthur. 1992. Busy Voters, Agenda Control, and the Power of Information. *American Political Science Review* 86:390–403.

Lupia, Arthur, and Mathew D. McCubbins. 1998. *The Democratic Dilemma: Can Citizens Learn What They Need to Know?* New York: Cambridge University Press.

Luskin, Robert C. 1987. Measuring Political Sophistication. *American Journal of Political Science* 31:856–99.

————. 1990. Explaining Political Sophistication. *Political Behavior* 12:331–61.

————. 2002a. From Denial to Extenuation (and Finally Beyond): Political Sophistication and Citizen Performance. In James H. Kuklinski, ed., *Thinking about Political
Psychology*. New York: Cambridge University Press.

————. 2002b. Political Psychology, Political Behavior, and Politics: Questions of
Aggregation, Causal Distance, and Taste. In James H. Kuklinski, ed. *Thinking about
Political Psychology*. New York: Cambridge University Press.

Luskin, Robert C., and James S. Fishkin. 1998. Deliberative Polling, Public Opinion, and
Democracy: The Case of the National Issues Convention. Paper presented at the
annual meeting of the American Association for Public Opinion Research, St. Louis.

Luskin, Robert C., James S. Fishkin, and Roger Jowell. 2002. Considered Opinions:
Deliberative Polling in Britain. *British Journal of Political Science* 32:455–87.

Luskin, Robert C., James S. Fishkin, Roger Jowell, and Alison Park. 1999. Learning and
Voting in Britain: Insights from the Deliberative Poll. Paper presented at the annual
meeting of the American Political Science Association, Atlanta.

Luskin, Robert C., James S. Fishkin, and Dennis L. Plane. 1999. Deliberative Polling and
Policy Outcomes: Electric Utility Issues in Texas. Paper presented at the annual
meeting of the Association for Public Policy Analysis and Management, Washington, D.C.

Luskin, Robert C., and Suzanne Globetti. 1997. Candidate versus Policy Considerations
in the Voting Decision: The Role of Political Sophistication. Unpublished manuscript, Department of Government, University of Texas at Austin.

Luskin, Robert C., and Joseph C. Ten Barge. 1995. Education, Intelligence, and Political
Sophistication. Paper presented at the annual meeting of the Midwest Political Science Association, Chicago.

Maddala, George S. 1983. *Limited-Dependent and Qualitative Variables in Econometrics*.
New York: Cambridge University Press.

Mansbridge, Jane J. 1980. *Beyond Adversary Democracy*. New York: Basic Books.

McClosky, Herbert, and Alida Brill. 1983. *Dimensions of Tolerance: What Americans
Believe about Civil Liberties*. New York: Sage.

Mill, John Stuart. 1859 (1975). *On Liberty*. New York: Norton.

————. 1861 [1991]. *Considerations on Representative Government*. New York:
Prometheus Books.

Neijens, Peter. 1987. *The Choice Questionnaire: Design and Evaluation of an Instrument
for Collecting Informed Opinions of a Population*. Amsterdam: Free University Press.

Neijens, Peter, Jan de Ridder, and Willem Saris. 1992. An Instrument for Collecting
Informed Opinions. *Quantity and Quality* 26:245–58.

Nie, Norman H., Jane Junn, and Kenneth Stehlik-Barry. 1996. *Education and Democratic Citizenship in America*. Chicago: University of Chicago Press.

Page, Benjamin I., and Robert Y. Shapiro. 1992. *The Rational Public: Fifty Years of Trends
in Americans' Policy Preferences*. Chicago: University of Chicago Press.

Pateman, Carole. 1970. *Participation and Democratic Theory*. New York: Cambridge
University Press.

Popkin, Samuel L. 1991. *The Reasoning Voter*. Chicago: University of Chicago Press.

Price, Vincent. 1999. Political Information. In John P. Robinson, Phillip R. Shaver, and
Lawrence S. Wrightsman, eds., *Measures of Political Attitudes*. San Diego, Calif.: Academic Press.

Rahn, Wendy M., John H. Aldrich, Eugene Borgida, and John L. Sullivan. 1990. A Social-Cognitive Model of Candidate Appraisal. In John A. Ferejohn and James H. Kuklinski, eds., *Information and Democratic Processes*. Urbana.: University of Illinois Press.

Renn, O., H. U. Stegelmann, G. Albrecht, U. Kotte, and H. P. Peters. 1984. An Empirical Investigation of Citizens' Preferences among Four Energy Alternatives. *Technological Forecasting and Social Change* 26:11–46.

Schaffer, Stephen. 1982. Policy Differences between Voters and Non-Voters in American Elections. *Western Political Quarterly* 35:496–510.

Schumpeter, Joseph A. 1950. *Capitalism, Socialism, and Democracy*. 3d ed. New York: Harper and Row.

Smith, Eric R. A. N. 1989. *The Unchanging American Voter*. Berkeley: University of California Press.

Sniderman, Paul M., Richard A. Brody, and Philip E. Tetlock. 1991. *Reasoning and Choice: Explorations in Political Psychology*. New York: Cambridge University Press.

Sniderman, Paul M., and Joseph F. Fletcher, eds. 1996. *The Clash of Rights: Liberty, Equality, and Legitimacy in Pluralist Democracy*. New Haven: Yale University Press.

Spragens, Thomas. 1990. *Reason and Democracy*. Durham, N.C.: Duke University Press.

Sullivan, John L., James E. Piereson, and George E. Marcus. 1982. *Political Tolerance and American Democracy*. Chicago: University of Chicago Press.

Verba, Sidney, Kay Lehman Schlozman, and Henry E. Brady. 1995. *Voice and Equality: Civic Volunteerism in American Politics*. Cambridge: Harvard University Press.

Wilson, James Q., and Edward C. Banfield. 1964. Public-Regardingness as a Value Premise in Voting Behavior. *American Political Science Review* 58:876–87.

Wolfinger, Raymond E., and Steven J. Rosenstone. 1980. *Who Votes?* New Haven: Yale University Press.

Young, Iris Marion. 1996. Political Theory: An Overview. In Robert E. Goodin and Hans-Dieter Klingemann, eds., *A New Handbook of Political Science*. New York: Oxford University Press.

Zaller, John R. 1992. *The Nature and Origins of Mass Opinion*. New York: Cambridge University Press.

8

The Nature of Belief
in a Mass Public

Michael W. Traugott

Since the advent of the routine application of survey research to measure public opinion, social critics and political theorists have been concerned about the appropriate role of polls in guiding public policy. Virtually all of the literature on this topic deals with public opinion as an aggregate system-level attribute, often in relation to other institutional forces at work in a democratic society. Price (1992) has pointed out the difficulty that social scientists from a variety of disciplines have had in dealing with this concept as well as the fact that it has been virtually impossible to agree on a "standard" definition. Political theorists as far back as Machiavelli and including the framers of the Constitution discussed the importance of public opinion in organizing a political system. Although responsiveness to public interests is one of the most fundamental democratic norms, concerns about an appropriate scope and role for the expression of public preferences have been frequent and varied.

Twentieth-century theorists such as Key (1961), Lippmann (1922), and Schattschneider (1960) dealt with these issues, contributing in a more systematic way to the dialogue about the meaning of "public opinion" in a "mass society." Philip Converse (1964) described in some detail the stratified nature of personal beliefs and political ideology in the United States. One key feature of the almost forty years since he wrote that essay has been the rise of widely disseminated public opinion poll results. This has come about as the consequence of a number of coincidental trends. They include the establishment of independent polling operations at news organizations, the reduction in data collection costs through the use of the telephone, the increased expenditures on and professionalization of political campaigns, and the rise of interest groups and their engagement in independent data-collection activities as a means to advance their own agendas. The net result has been a flood of information at any given time about what the public is thinking about important (and many unimportant) issues of the day—or at least how individuals are responding to particular question content and formats that are presented to them. All of these factors have contributed to an ongoing reconceptualization of what "public opinion" is as a function of how it is measured.

One topic that has not received a great deal of attention is how the public feels its interests and preferences should inform government action and public policy making. Political theorists and practicing politicians frequently invoke this basic democratic norm when discussing the linkage between mass voting behavior and voting in a legislature. But almost no empirical research has been devoted to learning how citizens feel about the government's attention to public opinion polls, the most common manifestation of public opinion today, in the policy-making and legislative process. The analysis presented here focuses on public attitudes about polls and whether the government should pay attention to them in formulating public policy.

The notion of social and political stratification that Converse applied to attitude consistency and ideology takes on an additional meaning here, as it is extended to reflect differing levels of support for this particular form of government attentiveness to public opinion. In summary, while slight majorities of the citizenry support the notion of government attentiveness to polls, measured in a variety of ways, this support is not randomly distributed in the population. Politically knowledgeable and sophisticated citizens, a relatively small but politically active stratum of the population, are less likely to support this form of vertical communication to governmental leaders. A combination of analyses suggest that such citizens believe that some people's opinions should carry more weight than others' in conveying preferences to governmental leaders. This in turn raises interesting questions about how citizens view the role of public opinion in a democratic society—in terms of the value they attach to their own views as opposed to the weight that should be given to others'.

Theoretical Antecedents

The literature on the relationship between public opinion and the government in a democracy can be divided into two parts. One thread emphasizes the need for controlling or managing opinion (propaganda) and is somewhat distinct from another that describes different mechanisms for incorporating appropriate attention to public preferences in the development of laws and public policy (representation). Machiavelli was one of the first to acknowledge the importance of organizing public opinion to support a leader, as opposed to the use of force or deceit as a method for buttressing political power in a modern nation-state. In *The Prince,* he describes a top-down system of manipulation of the popular imagination in support of the ruling elite as a way of engendering and maintaining power. This work was the precursor of contemporary political propaganda (cf. Katz et al. 1954; Combs and Nimmo 1993) that manifests itself in political campaigns and getting elected (Mauser 1989; Bennett 1992; Morris 1999) as well as in governing (Hurwitz 1989; Kernell 1993).

The notion of attending to public opinion or preferences is also a central tenet of a representative form of government. While Edmund Burke argued for the independence of elected representatives from mandates expressed at the polls, the framers of the U.S. Constitution developed a document that emphasized the transmission of instructions to elected officials. "Equal representation" became a linchpin of their new political system, even though the national legislature was carefully crafted in such a way as to balance the interests of state constituencies that varied in size against equal-sized congressional district constituencies.

In his introduction to *The Paradox of Mass Politics,* Neuman (1986) describes two different schools or clusters of recent theoretical development about how opinions should be aggregated other than as a simple sum of preferences.[1] The oldest and most heavily populated consists of scholars who see a society stratified by levels of political interest and activity. The models of stratified pluralism describe general communication processes within and between strata where elites ultimately express and act on public views. A second set of models describes issue publics that divide and integrate members of the population on the basis of their shared interest in particular topics. These publics vary in size and membership depending on the particular issues involved.

The stratified pluralism models share a vision of the public that generally consists of at least three strata and sometimes more. Almost all have an elite stratum in which only a few citizens actively engage in political debate and dialogue and regularly participate in politics. There is also a relatively large group of individuals who have some interest in politics and political activity and who are intermittently engaged in the political process. And there is almost always a distinguishable group of citizens who are completely disengaged from political life in either intellectual or behavioral terms.

Different theorists have described these strata in different ways, resulting in different estimates of their size. Philip Converse (1964) found that the number of sophisticates in the citizenry was quite small and that they were much more politically active than the rest of the electorate. He discussed two types of "elites." One consisted of those whose views reflect a consistency and ideological constraint not generally found in the population at large, a group representing about 3 percent of the population and of voters. He also distinguished a subset of this group that publicly participates in political debate, numbering only a fraction of 1 percent. Neuman (1986) also described a group of political activists that comprises only a small percentage of the population; a middle group of interested and potentially engageable citizens, comprising about three-quarters of the population; and a base of "apoliticals," comprising about one-fifth of the citizenry. In the foreword to *Personal Influence* (Lazarsfeld and Katz 1955), Elmo Roper described a society composed of a very few great thinkers at the center, surrounded by great disciples who interact with great disseminators and then lesser disseminators. They, in turn, interact with a group of participating citizens who make up somewhere between 15 and 35 percent of the population, with the remainder politically inert.

The consensus view is that levels of attention to and sophistication about politics vary in the population and that the number of those with coherent and integrated political attitudes is small. In the past, political activists could express their views and have them counted in a distinguishable way through such behavior as political participation, especially by voting; through protests and demonstrations; and through letter writing and other forms of contact with elected officials. The common denominator in all of these forms of expression was that they required some form of political activism. In effect, the views of the active few were distinguished from those of the passive many by engagement with the political system. What has changed in the post–World War II period, especially since the 1970s, is the frequent and systematic collection of the public's opinions on a wide range of issues through polls. The results are widely disseminated through the mass media, often in the form of polls that news organizations themselves conduct. While this has altered the nature of communication between citizens and their government as well as with each other, there is disagreement about whether this has improved the quality of the resulting democratic government.

Polls as a Form of Expression or Manipulation of Public Opinion?

Since the development of public polls by Gallup and others in the 1930s, proponents have argued that the technique is an ideal forum for expression of sentiment outside the context of elections.[2] Writing just after George Gallup successfully challenged the *Literary Digest* in projecting the outcome of the 1936 presidential election, Archibald Crossley viewed the public opinion poll as a way to correct for "false presentations of public opinion" and as "the long-sought key to 'Government by the people'" (1937, 35). Gallup and Rae described public opinion as

> the reserve force in democratic politics [that] can play its part only if the common run of people are continually encouraged to take an interest in the broad lines of public policy, in their own opinions, and in those of their fellows, and if clear channels exist through which these opinions can become known. (1940, 127)

These pioneers claimed that polls had an important role because elections occurred systematically but infrequently. Politicians avoided or never discussed some issues during campaigns, and unanticipated issues arose during a presidency or legislative session that could not have been discussed because no one knew they would arise. Polls present an opportunity for citizens to express their opinions and preferences on these matters when the ballot box is not available. And the broad dissemination of results keeps the population informed about other citizens' views on important issues.[3]

There have always been critics of the development of public polling as well. Blumer was one of the earliest. In his presidential address to the American Sociological Association (1948), he railed against the simple aggregation of attitudes as a measurement artifact without any theoretical basis. Ginsberg is a more contemporary critic who is concerned about the ways that the act of polling has transformed the meaning of "public opinion." He describes the measurement of opinions as "externally subsidized" by polling agencies who formulate questions and field surveys on their own schedule rather than a voluntary form of expression precipitated by serious political concerns. This has also resulted in a transformation of political expression "from a behavioral to an attitudinal phenomenon." And when polling organizations formulate survey questions, they change opinion from "a spontaneous assertion to a constrained response." An important consequence of the trend toward increased polling, in his view, is the promotion of the "governance of opinion" rather than "government by opinion" (1989, 275, 293). This tendency is exacerbated by journalists' problems in accurately reporting public opinion, a result of inadequate methodological training and a lack of familiarity with important public opinion concepts and models. Journalists are also handicapped by the strategic behavior of some groups in misrepresenting the current state of opinion on issues of particular concern to them (Traugott 1998; Traugott and Powers 2000).

These concerns are also important because government has increasingly adopted the position that the public should be routinely consulted on important issues. Federal agencies require impact assessments of major projects, often conducted through polls and surveys. Legislators assess the potential consequences of likely legislation or policy changes through surveys of constituents or through the representation of public opinion in the form of the testimony of others presented before committee hearings (Traugott and Kang 1998). In all of these ways, public opinion has become more accessible but less meaningful, in the sense that it is too easily available through contemporary telephone survey methods but often devoid of the forethought and lacking the intensity that characterizes reasoned deliberation about politics.

Through these various mechanisms, however, the assessment of public opinion takes place under an operational assumption of the simple aggregation of attitudes and preferences through the mechanism of polls. Virtually no attention is paid to the weight of the views of politically active citizens compared to those who are inactive or to those who feel strongly about the issue at hand relative to those who have weakly held or nonexistent views on the topic. As Blumer said in his presidential address, "in the process of forming public opinion, individuals are not alike in influence nor are groups that are equal numerically in membership alike in influence" (1948, 545). In virtually every contemporary case, the aggregation of measured attitudes to "public opinion" is treated as another element in a calculus of effects or consequences, often set against the views of organized interest groups or acknowledged experts in the area. And its impact is certified and amplified by the attention that politicians give to the data.

Jean Converse (1987) also discussed the ways that political leaders respond and react to measured public opinion in a contemporary society when data are easily available and politicians do not make a move without new poll results. She cited a series of cases where "congruence" between measured opinion and policy outcomes occurred while noting that indirect representation also has an important role. Most of that evidence is based on statements of elites or reviews of highly visible instances in which political leaders seemed to "respond" to the currents of opinion. What is generally missing from consideration in this area, both conceptually and operationally, is any treatment of how the public feels about the assembly of public opinion through polls as a way to inform the development of laws and policies. The following analysis addresses these issues and raises important questions about the relationship between a stratified society and views about public opinion's contribution to government operation.

Public Attitudes about Polls and Government Attention to Them

A recent analysis of public attitudes about polls and polling revealed the multidimensional nature of the phenomenon (Kang et al. 1998). A national survey conducted in April 1998 made it empirically possible to distinguish between one attitudinal dimension that measured the public's interest in polls as a way of keeping informed about what other citizens are thinking and another relatively independent dimension that measured attitudes about how much attention the government should pay to polls when formulating policy. Building on the theoretical antecedents of Goyder (1986) and Dran and Hildreth (1995), two scales were constructed through the factor analysis of several items measuring different aspects of these two dimensions.

The questionnaire contained items related to assessments of different aspects of the role of polls in a democratic society. A series of factor analyses were run to ascertain the underlying structure associated with several attitudinal items in the survey. The intent was to form scales that represent these two specific dimensions. While a number of alternatives were evaluated, seven items were employed in the final factor analysis and a conceptually appropriate two-dimensional solution was produced.

The Interest in Others' Opinion Scale consisted of five items:

B1. News organizations often conduct polls to let readers or viewers know more about a topic or an election. Do you think these polls are a good way to inform readers?

D1a. Polls are a good way for me to learn what other people are thinking.

D1b. The predictions of pollsters add to the excitement of a political campaign.

D1e. Public opinion polls make the country more democratic.

D1f. A poll is an opportunity for the silent majority to express their opinions.

B1 was coded yes or no, while the other four items had agree/disagree response options.

The Government Attention to Polls Scale consisted of two items:

C1. Do you think opinion polls have too much or too little influence on Washington?

D1c. People in government pay too much attention to opinion polls when making new policies.

The first item had three response alternatives, while the second gave the respondent an agree/disagree set of alternatives.

Looking at individual items, the survey revealed that there was a high level of interest in media polling. Two out of three respondents (65 percent) felt that polls conducted by news organizations are a good way to inform readers or viewers. Equivalent proportions agreed that polls are a good way to learn what other people are thinking (68 percent) and that a poll is an opportunity for the silent majority to express its opinions (62 percent). A slight majority (51 percent) felt that "people in government pay too much attention to opinion polls when making new policies," while the public was relatively evenly divided over whether opinion polls have too much (46 percent) or too little influence (39 percent) on Washington.

The survey also contained two broader evaluations of the government's use of polls. More respondents (46 percent) felt that the nation would be better off if its leaders followed public opinion polls more closely than felt it would be worse off (36 percent), while one in six (17 percent) said it would not make any difference or they weren't sure. And four times as many respondents felt that public opinion polls are a "good thing for the country" as opposed to a "bad thing" (39 percent compared to 10 percent), while half indicated they don't think that polls make any difference one way or another. These two items were highly correlated with both the Interest in Others' Opinions and Government Attention to Polls Scales when entered in the original factor analysis. While these items were excluded from those scales for that reason, they nevertheless bear on the issue at hand, and some data will be presented for them. When all seven items were entered into the SPSS factor-analysis procedure using an oblique rotation option, analysis produced two factors that explained 52.3 percent of the variance. The resulting two factors were relatively independent ($r =$ .185).[4]

When the scales were constructed as additive indexes, responses on the Interest in Others' Opinions Scale were relatively evenly divided among the six categories. That is to say, the smallest of the categories (those least interested) comprised 12 percent of the respondents, while the largest (22 percent) was the midpoint on the scale. For the three-point Government Attention to Polls Scale, however, almost half of the respondents (45 percent) occupied the lowest category (least likely to think that the government should pay attention), while 30 percent occupied the intermediate category and 25 percent the highest. In some sense, the variance in the number of respondents in each category was greater because the number of categories was fewer. This also attenuated its correlation with other items because of the constrained variance in this scale compared to the Interest in Others' Opinions Scale.

Public Opinion about Polls

One surprising result from initial analysis was that virtually all of these individual items about government attention to polls were negatively correlated with socioeconomic status (SES). That is, respondents with higher levels of education, income, and political knowledge were less likely to believe that polls were a good thing, measured in these terms. The bivariate (Pearsonian) correlations ranged between −.07 and .14. Higher SES respondents were also more likely to believe that polls have too much influence in Washington and that the government pays too much attention to polls. The correlations ranged between .12 and .22 for these relationships. These negative relationships raised interesting questions about the linkages between the respondents' status and views and those they hold about others'. These relationships also suggested some level of concern about the weight that others' views receive in policy deliberations.

These concerns could arise for any number of reasons that are not mutually exclusive. Some respondents may feel that others' views are less well considered than their own. Some citizens may believe that polls are inaccurate and unreliable; therefore, bad data should not be incorporated into policy decisions. These views may in turn be related to either a lack of familiarity with the methodology of contemporary polling or a disbelief in the methods. Another view could be concern about the accuracy of particular polls in relation to such issues as sponsorship, the organization that collected the data, or the actual results in relation to a citizen's own views on the issue. Still other explanations could include partisanship or general political ideology as well as political sophistication. All of these explanations are subsequently evaluated in multivariate analysis, looking at the general issue of whether or not the government should pay attention to polls (Government Attention to Polls Scale) and whether elected officials should pay attention to poll results in specific issue areas.

Attitudes about the Quality of Polling and Concern about Government Attention to Polls

One explanation for a lack of interest in having the government pay attention to polls could be that many respondents have concerns about the quality of the data. This could manifest itself as either a concern about methodological limitations or a belief that pollsters try to influence results; in either case, polls might not be accurate. This hypothesis could be tested in the survey, and it did not appear to hold. Past research has shown that the public generally has very low levels of knowledge about survey methods (Lavrakas, Holley, and Miller 1990; Traugott and Kang 2000), making it difficult to construct adequate measures to evaluate what people know. Some of these measures were present in the April survey as well. These included assessments of the respondents' knowledge of survey methodology as well as of their belief that respondents usually told the truth when they were interviewed. For example, 80 percent of the survey respondents said they did not think it was possible for a sample of 1,500 or 2,000 people to accurately reflect the views of the nation's population, while only 15 percent said it was. Only one-third of the respondents indicated that they understood "completely" what the concept of the "margin of error" is, while 41 percent said they understood it "somewhat," 14 percent "only a little" and 12 percent "not at all." Responses to these two items were barely correlated with each other ($r = .06$).

The data presented in table 8.1 show the result of a regression that includes personal demographic characteristics, including education, political knowledge, and knowledge and attitudes about polls, on the Government Attention to Polls Scale. These results demonstrate two things. Methodological knowledge itself (knowledge of sampling and an understanding of the margin of error) does not predict a belief that the government should pay attention to polls when deciding on laws, although a perception of accuracy associated with a sense that polls can accurately predict elections or that pollsters do not try to influence the results of their polls does. After controlling for these modest effects of methodological skills, political knowledge, education, age, and race were all negatively predictive of a belief that the government should pay attention to polls, although only the coefficients for knowledge and age were statistically significant. And women were more likely than men to have higher scores on the Government Attention to Polls Scale. In summary, the lack of general interest in having the government pay attention to polls cannot be attributed to a lack of knowledge or confidence in polling methodology, but it does seem to be related to a lack of faith in the independence of poll data and negatively to SES.

The survey also permitted assessments of whether the respondents felt that particular poll results were accurate and should be used by government officials in the formulation of public policy. As part of an analysis to explain the process by which people evaluate poll results, the survey contained an experimental manipulation of several attributes of hypothetical polls reported to the respondents (Presser et al. 1998). At the beginning of the survey, respondents were asked about their views on six issues of the day: legalization of homosex-

TABLE 8.1. The Regression of Personal Demographic Characteristics, Knowledge of Polling Methodology, Perceptions of Polls, and Political Knowledge on the Government Attention to Polls Scale

Predictor	Beta	t
Constant	.610	.167
Political knowledge	−.120	−3.072***
Education	−.023	−.654
Age	−.062	−1.840*
Race (1 = white)	−.034	−1.029
Gender (1 = female)	.055	1.668*
Knowledge of margin of error (4 = understand completely)	.032	.920
Confidence in sampling (1 = not possible to reflect views accurately)	.008	.248
Accuracy of election predictions (2 = right most of the time)	.066	1.963**
Respondents generally tell the truth (4 = very few)	−.034	−.964
Belief that pollsters influence their results (4 = hardly ever)	.155	4.724***
$R =$	.244	
$R^2 =$	.059	
$F =$	5.783***	

$*p < .10; **p < .05; ***p < .01.$

ual relationships, abortion, affirmative action, banning the possession of hand-guns by anyone other than a police officer, allowing children of illegal immigrants to attend public school, and government efforts to prevent smoking. These items were selected because a review of previous poll results showed that the public's opinions were relatively evenly divided on these issues, at least in the way that certain previous survey questions were worded. This expected division was important for the random assignment of respondents to subsequent experimental treatments.

Later in the survey, respondents were presented with the results from a hypothetical survey on two of these issues: a random selection from one they earlier indicated they felt strongly about and another they earlier indicated they did not feel strongly about. The hypothetical survey results appeared in a vignette in which there were other randomly manipulated factors. These included the side of the issue that the majority of the public favored; whether there was a sponsor of the poll and what side of the issue the sponsor favored (a group that favored one side, a group that favored the other side, or no mention of a sponsor); and the organization that conducted the survey (the Gallup Organization or a nondescript market-research firm). In all, there were twelve experimental conditions ($2 \times 3 \times 2$).

To summarize briefly the findings from that earlier analysis, believing the result of a poll is accurate is unrelated to the poll's substance. Portraying a majority as favorable versus opposed had no impact on believability for any of the six issues. For four of the six issues, respondents were more likely to believe the poll when it showed that their view was in the majority; the two exceptions were affirmative action and schooling for children of illegal immigrants, the only issues that involved race and ethnicity. Respondents' general opinion of polls, measured by a variety of other questions, was significantly related to belief in the accuracy of the poll results. The more favorably respondents judged polls in general, the more likely they were to believe each of the vignette polls, irrespective of the issue involved. Sponsorship was a significant predictor of believability in four of the six cases—overall, mentioning a client that has taken a stand on the issue reduced believability. But this effect resulted mostly from learning that the poll supported the sponsor's position. The difference between believing polls whose results were at odds with their sponsors' positions and those with no sponsor mentioned is much smaller, and for some of the issues it washed out entirely. Finally, the organization that conducted a poll had no effect on its believability.

From the perspective of marginal frequencies, the survey respondents were about evenly divided in their perceptions of the accuracy of the hypothetical polls. There were four responses to the question about each poll. Few respondents thought the scenario they were given described a poll that was "extremely accurate," but a majority of respondents (between 50 and 61 percent) thought that any particular survey was "fairly" or "extremely" accurate.[5] Given the information about the distribution of scores on the Government Attention to Polls Scale, it is not surprising that opinions were divided about elected officials considering the results in deciding laws. On four out of six issues, a bare majority of respondents indicated that the poll should not be used, and on one issue—legalizing homosexual relations between consenting adults—60 percent were opposed to use of the poll results. For one issue—affirmative action programs—a slight majority (52 percent) favored use of the poll.[6]

The final analytical step was to run a series of multiple regressions in which the dependent variable was whether elected officials should consider the results of a poll on a particular topic in deciding laws. The main independent variables were the respondents' perceived accuracy of a specific poll (which replaced their generic assessments of accuracy) and the score on the Government Attention to Polls Scale, as well as the two measures of knowledge of polling methodology and beliefs about pollsters' influence on their data. In addition, party identification was added as a proxy for political ideology; given the coding as Democrat = 3, it was expected to be negatively related to officials' consideration of the poll. Political knowledge was included as an indicator of political sophistication; based on the previous analysis, it should be negatively related to a belief that elected officials should consider the result of the poll in deciding laws on that issue.

In these analyses, the dependent variable represents a measure of whether the results of a particular poll should be considered in the development of new laws in that area. Analytically, the interest is in patterns of relationships for specific independent variables across the set of regressions. The results of six regressions are presented in table 8.2, and they show that both perceptions of accuracy and the government attention scale consistently exert strong independent effects in the expected directions on beliefs that elected officials should consider the results of a particular poll in deciding laws on that topic. Perceptions of the poll's accuracy were a stronger influence than the respondents' position on the government attention scale. In these regressions, political knowledge was not a statistically significant factor in any of the equations. Party identification was related in the appropriate direction, but it achieved statistical significance at the standard level for only one issue (allowing the children of illegal immigrants to attend public schools). It achieved marginal significance for abortion and government efforts to regulate possession of handguns. A belief that pollsters influence the results of their polls was significant in two equations. It had the appropriate negative sign for affirmative action but the wrong sign for allowing the children of illegal immigrants to attend public schools. Confidence in sampling was related to the belief that poll results should be used in deciding laws about homosexual relations, affirmative action, or the availability of abortions. Overall, these models explained proportions of variance in these equations ranging from 18 to 33 percent.

Summary

This analysis has shown that support for the democratic norm of direct representation of all citizens' views is not widely shared in the American public, at least when it is operationalized as the use of polls measuring public opinion to influence lawmaking. While it is possible to construct a general scale that reflects citizens' interest in having the government pay attention to polls as well as measure how the public feels about specific polls on particular topics, there are not large proportions of society who subscribe to this view. Of even greater importance, these concerns about polls as a procedure that simply aggregates and transmits public preferences to elected officials are not randomly distributed in society. Individuals with greater political capital are more likely to express reservations about this process. This reflects a kind of stratification in

TABLE 8.2.   The Regression of Beliefs that Elected Officials Should Consider Poll Results in Deciding Laws about Specific Issues on the Government Attention to Polls Scale, Perceived Accuracy of Polls on Particular Issues, Attitudes about Poll Quality, Party Identification, and Political Knowledge

	Homosexual Relations	Affirmative Action	Possession of Handguns	Availability of Abortion	Immigrants in Schools	Smoking Cessation
Government Attention to Polls	−.259*** (−4.780)	−.128*** (−2.527)	−.102* (−1.779)	−.168*** (−3.090)	−.116** (−2.211)	−.101* (−1.781)
Perceived accuracy	.297*** (5.502)	.447*** (8.955)	.382*** (6.795)	.390*** (7.057)	.431*** (8.255)	.374*** (6.678)
Political knowledge	n.s.	n.s.	n.s.	n.s.	n.s.	n.s.
Party identification	n.s.	n.s.	−.099* (−1.763)	−.097* (−1.806)	−.138*** (−2.609)	n.s.
Confidence in sampling	.180*** (3.338)	.183*** (3.714)	n.s.	.154*** (2.880)	n.s.	n.s.
Understanding margin of error	n.s.	n.s.	n.s.	n.s.	n.s.	n.s.
Belief that pollsters influence their results	n.s.	−.133*** (−2.610)	n.s.	n.s.	.111** (2.137)	n.s.
R	.464	.573	.453	.496	.505	.422
R^2	.216	.328	.205	.246	.255	.178
F	11.124	19.764	9.737	12.640	13.949	8.517

Note: The entries for each independent variable are beta coefficients; and the parenthetical entries, when appropriate, are the values of the *t*-statistic. The abbreviation n.s. indicates "not significant."
*$p < .10$; **$p < .05$; ***$p < .01$.

society, where political elites are more concerned about broad-scale representation than are citizens with lower levels of education, income, or political
knowledge.

A number of possible explanations for these relationships were explored.
Concerns about polling methods and the representativeness of the views they
report is not correlated with these concerns. However, a significant proportion of respondents believe that pollsters often try to influence their results,
and these views are correlated with concerns about attention to the results. A
multivariate analysis based on specific policy areas showed that the most consistent explanation for supporting the consideration of polls in the development of legislation was their perceived accuracy, a much more important
predictor of such beliefs than the Government Attention to Polls Scale, the
second-most-important factor. Methodological concerns were not generally
associated with a concern about whether elected officials should consider
these polls in deciding laws regarding these issues, nor was a concern that
pollsters could influence their results. For some topics, party identification
was also important, while confidence in the representativeness of sampling
was important for others.

These results place the public in as ambiguous a position as the Founding
Fathers with regard to views about public opinion's appropriate role in the legislative process. There is caution about the simple and straightforward aggregation of preferences and their direct application to making laws. There is both
an elite bias against counting the views of all equally as well as a concern about
the accuracy of any particular poll result. These concerns exist across a number
of policy areas, suggesting that they probably have a general applicability to
public views about the representation process rather than being narrowly
restricted to a particular policy domain.

This analysis raises a number of interesting questions that require additional
attention in an era when the number of legitimate polls is increasing and the
number of bad data collections is on the rise as well. With hardly any detailed
knowledge about appropriate polling methodology, the public is already
stratified about the appropriate use of poll data. Public concerns about accuracy seem appropriate in light of the growing strategic uses of poll data, even if
such concerns are not well grounded in sound methodological knowledge. The
number of bogus polls is on the rise—through dial-in mechanisms, misuses of
the Internet, and the like. We may be on the verge of a Gresham-like phenomenon where bad data will increasingly drive out good under the burden of frequent reports. We need to know more about how the public feels in direct and
indirect terms about polls as well as about its perceptions of how polls are being
used by government. The survey reported here did not explicitly link attitudes
about polls to attitudes about representation, a worthy topic of further
research.

Finally, this analysis is based only on data from the United States at a single point in time. Additional attention should be devoted to comparative work that includes political settings that vary in their level of political representation as well as the state of development of the polling industry and media reporting of polls. The length of time that democratic procedures and institutions have been in place could also be an important correlate of the public's views about the appropriate role of polls in a society. And data collection over time, even in the United States, would illuminate how changes in the number and reporting of polls is associated with views about polls and representative government. These are all important research topics whose ancestry can be traced directly to Philip Converse's work on mass publics and changing conceptions of public opinion in the political process.

NOTES

The data reported here were collected under a grant from the Pew Charitable Trusts, whose support is gratefully acknowledged, as is the research assistance of Mee-Eun Kang. Paul Lavrakas, Stanley Presser, and Vincent Price consulted on the design of the survey. The analysis and views expressed here are the sole responsibility of the author.

1. Neuman describes two additional models or schools that do not merit significant further attention. The methodological critique of previous theoretical development is not itself very theoretically oriented, and the changing American voter model is itself subject to a number of methodological criticisms that weaken the independent strength of the observations on which it is predicated.

2. A brief treatment of these developments appears in Cantril 1991, and J. Converse 1987 provides an extended discussion.

3. The most recent extreme form of blind faith in such data can be found on Dick Morris's Web site, www.vote.com, which is also the title of his new book. He collects opinions without any regard for their representativeness and forwards them to members of Congress.

4. These two factors were quite robust through multiple tests of the factor structure and scoring procedures. The simple additive indexes correlate with their more detailed regression-scored equivalents at .945 and .983. And the additive indexes were correlated at .223 with each other and with their opposite regression-scored scales at .204 and .191. The reliability (measured by Cronbach's alpha) for the Interest in Others' Opinions Scale was .66, and it was .58 for the Government Attention to Polls Scale.

5. Perceptions of accuracy were not correlated with the relationship between the respondents' views and the results of a hypothetical poll reported to them (r's ranging from 0.0 to .10)

6. A belief that elected officials should consider a poll was slightly related to the relationship between a respondent's view on an issue and the reported poll result. For four issues (abortion, affirmative action, handgun control, and government action to prevent smoking) the correlations were between .11 and .32, while they were smaller for the other two issues.

REFERENCES

Bennett, W. Lance. 1992. *The Governing Crisis: Media, Money, and Marketing in American Elections.* New York: St. Martin's.

Blumer, Herbert. 1948. Public Opinion and Public Opinion Polling. *American Sociological Review* 13:542–54.

Cantril, Albert H. 1991. *The Opinion Connection.* Washington, D.C.: CQ Press.

Combs, James E., and Dan Nimmo. 1993. *The New Propaganda: The Dictionary of Palaver in Contemporary Politics.* New York: Longman.

Converse, Jean M. 1987. *Survey Research in the United States: Roots and Emergence, 1890–1960.* Berkeley: University of California Press.

Converse, Philip E. 1964. The Nature of Belief Systems in Mass Publics. In David E. Apter, ed., *Ideology and Discontent.* New York: Free Press.

———. 1987. Changing Conceptions of Public Opinion in the Political Process. *Public Opinion Quarterly* 51 (supp): 12–24.

Crossley, Archibald M. 1937. Straw Polls in 1936. *Public Opinion Quarterly* 1:24–35.

Dran, Ellen M., and Ann Hildreth. 1995. What the Public Thinks about How We Know What It Is Thinking. *International Journal of Public Opinion Research* 7:128–44.

Gallup, George, and Saul Rae. 1940. *The Pulse of Democracy.* New York: Simon and Schuster.

Ginsberg, Benjamin. 1989. How Polling Transforms Public Opinion. In Michael Margolis and Gary A. Mauser, eds., *Manipulating Public Opinion.* Pacific Grove, Calif.: Brooks/Cole.

Goyder, John. 1986. Surveys on Surveys: Limitations and Potentialities. *Public Opinion Quarterly* 50:27–41.

Hurwitz, Jon. 1989. Presidential Leadership and Public Followership. In Michael Margolis and Gary A. Mauser, eds., *Manipulating Public Opinion.* Pacific Grove, Calif.: Brooks/Cole.

Kang, Mee-Eun, Paul Lavrakas, Stanley Presser, Vincent Price, and Michael Traugott. 1998. Public Interest in Polling. Paper presented at the annual conference of the American Association for Public Opinion Research, St. Louis.

Katz, Daniel, Dorwin Cartwright, Samuel Eldersveld, and Alfred McClung Lee. 1954. *Public Opinion and Propaganda.* New York: Dryden Press.

Kernell, Samuel. 1993. *Going Public: New Strategies of Presidential Leadership.* Washington, D.C.: CQ Press.

Key, V. O. 1961. *Public Opinion and American Democracy.* New York: Knopf.

Lavrakas, Paul J., Jack K. Holley, and Peter V. Miller. 1990. Public Reactions to Polling News during the 1988 Presidential Election Campaign. In Paul J. Lavrakas and Jack K. Holley, eds., *Polling and Presidential Election Coverage.* Newbury Park, Calif.: Sage.

Lazarsfeld, Paul, and Elihu Katz. 1955. *Personal Influence.* Glencoe, Ill.: Free Press.

Lippmann, Walter. 1922. *Public Opinion.* New York: Harcourt Brace Jovanovich.

Margolis, Michael, and Gary A. Mauser, eds. 1989. *Manipulating Public Opinion.* Pacific Grove, Calif.: Brooks/Cole.

Mauser, Gary A. 1989. Marketing and Political Campaigning: Strategies and Limits. In Michael Margolis and Gary A. Mauser, eds., *Manipulating Public Opinion.* Pacific Grove, Calif.: Brooks/Cole.

Morris, Dick. 1999. *Vote.com: How Big-Money Lobbyists and the Media Are Losing Their Influence, and the Internet Is Giving Power to the People.* New York: Renaissance Books.

Neuman, W. Russell. 1986. *The Paradox of Mass Politics.* Cambridge: Harvard University Press.

Presser, Stanley, Paul Lavrakas, Vincent Price, and Michael Traugott. 1998. How Do People Decide Whether to Believe the Results of a Poll? Paper presented at the annual conference of the American Association for Public Opinion Research, St. Louis.

Price, Vincent. 1992. *Public Opinion.* Newbury Park, Calif.: Sage.

Schattschneider, E. E. 1960. *The Semi-Sovereign People: A Realist's View of Democracy in America.* New York: Holt, Rinehart, and Winston.

Traugott, Michael W. 1998. The Role of the Mass Media in Conveying Public Opinion Accurately. Paper presented at the Conference on Data Quality, sponsored by the World Association for Public Opinion Research, Cadenabbia, Italy.

Traugott, Michael W., and Mee-Eun Kang. 1998. Monitoring the Use of Public Opinion Polls in Congress. Unpublished manuscript. Institute for Social Research, Ann Arbor, Mich.

———. 2000. Public Attention to Polls in an Election Year. In Paul Lavrakas and Michael Traugott, eds., *Election Polls, the News Media, and Democracy.* New York: Chatham House.

Traugott, Michael W., and Elizabeth C. Powers. 2000. Did Public Opinion Support the Contract with America? In Paul Lavrakas and Michael Traugott, eds., *Election Polls, the News Media, and Democracy.* New York: Chatham House.

9

Electoral Democracy during Politics as Usual—and Unusual

John Aldrich

Equilibrium and Change in Theories of Electoral Democracy

In broad brush, U.S. political history, especially the study of what we might call electoral democracy, has been essentially the study of party systems. Within the study of party systems, two theoretical questions predominate. One approach is based on the assumption of a reasonably unvarying equilibrium over some extensive period of time, and the research objective is to understand behavior holding that equilibrium constant. The other imagines and theorizes about the disruption of equilibrium and change in behavior causing that disruption and/or reacting to the resulting disequilibrium. I associate these with the theoretical contributions of Converse and of Key, respectively. I hope here to begin to unite our understanding of electoral democracy within and across the dynamics of equilibrium values. I discuss the theoretical issues in general, but I mostly embed this discussion in consideration of a particular case, electoral democracy before, during, and after the 1960s.

By *electoral democracy* I mean the beliefs and choices of the members of the mass public, the beliefs and choices of elected elites as candidates and as officeholders, the policies (and other governmental outputs) they chose, and the consequences of those selections for subsequent beliefs and choices. It seems to me that the fruits of the labors of our discipline over the past fifty years—in particular, the behavioral and choice-theoretic revolutions—have now made serious consideration of this notion of electoral democracy viable. I also think that the uniting of electoral democracy in and out of equilibrium is possible only within this larger context. The following pages seek to make these claims intelligible.

Insofar as I understand its intellectual history, the view that there is a basic and constant "equilibrium" value in the near or actual totality of U.S. politics was once rather common but is now decidedly out of fashion. To be sure, there is a general sense in which U.S. electoral democracy has been at an extremely long-term equilibrium value. The persistence of a two-party system at all (e.g., the various Duvergerian accounts [1954]) and the nearly 150-year continuation of competition between the Democratic and Republican Parties in particular are, in a sense, unvarying equilibrium accounts. Formally, Cox (1997) and Stokes and Iversen (1966) provide examples of such models. But the generally discredited view of long-term equilibrium made stronger claims that dealt not just with the form of electoral democracy (e.g., two-party competition), but with its content. Perhaps the most precise (and perhaps the last) version of such an account is that of Sellers (1965). He viewed this history as primarily cyclical, oscillating around a long-term equilibrium value. The greatest evident observations were increasing strength at the emergence of a new majority party, followed by it peaking and then subsequently declining from that peak, a crossing at the balance point such that the other party assumed a majority, which in turn increased in value, and so on. That is, he drew attention to the oscillations themselves. That view, however, was one of oscillation around a common and constant equilibrium value. Even if the system was rarely at that equilibrium value, it nonetheless governed the system.

Key rejected claims such as the sinusoidal pattern Sellers drew and replaced truly cyclical behavior with other dynamics. Most famously, he popularized the notion of critical elections (1955), in which a period of stability is punctuated by a short but dramatic burst of change, only to be followed by a lasting new period of stability. Unlike Sellers, however, this new period of stability was a return not to the long-run equilibrium value of the historical system but to a new and distinctly different equilibrium value. This notion became understood as partisan realignment, resulting in no small measure from the impact of *The American Voter* and other writings of the Michigan school (Campbell et al. 1960, 1966) as well as those of Burnham (1970) and Sundquist (1983). This transition was from defining disequilibrium based on sharp change in voting choices to one based on a sharp change in the distribution of partisan identification underlying those electoral choices.

This dramatic-change model of political history is, however, more general. For example, Carmines and Stimson (1989) explicitly reject the idea that there was a partisan realignment or a critical election in the mid-1960s. Nonetheless, their process of "issue evolution" is characterized as a "punctuated equilibrium." While the result after the punctuation may not be as wholesale a difference as in a partisan realignment, the new equilibrium nonetheless differs from that which went before. In their example, the two parties switched sides on civil rights in Congress and presumably at the elite level more generally. Further, (especially southern) blacks were effectively enfranchised and became overwhelmingly Democratic in near critical election form, and partisanship in the electorate more generally gradually adjusted to the elite changes on civil rights. Adams (1997) has more recently developed a second example of issue evolution, demonstrating the switch of parties on abortion in the 1970s and the series of consequences that resulted. Neither of these is anything like a complete partisan realignment, to be sure, but they are dramatic changes, defining new political realities. They indicate, that is, a change in the equilibrium of politics as usual. Sanbonmatsu (2002) offers one measure of the dominance of the theoretical position that equilibrium change is central, as she writes of gender issues in terms of a punctuated equilibrium that did not happen.

Key developed a second model of change, which he called "secular realignment" (1959). This process was more gradual and continuous (in the mathematical as well as the common language sense). It is nonetheless only a slower version of a critical election, in which the politics characterizing that which is undergoing a secular realignment is changing permanently. In the civil rights issue evolution in the 1960s, partisanship of the white South began to change fundamentally in response to the alteration in politics among blacks. Most especially, native-born white southerners began what was to become the clearest example we have of a secular realignment toward the GOP (see Stanley and Niemi 1995; I will return to this subject later in the chapter). Unanswered is the question of how to understand more fully circumstances that led to rapid, critical change among some people and to delayed, gradual, secular change among others. Even more pressing is the question of how we might know that the disruption of one equilibrium would settle to a new equilibrium at all. In any case, both of Key's theoretical contributions are models of change in equilibrium, and the objective is to assess changes in equilibrium as the theoretically privileged challenge.

The American Voter and related work, especially *Elections and the Political Order* (Campbell et al. 1960, 1966), differ from and complement Key's realignment writings. Where he was most interested in the nature of changes in political equilibria, much of Campbell and his coauthors' work concerned politics within one party era. Indeed, they studied times that lacked not only critical elections or partisan realignments but largely also significant cases of secular realignments. Thus, Campbell's classification of presidential elections (1966) points to realigning elections, all of which lie outside his data. Inside the Michigan school's data are maintaining elections (1948, 1960, and presumably 1964, 1976, and the elections of the 1990s) and deviating elections (1952, 1956, and presumably 1968, 1972, and the elections of the 1980s and 2000). Both maintaining and deviating elections reflect either no significant change or only temporary, inconsequential-in-the-long-term perturbations about a fixed distribution of party loyalties. And, while Converse (1966b) noted some slow convergence between the (white) South and non-South, it was not yet time to declare a southern realignment, whether critical or secular, only its possibility.

Thus, it is not unfair to characterize the Michigan accounts as analyses of politics as usual.

Their point can be made stronger. In particular, theirs is a theory of politics at equilibrium. I believe it is indeed fair to say that Converse's greatest contributions have been to theorize about politics in equilibrium. His development of the normal vote (1966a) is quite explicit in this regard, but "Of Time and Partisan Stability" (1969) also presents an equilibrium model. In this work, the properties he studies most closely and finds most interesting are the commonality of an equilibrium distribution of party identification across nations and the rapidity of convergence to that equilibrium distribution. It is significant, of course, that he develops equilibrium models of partisan identification, because this particular concept holds the key (as it were) to the stability of equilibrium of a party system in between realignments (or more general forms of punctuation).

The combination, then, of critical elections/issue evolutions/realignments (whether partisan or secular) and of normal-vote-dominated eras ought to provide something of a unified account. At the very least, their intersection is empty by definition, and it is reasonable to infer that the respective authors would concur that their union is exhaustive. Thus, Converse and Key together provide something of an exclusive and exhaustive account of electoral politics, if not quite electoral democracy more generally. One deals with politics as usual, when the system is in equilibrium. The other explains the politics of changing equilibrium.

Electoral Democracy in and out of Equilibrium

Suppose for the moment that it is, in fact, reasonable to divide our theorizing about the political world into those parts dominated primarily by a reasonably stable equilibrium and those primarily concerned with change in that equilibrium. Call them the theories of Converse and Key, respectively. Our thinking in the discipline about electoral democracy and how well it works is quite different in and out of equilibrium. To the extent that we can say there is anything like a collective understanding in our discipline, we would say that elections during politics as usual—the elections of *The American Voter*—are elections in which democracy is at best barely satisfying. Citizens are relatively disinterested and relatively uninformed and make relatively weakly grounded decisions. Were it not for the stabilizing force of partisanship, we might have reason indeed to worry about the viability of electoral democracy, just as Berelson did so worry in his prepartisanship view (1954). To be sure, such an account is broadly brushed, and numerous individuals make considered judgments in elections. Many more, however, appear to be making weakly considered and all too nearly insubstantial judgments.

Conversely (as it were), change in that equilibrium—most notably change as a result of partisan realignment—appears to be electoral democracy working at its finest. Intensely concerned and involved people respond to dramatic events with high levels of participation and, insofar as we can judge without decent surveys on hand, high levels of information. They make basic judgments that are clearly understood in retrospect to be sensible, if not fully rational, in the short run and that reshape the fundamentals of politics for a generation. Merely listing the elections of 1860, 1896, and 1932 makes the point sufficiently. It is too bad, this line of argument would run, that we have not had good, high-quality surveys run during even one such election, so that we could observe citizens acting at their finest.

Here I will dispute a number of these points. In particular I will argue:

1. We actually have observed electoral behavior in nonequilibrium cases.
2. The observed picture of the public is not distinctly different in such cases. Indeed, for decades, we were unable to detect that we were observing an out-of-equilibrium case in the 1960s. There were observed differences, but they seemed slight.
3. Politics was, however, very different, in ways we still are only coming to understand.
4. Theoretically, the dichotomy between electoral choice in normal and non-normal times is, I hope to show, false. The alleged low quality of choice in the first case is an underestimate resulting from misunderstanding of what it means to make choices at an established equilibrium. The potentially finest moments of electoral democracy during realignments may be an incorrect inference (since never observed, it is not correct to call it a misestimate), at least if the evidence we do have from choice in an out-of-equilibrium case is any guide. This should be no surprise, anyway. Theoretically, I believe, we should observe apparently more ephemeral choice in equilibrium, even if citizens are, in all cases, fully rational.
5. The reason we have been "misled" may be that we have all too often studied elections too nearly in isolation. We have also all too often studied legislative and executive politics in near isolation from public opinion and electoral democracy. To use Key's terms again (1964), we have kept all too separate the study of parties in the electorate from the study of parties in government.

A Change in Equilibrium Politics?

The 1960s and an Issue Evolution on Civil Rights

Carmines and Stimson (1989) apply their account of punctuated equilibrium to the case of the two parties on civil rights in the 1960s. Their general position is that there is some notable exogenous shock, the "punctuation" in punctuated equilibrium, followed by change over some extended period of time. Their more specific application began with elite change. In particular, the congressional parties switched ideological sides on civil rights as a result of shocks (rising salience of civil rights because of the movement and, perhaps, the 1958 elections). This elite change was followed by an enhancement of the public's ability to see more clearly the party positions on civil rights, leading in turn to changes in the public's affective orientations toward the two parties. The process culminated with the equilibrium shift in the mass public, in which party identification became more consonant with the new party positions on civil rights. Change in the Senate, but not the House, began with a sharp moderation in both parties after the 1958 election (see fig. 9.1, discussed subsequently), followed by the shift of sides in both chambers after the 1964 elections. Carmines and Stimson report that clarity of position began to be seen around mid-1963, with the affective shift in partisanship occurring just after 1964. Their measures indicate an increasing coincidence of racial liberalism and partisanship in the electorate that emerged sharply in 1964, and it then evolved more slowly until their data end in 1980.

Niemi and I overlaid Carmines and Stimson's elite calculations—that is, the four lines for the two parties and two chambers that measure the respective party in chamber's voting-based measure of racial liberalism (Aldrich and Niemi 1990, fig. 7, adapted here as fig. 9.1). As the figure shows, the shifts were remarkably precise. The four lines that connect the dots between the Congress-by-Congress scores intersected in an exact, common point—the Great Society Congress. This was the first time conservative southern Democrats were outweighed by liberal northern Democrats on behavioral manifestations of commitment to more liberal racial policies. Republicans also changed, voting increasingly often against civil rights measures. As I will discuss shortly, several other significant changes in congressional behavior also appeared at this moment, but I concur so far with Carmines and Stimson's account.

I turn at this point to add some complications to Carmines and Stimson's claims on civil rights per se. I propose that viewing civil rights in a larger policy and behavioral context might lead to modifications to their basic theoretical explanation. First, though, I will reconsider the question of causal direction between democratic leaders and followers.

Carmines and Stimson provide considerable evidence for the hypothesis that mass behavior changed in response to changes in elite behavior. While elite behavior changed at several points, it appears to have changed most significantly in the Great Society Congress. The authors therefore conclude that changes in public partisanship, which they found began in 1966, follow the changes in elite partisan behavior. In this way, they were led to conclude that over time, the public reacts, albeit slowly, to changes in elite behavior.

Even if we accept that elite behavior affects mass attitudes and behavior, it

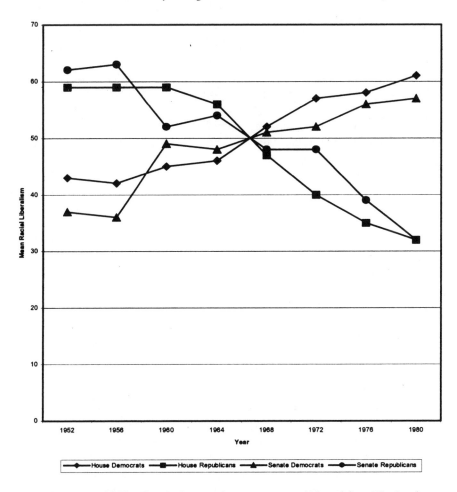

Fig. 9.1.   Racial liberalism in Congress by party, 1952–80. (Adapted from Niemi and Aldrich 1990, fig. 7, which was based on Carmines and Stimson 1989, 163.)

does not necessarily follow that elite behavior is not also responsive to that of the public. Indeed, why would members of Congress change the patterns that got them to Congress unless public attitudes and behavior had already changed or unless members could reasonably infer that the public would react to elite change with a new and (for the elite) more desirable behavioral response? Or it could be that any change in equilibrium behavior is so intertwined and simultaneous and interactive that who responds to whom is indeterminable. Consider two items.

Kessel (1991) has used the likes-dislikes questions (similarly to Stokes,

Campbell, and Miller 1958 and Stokes 1966) to assess the components of electoral choice for individual elections, dividing issues into a series of specific dimensions. In 1964, civil liberties (his name for the category that included and in 1964 consisted nearly exclusively of civil rights) was at a high point. It was, he showed, at its most salient, its most pro-Democratic, and its most influential in affecting the vote (ceteris paribus, i.e., in an extensive, multivariate probit model). Thus, it is not entirely clear that elite behavior changed prior to mass behavior. Rather, elite voting in the Great Society Congress might have differed from preceding Congresses at least in some significant part because mass voting behavior was different in the election that chose the Great Society Congress. Indeed, as I asked earlier, why else would elected politicians change their actions unless they believed such changes would be well (or at least well enough) received by the public?

One might object to this small caveat to the simple story of elite to mass equilibrium shift by saying that casting a vote is ordinarily subject to short-term perturbations. After all, that is precisely the point of the normal vote, deviating and reinstating elections, and the partisanship-based account of electoral equilibrium in general. Applied here, the claim would go, the public might have voted differently (in this case for Democrats as liberals on civil rights) in 1964, but the equilibrium is not altered until party identification alters.

Item two, then, is that party identification did change on or before the 1964 National Election Study (NES) survey and in just a fashion that one might want to claim as a "critical event." Figure 9.2 extends figure 1 from Niemi and Aldrich 1996 (89) to show that party identification among blacks altered dramatically in the early 1960s. Indeed, the change was so dramatic that had blacks constituted the entire electorate, 1962–64 would have been seen immediately as a critical election. Black partisanship changed in two ways. First, the percentage classified as apolitical made a step change in 1964 from a reasonably constant 16 (±2) percent from 1952 through 1962 to a nearly flat 1 to 4 percent from 1964 on. Significantly, this decline was to a percentage essentially the same as among whites. The entire change, that is, happened between 1962 and 1964. Not only was that change of short duration, but it was also as substantial in magnitude as mathematically possible; furthermore, the change ended at a new level that was sustained over a considerable period of time. Change in Democratic identification among the rest of the black electorate was not as clean a step change, but it was close. The percentage of all black partisans who were strong or weak Democrats varied from 50 to 53 percent in the 1950s and dipped to 44 percent in 1960. It then climbed to 60 percent in 1962 and 74 in 1964. It never dipped below 60 percent thereafter. Thus, there was certainly a dramatic and durable change in black partisanship in this second way between 1960 and 1964, and it appears to have been well under way by the 1962 postelection survey.

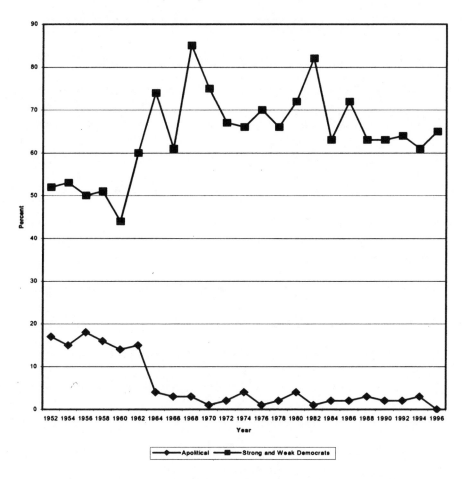

Fig. 9.2. Partisanship among blacks, 1952–96. (Data from American National Election Studies, compiled by author.)

Hence, at least among blacks, there was a permanent change in party identification, including a massive shift to the Democratic Party, before Democrats in either chamber voted more liberally on civil rights than did Republicans.

To be sure, this critical-election-style change is not apparent in the full electorate. Significantly for the main story Carmines and Stimson tell, white partisanship did not change in the aggregate until 1966—precisely when their theory leads them to expect a change to begin (see fig. 9.3). And even more clearly than among blacks, the change is gradual, and thus the pattern among whites as a whole—and therefore in the full sample—is precisely as issue evolution predicts. The change begins in 1966, but the growth in independence and

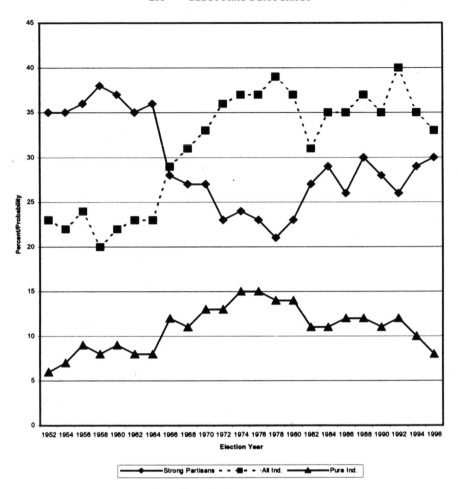

Fig. 9.3. Partisanship among whites, 1952–96. (Data from American National Election Studies, compiled by author.)

decline in strength of partisanship among whites was fairly well accomplished by the end of 1972. Whether the decline in independence and restrengthening of partisanship among whites in 1996 to return to pre-1972 levels will be sustained is an open question (see Bartels 2000; Aldrich 1999).

There is another minor caveat. Stanley and Niemi (1995, 1998) find that the incremental probability that a native white southerner would identify with the Democratic Party declined sharply and nearly linearly from 1960 through 1970 (bouncing back and forth between the 1968 and 1970 levels through the 1980s). Figure 9.4 presents their estimates. Thus, this one measure of partisanship among a second select group in addition to blacks changed in some genuine measure by 1964 compared to 1952–60 (unfortunately, their measure cannot be

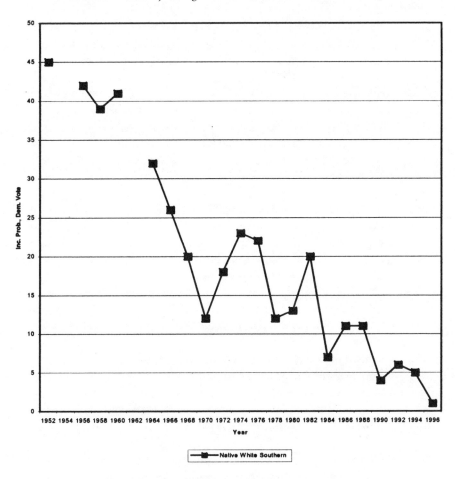

Fig. 9.4.   Democratic voting probabilities among native white southerners, 1952–66. (Adapted from Stanley and Niemi 1998.)

estimated for 1962, so we do not know if the change began before or after the 1962 survey).

At this point, the amendments to the straight issue-evolution account of civil rights are that change in the electorate began before 1964 (or before the 1964 NES survey, at least) among blacks and among native-born southern whites. For blacks, the changes were largely complete by the mid-1960s, although that certainly was not true for whites in general and for native-born white southerners in particular. It strikes me as significant that black apoliticals vanished to the usual trace levels before the passage—let alone the implementation—of the Voting Rights Act of 1965. Perhaps the Civil Rights Act of 1964 and actions of Goldwater and Johnson in particular were sufficient. The clear change in Democratic identification among blacks by 1962 suggests, however, that these changes also might not have resulted solely from those acts, although surely all were relevant.

The next amendment to the argument is thus that at least some significant changes in mass political beliefs and behavior changed before the largest changes in congressional partisan behavior and that some of these changes, in turn, reflect the civil rights movement and its impact on public opinion. In his study of Equal Employment Opportunity legislation Burstein (1985) presents data on actions associated with the civil rights movement (demonstrations, riots, and acts of violence against demonstrators). Demonstrations emerged with a significant, short peak in 1956, increased dramatically in 1958, declined in 1960, and rose through 1962 to their peak in 1963, from which they declined rather consistently back to the trace, premovement levels by 1972. Riots began to emerge as a way of action only in 1963 and 1964, declined in 1965, and then really took off in the long, hot summers of 1966 and 1967 before declining again by 1972. Antiriot demonstrations, injury, deaths, and property damage emerged in 1956 and were a "fluctuating constant" (i.e., varied about what my eyeballing suggests is a trendless mean) from 1956 through the end of the civil rights era in 1972.

Burstein used these data and others to examine the sources of congressional support for equal employment leading to passage of measures (in 1964 for blacks and in 1972 for women). He argued for the importance of public opinion and the civil rights movement in generating congressional action and the importance of ideas for shaping the particular form that action took.

> Public opinion appears to have been the fundamental determinant of congressional action. . . . The civil rights movement also appears to have affected Congress, however, in two ways. First it probably drew the attention of members of Congress to the issue of civil rights, leading them to monitor public opinion closer than they might otherwise have, and strengthening the link between public opinion and congressional action. Second, the civil rights movement also provoked a violent response that increased the salience of the issue for the public, which then demanded congressional action. (1985, 95)

It is significant not only that his data and conclusions are consistent with the emendations I have been posing to Carmines and Stimson's account but also that the movement had its impact before 1964. It thus preceded and presumably could have been a cause of the "punctuating event" they examine. It certainly seems plausibly related to the decline of apoliticals among blacks

between 1962 and 1964. It could also have been related to the increase in Democratic identification among blacks even earlier—at least as the movement's
impact was filtered through the actions and reactions of partisan elites (e.g.,
Kennedy's support of King in 1960). These, in turn spurred Johnson and northern Democrats in 1964 and thereafter to push for stronger legislation on civil
rights as well as possibly emboldened Goldwater to oppose the Civil Rights Act
of 1964.

The civil rights movement, of course, did not just coincidentally happen in
the mid-1950s, peak in the early to mid-1960s, and putter on and out by 1972. It
began with the courageous actions of Rosa Parks, Martin Luther King Jr., and
many other individual citizens. But it also began in part because of the actions
of elites. Such actions as Truman's integration of the armed services,
Humphrey and other northern Democrats' activities at their 1948 convention,
and the Supreme Court's decision in *Brown v. Board* and other cases. One can
continue to push further back (e.g., to tensions in the New Deal coalition with
the addition of blacks into a coalition with the white South and the [partially]
consequent emergence of the congressional conservative coalition). Indeed,
path-dependent historical explanations constantly pressure for ever-earlier
beginning points, in no small measure because of the importance of the beginning point in any path-dependent explanation. Thus, did congressional and
presidential politics of the mid-1960s "matter?" Or was it public opinion and
the civil rights movement that preceded that politics? Or was it even earlier
actions by political elites after World War II, . . . the Civil War, . . . the slave
state compromise, . . . the arrival of the first slaves from Africa? And, this first
point would not be so consequential if the explanation did not follow (path
dependently) from that initial observation and that initial observation were not
necessarily exogenous and unexplained within the theory. In this case,
Burstein's analysis at least reopens the crucial question of this inquiry—how
does electoral democracy work, and in particular what are the roles, importance, and impact of the public and the elites?

To this point, I have focused on the changing of an equilibrium in the 1960s,
understood as issue evolution, as a way of examining the balance of forces in
shaping political outcomes between the public and the elites. As I have demonstrated, Carmines and Stimson correctly said that critical events in Congress
shaped public opinion and changed party identification in permanent ways
and that these congressional events had been shaped by public opinion and
behavior and by the actions of those in the public who participated in the civil
rights movement or resisted it with force. I stop this particular part of the
investigation at this point, however, because another way in which we may fail
to understand fully the nature of electoral democracy in this period is by looking at civil rights in isolation. The critical moment Carmines and Stimson iso-

late for their punctuation is a moment when other major changes also occurred. I will now turn to those changes in the government, in policy-making, and in the electorate—that is, changes in electoral democracy.

The 1960s and (Other) Electoral Changes

The major point Niemi and I were making (Aldrich and Niemi 1990, 1996) was that there was something remarkable about the 1960s, something so remarkable that we called it a critical era that induced a change in party systems. We called it a critical era to distinguish it from a partisan realignment—that is, we agreed that the changes were not those that constitute a realignment. In particular, there was no large shift in the net balance of partisanship. Instead, while we called it an era rather than an election, we were basing our account on the original version of Key's critical elections concept. In particular, we argued for a relatively short, sharp, and sustained change in what I am here calling electoral equilibrium. Our general account included changes in leaders, policy, and institutions (for further elaboration, see Aldrich 1995, 1999). I will return to this larger set of claims in later sections. This section focuses on the electoral aspect.

Niemi and I attempted to demonstrate our claim empirically. We began our project having discovered that we had shared a common observation. The end of what Converse (1976) called the "steady-state period" in partisanship in 1966 (consistent with Carmines and Stimson) was often considered the beginning of a period of volatility. Many considered this period of volatility to have continued for decades, perhaps even through today (e.g., Wattenberg 1994; Abramson, Aldrich, and Rohde 1999). These were claims of electoral volatility in particular—that is, changes in public attitudes and behavior, notably those summarized by such terms as *party decline* and *dealignment.* Niemi and I had observed that many of the individual changes that began in the 1960s seemed to have slowed or stopped altogether in the 1970s—perhaps early in the 1970s, as illustrated by figures such as 9.2 and 9.3. Of course, each individual variable reflected its own pattern, so we decided to see if we could aggregate them in some fashion to achieve a new accounting, what we called the "macro-pattern."

We began by combing the literature to assess what variables scholars had analyzed. We eventually isolated twenty-nine indicators, with twenty-seven of them measured sufficiently often during (presidential) election years to incorporate them into the macro-pattern. All twenty-seven were measures of the beliefs or actions of the general public. Each variable had a unique post–World War II pattern. To see how it all added up, however, we created the macro-pattern by standardizing each variable to have mean zero variance one over time (originally 1952–88, more recently 1952–92). We then simply took the average of all standardized scores at each election. The results are reported in figure 9.5, which also includes a graph of a function fit via regression that is flat for

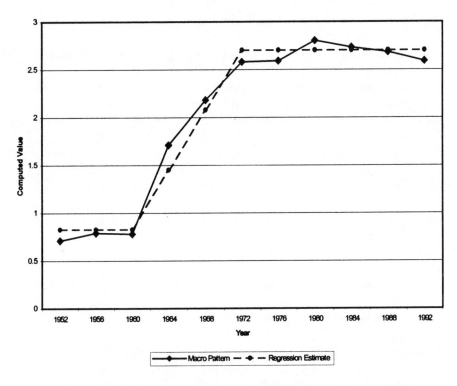

Fig. 9.5.   The macropattern in electoral attitudes and behavior, 1952–92. (Adapted from Aldrich and Niemi 1996, 99.)

1952–60 and increases by one-third in 1964, 1968, and 1972, at which point it is a constant for the rest of the period. This pattern is added merely to indicate how closely the macro-pattern fits our hypothesized "critical era" pattern that is constant during one stable era, changes over a critical era, and then culminates in a new and different steady state over time—in this case, the 1970s, 1980s, and into the 1990s.

The individual variables covered a range of matters (turnout, interest in the election, and so forth) but were heavily skewed toward partisanship. There were a few less immediately evident variables in addition to the already discussed measures and to other measures that are obvious for this purpose. One, for example, was a measure from Wattenberg (1994) on the use of issues in responses to candidate versus party "likes-dislikes" questions, and another is from Geer (1992) on the use of New Deal party-system issue responses. These measures were intended to see if the claims of continued electoral volatility, perhaps visible in some individual variables, could be sustained when viewing the electorally relevant universe as a whole. Figure 9.5 indicates our conclusion: No.

Bartels (2000) argues that the weakening of partisanship in the electorate has not followed the path claimed by advocates of the party-decline thesis, which is often at the heart of the electoral volatility argument. In particular, he claims that party identification has rebounded significantly since its nadir in the 1970s (see also Aldrich 1999 for a version of this claim and some evidence) and that it is more strongly correlated with the vote in both presidential and congressional elections now than then.

The first of Bartels's claims (1998, fig. 4) concerns a way to look at party identification in the whole electorate that is even closer in form to our macro-pattern than the measures we used to create it. In particular, he argues that one should distinguish the dynamic pattern of partisanship among voters from that among nonparticipants. He finds that among voters, the proportion of strong and weak identifiers in the NES sample was essentially a constant from 1952 through 1964 but dropped in 1968 and 1972. While it also did slightly in 1976, it rebounded so that it was essentially at the same level as 1972 from each election until 1996 (when the proportion jumped markedly). The pattern differs slightly among nonvoters (instead of flat from roughly 1972 to 1992, there is a slight slump in that period, albeit a lesser decline than in the 1960s). Overall, by distinguishing between participant categories rather then between racial groups, Bartels finds something much closer to the clear-cut critical-era pattern in partisanship. The 1950s, that is, were very different from the 1970s. The 1970s, however, were not much different at all from the 1980s and at least the early 1990s. The 1960s, meanwhile, were the decade of transformation.

Bartels's second claim concerns the increasing importance of partisanship for determining the vote. As I will discuss shortly, his claims strikingly resemble other patterns of party voting—the levels of party voting in Congress. For now, it is sufficient to note that his basic point is that party identification retains a robust relationship with the vote. Regardless of any arguments (and evidence) for the decline of party in the electorate, the original concept retains a great deal of vitality. Furthermore, after waning somewhat, its vitality has recovered to reach once again close to its highest impact. Partisan beliefs, therefore, remain consequential for determining the most basic element of electoral behavior, the vote.

This exercise of expanding the view of issue evolution in the 1960s to be more general than about race and civil rights per se permits an expansion of one other aspect of the account told by Carmines and Stimson. One of the first consequences of the elite shift they found was that the public began to see more clearly the (new) party positions on civil rights. Pomper (1972) in his paper "From Confusion to Clarity" demonstrated the shift in the public's perceptions of the stands of the two parties on numerous issues from 1956 to 1968. While acknowledging that those who saw party positions did see them more clearly in the mid-1960s than in the late 1950s, Margolis (1977) was struck by the large numbers who did not report any perceptions of party positions. As a result, he stated, the total increase in clarity was considerably less than it originally seemed. This is roughly akin to a glass half full of murky water being filled to the top with clear water. Are we struck more by the addition of clarity or by the fact that the glass still contains cloudy water?

Conclusion

This section argues that changes occurred in a broad array of mass public attitudes and behaviors during the 1960s. In most cases, these changes were concentrated between 1962 and 1972 and thus were relatively rapidly accomplished. A few were more like secular realignments, but most of the changes were more like those expected during a critical period—short, sharp, and sustained. In either form, these changes cumulated in such a fashion that there was a durable change—there was no going back. This durability of change across such a wide array of attributes in the general public led Niemi and I to conclude, as I now reaffirm, that a fundamental change in electoral politics occurred during the 1960s (with much happening in the public by 1964). It happened not to be a partisan realignment, as least not as a partisan realignment is classically understood, but it was a major change in the balance of forces. The change altered the equilibrium that seemed to describe electoral politics from the end of World War II to the civil rights era. The constancy of the macro-pattern for the next two decades after achieving its new balance in 1972 supports the inference that the disruption of the equilibrium in electoral politics in the 1960s resettled to a new and different equilibrium by about 1972.

This shape of dynamic change describes a broad swath of electoral politics, especially that centered on partisanship, as well as one piece of legislative politics so far—that of party stances on civil rights. I now turn to a more general consideration of governing and policy-making and thus to a more nearly complete consideration of electoral democracy. This investigation will uncover a mixture of patterns. Some elite patterns will be seen to resemble those in the mass public (and on congressional evolution on civil rights), but some reflect a second major dynamic pattern. The challenge then will be to consider how, if at all, the two dynamics can tell a consistent story about electoral democracy.

A Second Form of Change in the 1960s and Thereafter

The 1960s and Changes in the Party-in-Government and in Policy-Making

In addition to the civil rights issue evolution in Congress, a number of other relevant changes in congressional policy-making occurred during this period.

These changes are of a different form from the equilibrium shift forms so far described—that is, they do not fit either the critical or secular forms of realignment or the issue-evolution pattern. I consider two elite and one public pattern in this section.

The most impressive aspect of the Great Society was the volume of legislation undertaken in that Congress in particular and in the 1960s in general. This aspect of legislating can be addressed through the argument elegantly presented by Mayhew (1991; see also Krehbiel 1998 for an equally elegant extension and explanation). Mayhew documented one basic, very general, and surprising claim: the existence of divided government slowed government productivity barely if at all. There is little evidence of gridlock when each party has an effective veto over actions taken by the other, or at least no greater gridlock with a divided government than with a unified one.

Howell et al. (n.d.) extended Mayhew's original data (and questioned his basic claim). They included all 17,663 public laws enacted from 1945 through 1994 and extended Mayhew's typology of legislation. They created four categories: A-level bills consist of landmark legislation (à la Mayhew); B are "important" (or what Howell et al. call "non-landmark but nonetheless highly consequential legislation" [2]); C are ordinary matters; and D are minor pieces of legislation.

In figure 9.6, I report the frequency of A and B laws, both separately (fig. 9.6A) and combined (fig. 9.6B), passed in each Congress from the 1953 opening of the 83d Congress through the 103d Congress, which convened forty years later. Most striking is the dramatic rise in the number of important and landmark laws passed in the mid- and late 1960s. Landmark legislation increased sharply after Kennedy's election and the emergence of a unified Democratic government. The actions of the two Congresses of his administration are often thought to reflect pent up demand from northern Democrats for more liberal legislation, expressing frustrations that grew during the Eisenhower administration (especially, as per Carmines and Stimson [1989], after the Democratic victory in the 1958 elections). Also consistent with that alleged cause, the most evident datum in the A-level time series is the spike associated with the Great Society Congress, where the number of "landmark" bills exceeded those thought to be merely "important." Together, the two categories of legislation peaked in the Great Society Congress. The Congress elected in 1966 passed many landmark bills, although nowhere near as many as its predecessor. By this measure, however, this Congress still passed the second largest number. Equally striking, however, was that the total of categories A and B remained at nearly the same level in this and the succeeding congress as in 1965–66. Landmark legislation remained a constant possibility throughout this era: although its levels declined, by the late 1970s they had only reached a level reminiscent of the 1950s. It wasn't simply that the enthusiasms of 1965–66 slowly atrophied. Rather, the remainder of the decade saw moderately to very large numbers of

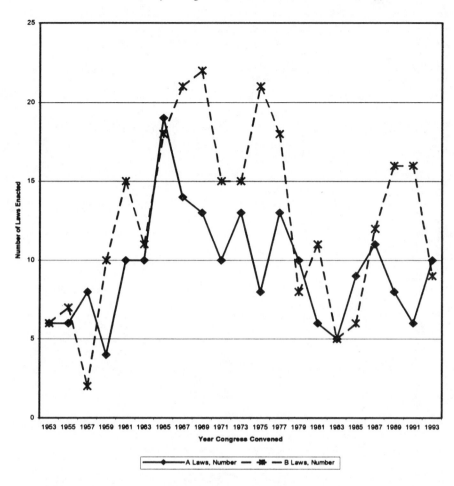

Fig. 9.6.   Major and landmark legislation enacted, 1953–94. (*A*) Types A and B, separate;
(*B*) Types A and B, combined. (Data from Cameron, compiled by author.)

important laws enacted along with numerous landmark bills. Only after the
1978 midterm did the bulge of significant activity finally slow.

This pattern is largely unrelated to the presence or absence of divided government. The relative peaks after Kennedy's, Johnson's, and Carter's elections
and the resurgence of legislating that occurred after the reunification of the
Democratic Congress in 1986 (see fig. 9.6B) imply some effect when Democratic majorities are newly elected. In any case, it is clear that the 1960s and
1970s were times of active legislating. The 1965 through 1972 period (that is, the
critical era) was distinctive in its activity, although 1974–77 was nearly as distinctive and both were distinct from other Congresses in this time frame. From
these data, however, the 1960s clearly were important for the federal govern-

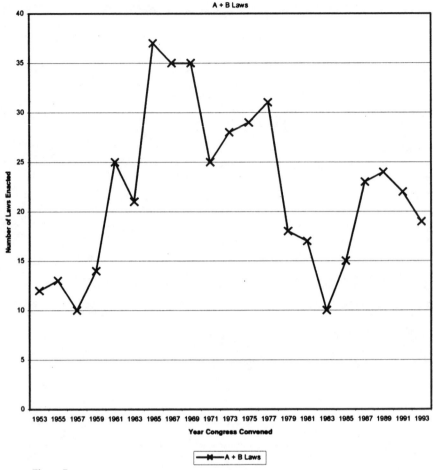

Fig. 9.6B

ment, which was highly active and involved in creating a very large change in public policy. As Erikson, MacKuen, and Stimson (2002) demonstrate, this large burst of legislation was the product not merely of active Congresses but of active Congresses passing primarily liberal legislation—a point to which I will return.

Some would argue that the Great Society Congress also marks the beginning of the end for unity in the Democratic Party. The potential voting alliance between southern Democrats and Republicans was, of course, a regular feature from the conservative coalition's origins in the mid-1930s. Northern Democrats' inability to achieve their political goals, whether on civil rights or on other matters, was a continuing source of frustration to them throughout the postwar period. Indeed, precisely because of the alliance's emergence as a working majority within the Democratic congressional delegations in 1958, frustration built so clearly. This observation led Carmines and Stimson to mark 1958 as the beginning of their issue evolution, and the first signs of the evolution did appear in the Senate—but not in the House—in 1959, as figure 9.1 demonstrates. This division within the then dominant majority party also plays a great role in what we consider when we think about divided government and thus serves as backdrop to the time period covered by Mayhew (1991) and in Howell et al. (n.d.). The spike of A-level legislation in the Great Society Congress was so prominent, in this view, precisely because northern Democrats could legislate without regard to the conservative coalition. Indeed, they could act without regard to their solid southern base at all, potentially for the first time since the Civil War.

Rohde and I (Aldrich and Rohde 1996, 1997, 1997–98, 1998, 2000) have examined the homogeneity or heterogeneity of the two parties in our analysis of what we call "conditional party government." We believe that the relative homogeneity of preferences within at least the majority party serves as the "condition" in conditional party government. And, we argue, when that condition is relatively well met, the majority party will weigh unusually heavily in governing and in policy-making. We were not the first by any means, however, to have taken note of the continuously growing heterogeneity of the Democratic Party's majority in Congress from the end of World War II into the 1970s. We developed a number of measures of this concept and examined it in these Congresses (Aldrich and Rohde 1998), using both the Poole-Rosenthal (1985, 1997) and Heckman-Snyder (1997) estimates of ideal point locations of members. In both cases we examined primarily the first and most important dimension in their estimates, which are based on actual behavior—that is, on roll call votes cast on the floor of Congress. (Here I report only the House; see Aldrich and Rohde 1998 for a bit of evidence about the Senate.) In figure 9.7, I report one of these measures, the R^2 that results from regressing ideal point location on the first (most important and partisan) dimension on party affiliation. Other measures show very comparable patterns (see Aldrich and Rohde 1998). The point is the decline of cohesion within the two parties over the 1950s and 1960s, a decrease that bottomed in or around 1970. The overall (dis)similarity of voting within each party then ceased its decline and began to increase steadily over the remainder the 1970s through today. The decline and resurgence of party homogeneity is more or less smooth and uniform in the Poole estimates, bottoming in the Congresses elected in the early 1970s and peaking in the 104th Congress. The Snyder estimates show a much starker decline that began in 1962, bottomed sharply in 1970, and then climbed more continuously into the 1990s.

The previous sections on the 1960s emphasized one kind of dynamic, that associated with a shift in equilibrium that was concentrated in the 1962–72 period. That dynamic is primarily one of short, sharp, and sustained change, akin to the existence of a critical era or to a punctuated equilibrium shift of the

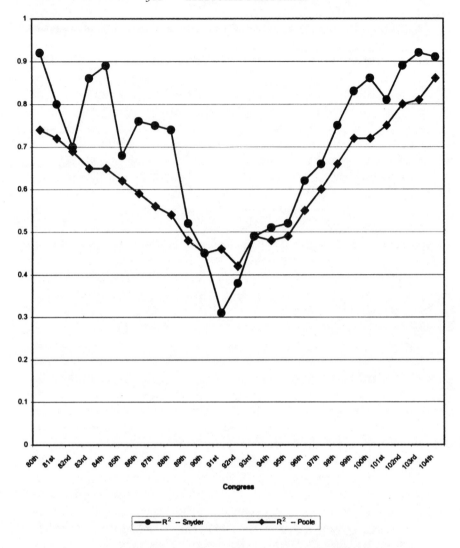

Fig. 9.7.   Cohesion of parties in the U.S. House, 1953–96. (compiled by author.)

issue evolution sort. Each of these instances of this first dynamic occurs within that decade. To be more precise, the ordering of these variables is an important element of the argument, but what is equally important is that the old stable pattern was disrupted during that decade and that the decade ended with a new typical value in place. Here, I have pointed to a second dynamic, one of dramatic change of a different type. It is neither short nor necessarily sharp—the Poole measure in figure 9.7, for example, is of a nearly linear decline over the first twenty years, followed by a nearly linear increase over the last twenty years. With Snyder's estimates, the decline is quite rapid in the 1960s but the "recovery" is nearly as long and as slow as with the Poole estimates.

What is really important, however, is less the magnitude or even the duration of the change but that, at the end, the measure has typically returned to a value not unlike that at which it began. It does not appear that the new levels of homogeneity within the two parties' congressional delegations are an equilibrium change of the sort envisioned in either realignment or issue-evolution theories. Much the same is true with respect to the volume of legislation. The growth in bill making in the 1960s and 1970s marked a dramatic surge from the 1950s, but instead of moving to some new level of legislating, the 1990s marked a return near to the levels of the 1950s.

This argument has one further element. I previously reported that Bartels (1998, 2000) made two claims, and I discussed the first. His second claim concerns the relationship between partisan identification and the vote. I earlier reported his emphasis on the fact that the correlation between party identification and the vote has been consistently high. But he also noted some variability. In particular, the correlation begins high, sags from the middle of the 1960s through the 1970s, and then climbs again. In figure 9.8, I plot this relationship between party identification and the congressional vote (actually a regression coefficient estimate that therefore is not bounded by +/1) alongside the measure of party homogeneity in the U.S. House. Figure 9.8 clearly supports two conclusions. One is that the Bartels's measure of the impact of party identification in the electorate follows a very similar pattern to the impact of partisan affiliation in Congress. The second is that the electorate's pattern seems to follow closely that at the elite level but lags by a decade.

Reconciling the Two Dynamics

We have observed two basic time dynamics (ignoring fig. 9.4 for the moment). One dynamic is that which we would expect to observe if there were a change in equilibrium. Figure 9.5 is one prime example of this pattern. This figure includes a small element of behavior, but it is dominated by measures of various aspects of the attitudes and beliefs of the public. So, too, are figures 9.2 and 9.3 meant to illustrate changes from one equilibrium to another, and these also are changes in beliefs—here, partisan beliefs. Only figure 9.1, the core evidence of issue evolution on civil rights, is a measure of behavior and yet meant to be of this first dynamic. I will subsequently return to it.

Figures 9.6, 9.7, and 9.8 present the second major pattern of a time path— major change away from some particular value but then a return to or nearly to that value. While it is common to infer patterns of beliefs among members of Congress from the Poole and Rosenthal and the Heckman and Snyder data,

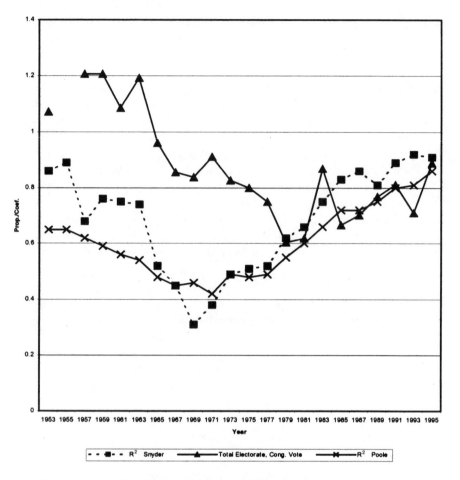

Fig. 9.8. Party and voting in the U.S. House and electorate, 1953–94. (Data from Larry
M. Bartels, Keith T. Poole, and James Snyder, compiled by author.)

these measures are based on votes cast. Therefore, they, like the Bartels measure in figure 9.8, are measures of behavior. Even more, all three variables are
actually measures of the relationship between party affiliation and the vote.
The figure 9.6 measures are various accounts of what members of Congress
selected. Thus, the two basic time paths observed are, first, a change in equilibrium and, second, a change-and-return pattern. In addition, there is a substantive component associated with each dynamic. The shift in equilibrium
dynamic is composed of measures of beliefs. The long-term change-and-return
pattern is composed of measures of the relationship between (partisan) beliefs
and behavioral choices.

There is a possible reconciliation between these two time dynamics, given the distinction just drawn. All contemporary theories of politics—behavioral, social or cognitive psychological, limited, bounded, and full rational choice theories—rest on a common and very basic assumption: attitudes/beliefs/preferences determine behavior. The reconciliation, then, is simple. The disequilibrium, which appears to be a disjunction in beliefs, is also marked by a growing discrepancy between the ordinary relationship between beliefs and behavior. The fundamental issue is that beliefs are growing away from their status quo, defining politics as usual. Especially among the mass public, however, beliefs change only rarely, and when they do it is under stress and in patterns that are of the changing equilibrium sort. Belief change is politics as unusual. Presumptively, politics as usual is marked by, perhaps even defined by, relatively constant beliefs, or at least by one particular class of beliefs, partisan beliefs. Behavior, conversely, follows beliefs. Thus, over time, once beliefs change, the pattern of behavior adjusts to the new set of beliefs (but why so slowly? because it must be filtered through institutions?). Politics as usual, therefore, is politics under largely unchanging beliefs, with the connection between beliefs and behavior more or less at full adjustment. What we observe in the 1960s, then, was the disruption of stable beliefs, with the result that mass political behavior was thrown into disarray with respect to its fit to those beliefs. Those beliefs settled reasonably quickly, with behavior more slowly adjusting (at both mass and elite levels, as in fig. 9.8) to accord with beliefs.

Under this interpretation, the driving force appears to be the mass public. Its beliefs changed during the critical era, and its beliefs-behavior connection was brought into alignment. The key question, then, is why the adjustment of the public was slow. The answer implied in figure 9.8 is that the time lag in the public resulted in some measure from the elites. Most especially, that means a sorting out of the beliefs among affiliates of the two parties—the increased homogeneity within political parties. Only then did the public connection between partisan identification and votes come back into an alignment typical, I believe, of politics as usual. It appears that the decline in the connection between party and vote in the public lags the comparable decline between party affiliation and vote among members of Congress by four to eight years. Thus, the slow adjustment of the public can be attributed—but only in part—to the adjustment among the elites.

While this line of argument implies that the mass public responds to elites, that is only part of the story. The elites also respond to the masses. In particular, the growing homogeneity within the parties in Congress appears to be a response to the electorate in several ways. The fundamental story as told by Rohde (1991) is that the enfranchisement of southern blacks led to the change in the selection of southern members of Congress. That delegation came to reflect the rest of the nation more closely by virtue of including the region's full electorate, and, in reaction, an increasingly two-party region arose. The result was an expansion of liberal votes in the Democratic electorate, the selection of more moderate to liberal Democrats to Congress, and/or the switch to Republicans as the choice of conservatives. The fundamental story told by Poole and Rosenthal (1997) is a more general account consistent with Rohde's account—change in congressional voting patterns results not as much from changing preferences among continuing members as from changing the members themselves. In this view, then, only after the congressional delegations came to be more internally homogenous—after, that is, party identification could be more meaningful as a basis of one's standing decision—did the impact of party identification on the vote surge back to its more common, high, level.

The decline in elite partisan homogeneity is, in this view, an interaction between the structurally imposed absence of two-party competition in the South that perforce led to the selection of Democrats to Congress and the inability to keep civil rights off the congressional agenda. The New Deal coalition was forged with southern Democrats as central members, so liberal, welfare-state-style, economic issues were not what made the conservative coalition a major force. Put another way, southerners could select Democrats not very atypical from the party as a whole when economic concerns were paramount. Consequently, unlike elsewhere in the nation, the entire enfranchised southern electorate selected these Democrats—not the full electorate but also not an electorate that had two viable parties between which to select. Given the South's economic status, however, a party base composed of all whites was not very distinct in economic terms from the northern Democratic base, which was at least partially multiracial but, given party compositions, was disproportionately less well-off. Rather, what made the southern Democratic electorate distinct from its northern partisan peers was race. Therefore, the potential tensions within the Democratic Party were manifested concretely as the party became more unable to keep (or to want to keep) civil rights off the agenda. Thus, in this view, the electoral democratic system was consistently on the verge of being out of equilibrium, but this situation arose over concerns that did not materialize. Thus, its potential disequilibrium was not realized often enough to disrupt the connection between the electorate's beliefs and behavior. The issue evolution on civil rights, in this account, is a story of the breakdown of the safeguards among elites, especially within the majority party, that kept that potential disruption from being realized. The breakdown occurred not within the party in government, however, but outside of Congress, whether in presidential politics (the 1948 convention and integration of the armed forces), the Supreme Court, or the mass public and civil rights movement therein spawned. More accurately, this stream of forces joined together with numerous (but not universal) years of economic good times in the fabulous 1950s and go-go 1960s to raise the public salience of civil rights relative to economic issues. Only then did electoral-democratic elites (both presidents and members of

Congress in their legislating roles) respond with the civil rights issue evolution. And, this evolution did not so much change the ideological beliefs of those elites as change those elites via election and change the issue agenda, so that Democrats were forced to vote on civil rights issues that divided their two regional wings rather than on other issues that united the party.

One other force is also at work, the burst of legislation of the 1960s through mid-1970s. Elections made this burst possible. The 1958 election was the start, important for strengthening the northern wing of the Democratic Party especially in the Senate, as Carmines and Stimson (1989) note. The 1960 election was also significant. It not only reunified control for that party but also selected a Democratic president who chose to support King in jail when doing so was not obligatory and when seemingly similar predecessors such as FDR might not have. The 1964 election was, of course, the most consequential. It gave the northern Democrats effective control over each of the three legislating wings, even if that meant a southern president acting (as third legislative wing) against his region's partisan imperative.

But this is merely to repeat the account of the issue evolution on civil rights. The burst of legislation included a very wide variety of important and landmark legislation. The Civil Rights Act of 1964 was the 87th and 88th Congresses' only legislation in this area, and it is "merely" one of five landmark bills (or one of twenty-eight important or landmark bills) by Mayhew's count (1991, table 4.1). The Great Society Congress enacted twenty-two major bills, of which Mayhew considered three to be historically significant. The Voting Rights Act was only the one that was clearly a civil rights measure, although War on Poverty legislation (e.g., model cities, housing and urban development) made the distinction less than clear-cut. (The 90th Congress added sixteen more important bills, with only the Open Housing Act clearly a civil rights measure and, to Mayhew, the only one of landmark status.) In short, governing in the Kennedy and Johnson years was extremely active, and it was also much more diverse than the focus here on civil rights would imply.

Two points seem most relevant. The first is another take on shifting agendas. The first assessment was that the civil rights movement forced civil rights onto the political agenda, revealing the divisions between North and South in the Democratic Party. In this view, elites sought to keep specific issues off the agenda, much as in the Democrat and Whig era a century earlier (Aldrich 1995). Some major elected elites did, of course, take an active role in seeking this change in the agenda (as was true in the age of Jackson, too—e.g., David Wilmot). That is why Johnson (and Humphrey) looms large in that issue evolution. Burstein's (1985) point was, however, that the civil rights movement increased the issue's salience in the public and thereby among elected officials.

The Great Society Congress passed five important (level-B) bills on environmental issues, at least as many as on civil rights when War on Poverty measures are counted in that group and far more (although none as historically important) as on civil rights directly. (These are the Highway Beautification Act, Motor Vehicle Pollution Control Act, the Water Quality Act, the Clean Water Restoration Act, and air pollution control.) The 88th Congress also passed an important environmental measure (the Clean Air Act of 1963). Even more, the Equal Pay Act of 1963 was the first important gender-discrimination-reduction measure in the modern era. Not unlike the Civil Rights Act of 1957, then, the elected elite passed notable measures that at least coincided with or even preceded the emergence of major movements that arose during the Nixon years. One could make arguments for new (or revived) agenda dimensions on other aspects of the burst of legislation in this period, but the actually rather substantial series of actions on the environment makes the points needed here. First, the agenda was large and diverse. Second, while the issue evolution on civil rights was pushed into being in part by sustained public pressure and movement politics, elected officials could also play leadership roles in major changes in the agenda. Third, therefore, there is more to the 1960s than an issue evolution on civil rights, and the break with the past—the breaking of the old equilibrium—was of a broader scope and more complex than the story of civil rights suggests.

The first point is that the subject matter of what was passed into law in the 1960s changed. The second point is that there was a clear directionality to that change. Erikson, MacKuen, and Stimson (2002) have assigned an ideological direction to the one of Mayhew's measures of important legislation. From 1960 (with only one important bill) through 1980 (with two), they consider every piece of important legislation to be liberal. In terms relevant here, then, with every piece of legislation in the vast burst of activity in this period of a critical era (plus several Congresses thereafter), the government not only was active but was changing the status quo in a liberal direction. Once again, this accounting is far more general than civil rights. The liberal shift in policy in the United States continued long after civil rights was effectively removed from the agenda. In fact, the only civil rights legislation in the Erikson, MacKuen, and Stimson measure during the Nixon, Ford, and Carter administrations was the two extensions of the Voting Rights Act in 1970 and 1975. In addition, the more modest but detectable surge in the enactment of important legislation between the Democratic recapture of unified control of Congress in 1986 and the party's loss of it in 1995 is entirely in a liberal direction. To be sure, there is an element of subjectivity in Erikson, MacKuen, and Stimson's coding exercise. One might also reasonably claim that important new legislation is a concept predisposed toward a liberal direction (one can almost hear Reagan intone that government is not the solution to our problems, government *is* the problem). Nonetheless, neither point is necessarily binding. The authors do find conservative directions in important legislation in the remaining years—those of the Eisenhower administration, the first six years of the Reagan administration, and the 104th Congress.

It seems clear that this volume and direction of change in governmental policy must play a substantial role in the story. Here, I agree with Erikson, MacKuen, and Stimson's account. They claim (with considerable supporting evidence) that legislation enacted is the consequence both of public preferences and of partisan control of office, and they find the former more substantial. For one, the independent effect of control of office is less than the effect of public mood on policy. Second, public preferences affect not only legislation but also and more directly partisan control of office. This part of the story closely resembles what Rohde and I call conditional party government: elections determine the relative homogeneity of the parties in office, and when that condition is particularly well met, the parties in government add to that electoral force. Erikson, MacKuen, and Stimson further claim that legislating impacts public mood. For example, the Great Society Congress enacted even more liberal laws than the previously receptive public desired. The result was a reactionary shift in mood on policy back toward a more conservative set of wishes.

I think it reasonable to suppose that both the dramatic volume of legislation and its consistent liberal nature are significant parts of the cause of the disalignment between the public's partisan beliefs and behavior in and after critical eras. As the parties in government became more cohesive in their voting behavior on the floor of Congress and as the volume and direction of that which their votes created slowed to what were seemingly more typical levels, public beliefs and behavior began to adjust to their more typical—and very high—levels.

Conclusion

There are, to be sure, more than a few loose ends in this account. Still, several conclusions are worth tentative consideration. First, electoral democracy is not purely of the more populist sort, in which public wishes tightly constrain elected officials. But this is also no elite-driven account of electoral democracy. Rather, the public and those it elects are both important. While I have kept this chapter as soft a rational choice account as possible, the evidence seems persuasive that both sets of actors are strategic actors and they are in an ongoing game—that is, they are in a strategic setting. That, it seems to me, is the essence of a republican democracy. Second, it may be true that the public is susceptible to perhaps even demagogic appeals from candidates and officeholders. Narrow ambition for reelection may also be the best description of the at least short-term motivations of those elites. Even so, I am persuaded that the beliefs of both sets of actors together are what most fully determine policies adopted, and I am persuaded that the public's beliefs are, in turn, affected by policies that have been adopted. Third, the ongoing patterns of electoral democracy are typified by an ongoing politics as usual for most of the time, with dramatic bursts of change, of politics as unusual, for some of the time. Whether this pattern of stability, change, and then new and different stability is really the equilibrium–disequilibrium–new equilibrium of punctuated equilibrium or critical eras is less certain. We lack a well-enough developed theory of macropolitics to know what a macropolitical equilibrium even would be. Whatever the theoretical case (and we are closing in on the ability to pose such questions seriously if not yet to answer them), the substantive case seems undeniable. Yet nothing special differentiated the public of the 1950s from that of the 1960s from that of the 1970s and thereafter. Beliefs determined behavior, the public was only barely more interested and involved in politics in one decade than another. What did differ was that the public's partisan beliefs were disrupted in the 1960s, making them a less useful guide to behavior. When, in time, the party in government returned to levels typical of the late New Deal, partisan beliefs returned to levels of alignment with behavior typical of the late New Deal. Thus, finally, party identification, even in this new age, is as consequential for guiding public behavior as it was in the days examined in *The American Voter*. It took, however, an appreciation of the connection between the party in the electorate and the party in government to realize that.

NOTE

I thank Bill Flanigan for his helpful comments.

REFERENCES

Abramson, Paul R., John H. Aldrich, and David W. Rohde. 1999. *Change and Continuity in the 1996 and 1998 Elections.* Washington, D.C.: CQ Press.
Adams, Greg D. 1997. Abortion: Evidence of Issue Evolution. *American Journal of Political Science* 41:718–37.
Aldrich, John H. 1995. *Why Parties? The Origin and Transformation of Party Politics in America.* Chicago: University of Chicago Press.
———. 1999. Political Parties in a Critical Era. *American Politics Quarterly* 27: 9–32.
Aldrich, John H., and Richard G. Niemi. 1990. *The Sixth American Party System: The 1960s Realignment and the Candidate-Centered Parties.* Duke University Working Paper in American Politics no. 107.
———. 1996. The Sixth American Party System: Electoral Change, 1952–1992. In *Broken Contract: Changing Relationships between Americans and their Government,* ed. Stephen C. Craig. Boulder, Colo.: Westview.
Aldrich, John H., and David W. Rohde. 1996. A Tale of Two Speakers: A Comparison of Policy Making in the 100th and 104th Congresses. Paper presented at the annual meeting of the American Political Science Association, San Francisco.
———. 1997. Balance of Power: Republican Party Leadership and the Committee System in the 104th House. Paper presented at the annual meeting of the Midwest Political Science Association, Chicago.
———. 1997–98. The Transition to Republican Rule in the House: Implications for Theories of Congressional Politics. *Political Science Quarterly* 112:541–67.

————. 1998. Measuring Conditional Party Government. Paper presented at the annual meeting of the Midwest Political Science Association, Chicago.

————. 2000. The Republican Revolution and the House Appropriations Committee. *Journal of Politics* 62:1–33.

Bartels, Larry M. 1998. Party Identification and Voting Behavior, 1952–1996. Unpublished manuscript, Princeton University.

————. 2000. Partisanship and Voting Behavior, 1952–1996. *American Journal of Political Science* 44:51–65.

Beck, Paul Allen. 1974. A Socialization Theory of Partisan Realignment. In *The Politics of Future Citizens,* ed. Richard G. Niemi. San Francisco, Calif.: Jossey-Bass.

Berelson, Bernard R. 1954. Democratic Theory and Democratic Practice. In *Voting,* ed. Bernard R. Berelson, Paul F. Lazarsfeld, and William N. McPhee. Chicago: University of Chicago Press.

Burnham, Walter Dean. 1970. *Critical Elections and the Mainsprings of American Politics.* New York: Norton.

Burstein, Paul. 1985. *Discrimination, Jobs, and Politics: The Struggle for Equal Employment Opportunity in the United States since the New Deal.* Chicago: University of Chicago Press.

Campbell, Angus. 1966 (1960). A Classification of the Presidential Elections. In *Elections and the Political Order,* by Angus Campbell, Philip E. Converse, Warren E. Miller, and Donald E. Stokes. New York: Wiley.

Campbell, Angus, Philip E. Converse, Warren E. Miller, and Donald E. Stokes. 1960. *The American Voter.* New York: Wiley.

————. 1966. *Elections and the Political Order.* New York: Wiley.

Carmines, Edward G., and James A. Stimson. 1989. *Issue Evolution: Race and the Transformation of American Politics.* Princeton: Princeton University Press.

Converse, Philip E. 1964. The Nature of Belief Systems in Mass Publics. In *Ideology and Discontent,* ed. David E. Apter. New York: Free Press.

————. 1966a. The Concept of a Normal Vote. In *Elections and the Political Order,* by Angus Campbell, Philip E. Converse, Warren E. Miller, and Donald E. Stokes. New York: Wiley.

————. 1966b (1963). On the Possibility of Major Political Realignment in the South. In *Elections and the Political Order,* by Angus Campbell, Philip E. Converse, Warren E. Miller, and Donald E. Stokes. New York: Wiley.

————. 1969. Of Time and Partisan Stability. *Comparative Political Studies* 2:139–71.

————. 1976. *The Dynamics of Party Support: Cohort-Analyzing Party Identification.* Beverly Hills, Calif.: Sage.

Cox, Gary W. 1997. *Making Votes Count: Strategic Coordination in the World's Electoral Systems.* New York: Cambridge University Press.

Duverger, Maurice. 1954. *Political Parties: Their Organization and Activities in the Modern State.* London: Methuen; New York: Wiley.

Erikson, Robert S., Michael B. MacKuen, and James A. Stimson. 2002. *The Macro Polity.* New York: Cambridge University Press.

Geer, John G. 1992. New Deal Issues and the American Electorate, 1952–1988. *Political Behavior* 14:45–65.

Heckman, James J., and James M. Snyder, Jr. 1997. Linear Probability Models of the Demand for Attributes with an Empirical Application to Estimating the Preferences of Legislators. *Rand Journal of Economics* 28:142–90.

Howell, William, Scott Adler, Charles Cameron, and Charles Riemann. N.d. Divided Government and the Legislative Productivity of Congress, 1945–1994. Version 4.1. Unpublished manuscript.

Kessel, John H. 1991. *Presidential Campaign Politics.* 4th ed. Pacific Grove, Calif.: Brooks/Cole.

Key, V. O., Jr. 1949. *Southern Politics in State and Nation.* New York: Knopf.

———. 1955. A Theory of Critical Elections. *Journal of Politics* 17:3–18.

———. 1959. Secular Realignment and the Party System. *Journal of Politics* 21:198–210.

———. 1964. *Politics, Parties, and Pressure Groups.* 5th ed. New York: Crowell.

Krehbiel, Keith. 1998. *Pivotal Politics: A Theory of U.S. Lawmaking.* Chicago: University of Chicago Press.

Margolis, Michael. 1977. From Confusion to Confusion: Issues and the American Voter, 1956–1972. *American Political Science Review* 71: 31–43.

Mayhew, David R. 1991. *Divided We Govern: Party Control, Lawmaking, and Investigations, 1946–1990.* New Haven: Yale University Press.

Pomper, Gerald M. 1972. From Confusion to Clarity: Issues and the American Voter, 1956–1968. *American Political Science Review* 66:415–28.

Poole, Keith T., and Howard Rosenthal. 1985. A Spatial Model for Legislative Roll Call Analysis. *American Journal of Political Science* 29:357–84.

———. 1997. *Congress: A Political-Economic History of Roll Call Voting.* New York: Oxford University Press.

Rohde, David W. 1991. *Parties and Leaders in the Postreform House.* Chicago: University of Chicago Press.

Sanbonmatsu, Kira. 2002. *Democrats, Republicans, and the Politics of Women's Place.* Ann Arbor: University of Michigan Press.

Sellers, Charles G., Jr. 1965. The Equilibrium Cycle in Two-Party Politics. *Public Opinion Quarterly* 29:16–38.

Stanley, Harold W., and Richard G. Niemi. 1995. The Demise of the New Deal Coalition: Partisanship and Group Support, 1952–1992. In *Democracy's Feast: Elections in America,* ed. Herbert F. Weisberg. Chatham, N.J.: Chatham House.

———. 1998. *Vital Statistics on American Politics, 1997–1998.* Washington, D.C.: CQ Press.

Stimson, James A. 1991. *Public Opinion in America: Moods, Cycles, and Swings.* Boulder, Colo.: Westview.

Stokes, Donald E. 1966. Some Dynamic Elements in Contests for the Presidency. *American Political Science Review* 60:19–28.

Stokes, Donald E., Angus Campbell, and Warren E. Miller. 1958. Components of Electoral Decision. *American Political Science Review* 52:367–87.

Stokes, Donald E., and Gudmund R. Iversen. 1966 (1962). On the Existence of Forces Restoring Party Competition. In *Elections and the Political Order,* by Angus Campbell, Philip E. Converse, Warren E. Miller, and Donald E. Stokes. New York: Wiley.

Sundquist, James L. 1983. *Dynamics of the Party System.* Rev. ed. Washington, D.C.: Brookings Institution.

Wattenberg, Martin P. 1994. *The Decline of American Political Parties, 1952–1992.* Cambridge: Harvard University Press.

10

Coming to Grips with V. O. Key's Concept of Latent Opinion

John Zaller

When the late V. O. Key Jr., wrote that "to speak with precision about public opinion is a task not unlike coming to grips with the Holy Ghost" (8), he gave the behavioral revolution then gaining force just the excuse it needed to ignore his important concept of "latent opinion." This paper attempts a revival of that concept.

Key (1961) defined public opinion as "those opinions held by private persons which governments find it prudent to heed." He went on to introduce the concept of "latent opinion," which "in the practice of politics and government . . . is really about the only type of opinion that generates much anxiety" (262). Key offered several understandings of the "singularly slippery" idea of latent opinion, but all reduced to essentially this: latent opinion is opinion that might exist at some point in the future in response to the decision makers' actions and may perhaps result in political damage or even defeat at the polls. This is why officeholders care about it and why Key made it central to his analysis.

Key pointed out that public opinion as measured in polls might often be a poor indicator of latent opinion. "Responses to survey questions," he explained, give no clue "as to the convertibility of opinion into votes." Thus

> if a legislator is to worry about the attitude of his district, what he needs really to worry about is, not whether his performance pleases the constituency at the moment, but what the response of his constituency will be in the next campaign when persons aggrieved by his position attack his record. (499)

If the private opinions that governments are most prudent to heed—and presumably do heed—are opinions that opponents might stir up at the next election, it is little wonder that Key compared the study of public opinion to coming to grips with the Holy Ghost. If anything, he underestimated the problem.

Writing at the same time, Philip Converse faced the same challenge as Key, noting, for example, that mass belief systems had never surrendered easily to empirical study (Converse 1964). But Converse didn't go on to talk about the Holy Ghost. He and his Michigan collaborators (Campbell et al. 1960) built models to show that it was, in fact, possible to speak with precision about public opinion. Nor can work in the Michigan tradition be faulted for failing to situate public opinion in the political process. *Elections and the Political Order,* published in the mid-1960s, still stands as a model of politically relevant political behavior research (Campbell et al. 1966). Also, although it is sometimes forgotten, Converse's seminal work on belief systems took as its focal task the interpretation of electoral mandates, whether in the nineteenth-century United States, in Nazi Germany, or in the U.S. election of 1956. Thus, his pathbreaking arguments that most voters are not ideological, and that they often have no attitudes at all, were in service of a larger point concerning the kinds of inferences that may and may not be legitimately drawn from expressions of public opinion. One finds comparably political concerns in all of Converse's major work.

The modeling tradition that the Michigan scholars helped to inaugurate has carried the day in public opinion research, but their central concern with politics has receded from much work in political behavior. Quite often, researchers are more concerned with pure psychology, elegant statistical models, or simply a high r^2.[1] Hence it is worth emphasizing that, as difficult as Key's conception of public opinion may be to implement in quantitative research, it has these important virtues: it focuses on what actually drives much of politics, which is gaining and holding public office in elections. It distinguishes electorally relevant opinion from mere survey responses, raising thereby the specter of nonattitudes. And finally, it highlights the complexity of the process by which politicians' estimates of public opinion affect their decisions. In these ways, Key's concept of latent opinion focuses squarely on the interaction between politicians and citizens in the democratic process, a topic that ought to be more central to the study of public opinion than it is.

For these reasons, then, this chapter attempts a revival of scholarly interest in latent opinion, a neglected element in the tradition of V. O. Key. The chapter has five main sections. The first explicates the concept of latent opinion and gives some examples. The second describes what I claim is a common type of latent opinion—namely, a propensity on the part of the public to resist painful trade-offs and to punish politicians who force choices. Even when the public seems to accept a trade-off, it may suddenly reverse course, especially when urged to do so by the opposition at election time. The latent opinion that exists on many issues is, therefore, to have one's cake and eat it too. Though sometimes difficult to observe in polls at the moment politicians must choose policies, latent opinion may later spring to life at the beckoning of skilled opponents.

The third part of the chapter attempts to specify some conditions that affect when politicians are controlled by public opinion as expressed in current polls and when they will disregard current public opinion to be responsive to latent opinion. For purposes of this section, latent opinion may involve the public wanting to have its cake and eat it too, or it may involve some other latent response propensity of the public. The key proposition is that when politicians believe that they know better than the public what means will lead to desired ends, politicians will ignore the polls and follow their own beliefs. President Clinton's executive authorization of forty billion dollars in loan supports to Mexico in his first term is a perfect example: although the policy was massively unpopular at the time he approved it, Clinton believed—or acted as if he believed—that the ripple effects of a crippled Mexican economy on the U.S. economy, which the bailout was designed to prevent, would be more politically damaging to him at reelection time than lingering resentment of the loan bailout. Several arguably similar cases in which Clinton ignored current opinion to play to latent opinion are examined.

The fourth part of the chapter returns to the notion of inconsistent opinion as embodied in the latent tendency to want to have one's cake and eat it too. In an analogy to market capitalism, in which consumers inconsistently want the highest quality goods at the lowest possible cost, the argument is that such inconsistency may often serve the public's interest. A fifth section argues for the continuing relevance of latent opinion in research and teaching on public opinion.

The bulk of the chapter consists of anecdotal evidence that publics and politicians behave in accordance with these propositions. There is no systematic testing. The aim is merely to explicate Key's concept, show some new ways in which it can be used, and thereby call attention to what seems to me an important avenue for future systematic research.

The Concept of Latent Opinion

Although Key drew a parallel between public opinion and the Holy Ghost, he was no mystic when it came to explaining public opinion. Nor did be believe that the politicians who heeded latent opinion—an entity that, by definition, was not directly observable—were responding to figments of their imaginations. His position, rather, was that the public has real propensities to respond to stimuli in particular ways, that savvy politicians learned or could at least sense many of these propensities, and that political scientists can, to a limited extent, generalize about them.

> The citizen is equipped with ingrained sets of values, criteria for judgment, attitudes, preferences, dislikes—pictures in his head—that come into play when a relevant action, event, or proposal arises. To know how the public will respond to a contemplated course of action, those in positions of leadership and authority need only to relate that action to their estimate of the pictures in people's heads—and adjust their strategy accordingly. (1961, 264)

Some of the public's propensities were, as Key said, "more or less Pavlovian" or "mechanical" in character (271); others "depend on the broad kinds of values and expectations held by people" (274); and some involve a willingness to take cues from "that vaguely defined category we call the 'political elite'" (286). Some forms of latent opinion were so basic (e.g., a propensity to react defensively to threat) that Key doubted whether anything was gained by applying his term to them; others involved novel events for which people lacked "the comforting guidance of grooves in the brain," thus rendering their responses "utterly unpredictable" (267).

Notwithstanding Key's hesitations, his pivotal decision to define public opinion in terms of its response propensities rather than fully formed opinions, on the grounds that politicians' estimates of these propensities are what drive politics, presents no deep theoretical difficulties. The difficulties are on the practical side—having sufficient data and wit to reliably detect the response patterns that exist.

One well-known and important form of latent opinion is the reliable propensity of voters to punish presidents at election time for good or bad economic performance. Since the nineteenth century, incumbent politicians have known about this response propensity and exerted themselves to make sure performance was good (Tufte 1978). Although my use of the concept of latent opinion to characterize this phenomenon sheds no new light on it, the reference does reinforce the point that there is no difficulty in principle in studying latent opinion. It is simply a matter of identifying and measuring particular response regularities.

The "rally round the flag" effect in foreign policy crises is another notable case of latent opinion. Following the imaginative work of Mueller (1973) and armed with an abundance of surveys measuring presidential popularity, scholars now recognize a reliable, general tendency for the public to support the president in times of crisis (Oneal, Lian, and Joyner 1996; Baum 2000). Whether this tendency is rooted in a "Pavlovian" instinct, or, as Brody and Shapiro (1989) have suggested, an inclination to follow elite cues in crisis, it seems another straightforward example of a reliable propensity that Key would call latent opinion.

"Rally events" usually refer to upward spikes in presidential job approval, but the public's propensity to support presidential policy initiatives in foreign policy crises may be even greater. In 1988, a national poll found that only 18 percent of the public favored sending U.S. troops to Saudi Arabia if necessary to defend it from Iran. But two years later, when the threat to Saudi Arabia was from Iraq rather than Iran, 75 to 80 percent of the public supported President Bush's decision to send U.S. troops virtually as soon as he announced it (Mueller 1994). Most rally effects are considerably smaller than this 60-per-centage-point surge, but this is probably because few rallies develop from such a low base of initial public support.

As I understand Key's concept, the latent opinion in this example is not the high level of support that Bush enjoyed after announcing his policy. It is the public's reliable propensity to provide such support—a propensity that was not immediately observable in polls at the time Bush acted but might have been inferred from the public's response to past crises. Thus, one would say that latent public opinion supports presidential policy in foreign policy crises, at least at the beginning. A president's task in such crises is then to activate this latent opinion. More generally, the task of ambitious politicians is to activate latent opinions that are helpful to their cause and steer clear of latent opinions that may damage them politically.

The argument for Key's approach is, as I have indicated, that it fruitfully focuses research attention on the particular form of public opinion that often really drives politics. Thus, it is important to note that, in the case of rally effects, politicians are well aware that such effects occur and act in conscious anticipation of them. For example, at the time that the United States attacked Iraq in early 1991, polls indicated that only about half of the public supported this policy. When, in the course of another study, I asked a high Pentagon official whether this lack of support was a problem, he insisted it was not. "We felt the country basically supported the military effort," he said, "and that as soon as the fighting started, there would be a surge of increased support." Then, if the war could be won quickly enough, public support would never become an issue (Zaller 1995, 258).

But if, as these examples make clear, it is easy to point to important, well-established forms of latent opinion, it does not follow that all forms are so easy to identify, either for politicians or for academics. Yet, as I show in the next two sections, other important forms of latent opinion can be identified and described in general terms.

Latent Opinion and Presidential Decision Making on Vietnam

Many political issues are endogenous. That is, they arise from the strategic decisions of politicians who either do or do not want to face the issue based on their estimates of latent opinion. If politicians behave with sufficient shrewdness, the latent opinions that become actual opinions will be a very biased sample—biased toward issues that make decision makers look good and away from issues that make them look bad. This may be true even in the domain of foreign policy, where crises tend to rise exogenously. For even here, presidents may respond to some international provocations and not others. For example, when the North Vietnamese attacked U.S. naval forces in the Gulf of Tonkin shortly before the 1964 election, President Johnson responded vigorously. But when the North Koreans not only attacked but also seized the U.S.S. *Pueblo* in 1968, Johnson's response was low key and unassertive. This sort of endogeneity bias in the potential issues that become actual issues complicates the study of latent opinion.

In this section, I examine presidential decision-making in the early stages of the Vietnam War. The section has three aims: (1) to show that Presidents Kennedy and Johnson followed political strategies based on a particular reading of what public opinion toward future policies would be—that is, a particular reading of latent opinion; (2) to lay the groundwork for a claim that latent opinion often takes a particular general form that it had in the Vietnam case; and (3) to deal, as best I can, with the endogeneity issue just raised.

Following the adage that hard cases make bad law, one should perhaps avoid using the Vietnam War as a case study. It not only produced arguably the greatest policy disaster of the post–World War II era[2] but also presented an unusually severe policy trade-off: Most Americans wanted to contain the expansion of communism, but few wanted to fight a land war in the jungles of Vietnam to achieve that goal.

Yet because part of this chapter's purpose is to examine the public's latent response to policy trade-offs, the Vietnam War makes an excellent case to study. The fact that it is an unusually important case merely means that, for my purposes, it is an easy case to get information about.

In his political biography of President John Kennedy, Richard Reeves, a journalist, provides abundant evidence concerning Kennedy's political calculus on Vietnam. Reeves never mentions latent opinion, but he depicts a president in constant dread of what his Republican opponent in the next election might say about him. With the memory of the McCarthyist 1950s still fresh, many of Kennedy's fears centered on U.S. involvement in Vietnam, a conflict he felt he could neither win nor afford to lose:

> [Kennedy] told [Walt] Rostow he did not need stacks of memos to understand political consequences, that was his business. American withdrawal

[from Vietnam] would destroy him and the Democratic party in a replay of "Who Lost China?" debate in the early 1950s . . . (Reeves 1993, 261)

That evening over a drink, Kennedy brought up Vietnam again with Charlie Bartlett: "We don't have a prayer of staying in Vietnam. Those people hate us. They are going to throw our asses out of there at almost any point. But I can't give up a piece of territory like that to the Communists and then get the American people to re-elect me." (484)[3]

Politically, he could not afford to look weak militarily. Whatever he truly thought . . . about the commitment of Americans on the ground in Asia, he was not ready, as he had told CBS only a month before, to be accused of losing Vietnam to the Communists, as other American politicians had only ten years before been accused of losing China to the Communists, and had been destroyed. (604)

But although Kennedy feared the public would punish him for "losing Vietnam," he also feared electoral retribution if he undertook a military effort to save it. As he told a confidant in another context, "we all know how quickly everybody's courage goes when the blood starts to flow." (Reeves 1993, 416). (Political scientist John Mueller [1973] would soon provide the exact mathematical form for the rate at which courage declines as a function of casualties, another way in which Mueller studied latent opinion without using this term.)

From Kennedy's reading of public opinion, the dilemma he faced was as follows: Any attempt to "save" Vietnam would encounter unacceptable domestic political consequences because the public was not willing to support sustained use of military force. Yet at the same time, if my analysis is correct, the public also would not tolerate the loss of Vietnam. The public, in other words, wanted to have its cake and eat it too—to contain communism without paying the cost for doing so. Or, in a different metaphor, it wanted a free lunch.

After Kennedy's death, President Johnson faced the same predicament in Vietnam and, as secretly recorded tapes make clear, he parsed it exactly as Kennedy had. "We haven't got any mothers that will go with us in a war" he told the Joint Chiefs of Staff (Beschloss 1997, 267). To his friend Richard Russell he confided, "I don't think the people of this country know much about Vietnam and I think they care a hell of a lot less" (365).

But Johnson felt political pressure to maintain the U.S. position: "I'm confronted. I don't believe the American people ever want me to run [from Vietnam]. If I lose it, I think they'll say I've lost. I've pulled in" (Beschloss 1997, 401). "They'd impeach a president though that would run out, wouldn't they?" he asked Russell (369).

Johnson was particularly worried about Barry Goldwater, the 1964 Republican presidential nominee who regularly criticized Democrats for being soft on defense and seemed to thrive politically by doing so. As one of Johnson's advisers told him, "You're going to be running against a man who's a wild man on this subject. Any lack of firmness he'll make up." Hence, in any crisis, it was imperative, as the adviser said, for the United States to act tough: "You've got to do what's right for the country. . . . But whatever you can do to say, when they shoot at us from the back, we're not soft, . . . we're going to protect ourselves, we'll protect our boys, . . . I think it's all to the good" (Beschloss 1997, 495). Even after the 1964 election, Johnson continued to worry about attacks from the right. As he told George Ball in 1965, "George, don't pay any attention to what those little shits on the campuses do. The great beast is the reactionary elements in the country. Those are the people that we have to fear."[4]

Although Johnson felt Republican pressure to be tough in Vietnam, he also believed that the opposition would criticize him for it, too. When Robert McNamara urged Johnson to "educate" the public about the need for a sustained effort in Vietnam, Johnson responded, "I think if you start doing [that], they're going to be hollering 'You're a warmonger.' . . . I think that's the horn Republicans want to get us on" (Beschloss 1997, 388). Even worse would be if American soldiers began to suffer casualties. "You get a few [soldiers] killed. . . . The Republicans are going to make a political issue out of it, every one of them, even [anticommunist Republican leader Everett] Dirksen" (365).

Nor were Republicans the only opposition group Johnson had to fear. Under the new leadership of Robert Kennedy, the Kennedy wing of the Democratic Party had, to that point, impeccable anticommunist credentials and was prepared to assert them to retake the presidency. "Members of the Kennedy team," as Gelb has suggested, "would be in the front line in charging Johnson with being soft" (Gelb and Betts 1979, 222), but as Bobby would show in 1968, that wing would also take the front line in charging Johnson with waging an immoral war.[5]

There was, finally, another opposition group poised to criticize Johnson, the press. As Gelb observes,

> Past experience with domestic reaction to anything that resembled a gain for communism showed what could be expected. Congress and the press would not talk about anything else. The "loss" would be the number one news story for months at the least. The administration would have to try to show that the loss was not a defeat . . . consum[ing] invaluable time and energy in its own defense. That was the key. The president would be on the defensive, making him look vulnerable to attack on other issues as well. (Gelb and Betts 1979, 223)

Johnson, then, read public opinion as wanting to save Vietnam without paying a price to do so, and he saw other elites as eager to play to that view, lambasting him for either losing Vietnam or incurring costs to prevent that outcome. The architecture of Johnson's Vietnam policy reflected this balance of pressures: public assurance that the United States would prevail in Vietnam, combined with refusal to authorize the level of military force requested by the Pentagon or even to admit the level of military force that he had approved. Other factors obviously played a role in Vietnam policy, but the congruence between a public opinion passively committed to a free lunch and policies that aimed at providing one should not be overlooked as a primary determinant of U.S. policy in that conflict.

What makes Vietnam a case of responding to latent opinion rather than actual opinion as measured in polls is that, in the critical period prior to the introduction of combat troops, opinion polls, when they existed at all, were of little relevance. Probably because Kennedy and Johnson feared that anticommunist hotheads would dominate an open discussion of Vietnam—another bow to latent public opinion—neither sought debate of the issue. Attempts along these lines would, as Johnson put it, lead only to charges that he was a warmonger. And in the absence of discussion, few Americans had opinions that were worth taking seriously. As Johnson complained to one of his advisers in May 1964,

> Did you see the poll this morning? Sixty-five percent of 'em don't know any-thing about [Vietnam] and of those that do, the majority think we're mis-handling it. But they don't know what to do. That's Gallup. It's damn easy to get in a war but it's gonna be awfully hard to ever extricate yourself if you get in. (Gelb and Betts 1979, 372)

Public opinion was, of course, even less crystallized in Kennedy's term. Thus, both Kennedy and Johnson were forced to navigate by their readings of latent opinion.

The political pressures present in this situation—an ambivalent public that would be encouraged by opposition elites to insist on having it both ways—arise with some frequency in U.S. politics and constitute an important general instance of Key's concept of latent opinion. But before making that argument, I first need to clarify some issues relating to the Vietnam case.

As I noted earlier, Key's concept of latent opinion is not about politicians' perceptions of public opinion but about the actual propensities of public opinion that politicians are prudent to heed. This, in turn, brings us to the endogeneity problem also mentioned earlier: If politicians heed the propensities of public opinion, they never become manifest, even if they are real. The only thing that can be directly observed is politicians acting to head off what they perceive to be real propensities.

How, then, can we confirm that the propensities are real? In the case of Vietnam, in particular, how can we know that the public would punish any politician who "lost Vietnam?" Might not Americans have applauded a unilateral withdrawal from Vietnam in 1965 and rewarded Johnson with a triumphal reelection in 1968? Perhaps Kennedy and Johnson both made mistaken readings of public opinion.

Polls from the period in which Kennedy and Johnson made fateful decisions concerning Vietnam do show majorities against permitting a communist takeover anywhere in the world, including Vietnam. But such polls offer little help because what we need to know is how the public would have responded if Kennedy or Johnson had tried to lead the country out of Vietnam. One might contend that either president could have done so because, as other evidence shows, presidents are often effective in leading or "educating" public opinion on foreign policy (Gamson and Modigliani 1966; Mueller 1973). Yet this evidence is also suspect, since cases in which presidents attempt to educate public opinion are a selected sample—cases, that is, in which presidents have believed, quite possibly with reason, that they could effectively lead mass opinion.[6] In cases in which leadership appears hopeless, as it may have been in the case of Vietnam, no leadership is attempted. We are left, then, with no untainted evidence on whether Kennedy and Johnson's readings of future public opinion were accurate. In the normal absence of experimental evidence, we are unlikely ever to get such evidence either for this or other similar situations.

Yet attention to latent opinion is not entirely without recompense. If nothing else, it forces recognition that realistic analysis of the relationship between public opinion and policy-making must examine not only hard poll data but also more amorphous evidence concerning latent opinion. And that evidence, though not untainted, does have clear value. For there is enough evidence to make clear that Kennedy and Johnson faced actual dangers if either had decided to pull out of Vietnam. We know this because we can, as latter-day analysts, look at the same evidence they did and recognize in it the same dangers: a replay of the 1950s debate over who lost China, charges that Democratic presidents were incompetent stewards of Cold War foreign policy and soft on communism, and so forth. Kennedy or Johnson might have been able to effectively manage these charges, which Goldwater was already hurling at them, but the dangers these charges posed are, in light of events of the previous period, hard to doubt. This is because, quite apart from the Vietnam case, the evidence from the first years of the Cold War indicates that the public had some propensity to punish presidents who allowed communist gains, whether or not it would have done so in the particular case of Vietnam. If the evidence of this latent opinion is not stronger, it is probably because, even in the late 1940s and 1950s, policymakers exerted themselves to heed it. Yet we can also see that, even so, Truman's popularity plummeted amid his attempts in 1950 and 1951 to save Korea from communism, thus suggesting little public tolerance for anticommunist wars that involve heavy loss of American lives.

Scholars have devoted much energy to the counterfactual question of whether Kennedy or Johnson could have engineered a politically safe withdrawal from Vietnam. They make an especially plausible case that, in the political context of early 1965, other politicians and the media would have provided enough cover to induce the public to accept a well-crafted presidential decision to withdraw.[7] Even opposition politicians might mostly have gone quietly along, since arguing against peace would have made salient the cost of not withdrawing. However, a claim that a president could have managed a politically safe withdrawal cannot stop here. How would international events have played out over the next few years? How would political opponents have responded at the next election? And how would voters have responded at that time? It might have been safer to attack a withdrawal decision from a distance of several months or years, when the danger of actually sending troops had passed, and harder to defend at that time, when arguments about cost might have seemed to voters like excuses for inaction.[8] One can, to be sure, imagine a counterfactual scenario in which Johnson led the country out of Vietnam, Cold War tensions abated, and racial disturbances in the cities became the big issue of the 1968 election. However, one can equally well imagine a 1968 campaign in which alleged defeat in Vietnam, racial disturbances in the cities, and seizure of the U.S.S. *Pueblo* by North Korea in early 1968 were rolled into one grand theme of national humiliation. Presidential campaigns often roll many issues into one—of which Kennedy's 1960 promise to "get the country moving again" is a good example—and it is difficult to anticipate what combinations will arise. It may be precisely this uncertainty that makes presidents loathe to concede anything to the opposition that can be retrospectively interpreted as failure and packaged with other apparent failures, as withdrawal from Vietnam could easily have been.

Thin as it is, then, I believe the evidence is sufficient to show that, as regards the Cold War, the public wanted to contain communism without having to fight continual wars to do so and that Kennedy and Johnson were not simply imagining that this propensity existed. It thus tends to uphold the key point in this analysis: that the principal contours of U.S. policy on Vietnam—doing enough to avoid losing without making a wholehearted commitment to winning—are interpretable as a response to the public's latent preference to avoid painful trade-offs.

Summary

The Vietnam case shows both the importance of taking latent public opinion into account in the study of democratic politics and the pitfalls in trying to do so. It also reveals three specific factors that may arise with some frequency in American politics: first, a mass public that is inclined to avoid trade-offs between competing values; second, opposition politicians eager to encourage the public in this propensity; and third, government decision makers more interested in future opinion than in present opinion. How often these factors arise, whether in foreign policy crises or elsewhere, is obviously uncertain.

To learn more about latent opinion, we shall need to examine a greater number of cases and to generate something closer to testable predictions. I now turn to both tasks.

When Politicians Should Ignore the Polls

When public opinion is inconsistent or poorly crystallized, as in the case examined in the previous section, presidents may feel relatively free to ignore the polls. Yet there are cases in which savvy politicians ignore one-sided expressions of apparently firm and clear opinion. One involved the so-called Mexican bailout in early 1995. The problem arose after Mexican politicians maintained the value of their national currency at an artificially high level for electoral purposes. This device propped up the Mexican economy for some months but eventually led to a spectacular crash of the peso on the international currency markets. This, in turn, led to a banking crisis in Mexico and the threat of a domino effect on the currencies of other developing countries.

Arguing that economic collapse in the developing world would surely damage the U.S. economy, the Clinton administration asked Congress to approve a loan program that would stabilize the Mexican economy. The proposal involved loan guarantees rather than direct aid, but even so, it was massively unpopular. In the three polls I found, an average of 21 percent of those surveyed favored the loan program—probably disproportionately highly informed persons and persons of Mexican descent—and 74 percent opposed. In these circumstances, Congress, which had recently cut domestic spending and raised taxes to balance the federal budget, refused to go along with what seemed like a U.S. gift to Mexico.

The logic of the choice Clinton then faced was clear: He could heed public opinion as expressed in current polls but risk alienating the public opinion that would exist in November 1996 by increasing the likelihood of a U.S. recession at that time. Or he could ignore public opinion as expressed in polls and play to the public opinion that would exist at election time. The fact that Clinton had, by that time, linked the U.S. and Mexican economies via the North American Free Trade Agreement (NAFTA) increased the political stakes.

Despite Clinton's reputation for pandering to polls, he ignored them in this instance and, on the basis of his executive power, authorized twenty billion dollars and concessions worth perhaps another twenty billion dollars. For his pains, Clinton was immediately attacked by Rush Limbaugh, Ross Perot, and

Pat Buchanan (though not Republican Senate Majority Leader Bob Dole, who supported Clinton on this issue). If Clinton's choice was between giving some of the biggest mouths in U.S. politics an emotionally charged round of ammunition to use in the context of a basically good economy or denying them that ammunition at the cost of a sound economy, we should not be surprised by his decision.

This case suggests a generalization about how politicians should think about latent opinion: For cases in which presidents can alter the real-world situation that will shape public opinion at the time of the next election, they should ignore public opinion as expressed in current polls and cater to future opinion. When, however, presidents are powerless to affect the real-world basis of future opinion, they should be wary of ignoring current opinion because it may still be in place at the time of the next election. The idea behind this proposition is that, as Fiorina (1981) pointed out, the public opinion that expresses itself in elections tends to be more concerned with ends than means.

Although I have not systematically studied Clinton's inclination to follow or ignore polls on tough issues, I have collected several important cases that seem to fit this generalization. Here are four that fit the scenario for ignoring public opinion:

1. As a candidate for president in 1992, Bill Clinton promised to increase "investments" in people, cut taxes for the middle class, and cut the budget deficit in half. In his first budget after taking office, he proposed some new investments as well as a significant tax increase for the middle class (mainly in the form of an energy tax), new taxes on Social Security benefits, and cuts in Medicare. Clinton wanted to cut cost-of-living adjustments or Social Security as well, but congressional Democrats vetoed the plan before it was publicly announced. Polls taken before and after Clinton announced his budget plan showed, as would be expected, that the tax provisions were unpopular but that other elements of the plan, notably investments in education and tax increases for the rich, were popular. The interesting question is why, contrary to electoral promises and current polls, Clinton proposed the unpopular elements he did.

2. NAFTA never had great support in public opinion polls[9] and was extremely unpopular among one of Clinton's core groups, organized labor. Nevertheless, Clinton threw his full support behind NAFTA and won a close vote in Congress to pass it. Why?

3. With thousands of boat people fleeing a military regime in Haiti to come to the United States in the late summer of 1994, Clinton asked Congress for authorization to send U.S. troops to restore a democratic government in Haiti. Congress refused. Even though three recent polls showed that about 30 percent of the public favored unilateral U.S. military action and 65 percent

opposed it, Clinton made a televised speech to announce that he intended to order an invasion. Even after the invasion, however, public opinion remained nearly divided and quite dubious about the policy. Why offend public opinion over Haiti?

4.   Throughout Clinton's first term, the mass media broadcast disheartening images of civil war and atrocity in Bosnia. By 1995, the public was willing to support air strikes against the Serbian side but opposed sending U.S. ground troops to police a truce among the warring factions.[10] Nevertheless, Clinton instructed the State Department in the summer of 1995 to broker a deal among the contending factions that would be enforced by U.S. ground forces. By the end of the year, the U.S. Senate had ratified the Dayton Accords, committing U.S. peacekeeping forces to Bosnia. (Senator Dole, the likely Republican nominee for president in 1996, played a key role in securing Senate approval for the unpopular measure.) Why would an election-hungry president push to send U.S. troops into harm's way in an election year?

The answer in each of these cases is, as I maintain, that it was plausible for Clinton to believe that the policies he put into place would produce beneficial and visible results by the time of the 1996 election. In the cases of NAFTA, the Mexican loan, and the first budget proposal, the main expected benefit was a marginally stronger economy. In the cases of Haiti and Bosnia, the main expected benefit was an end to disturbing images on the evening news and restoration of Pax Americana at what the president thought would be very low cost.

These cases, two of which I will further discuss shortly, stand in contrast to two others, gays in the military in early 1993 and welfare reform in 1996. The first involved a campaign promise by Clinton to end discrimination against gays in the military; the second involved a Republican-sponsored initiative to terminate federal responsibility for Aid to Families with Dependent Children. In neither case is it plausible to believe that Clinton controlled policy instruments that would affect the basis of public attitudes. So when polls showed public opposition to positions he had staked out, the president worked out face-saving surrenders with congressional leaders and moved on to other matters.

I think that my theoretical explanation for these cases—that politicians will disregard public opinion when they think they can play effectively to its long-term propensities and defer to it otherwise—is quite plausible within a general paradigm of political rationality. However, the classification of cases (i.e., measurement) necessary to empirically verify the claim raises problems, especially as regards Bosnia and the budget proposal. Let me therefore examine these cases in more detail.

What exactly distinguishes Bosnia from Vietnam besides the fact that it was possible to "save" Bosnia at low cost and impossible to do the same in Vietnam, thereby satisfying the public in Bosnia and creating a nightmare in Vietnam?

Also, how do we know that Clinton acted from political pragmatism rather than, say, principle?

The answer to the first question is that very little distinguishes Bosnia from Vietnam except cost. Yet cost is no minor matter. The public may have been wiser about the dangers of intervention in Bosnia, but the key difference, according to my analysis, is not the nature of public opinion but the nature of the policy instruments at the president's disposal in relation to the problem at hand. Even though the public did not immediately realize it, the combatants in Bosnia, in contrast to those in Vietnam, were ready for peace, and the introduction of a few thousand U.S. ground troops was sufficient to achieve that peace. Thus, Clinton controlled a much more effective set of power levers in Bosnia than Kennedy and Johnson had in Vietnam. This section focuses on when politicians will ignore polls, and the key point is that they will do so when they believe they have the practical means of satisfying the public in the long run.

The question about motivation is more difficult. One can rarely be certain whether an individual politician in a particular case has acted out of pragmatism or principle—or anything else, for that matter. It is, however, reasonable to assume that a politician's ideological principles are relatively fixed, whereas opportunities and incentives to act on those principles vary. The latter, therefore, are the better bet to explain differences in behavior within the same individual. With this in mind, consider the following analysis of Clinton's Bosnia decision by *Washington Post* columnist Jim Hoagland:

> Few cliches are as dear to American politicians as the claim that politics stops at the water's edge. But good politics can be good foreign policy. Bill Clinton is proving that on Bosnia.
>
> The president's muscular intervention to get a cease-fire in Bosnia after two years of dithering owes a lot to events on the ground. When Croatia's summer blitzkrieg shattered an overextended Bosnian Serb army, Clinton saw his chance and took it. But senior administration officials also point to an uncharacteristically forceful presidential directive to them to "bring clarity" to the Bosnian crisis before reelection campaigning engulfs Clinton early next year. They admit this campaign-driven directive was a major factor in a new American activism on Bosnia that has not yet run its course. If this activism is both sustained and productive . . . it will cast a new light on . . . this president, who came to Washington tagged by the media, the public and himself as a policy wonk. Wrong. Clinton is a politics wonk. Politics—partisan and personal—energize, inspire and focus Bill Clinton in a way that the detached decision-making of foreign affairs (and many other things) does not. . . . The chance to hem in Bob Dole and other critics on Bosnia has at last given Clinton a passion and a drive on a foreign crisis that help stop the erosion of American leadership in global affairs—at least temporarily. (Hoagland 1995)

Sending U.S. troops to Bosnia was risky, but criticism from the Republican nominee for failing to clear up Bosnia was a certainty unless Clinton acted to defuse the issue. This, I suggest, is why Clinton ignored the polls on Bosnia.

The problem with this analysis is that the cost Clinton could expect to incur from U.S. casualties in Bosnia was almost certainly greater than the small gain he could expect from defusing the issue. But what were the expected chances of success if he sent U.S. troops? If they were high enough, the expected-utility calculation could still run in favor of intervention.

As later news accounts indicated, U.S. military leaders were reasonably confident that intervention could succeed—as, in fact, it has. If Clinton was acting on this expert opinion, as presumably he was, then Hoagland's inside account can be taken as evidence that Clinton was acting consistently with my rule: The president disregarded current polls on Bosnia because he had the means of affecting the real-world situation to which the public would be responding once the presidential contest heated up, thereby hemming in his opponent.

The unexpected fiscal conservatism of Clinton's first budget also bears closer analysis: Was Clinton a more instinctively principled and moderate Democrat than he has been given credit for? Or was he, as my analysis would suggest, merely a clever pragmatist? From Bob Woodward's inside account of decision-making in *The Agenda* (1994), the evidence points rather clearly to pragmatism. His key advisers—Alan Blinder, Alice Rivlin, Leon Panetta, and Lloyd Bentsen—plus Fed Chairman Alan Greenspan all warned of a potential fiscal crisis if the federal budget deficit were allowed to continue to grow. The economic team stressed that the long-term performance of the economy depended on interest rates and that interest rates in turn depended on the confidence of the bond market and the Federal Reserve that the federal government would bring its budget deficit under control. Clinton fairly consistently took the economic advice he received, but he did not enjoy doing so. During one presentation by his economic team,

> Clinton's face turned red with anger and disbelief. "You mean to tell me that the success of the program and my reelection [nearly four years off at that point] hinges on the Federal Reserve and a bunch of fucking bond traders?" he responded in a half-whisper.
>
> Nods from [Blinder's] end of the table. Not a dissent.
>
> Clinton, it seemed to Blinder, perceived at this moment how much of his fate was passing into the hands of the unelected Alan Greenspan and the bond market. (Woodward 1994, 84)
>
> By seizing control of the deficits and their economic future, Gore argued, they would be doing what was politically unpopular but right. . . . When people saw the boldness, there would be a surge of support for the plan. Gore, who had been saying that boldness was the essence of Franklin D. Roosevelt's

program, again pointed to the New Deal legislation. "Look at the 1930s," he reminded.

"Roosevelt was trying to help people," Clinton shot back. "Here we help the bond market, and we hurt the people who voted us in." (93)

According to Woodward, Clinton reviewed every important element of his budget proposal, complaining about its stringencies as he went:

> [Clinton said] that he still planned to propose an increase in the percentage of Social Security benefits subject to taxes, even though it would mean a big jump for middle-income retirees. "All the voters live in Florida," he noted, only half-jokingly. The implications for the 1996 election were clear. Clinton had lost the state in 1992, but it would surely be lost again. "Bye-bye Florida," he said. (135)

> At one point [the economic advisers] were reviewing rural and agricultural programs, cutting away at what most of them considered indefensible special-interest subsidies.
>
> "Mr. President," Rivlin said enthusiastically. "I've got a slogan for your reelection." Taking off on his campaign promise to "end welfare as we know it," she proposed: " 'I'm going to end welfare as we know it for farmers.' "
>
> Clinton stiffened, looked at her, and snapped, "Spoken like a true city dweller." The former governor of Arkansas leaned across the table dramatically in her direction and added, "Farmers are good people. I know we have to do these things. We're going to make these cuts. But we don't have to feel good about it." (138–39)

> Clinton still had qualms. Not only would he be unable to cut middle-class taxes as he had promised, but he would be raising taxes on the middle class. "These are the people who got screwed in the 80s," he said. "And it's a heck of a thing for me to propose this." (139)

In taking much of his economic advisers' advice, Clinton turned a cold shoulder to the advice of his political advisers, such as James Carville, Stanley Greenberg, Paul Begala, and Mandy Grunwald. According to Woodward,

> "Why did we run," asked Stan Greenberg, pounding the table [at a meeting at which Clinton was not present]. . . . Deficit hawks and the Washington establishment had stolen Clinton's presidency. "The presidency has been hijacked," Greenberg said flatly. A near-fatal disconnection had taken place. The team of political advisers that understood Clinton and his extraordinary mix of political traditions—true Democrat, populist, Southern pulse-taker, brainy policy student—was out in the cold. As a result, the vital link between Clinton and the voters was being severed [in Greenberg's view]. (97)

Mandy Grunwald, for one, did not share the jubilation [when financial markets reacted well to the Clinton plan]. She believed that the bond market thrived on bad news for the middle class. The reaction seemed to indicate that if Clinton didn't plan to screw the middle class, he was not serious about deficit reduction. (108)

Clinton liked frankness, and Begala was a natural with direct communication. . . .

"Mr. President," Begala said, "why are you listening to these people [the economic team]? They did not support you. It's not what you're about."

"We need them," Clinton said. . . . "We can't do anything for people unless we reduce the deficit."

. . . "Mr. President, we're just driving at a magic number [i.e., a deficit reduction target of $140 billion]. That number, it's like there's some magic in it." How did that happen? Begala asked.

"They love their country," Clinton said of his economic team. "They're working hard at this. What do you want me to do? We can't lie about the deficit. Can't do that."

"I agree," Begala said.

"Then stop," Clinton ordered. (136–37)

Since Woodward's account of these events is based heavily on the testimony of Clinton loyalists, it may be overly sympathetic to Clinton. Yet there is no reason to doubt the central theme—Clinton's political advisers were put out in the cold as the president made the political decision to govern, in this instance, on the basis of pragmatic criteria. Nor is there reason to doubt the reason that Clinton gave for doing so—that making the economy run well over the long term requires adopting the kinds of policies that please bond traders more, at least in the short run, than the voters who had supported him in the election.

In formulating his first budget, Clinton faced a public that, as is often the case, wanted a free lunch. Its inconsistent demands were not, in this case, latent but were openly expressed in polls about budget preferences. Clinton disregarded this expressed opinion, betting, in effect, that a strong economy was what the public wanted most of all.

Summary

In this section, I proposed a low-level generalization about when presidents may be expected to ignore polls and defer instead to their reading of latent opinion. The key idea is that when presidents possess policy levers sufficient to determine the real-world conditions on which the public will ultimately judge its actions at election time, presidents should ignore present opinion as expressed in polls and defer to their reading of latent opinion. Otherwise, they should do the reverse. I offered very short vignettes of seven policy decisions, five of which were intended to illustrate the first type of case and two of which were intended to illustrate the second.

I cannot claim that this brief exercise has strong evidentiary value, but I believe it nonetheless suggests how more rigorous testing might be done.

The Rationality of Inconsistent Preferences

It is commonplace to disparage the public for the inconsistency of its opinion. However, this disparagement may be unwarranted. In many cases, pressuring politicians to do the impossible could serve the public's interest as well as any feasible alternative.

Taxing and spending is perhaps the classic case in which opinion inconsistency arises. Majorities want low taxes, high levels of government service, and a balanced budget—and, for most of the 1980s and 1990s, a constitutional amendment to force a balanced budget. Depending on the particular question wording, citizens also want government to protect them from the health and safety hazards generated by the modern economy, but they also want government to keep small and let competition reign in the private sector. Voters want tariff walls high enough to protect American jobs, but they also want cheap foreign imports and free trade for U.S. exports. And citizens also want the higher level of economic prosperity that, as economists almost unanimously contend, derives from free trade. In the area of foreign policy, Americans generally want the benefits of an assertive national foreign policy without having to pay the costs of this benefit.

There is nothing obviously irrational about a preference for having your cake and eating it too. Commenting on the citizens who said that "the government should cut taxes even if it means putting off important things that need to be done" yet favored increased spending on social welfare, Key wrote,

> from their standpoint their position is comprehensible. A simple calculus of self-interest makes simultaneous support of tax reduction and expansion of welfare activities entirely consistent for them. (1961, 168)[11]

The same can be said for other instances in which the public makes apparently unreasonable demands. Who, after all, wouldn't prefer to have his enemies kept at bay without the need for expensive armaments and occasional wars? Who wouldn't prefer a lean government effectively looking out for everyone's health and safety rather than a bloated one? The fact that outparty politicians have an incentive to give voice to the public's "unreasonable" demands only encourages citizens in the natural propensity to try to get as much as possible out of government for the least possible cost.

The problem, if there is one, is the effect of the public's demands on those responsible for making policy. As Key comments on the preference for high spending and low taxes, "For the system as a whole . . . this combination is irrational and creates problems in program-making" (1961, 168).

In no case is the pernicious effect of inconsistent policy preferences more clear than in the case of Vietnam. Because the public was, in Johnson's estimation, unwilling either to accept a defeat in Vietnam or to pay the cost of winning, the country pursued a perverse policy of getting itself into a serious war without the level of commitment necessary to achieve the goal that presumably made war necessary. Similarly in the case of budget politics, the public's preference for high levels of government services with low taxes pressured politicians to indulge in a variety of accounting gimmicks and even constitutional amendments to hide their inability to live up to the promises that political pressure forced them to make.

Although these pernicious effects ought not to be minimized, one should, at the same time, recognize that potential benefits might also exist. Consider the following analogy to market capitalism: consumers entering the marketplace want high-quality goods—whether cars, computers, or hamburgers—at low cost. Consumers can generally recognize both low cost and high quality when seeing them. But, as in politics, consumers have no idea how either quality or cost is achieved and do not care to find out. They simply want the best of both worlds without paying a lot of attention to details. But since producers have an incentive to satisfy as best they can the unreasonable demands of customers, the result has been a history of steady improvements in both the quality and cost of consumer goods.

If consumers, in their ignorance, told producers that they wanted either the highest quality regardless of cost or the lowest cost regardless of quality, consumers would either go broke quickly or acquire countless products that failed to work as advertised. Consumers would, in other words, fare worse than they do in demanding both low cost and high quality.

Without wishing to make any grandiose claims about what exactly happens in the political marketplace, one can argue that the same general forces are at work. The public's perhaps unconscious strategy of making unreasonable demands, in combination with an electoral system that encourages politicians to exert themselves to satisfy those demands, may often lead to reasonably good outcomes. If, conversely, voters cheerfully agreed either to pay whatever taxes were deemed necessary by politicians to fund "essential" services or to be contented with only those services, including defense, that were affordable at very low cost, the result would be satisfactory to few or none.

Market failures do occur in business, and no doubt they do so as well in politics. Thus, to admit that "unreasonable" or inconsistent public demands on government sometimes lead to pernicious effects, as they appear to have done in the case of Vietnam, falls much short of a demonstration that such demands are, in general, self-defeating. Moreover, the United States did in the end win the Cold War and did so at much lower overall cost than was feared at its inception. It is conceivable that Vietnam, by upholding the credibility of U.S. alliances and thereby keeping pressure on the Soviet Union, contributed to that result. Or, even if Vietnam was a complete waste of American and Vietnamese lives, it may have been a much smaller disaster than would have been expected under some different system of political incentives. Furthermore, the federal government did eventually manage to achieve a balanced budget at relatively high levels of government service and then enacted a giant tax cut to cap off the achievement. My claim, then, is not that market competition is the answer to all the ills of democratic politics, including a woefully uninformed and apathetic public. It is only that the public's apparent propensity to make inconsistent demands on government decision makers may be a more effective strategy than it initially seems and a reasonably good general strategy overall.

In evaluating the efficacy of unreasonable demands, one needs also to consider the alternative. Is it reasonable to believe that any mass public will ever devote itself sufficiently to public affairs to be able to make informed, reasonable judgments on the vast number of issues on which it is called on to opine in polls? Obviously not. Suppose, though, that it were possible. Which, then, would be the better mechanism for democratic decision making: a mass electorate deliberating on an issue such as Vietnam under the shadow of the nuclear bomb, the tutelage of politicians like Johnson and Goldwater, and the guidance of the news media that have triumphed in the current environment of cutthroat competition for high ratings? Or the judgments of politician-presidents whose instincts and incentives are to anticipate what the public will want at the end of the day and after the dust has settled?

If forced to make a choice, one might reasonably prefer a government driven by inconsistent latent public opinion to a government driven by what would, under the best of circumstances, pass for informed public opinion. I do not assert this as a firm conclusion but rather as a suggestion to be evaluated.

The Future of Latent Opinion

Key's notion of latent opinion—that the public opinion politicians care most about is the public opinion that will exist at the next election—seems at first encounter sensible but scientifically retrograde. It seems sensible because it is obviously what office-seeking politicians should care most about but retrograde because of the difficulty of studying something that is latent rather than manifest. Key's cheerful admission of the seemingly mystic qualities of latent

332   ELECTORAL DEMOCRACY

opinion reinforced the latter impression and may well have contributed to its neglect over the years. Yet, as I have tried to show in this chapter, the public does have latent tendencies that are at least as real as many of its attitude statements, which, though manifest, are often best understood as nonattitudes. Latent dispositions to rally round the flag in crises, to vote on the basis of economic performance, and to resist painful trade-offs are all genuine response tendencies that politicians are prudent to heed and political scientists are therefore wise to study.

What is perhaps more open to dispute is whether Key's concept of latent opinion is necessary for this study to occur. After all, rally effects and economic voting—as well as the tendency of politicians to anticipate them—have been thoroughly studied without reference to the concept of latent opinion. Similarly, my conjecture that the public reliably resists painful trade-offs could be investigated as a freestanding assertion. Finally, my contention that politicians will sometimes ignore current opinion in order to play to future opinion has been investigated by scholars who appear to owe no debt whatsoever to Key's concept of latent opinion. These studies are worth pausing to review.

Jeffrey Cohen (1997) has undertaken an ambitious quantitative analysis of how presidents from Eisenhower to George Bush responded to public opinion. His argument, quite similar in flavor to mine, is that presidents will respond to public opinion on symbolic concerns but follow their own best judgment on policy matters on which the public may later judge them. His evidence on symbolic responsiveness is persuasive: at the level of rhetoric and ideological tone, presidents do seem to follow public opinion. (Evidence on presidential responsiveness to the public's ideological leanings in Stimson, MacKuen, and Erikson 1995 also follows this pattern.)

At the level of concrete policy proposals, Cohen's evidence—and particularly his case evidence—is somewhat mixed. Sometimes presidents ignore opinion, and sometimes they respond to it, depending, as Cohen argues, on the strength of their policy convictions.

The other important study to venture onto this turf is a formal analysis of presidential decision making by Canes-Wrone, Herron, and Shotts (2001). Its conclusions were also arrived at independently of mine but are strikingly similar. When the probability is high that voters will find out by the next election whether a president's policies serve the public's interests, presidents are rational to disregard short-term expression of public opinion and play to long-term public interests. When, however, presidents face close elections and problems having little chance of short-term resolution, they will sometimes find it rational to "pander" to voters—that is, to enact the policies voters want even if the presidents have private information that the policies do not actually serve voter interests. Even very popular presidents may find it rational to pander if they face problems that are unlikely to be resolved before the next election. Even very unpopular presidents may ignore public opinion if they believe the benefits of their decision may become clear to voters by election day. Thus, Canes-Wrone, Herron, and Shotts formalize much of my argument and, in some ways that I have not described, go beyond it.[12]

Given, then, that most of what I have described in this chapter as evidence for the importance of latent opinion can be—and mostly has been—discussed without reference to the concept of basic opinion, what is the value of keeping the concept of latent opinion scientifically alive?

One answer to this question is clarity. If, across a range of seemingly disparate situations from Vietnam to economic policy-making, politicians are doing roughly the same thing, it clarifies our understanding of these situations to point out the common feature and to have a concept for naming it.

Another answer is communication. One of the banes of political science is how much research is conducted by specialists—in foreign policy, the presidency, public opinion, and so forth—who are studying the same thing without knowing it. Specialization is obviously necessary to understand the unique features of each domain. But ways must be found for the specialists, all of whom have their hands full simply trying to keep up with their own subjects, to communicate with each other about what they have in common. Latent opinion, a concept that travels easily across domains, is useful for that purpose.

But a more important reason for retaining the concept of latent opinion is parsimony. If a concept can provide a convincingly unified account of seemingly disparate phenomena, the account is more persuasive by virtue of that fact. Consider my anecdotal account of U.S. policy in Vietnam. A vast body of research exists on this case, most of it done by specialists in international relations in general or even the Vietnam War in particular. This research has turned up dozens of explanations for U.S. policy. If, in this situation, a researcher were to write a new book on Vietnam stressing Johnson's fear of forcing the public to make a painful trade-off, it would stand as simply another explanation for an already overdetermined event. If, however, the researcher were to amass evidence that the public frequently resists making unwelcome trade-offs, that politicians always strive mightily to avoid forcing it to do so, and that Vietnam policy fits this pattern, this evidence would count as more than simply another argument about U.S. policy in Vietnam. It would count as systematic evidence about the cause of policy in Vietnam.

Systematic evidence cannot be gathered without concepts that span multiple cases. Many of the concepts used for this purpose in political science are simple, unimaginative ones, like war, budget policy, and economic policy, and can therefore span only a narrow set of cases. Latent opinion is a more general concept, in the sense that it can span a broader and more seemingly disparate set of cases. For example, it works in the study of congressional as well as presidential decision making (Arnold 1990; Zaller 1995).

It would make no sense, then, to assert that because political scientists are studying latent opinion in many contexts without reference to the concept that the concept is unimportant. The more sensible assertion is that latent opinion is especially valuable because it can help clarify and unify research that already exists.

My conclusion is therefore that latent opinion remains a valuable tool of public opinion analysis. Politicians do not always play to latent opinion, as Jacobs and Shapiro (2000) clearly demonstrate, but they often seem to do so. The clearest evidence of the importance of latent opinion is the disparate research it spans, some of which has as much precision as any in political science. The central idea of latent opinion—that politicians are normally most concerned with response propensities that will become manifest at some point after they act, most likely at the time of the next election—should be routinely taught to beginning and advanced students and should be better integrated into future studies of public opinion.

NOTES

This chapter is based on a paper presented at the Symposium in Honor of Philip Converse, Boston, Massachusetts, September 2, 1998. I thank Larry Bartels, Brandice Canes-Wrone, Charles Franklin, Ken Schultz, Ken Shotts, and Marc Trachtenberg for critical comments on the paper. Remaining errors are, of course, my own.

1. These sorts of shortcomings are as least as evident in my *Nature and Origins of Mass Opinion* (Zaller 1992), with its relentlessly top-down view of politics, as in most other behavioral research.

2. A case to the contrary would be that, although costly to the United States, the Vietnam War was useful in signaling American resolve, thereby keeping up the pressure that led to the demise of the Soviet Union.

3. Marc Trachtenberg offers an insightful interpretation of this remark by Bartlett, a journalistic friend of the president. Perhaps, Trachtenberg suggests, Kennedy was not so much confiding in Bartlett as using him to get out a message that would make it easier for Kennedy eventually to withdraw. If, after all, other elites came to believe that Kennedy believed that the only reason to stay in Vietnam was to avoid electoral embarrassment, it would make it harder for Kennedy to escalate and easier to withdraw. Trachtenberg cites another case in which Kennedy told journalist Arthur Krock in late 1961 that the "domino theory" would make no sense in Southeast Asia after the People's Republic of China got nuclear weapons. Again, Kennedy might have intended his remark to create pressure that would make it harder to escalate in Vietnam and easier to withdraw. Even if Trachtenberg's interpretation of Bartlett's remark is correct, it does not undermine my argument. It simply shows Kennedy trying to escape the pressure created by the public's wish for a free lunch by creating a sympathetic understanding of his dilemma among other elites.

4. Cited in Robert L. Jervis, H-Diplo Roundtable Discussion, posted February 1, 2000.

5. Gelb cites journalist Tom Wicker as the authority for this view.

6. For a formal statement and an empirical illustration of this problem, see Schultz 2001.

7. See review essay by John Garofano (2002) and Logevall 1999 (chap. 12). Given, however, the extent of U.S. military commitment, it should be pointed out that these scholars are essentially ignoring Fearon's (1994) incisive argument about audience costs, as if fifteen years of U.S. involvement in Vietnam had little importance.

8. The notion that opposition politicians may bide their time to see how events play out is developed in Zaller 1995.

9. In twenty-five national polls conducted in 1993, a plurality or majority opposed NAFTA in eighteen polls, supported NAFTA in six polls, and split evenly in the final case.

10. No questions from mid-1995 capture the decision Clinton faced at that time. However, there was strong opposition to any plan for sending U.S. troops "to try to end the fighting." Even after Congress had authorized sending troops, the public opposed by a margin of 52 to 43 percent the plan to send "up to 20 thousand U.S. troops to Bosnia, as part of a NATO peacekeeping force, to enforce the peace agreement between Bosnia, Serbia and Croatia" (Public Opinion Online, Roper Center, May 31, 1996).

11. Hansen (1998) demonstrated a high level of consistency in the public's attitudes on a series of taxing, spending, and deficit issues in the early 1990s. However, the consistency indicated mainly support for a status quo in which there was a very large budget deficit.

12. In a subsequent paper, Canes-Wrone and Shotts (2002) find support for the predictions of this theoretical model. When elections were distant, presidents from Nixon to Clinton ignored public budget priorities across eleven domains, tending instead to follow their own ideological proclivities or private information. But in the later halves of their terms, presidents facing close elections were less ideological and more responsive to public preferences. Notably, the empirical analysis is carried out at the level of discrete policy choices rather than broad indices, and presidential responsiveness is not uniform but instead varies by the immediacy of electoral risk.

REFERENCES

Arnold, R. Douglas. 1990. *The Logic of Congressional Action.* New Haven: Yale University Press.

Baum, Matthew. 2000. Who Rallies? The Constituent Foundations of the Rally-round-the-Flag Phenomenon. Paper presented at the annual meeting of American Political Science Association, Washington, D.C.

Beschloss, Michael. 1997. *Taking Charge: The Johnson White House Tapes, 1963–1964.* New York: Simon and Schuster.

Brody, Richard, and C. R. Shapiro. 1989. A Reconsideration of the Rally Phenomenon in Public Opinion. In *Political Behavior Annual,* vol. 2, ed. S. Long. Boulder, CO: Westview.

Campbell, Angus, Philip Converse, Donald Stokes and Warren Miller. 1960. *The American Voter.* New York: Wiley.

———. 1966. *Elections and the Political Order.* New York: Wiley.

Canes-Wrone, Brandice, Michael C. Herron, and Kenneth W. Shotts. 2001. Leadership and Pandering: A Theory of Executive Policymaking. *American Journal of Political Science* 45:532–50.

Canes-Wrone, Brandice, and Kenneth W. Shotts. 2002. A Time to Lead and a Time to Pander: The Conditional Nature of Presidential Responsiveness to Public Opinion. Paper presented at the annual meeting of the Midwest Political Science Association, Chicago, Illinois.

Cohen, Jeffrey E. 1997. *Presidential Responsiveness and Public Policy-Making: The Public and the Policies That Presidents Choose.* Ann Arbor: University of Michigan Press.

Converse, Philip. 1964. The Nature of Belief Systems in Mass Publics. *Ideology and Discontent,* ed. David Apter, 206–61. London: Free Press.

Fearon, James. 1994. Domestic Political Audiences and the Escalation of International Disputes. *American Political Science Review* 88:577–92.

Fiorina, Morris P. 1981. *Retrospective Voting in American National Elections.* New Haven: Yale University Press.

Gamson, William A., and Andre Modigliani. 1966. Knowledge and Foreign Policy Opinions: Some Models for Consideration. *Public Opinion Quarterly* 30:187–99.

Garofano, John 2002. Tragedy or Choice: Learning to Think outside the Archival Box. *International Security* 26:143–68.

Gelb, Leslie H., with Michael Betts. 1979. *The Irony of Vietnam: The System Worked.* Washington, D.C.: Brookings Institution.

Hansen, John Mark. 1998. Individuals, Institutions, and Public Preferences over Public Finance. *American Political Science Review* 92:513–31.

Hoagland, James. 1995. The Bosnia Turnabout. *Washington Post,* October 8, p. C7.

Jacobs, Lawrence, and Robert Shapiro. 2000. *Politicians Don't Pander: Political Manipulation and the Loss of Democratic Responsiveness.* Chicago: University of Chicago Press.

Jervis, Robert L. H-Diplo Roundtable Discussion, posted February 1, 2000. www2.h-net.msu.edu/~diplo/.

Key, V. O. Jr. 1961. *Public Opinion and American Democracy.* New York: Knopf.

Logevall, Fredrik. 1999. *Choosing War: The Lost Chance for Peace and the Escalation of War in Vietnam.* Berkeley: University of California Press.

Mueller, John. 1973. *War, Presidents, and Public Opinion.* New York: Wiley.

———. 1994. *War, Presidents, and Public Opinion.* Chicago: University of Chicago Press.

Oneal, John R., Brad Lian, and James H. Joyner Jr. 1996. Are the American People "Pretty Prudent?" Public Responses to U.S. Uses of Force, 1950–1988. *International Studies Quarterly* 40:261–80.

Reeves, Richard. 1993. *President Kennedy: Profile in Power.* New York: Simon and Schuster.

Schultz, Kenneth A. 2001. Looking for Audience Costs. *Journal of Conflict Resolution* 45:32–60.

Stimson, James A., Michael B. MacKuen, and Robert S. Erikson. 1995. Dynamic Representation. *American Political Science Review* 89:543–65.

Tufte, Edward. 1978. *Political Control of the Economy.* Princeton: Princeton University Press.

Woodward, Bob. 1994. *The Agenda.* New York: Simon and Schuster.

Zaller, John. 1992. *Nature and Origins of Mass Opinion.* New York: Cambridge University Press.

———. 1995. Strategic Politicians, Public Opinion, and the Gulf War. In *Taken by Storm: The News Media, U.S. Foreign Policy, and the Gulf War,* ed. Lance Bennett and David Paletz. Chicago: University of Chicago Press.

Contributors

John Aldrich is Pfizer-Pratt University Professor of Political Science at Duke University and is a member of the American Academy of Arts and Sciences.

Larry M. Bartels is Stokes Professor of Politics and Public Affairs at Princeton University, and is a member of the American Academy of Arts and Sciences.

Holly Brasher is Assistant Professor of Political Science at George Washington University.

Robert S. Erikson is Professor of Political Science at Columbia University.

Steven H. Greene is Assistant Professor of Political Science at North Carolina State University.

Donald R. Kinder is Philip E. Converse Collegiate Professor of Political Science and Psychology at the University of Michigan.

Kathleen Knight is Associate Professor of Political Science at Barnard University.

Milton Lodge is Distinguished University Professor of Political Science at the State University of New York at Stony Brook.

Robert C. Luskin is Associate Professor of Government at the University of Texas at Austin.

Stuart Elaine Macdonald is Professor of Political Science at the University of North Carolina at Chapel Hill.

Michael B. MacKuen is Burton Craige Professor of Political Science at the University of North Carolina at Chapel Hill.

George Rabinowitz is Burton Craige Professor of Political Science at the University of North Carolina at Chapel Hill.

Marco R. Steenbergen is Associate Professor of Political Science at the University of North Carolina at Chapel Hill.

James A. Stimson is Raymond Dawson Professor of Political Science at the University of North Carolina at Chapel Hill and is a member of the American Academy of Arts and Sciences.

Michael W. Traugott is Professor of Communication Studies at the University of Michigan and is past-president of the American Association for Public Opinion Research.

Herbert F. Weisberg is Professor of Political Science at the Ohio State University and past president of the Midwest Political Science Association.

John Zaller is Professor of Political Science at the University of California at Los Angeles and is a member of the American Academy of Arts and Sciences.

Name Index

Harding, David, 115n. 4
Hasecke, Edward B., 89
Hastie, Reid, 132, 149, 154
Heckman, James J., 299, 301
Hensler, Carl P., 18
Hermann, Margaret, 115n. 4
Herron, Michael C., 332–33
Herstein, John A., 133, 160n. 1
Hertel, Guido, 161n. 22
Higgins, E. Tory, 139, 142
Higham, John, 24, 38
Hildreth, Ann, 267
Hinich, Melvin J., 126, 128, 139–40
Hoagland, Jim, 325–26
Hodges, Sara D., 56, 152, 161n. 21
Hogg, Michael, 89
Holbrook, Allyson, 97
Holley, Jack K., 270
Horowitz, M., 88
Hovland, Carl I., 136
Howell, William, 296, 299
Hsu, M. L., 18
Huddy, Leonie, 131
Hurley, Norman L., 158, 161n. 16
Hurwitz, Jon, 18, 264
Hussein, Saddam, 30, 32–33, 37
Hyman, Herbert H., 42n. 10, 57, 75n. 6, 87

Insko, Chester A., 90
Isbell, Linda M., 150
Iversen, Gudmund R., 280
Iyengar, Shanto, 67, 130, 133–34, 143

Jackson, John E., 84, 96, 107
Jacobs, Lawrence, 334
Jacoby, William G., 196, 208
Jahoda, Marie, 42n. 10
Jamieson, Kathleen Hall, 132, 162n. 23
Janis, Irving L., 136
Jervis, Robert L., 334n. 4
Johnson, Eric J., 133, 140
Johnson, Lyndon, 316–21, 330
Johnston, Richard, 67–69, 77n. 21
Jones, Calvin C., 84, 109
Jones-Lee, M. W., 53
Jowell, Roger, 245, 249, 255
Joyner, James H., Jr., 315

Judd, Charles M., 92, 97, 128, 143, 160n. 8
Junn, Jane, 247, 256nn. 1, 3
Just, Marion R., 126, 154–55

Kagay, Michael R., 210
Kahneman, Daniel, 49, 51–54, 56–57, 60, 64, 139
Kam, Cindy D., 22, 25, 38, 40, 42nn. 14, 17
Kang, Mee-Eun, 266–67, 270
Kaplan, K. J., 97
Katz, Daniel, 105–6, 264–65
Keane, Mark T., 127
Keeter, Scott, 126, 161n. 11, 248, 250–52
Keith, Bruce, 96, 116n. 14
Keller, A. G., 20, 41n. 7
Kelley, Harold H., 136
Kelley, Stanley, Jr., 97, 145–47
Kelly, Caroline, 89, 91–92, 116n. 7
Kennedy, George A., 77n. 18–19
Kennedy, John F., 17, 316–21, 334n. 3
Kennedy, Robert, 318
Kerlinger, F. N., 97
Kernell, Samuel, 264
Kessel, John H., 96, 285–86
Key, V. O., 11, 86, 262, 279–83, 292, 311–15, 319, 329–32
Kiewiet, R. Roderick, 244
Kinder, Donald R., 5–6, 16, 18, 22, 25, 27, 32, 36, 38–40, 40nn. 2–4, 41n. 5, 42nn. 9, 14, 17–18, 48, 63–65, 67, 75n. 1, 76–77n. 17, 86, 94, 99, 105, 116n. 6, 126, 134, 140, 143, 159, 160n. 1, 244
King, Gary, 197
King, Martin Luther, Jr., 291
Kitayama, Shinobu, 148, 150, 161n. 20
Klayman, Joshua, 142
Kleugel, James R., 39
Klingemann, Hans-Dieter, 256n. 1
Knetsch, J. L., 49, 53
Knight, Kathleen, 9, 206, 208
Korchin, Sheldon, 115n. 1
Kramer, Gerald H., 197
Krehbiel, Keith, 296
Krock, Arthur, 334n. 3
Krosnick, Jon A., 41n. 5, 63, 99–101, 103–4, 115n. 4, 128, 134, 143, 148, 151, 160n. 8
Kruglanski, Arie W., 135

Subject Index

Agenda, The (Woodward), 326–28
American Voter, The (Campbell et al.), 83, 86, 113, 126, 172, 175, 207, 210, 239, 280–82, 312
antisemitism, 19, 21–22
associative network model, 129–31
attitudes
  about public opinion polls, 267–69
  attending to important, 134
  context dependency of, and framing effects, 56–69
  defined, 51–52, 94–96
  democracy and, 5–6, 48–49, 67–75
  partisan (*see* partisan attitudes)
  party identification and attitude theory, 84, 113–14
  vs. preferences, 49–56
  See also beliefs; public opinion
Attitude Strength (Petty and Krosnick), 99
Authoritarian Personality, The (Adorno et al.), 19, 22, 37

beliefs
  Converse's analysis of, 14–18 (*see also* Converse, Philip E.)
  ethnocentrism (*see* ethnocentrism)
  groupcentrism and, 16–19, 37–38
  of mass publics and democracy, 13, 37
  stability/dynamics of change in electoral politics and, 303
  See also attitudes; public opinion
bin model, 132
Bosnia, 324–26

bounded rationality, cognitive miserliness vs., 160n. 4
budget, federal, 326–31

candidate evaluation, 8
  hybrid models of, 153–54
  information-processing mode, determinants of, 154–55
  memory-based models of, 145–48, 158
  modified memory-based model of, 155–57
  on-line model of, 148–53, 158
  policy-based (*see* policy issues)
  weighted additive model of, 140–41
  See also political cognition
citizenship
  cognitive research, normative implications for, 157–59
  ideal citizens (*see* ideal citizens)
  See also democracy; electoral democracy; voters
civil rights, 283–92, 304–6
cognition
  contingent-valuation methods, insensitivity to scope, 53–54
  by the ideal citizen, 238 (*see also* ideal citizens)
  party identification and, 95–96 (*see also* party identification)
  political (*see* political cognition)
  preferences, brain structure and formation of, 55–56
  self-categorization theory, 89

psychology of voters
attitudes vs. preferences, 49–56
electoral democracy and, 5–7
party identification (see party
identification)
political cognition and, 125 (see also
political cognition)
public opinion
attitudes vs. preferences, 49–56
congressional partisan behavior and
changes in, 290
democracy and, 2–5, 13, 39–40, 48–49,
262–63, 274–76
ethnocentrism and, 24–37
framing effects and, 56–69
on immigration, 24–31
as an institution, 3
Key's definition of, 311
latent (see latent opinion)
partisan attitudes (see partisan attitudes)
on the Persian Gulf War, 30, 32–37
polls (see polls)
rationality of inconsistent, 329–31
See also attitudes; beliefs; Converse,
Philip E.
public policy
directional voting and, 197
framing effects and public opinion,
56–69
ideal citizens and, 249–55
ideology and (see ideology)
issue evolution (see issue evolution)
See also policy issues
punctuated equilibrium, 280–81,
283–84

race
groupcentrism and beliefs relating to,
17–19
stability of public opinion on, 41n. 6

rally effects, 315
rational choice theory
limited information and, 133–34
party stability, explanation of, 111–12
working memory and, 128
recognition, 137–38
reference-group theory, 17, 85–86, 92–94,
113. See also intergroup relations
Reform Party, 112

Saris, Willem E., modified on-line model
of, 153
schema concept, 132
selectivity effects, 104–5
Social Choice and Individual Values
(Arrow), 51
social identity, 88–90
sociotropism, 244–45
stereotypes, 22–23, 137
stories, 132
succession effect, 107

valence, criteria for, 139–40
Vietnam War, 316–21, 330–31
Voter Decides, The (Campbell, Gurin, and
Miller), 85
voters
ideology and (see ideology)
independents, 86, 93, 96, 114–15
mental processes of (see political cognition)
participation, significance of, 243
party identification (see party
identification)
policy issues and (see policy issues)
psychology of, 5–7, 49–56, 125
See also electoral democracy; public
opinion

weighted additive model, 140–41
working memory (WM), 127–32, 146